# WHITE WATER RED HOT LEAD

On Board U.S. Navy Swift Boats
in Vietnam

DAN DALY

CASEMATE | publishers
*Philadelphia & Oxford*

Published in the United States of America and Great Britain in 2017 by
CASEMATE PUBLISHERS
1950 Lawrence Road, Havertown, PA 19083, USA
and
The Old Music Hall, 106–108 Cowley Road, Oxford OX4 1JE, UK

Hardcover Edition: ISBN 978-1-61200-478-5
Digital Edition: ISBN 978-1-61200-479-2

A CIP record for this book is available from the British Library.

Photography by Dan Daly unless otherwise stated
Map illustrations by Maritime Museum of San Diego

Printed and bound in the United States of America

For a complete list of Casemate titles, please contact:

CASEMATE PUBLISHERS (US)
Telephone (610) 853-9131
Fax (610) 853-9146
Email: casemate@casematepublishers.com
www.casematepublishers.com

CASEMATE PUBLISHERS (UK)
Telephone (01865) 241249
Fax (01865) 794449
Email: casemate-uk@casematepublishers.co.uk
www.casematepublishers.co.uk

This book is dedicated to all my Swift Boat shipmates with whom I had the honor to serve. To all veterans, a sincere "Thank you for your service." To my fellow Vietnam veterans, "Welcome home."

# CONTENTS

# ACKNOWLEDGEMENTS

My appreciation to Mike Zak: friend, venture capitalist, military historian and former Marine, for his support, comments and realistic guidance. My thanks to David Gallagher for his ongoing effort in many areas, both mechanical and manuscript. In terms of content, Ed Bergin and his description of his crew's capture of the enemy trawler was invaluable. Thanks also to Tom Jones and his crew for describing the rescue of four of my crew, which fine-tuned the story. Joe Patton, Bill Franke, Virg Irwin, Larry Irwin, Stirlin Harris and Michele Bernique provided not only the first-hand combat content, but photographs for the composite story of Swift operations out of An Thoi.

Neva Sullaway applied her personal writing and editorial experience, along with insight gained from her years publishing the Maritime Museum of San Diego's Pacific Maritime History Journal. She has made our product better and the experience more enjoyable and now she is a senior scholar of Swift Boat history.

My sincere thanks to them and other friends for their comments and encouragement.

# PREFACE

This nonfiction story is not a broad-based history of the Vietnam conflict; it is the story of young men from across the United States who volunteered to serve their country in a type of duty that had not been seen since the PT Boats of World War II.

In Vietnam, those in Swift Boats experienced naval combat in the closest confines imaginable, where the enemy was hidden behind a passing sand dune or a single sniper could be concealed in an onshore bunker, mines might be submerged at every turn and fork in the river. The enemy was not over the horizon or miles away; he was all around you, right in front of you at the next turn, hiding, waiting, while your fifty-foot Swift Boat works its way upriver. In many cases, the rivers became so narrow there was barely room to maneuver or turn around. The only way out might be straight into a deadly ambush.

The average Swift Boat skipper was twenty-four years old and enlisted crewmembers averaged about the same. A routine day could start with sunshine and calm seas, switch instantly to deadly combat, be torn apart by a terrifying storm and end with a well-deserved beer back at the base.

These stories make you part of the Swift Boat crew. You're at the helm doing 30 kts with your left hand locked on the throttles. Firing the .50 caliber machine gun is now your responsibility. Your eyes ache and your brain is dizzy from searching the shoreline with binoculars. Wind is up, you're 90 miles from base and the horizontal monsoon rain has just returned. It suddenly dawns on you that the enemy is hidden on shore just 100 yards away and he intends to kill you. At day's end, you and your shipmates are flat ass tired but you're glad to be alive, if only to fight another day.

This book is composed of actual stories that I had the honor to be part of, or they were stories that were told to me by first-hand participants. I did not serve in the southern patrol areas, but the individuals mentioned and their crews did serve there and it is their stories that I have woven together.

Bob Mack is a composite character who provides continuity to a fifteen-month story. Navy nurse Kate Hancock is a fictional name, but her story contains a great deal of real memories for me and she is someone who has been dear to me for over fifty years and knows this story well.

Dan Daly

# SWIFT BOAT TERMINOLOGY

Intending no insult, the *bow* is the pointed front end of the boat/ship; the *stern* is the flat backend of the boat/ship. The *port* side is the left side of the boat as you face forward and the *starboard* is the right side as you face forward. One does not go "back aft" or "down below" because one word is sufficient. One goes aft or one goes below.

*Big Jimmie diesels* were the main propulsion engines of the Swift Boat, each 480 hp. The term "Jimmie" refers to the manufacturer, General Motors Detroit Diesel. Swifts also had a small Onan diesel generator that put out 110 volts of electricity and carried 750 gallons of diesel fuel which would allow approximately 30 hours of long-range patrol, transit and on station.

*Electronics on Swift Boats* were very basic and included commercial non-military Decca (British) 202 radar with an accurate range of 12–15 miles. The main radio was a single-sideband model with a range of 50 to 100 miles. We had numerous short-range FM radios with clearer transmissions that we used to communicate with onshore troops. Swifts also had a single depth sounder (fathometer). There were no other navigation devices on board other than the compass.

*The gun tub* was the small round circular structure on top of the pilothouse and was the location for the twin .50 caliber mount.

*The radar mast* was located just behind the pilothouse and the gun tub. It was a platform for the radar antenna along with various signal lights and the American flag.

*The fantail or aft deck* was the flat area that extended from the main cabin to the stern. In the middle of that area was located the 81mm mortar and a single .50 caliber machine gun. Closer to the main cabin were the large hatches that opened to the engine room. The large horizontal locker storing mortar ammunition was located at the stern.

*A Swift Boat had two wheels or steering stations*, one in the pilothouse and a stand-up wheel located port side at the rear of the main cabin. Throttles and gear shifts were available at both locations.

In the Navy, *lines* are used to tie up ships and boats. Ropes are for cowboys.

*The Navy and the Air Force* use charts, the *Marines and the Army* use maps.

*Telling time:* military time is calculated in terms of a 24-hour day. For example, 2 A.M. is 0200, 2 P.M. is 1400. PM time is simply the hour 2 added onto 1200, ergo 1400.

## Weapons

The twin .50 caliber machine guns on a Swift Boat were located in the gun tub, which could be entered by crawling up from inside the pilothouse or by climbing into it from the main cabin roof top. Each gun fired approximately 500 rounds a minute. A fired .50 caliber round is about the size of your thumb and it is classified as a heavy machine gun. Stored below the deck in the main cabin we carried 15,000 to 20,000 rounds of belted (linked together) .50 caliber ammunition. The other .50 caliber was a single gun located on a fixed pedestal in the middle of the after deck. Below that gun was the 81mm mortar which could be trigger or drop fired, one round at a time. It had a range of up to two miles and we carried anywhere from 80 to 100 rounds in a large ammunition locker located "aft on the fantail."

In addition, we had numerous small weapons: six M-16 fully automatic assault rifles (also called the AR-15), two pump shotguns, two M-79 grenade launchers and several .38 caliber pistols. In addition, we had thermite (high temperature grenades), to destroy the engines and weapons if the boat was disabled and subject to capture.

## Call Signs

There were three sets of call signs, two official and one very unofficial. When a boat was traveling to or from her home base to a specific patrol area, it carried a call sign plus the number of the boat. Up north, this would be "Newsboy India 76," meaning PCF 76 was traveling to or from a specific patrol area. Upon arrival in the patrol area, you would switch to another call sign specific to that patrol area. Again, up north, this would be Enfield Cobra plus Alpha, Bravo or Charlie, etc., with no boat number included.

The unofficial call signs, often derogatory in nature, were assigned to individual boat skippers by their peers. In addition, specific geographic locations were assigned names from Disneyland. The use of these call signs was efficient and not encrypted, which never sat well with the communications security types. For example: "Big Ben will rendezvous with Surf Rider at Minnie Mouse at 0200 hours."

In most cases, call signs were used because they were easy to under-stand during radio transmissions that were often weak and garbled and, at other times, they simply brightened your day.

## Specific Words, Phrases and Nicknames

| | |
|---|---|
| *Admiral's Barge* | A small 35- to 40-foot boat, somewhat formal in nature, belonging to an admiral. |
| *Affirmative* | I agree with your last statement. |
| *Aft* | A location or movement toward the stern of a vessel. |
| *Airdales* | Navy pilots. |
| *APL* | Navy barges used for living quarters in Vietnam, also referred to as "The Apple." |
| *Below* | A location below the main deck of a vessel. |
| *Brass/spent brass* | A term describing the metal cartridges left behind when the .50 caliber or other weapon was fired. |
| *Boats* | A commonplace nickname for a U.S. Navy boatswain mate. |
| *CAPs* | Civilian Action Patrols, small independent USMC units that worked in and protected Vietnamese villages. |

| | |
|---|---|
| *Cease-Fire* | Immediately stop shooting any weapon. |
| *CO* | Short for the Commanding Officer of a specific ship. |
| *Column* | A group of Swift boats/ships one following the other bow to stern. |
| *Commence fire* | Immediately start shooting the designated weapon. |
| *Coordinates* | Usually a position measured in latitude and longitude on a chart or map. |
| *CSC* | Coastal Surveillance Center, the six onshore groups that coordinated most U.S. maritime activities in Vietnam. |
| *Cumshaw* | A Navy term describing the questionable acquisition of any item. |
| *DIW* | Dead in the water. |
| *DMZ* | Demilitarized zone between South and North Vietnam, established by the 1954 Geneva Accords. |
| *ETA* | Estimated time of arrival. |
| *Fix* | In Navy terms, the location of a vessel usually on a chart or map. |
| *Forward* | A location or movement toward the bow of a vessel. |
| *Gen. Quarters* | A Navy term meaning the crew is fully ready for battle. |
| *Guns* | A commonplace nickname for a U.S. Navy gunner's mate. |
| *Guns Free* | Permission given for any weapon to fire at the enemy. |
| *Guns Tight* | Specific order stating that all guns would not be fired until another order was given such as "guns free" or "commence fire." |
| *HE* | High explosive—describing an artillery round or bomb. |
| *Hooches* | Lightly built cabins usually with screened-in sides used for living in Vietnam. |
| *Illumination* | A parachute flare or artillery round used to light up a dark position. |
| *Interrogative* | I am asking you a question. |
| *KIA* | Killed in action. |

xiv • WHITE WATER RED HOT LEAD

| | |
|---|---|
| *Klick* | 1 kilometer, a distance of slightly over 1,000 yards, used for on-land distances. At sea, yards or miles are usually used. |
| *Lima Charlie* | Loud and Clear. |
| *Line Abreast* | A group of Swift boats/ships running alongside each other. |
| *LOP* | Line of position, a line from a vessel usually to a point on land. |
| *Mayday* | I am in trouble and need immediate assistance. |
| *Medevac* | The process of using a vehicle or aircraft to evacuate wounded. |
| *Midship* | A location usually halfway along the length of a vessel. |
| *Mike Mike* | Millimeters, usually the measurement of ammunition or a weapon. |
| *Negative* | I disagree with your last statement or you are wrong. |
| *NSAD* | The Naval Support Activity Da Nang, the large shore-based group that provided logistical support to all the Marines in Vietnam. |
| *NVA* | The more sophisticated and better-equipped North Vietnamese Army. |
| *O-in-C* | Abbreviation for Swift Boat Officer-in-Charge. |
| *Out* | A radio term meaning that the two-way conversation is over. |
| *Over* | A radio term meaning my part of the conversation is complete, start yours. |
| *Recon* | To reconnoiter or check something out, the act of reconnaissance. |
| *Roger That* | I heard you and understand. |
| *ROKs* | Troops from the Republic of South Korea. |
| *Romeo, Romeo* | The act of setting up a meeting, a rendezvous. |
| *Say Again* | Repeat yourself, I am not sure what you just said. |
| *Semper Fi* | A Marine Corps term of greeting or brotherhood meaning "Always Faithful." |
| *Snipe* | A commonplace nickname for a U.S. Navy engine-man or machinist mate. |

| | |
|---|---|
| *Stand by* | Wait for the next order or communication. |
| *That's a Charlie* | You are correct. |
| *Top Side* | A location, usually the main deck of a vessel. |
| *VC* | Victor Charlie or Viet Cong, the enemy. |
| *VT* | Variable time fuse on a bomb or artillery round causing it to go off above ground. |
| *Wilco* | I heard you, understand and will comply. |
| *Will Advise* | I will get back to you in the future with further information. |
| *Your Last* | Refers to the last statement that you made. |

# MAPS AND CHARTS

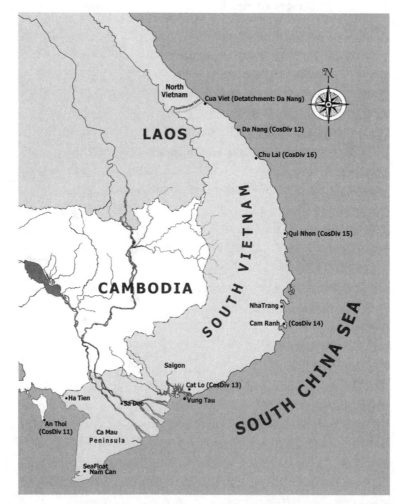

*Vietnam Coastal Map and Swift Boat Bases. (Courtesy Maritime Museum of San Diego)*

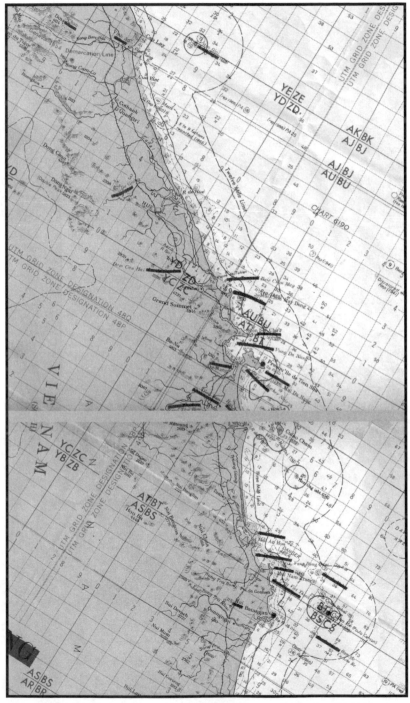

*Grid Coordinate Chart, Northern Patrol Sectors (Author's collection).*

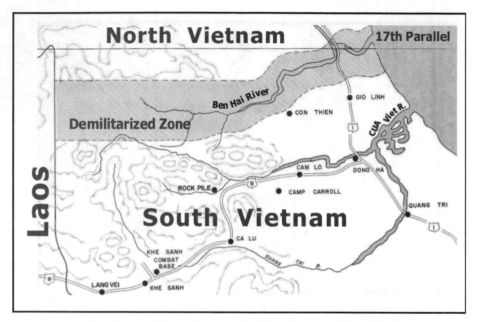

*Demilitarized Zone. (Courtesy Maritime Museum of San Diego)*

# Section I
# Swift Boat School

## CHAPTER I

# CORONADO SETTLING IN

We were close in, no more than 100 yards off the beach, less than the length of a football field. We were eyeball to eyeball with the enemy. This was no standoff gun battle and unfortunately the bad guys had some cover while we were on the boat out in the open. The constant clattering from our three .50 caliber machine guns was damn near deafening, even without being combined with a similar racket coming from the other Swift Boat a short fifty yards ahead. Just behind me, the spent brass cartridges from the fired rounds jumped up out of the after gun's breach then clanged onto the deck where they rattled and rolled, scattering underfoot surrounding the gun mount.

Driving at the after steering station, I had a clear view of the shoreline to port. My right hand was locked onto the big steering wheel and my left hand had a death grip on the throttles. I didn't have a gun and I wasn't shooting at the enemy; my job was to drive and try to think our way out of this bucket of shit. It was easy to see that the rounds from our boat were tearing up the top ridge of the sand dune, lifting grass and dust into a swirling blanket ten feet in the air. The other Swift Boat had targeted the jungle right behind the dunes and its guns were making chopped coleslaw out of the dark green foliage.

Suddenly, out of the corner of my eye, astern of us about thirty yards, I saw what appeared to be small puffs of smoke rising from the beach leading down to the water. In seconds, I recognized that these puffs of smoke were in fact the rounds from another enemy machine gun hitting the soft sand. This was the classic ambush; they had waited for both boats to engage their first firing position and now had opened fire on us, the second boat from their second position in a cross fire. The slugs rapidly continued their deadly march out across the water, marking each step with their foot-high splashes. In the next moment, the slugs started hitting amidships on our boat, each one making a high-pitched squeal as they twisted and penetrated the thin quarter-inch aluminum hull. Swift Boats had no protection of armor plating, just their return fire and speed.

This enemy gunner was good, despite his constant firing he controlled the climb of his machine gun as he swept forward to the main cabin, knocking out both our sliding windows. Fortunately, they were held in place by overlapping strips of tape that prevented razor-like shards of glass from filling the cabin. Now it occurred to me—his target was not the cabin or the windows but me! He had calculated that our boat would move forward across his line of fire and was leading the target with his weapon. Fortunately for us, he had misjudged our speed, but I guessed he would rapidly correct his aim, moving back to the steering position where I was standing. In response, I jammed the throttles full forward while I spun the large wheel hard to the right. I had no intention of being at that location.

As our big diesels roared to life and the bow of the boat started to lift, our gunner on the after deck spread his legs apart and planted both feet solidly on the deck. In one motion, he swung his big .50 caliber hard to the left following the enemy rounds back up the beach to the sniper's location. Now, there were two players in this deadly poker game. No question, we were out in the open, fully exposed, but our hand held the higher card—the big .50 caliber machine gun with its belt of 400 rounds.

I awoke with a jerk. Instinctively, both my hands grabbed the seat in front of me. At the time, my thinking was somewhat muddled by several drinks consumed earlier in the flight, so my brain vacillated between overdrive and idle speed. Despite this, I still recognized that the plane's four jet engines had begun to whine louder as well as increase in pitch as the pilot increased power. Looking out the cabin window on the port side of the aircraft, I saw the high-rise office buildings of what I assumed was downtown San Diego now rising above the plane and we were coming down hard. My first thought was, *Dammit, we're going to crash right here at the edge of the city and I haven't even reported for duty yet.* While at the time, I was ignoring the fact that the day was perfectly clear, I did recall reading that landings and takeoffs were statistically the most dangerous part of any plane trip.

Adrenaline pumping, I looked quickly around the cabin to see who else was taking any emergency action. To my shock, the other passengers surrounding me appeared remarkably calm and those in window seats were actually casually gazing out. This placid image was then reinforced by a light bounce as we touched down safely and uneventfully at San Diego International Airport.

After a struggle to get my bearings in place, it became apparent to me that the airport was in fact located right along the edge of the city of San Diego. Our landing approach was indeed a clear one, but just happened to run parallel to a row of downtown high-rise buildings.

I surmised that this type of runway approach must have been a Southern California thing, most likely based on their consistently good weather. Airports in the northeast that I was used to, like Boston's Logan and New York's LaGuardia with their rain, fog and snow were nothing like this. First Lesson Learned—things were going to be somewhat different out here in sunny Southern California.

Head cleared, now fully awake, my goal was to reestablish some patina of sophistication after my very public knee-jerk "impending death" display. Fortunately for my warrior image, I was in civilian clothes, blue blazer, grey slacks with a blue button-down shirt and striped tie, more Nantucket than military. My father, in his usual kind way, had thoughtfully purchased a full fare ticket for me so that I wouldn't run the risk of being delayed by military standby, which also would have required my flying in uniform. Doing a quick postmortem, I determined that the three Jack Daniels and water on route had undoubtedly made the six-hour flight more relaxing, but may well have contributed to my recent in extremis display.

Somewhat humbled, I began the process of deplaning. I carefully checked under my seat, scanned the overhead bin, and pulled back the pouch of the seat in front "to ensure that all personal items were removed" and that I was leaving nothing on board. Most important, I had my official orders to Swift Boat duty close at hand. In the military, orders are the paperwork that gets you from one place to another quite smoothly. If and when you lose your orders you are classified a non-entity until your last command forwards a replacement copy. This was definitely not going to happen.

Lastly, I reached down to the deck and picked up my carry-on bag that had been stowed under the seat in front. I zipped it open and shoved in my military orders alongside the latest James Bond 007 book *Goldfinger*. This was nestled appropriately beside my holstered pistol that I had purchased several weeks earlier in Boston. It was a serious handgun, a .357 Magnum with a 4-inch barrel, along with 500 rounds of packaged ammunition. San Diego take note, Dan Daly has arrived.

At the baggage claim, I picked up my large suitcase and manhandled a cumbersome but required steamer trunk containing a full complement of Navy uniforms. My guess was that the Washington wonk who generated these packing lists had never been to San Diego and probably thought a Swift Boat was some high-speed yacht club launch.

With the help of a luggage "Red Cap," I grabbed a taxi for the short trip to the naval base on the nearby island of Coronado. Walking through the sliding doors, I was immediately greeted by a gentle breeze, swaying palm trees, bright sunshine and 72°, in January no less. All this was in sharp contrast to the freezing temperatures, grey skies and dirty snow banks that I had left behind in Boston just seven hours earlier. The adventure was about to begin and things were definitely looking up.

The Navy's main base was located nearby on the east side of San Diego harbor and this was where all the large ships were berthed. In contrast, all the oddball Navy commands (grouped under Special Warfare), which included Swift Boats, were located on the island of Coronado about two miles away on the west side of the harbor. Soon my taxi and I rolled onto the ferry for the short thirty-minute trip to the base.

Pulling up to the main gate at Coronado, I showed my orders to the guard who quickly read them, saluted smartly and directed us to the Bachelor Officers Quarters (BOQ). After checking in, I dumped both my bags and the massive trunk in my assigned double room, which was fortunately located on the first deck. While not glamorous, it was certainly adequate with a shared head between two bedrooms. It was a beautiful Friday afternoon in early January and I had purposely arrived early so that I could settle in, do a little base reconnaissance and get the lay of the land before reporting for duty at 0700 on Monday morning. In military decorum, especially at the junior officer level, one arrives early, not late.

Even to the non-military observer, Coronado was a serious working base and civilian clothes definitely seemed out of order, so I decided on a working uniform of wash khakis. First, I unpacked, which was a relative term, quickly filling up the room's small bureau and even smaller closet. However, I had just spent the last eighteen months serving on a destroyer, which were not known for their sumptuous living accommodations, so I knew space efficiency. Navy storage guidelines: wear it—goes on top; maybe—on the bottom; and highly unlikely—remains in the trunk. This would be the wardrobe game plan for the next ninety days.

Coronado, by Navy standards, was a small base because there were no significant ships stationed there. Instead, there was a collection of small water craft of all shapes, sizes and designs. Earlier, when we passed through the main gate looking between several of those glamorous "West Coast beige" concrete buildings, I had gotten got a quick glimpse of the piers where I saw one of the Swift Boats tied up. So, I decided that my next move would be to walk down to the piers and check things out firsthand.

In uniform, I looked somewhat like I fit in, except for the frogman/ SEAL types. These guys called Coronado their West Coast home base and therefore they set their own fashion standards. Most of the time, they were strolling around either in Navy issue khaki shorts with blue t-shirts (I found out later they were in fact bathing suits) or custom-tailored green utilities, both finished off with combat boots. Nothing baggy or ill-fitting for these guys.

As I walked down to the piers, I looked out at the narrow entrance of Coronado harbor and saw that four or five Swift Boats were returning to the base, presumably from some training operation. I had enough sea time in the Navy to understand that when you knew nothing and are the new kid on the block it is extremely difficult to look "with it and cool." Therefore, I stood off to the side at the edge of dock as the boats maneuvered one by one alongside the pier and tied up. Other than seeing them in a picture, this was my first exposure to Swift Boats and naturally I made a series of rapid-fire observations.

That afternoon, there were actually six boats arriving and one of the first things I noticed, or actually heard as they approached at idle speed, was the deep and rolling rumble of the diesel engines. I learned later that everyone in the program felt this engine sound was unique and it had become a trademark of Swift Boats. It was generated by the twin Detroit Diesel 12V-71 series engines, which were manufactured by General Motors. The "12" was the number of cylinders and the "71" was the size of the cylinder bore. The result was two large hunks of metal weighing a couple of tons, each of which generated about 485 HP. Over time, we would grow to love these machines and their thunderous roll and roar.

At first glance, I could hardly describe the boats as beautiful; they had a short bow, actually a very short bow for a fifty-foot boat. If you were being unkind, "stubby" would be the appropriate word. After six feet, the bow butted up against a small pilothouse with five windows that connected to a second longer and lower cabin extending fifteen feet behind.

I knew a fair amount about small boats having spent summers on Cape Cod and having been through two major storms on my first ship. I clearly remember thinking at that time that the short bow of the Swift Boat might be a real problem in heavy seas. In those conditions, the force and weight of an oncoming wave would hit the pilothouse head on, rather than being displaced by a larger bow where the seas could roll off.

Cut out and welded on top of the pilothouse was a circular gun tub that held a serious-looking set of twin .50 caliber machine guns. The aft deck was long and uncluttered with another single .50 caliber combined with an 81mm mortar attached underneath it. Both of these stern weapons were fixed on a sturdy-looking three-legged swivel pedestal that was welded to the middle of the main deck. For a small fifty-foot boat there was no question that this was an impressive amount of fire-power. To a young naval officer, who had just volunteered to spend the next fifteen months involved in this program, the Boats passed my first inspection just fine.

Even to the casual observer, which I was not, all the crews, both officers and enlisted, seemed very squared away and knowledgeable. They quickly and smoothly tied up the boats; three alongside the pier and three more outboard of the first boats. No yelling, no confusion, just a very orderly process undertaken by all hands. I was impressed, but somewhat taken aback that this was such a "by the numbers" operation, not the usual "asses and elbows" that you might see in some training commands.

As the crews walked by me, the other boat officers acknowledged my humble presence with either a knowing nod or brief "Hi." Certainly it was not a "Welcome to the Club" greeting that was followed by some sort of secret handshake. Then, it occurred to me that this was Friday afternoon and it was fast approaching time for happy hour (discount drinks) at the O'Club. Most likely they had concluded, if I couldn't tell time, then that was my problem. Once again, the challenges of being the new kid in town.

Not wanting to appear overly anxious to be one of the guys and simply jump in line, I walked back alone to the BOQ. My decision was to fine-tune my unpacking and then head over to the O'Club. The formal Navy travel instructions I had been sent required enough sets of uniforms, both dress and work plus civilian clothes, for a very full twenty-year career in the U.S. Navy. I later learned that most of these would be shipped home when we finished Boat School and left for Vietnam.

Completing my unpacking did not take long because I left many items either in the trunk or in the accompanying suitcase. Both of these I had muscled under my bunk with just an inch to spare because off-site storage was not an option. No Navy dress sword, but just about everything else was "present and accounted for."

As I headed out my door, I noticed that across the hall were two other new arrivals apparently over packed like me. Working on that psychological dictum that "misery loves company," I introduced myself to LT Ed Bergin and LTJG Bob Mack. After handshakes all around, Bob mentioned he was a West Coast sailor, while Ed was East Coast like me. We swapped the mandatory but brief war stories and I quickly learned that all of us had several prior years of destroyer experience, which seemed to be de rigueur for Swift Boats. Our seafaring commonality combined with being the new kids on the block was enough to plant the seeds of a friendship and certainly more than enough to justify joining the other troops for happy hour at the nearby O'Club.

Now that we had an agreed-upon mission (cocktails), we got under way. While our specific surroundings were new to us, we were salty enough so that none of us felt like college freshmen arriving for their first day of classes. Also, Coronado was a very different type of base—it was home for both operating and training commands, but they were all small and specialized. They included units such as Frogman (UDT) and SEALs, which was a new group that evolved from Frogs but one with more combat training. Then there was something called BeachMasters, who I think, were basically traffic cops trained to manage a Marine amphibious landing. Last, but certainly not least, was the Swift Boat School.

The Frog types "ruled" because this was their home base. If you calculated your strategic military importance and where you were in the social pecking order based on the size of their wrist watches and the number of sports cars they drove, there was no competition. These guys won hands down. From our standpoint, we were visitors just passing through. However, the most significant difference between Coronado and nearby San Diego was that there were fewer senior officers at Coronado because there were no big ships and therefore no big commands with big bureaucracies. This made the environment a lot friendlier and a lot less formal even for low-life transient students like us. Also factor in, this was laid-back Southern California with all that it implies.

The Officers' Club, like most structures on the base, was a cement two-story building, again painted that restful California beige. For some reason, which was lost on me, nothing on the base seemed to exceed three stories in height and most buildings were painted in that restful beige. Right inside the main door of the Club was the usual large heavy-duty mahogany bar finished with thirty coats of varnish, fronted by numerous small tables. Nearby was a casual dining room for breakfast, lunch and quick dinners and a more formal dining room was upstairs with a view of the harbor. I had no doubt that the O'Club on the San Diego side of the harbor was significantly larger and far grander. Looking around, we three new guys agreed that this environment was just fine and on first cut was just what we were looking for.

Ed was two years my senior and a full lieutenant from a military family. He had gone to Florida State University and then to Officers' Candidate School in Newport, Rhode Island. Bob was my age, and a Naval Academy grad who had grown up near Seattle, Washington. I was from Boston, graduated from Harvard, but had enough real world experiences so that I was more realistic about life than many of my fellow Ivy League alumni. Ed and I were single, Bob was engaged and very soon to be married. It soon became apparent that Ed had more great stories than a talk-show host, while Bob, in contrast, was more low-key and almost professorial in his demeanor.

Regardless, we were all on the same mission. We had volunteered without extensive investigation for Swift Boat duty, most likely basing our decisions on glamour, adventure and a real desire to serve our country, albeit in the fast lane. Just as important, sitting at the bar, the three of us, by the second drink, had swapped enough sea stories so that the solid foundations of a new friendship had definitely been laid.

The Navy had initially structured the Swift Boat program so that it was totally volunteer for both officers and, in most cases, enlisted men. Officers at a minimum had to have two years plus of experience, usually on a smaller ship such as a destroyer. On that assignment, hopefully you would have gained ship-handling knowledge and more importantly learned about people and leadership skills. This type of duty usually entailed being a division officer with anywhere from twenty to thirty people reporting to you.

I had some previous small boat experience as did Ed, having spent a lot of time in Florida, but most of the officers enrolled at the school did not. Therefore, significant exposure to small boat handling was one of the critical training goals of the school. It always amazed me that, even at the end of their twelve-month tour in Vietnam, there were certain boat officers who were generally quite competent but still made their dockside landings by ear rather than finesse. This approach, as you can imagine, took its physical toll on the thin aluminum hulls of the boats.

Directly across the street from the base was Coronado Beach, the "Silver Strand," which is one of the finest sand beaches in Southern California. The Navy still owns several miles, yes miles, of this incredibly valuable property. At the northern end of the beach was the historic Hotel Del Coronado, which today remains a magnificent hotel, world famous and a historical venue. It was built in the late 1800s in the Victorian fashion, replete with turrets, gables, ornate porches and railings painted white and with its signature red roof, all beautifully maintained. In stark contrast, just several hundred yards to the south, began the Navy's beach property which was used for all types of beach- and surf-related training operations. Obstacle courses of every description and burnt-out aircraft decorated the beach. Fortunately for the "Del," there was a buffer zone in between that was composed of several high rise and very expensive condominium buildings.

Swift Boat School was twelve weeks long and the curriculum was straightforward, basically "hands-on" practical. As a result, few if any nighttime visits were required to the nonexistent library. The days were taken up learning every detail about the boats: engines, electronics, and weapons. Because each crew was small—just six men (one officer and five enlisted)—cross-training of the men was critical, especially heading into a combat situation. I insisted that everyone be able to clean, load and fire every weapon, know the basics regarding maintaining the engines as well as how to use the radios and radar in the dark. All this training had to be accomplished surrounded by as much noise, yelling and confusion as I could generate. In time, they would each learn to drive the boat, but for the time being, understanding its equipment bow to stern was more important.

The Navy usually tried to assign an engineman, radioman and gunner's mate to each crew and they would have prime responsibility for that specific area of the boat, both from maintenance and operating standpoint. However, this "expert" would often be no more than twenty years old, so a team effort was non-negotiable, but it was also a concept well received by our crew. After we left school, the next twelve months would be spent together on a fifty-foot boat patrolling the coast and the rivers of South Vietnam or riding out a Pacific Ocean storm. I knew that we would often be at sea every other day for thirty hours or more. There would be no tolerance for bad-hair days and personality quirks.

I met my crew the afternoon of our first full day, realizing we would train together for the next several months. They were young, very young, except for Bos'n Mate Bill Fielder ("Boats"), who was a second-class petty officer. He appeared to be about twenty-eight and came from Texas with the appropriate twang. "Salty" would best describe Boats, from the swagger of his walk to the tilt of his white cap. The wrist of each hand had links of chain tattooed on it with a spider resting on the outer edge. The symbolism was lost on me and I found out later there was none. Not viewable at the time were two sharks on his chest facing each other. The tattoo "piece de resistance" was the list of girlfriends and one former wife on his upper left arm. A narrow line was drawn through each to indicate past tense.

Oscar Wells ("Snipe") was twenty-two, from Georgia and an engine-man second class who knew his trade well. He has now retired to Georgia after a stint as an officer in the Army, followed by parish time as a minister in Augusta, Georgia. Mike Newcomer was a twenty-year-old third-class radioman from Washington State who knew his electronic gear well, both from Navy schools and previous duty. Bob Buck and John Muller were both seamen in their late teens. They were a little short on sea duty but from the start they had a great attitude, ready to learn. Muller was from Oregon, knew something about guns, so I assigned him to weapons, with Buck, from Washington, as his protégé.

I had seen their personnel records beforehand and knew that Boats was the only one who had seen any significant Navy duty, most of it on cruisers and destroyers. As I said, he was the ultimate salty bos'n, resplendent with tattoos, the folding buck knife on his belt and whenever available, the coffee mug. The last item was always held firmly in the right hand by the index finger supported by the second finger and stabilized by the thumb resting on the top of the mug. It was a procedure that worked well, but I don't think it was an actual part of Navy regs.

I assumed correctly that someone with Boats' Navy experience had somehow illegally gained access to my personnel file. This was confirmed by his negative attitude toward me when we first met and was most likely based on what he read in my record as a lack of Navy experience calculated only in terms of years. This was the first and very big mistake on the part of Boats.

That first day, the crew (although young) was friendly and respectful except for Boats, whose standard answer in response to my questions was a curt "Yeh." As we reviewed the week ahead there was little change and his negative attitude continued. By the end of the day, I came to the conclusion that this attitude was going to be a real and unacceptable problem, and I decided now was the time to deal with it.

I pulled him aside, out of earshot of the rest of the crew and told him in no uncertain terms, "Boats, it has been a long, long day, which is not going to repeat itself tomorrow."

I then outlined for him two clear and simple options: "First, you can lead the crew and manage the boat while reporting to me and God willing, we would all return home together. Second, you can continue to be the asshole you have been today and either you'll come home in a pine box or at best, a broken-down seaman recruit."

I closed with: "0630, I want your answer. Now dismiss the men."

I then turned and walked away. No question, it was a gutsy ball play, but I had been down a similar road on my first ship and had received some great leadership advice from a chief petty officer that I had never forgotten.

When I arrived the next morning, my troops were all lined up and squared away. Boats stepped forward, his hat cocked just so and his uniform starched to such an extent it could stand on its own.

He snapped a salute and said, "Morning, Skipper, all men present and accounted for."

My response was a returned salute and a simple "Boats, I assume option one?" "Yes, sir, option one," he replied.

*Boat School in Coronado.*

That's how it began, a great relationship, both work and personal, based on mutual respect, trust and a team effort. This served us well in the months and trials ahead and remains one of my proudest accomplishments to this day. At that moment I prayed, with God's blessing, we would in fact all return home together.

As I said, the days in class would not be described as intellectually demanding but definitely taught us the myriad of critical things we needed to know both to operate and survive. At the same time, a Swift Boat would hardly be described as a sophisticated piece of military hardware. When they began the program, the Navy needed about 130 boats delivered quickly. As a result, they purchased them from a company in Louisiana called Sewart Seacraft. This type of boat was being used to deliver crews and supplies to offshore oil rigs in the Gulf of Mexico.

The boats were fast, about 30 mph, and could be built quickly with little design modification. Most of the equipment on board, except for the various weapons, was off the shelf commercial, not military, which made it readily available. My guess was that few, if any, in the senior Navy bureaucracy really understood or cared what the Swift Boat mission was. At the same time, the cost of buying these 130 Swift Boats, compared to the complex procurement contracts for Navy ships and aircraft, had to be considered "small change" and most likely received limited review. This concept of soft focus, operating under the bureaucratic radar scope, evolved to be one of the most attractive features of the entire Swift Boat program.

In school during the day, we disassembled, rebuilt, crawled under, and then crawled over, turned on, then turned off every piece of equipment, eyes open and then eyes closed. We went to the shooting range for small arms fire and into the outside unheated pool for survival swimming. Even in San Diego, in February, this was not a pleasant experience.

Each officer was responsible for PT (physical training) of his own crew, so at the end of the day we ran and did the usual pushups, sit-ups, etc. My goal was to get them in acceptable shape and cause enough pain to cut down on the cigarettes and beer. Muller and Buck were just nineteen and each weighed about 130 pounds, so debauchery was not an issue and they had no problem keeping up with me. I knew one of the frogmen stationed at Coronado from Harvard, Teddy Roosevelt IV (TR4), and he gave us several sessions on hand-to-hand combat. My crew thoroughly enjoyed seeing their 220-pound leader sent flying through the air launched by someone half his size. All for the good of the cause!

At night, we went our separate ways and I usually teamed up with Ed and Bob and some other sophisticates from the Boat class just ahead of us. In most cases, our target was The Mexican Village, a "watering hole" downtown frequented by the local Coronado femme fatales. Bob had just gotten married back home to a great girl named Connie, whom we would meet later on, so he was not a full partner in crime. Without question, Ed was our ringleader, a title according to him that was firmly based on his age and experience; it certainly wasn't his social sophistication.

One night, we met a group of teachers who taught in the local school and lived nearby in a rented house on the island. Somehow during maneuvers, Ed tried to lock in a weekend party at their place, but they were not buying into his game plan. Without question, this was a serious setback for our self-appointed social director.

*First time at the wheel.*

Available young macho males were hardly an endangered species on Coronado Island. To make matters worse, we were visitors in transit only (twelve weeks), so this negatively impacted our overall attractiveness rating. After the girls departed, we ordered another round and reviewed the battle plan, while candidly discussing its flaws. Conclusion: "They weren't interested."

Calling on my more subtle New England training and social development, I made the suggestion that we simply show up at their door next

Thursday with steaks (uncooked), along with an adequate inventory of red wine and simply ask them which night was better—Friday, Saturday, or Sunday night. I now realize this is called the "assumptive sales close," not "yes" or "no" but rather "when." Much to my relief and to the enhancement of my stature among my peers, the plan worked. Saturday it was. Obviously, our sophisticated presentation, along with a menu of fine food and drink, carried the day. I am pretty sure that, after the fact, Ed took credit for the idea. Regardless, the result was the start of an enjoyable friendship albeit by definition, a short one.

At dinner, we were informed by our hosts (hostesses) that on most Sundays, early in the afternoon, there was a mixer (for want of a better word) for officers and guests at the North Island Airbase. This facility to our surprise was in fact an *airbase*, which was appropriately located at the *north end of the island*. Damn clever, these airdales (Navy aviators). Adding to the mystery, for some reason the club was called the "Down Winds." The description "Club" was a bit of a stretch because the mixer was basically held outside in what might best be described as a block

*No instructors on board.*

house. It was a four-sided cement block building. It did have a roof, but the sides were those ornate open cement blocks that you see used on some fancy houses where the owners had too much money and not enough taste. Regardless, the beer flowed freely and the music was nonstop rock and roll. The dress code was casual, very casual. Kind of West Coast washable—not Cape Cod and definitely not the Hamptons.

I learned later, as evening approached and the setting sun slowly caressed the nearby blue Pacific, that there was a definite logic behind the physical structure of "Down Winds." It was based on the fact that this was indeed a Naval airbase. *Naval Air* being the operative words, as in pilots and low-flying planes.

As the music beat faster, the crowd grew louder and louder, sweat flowed and the good times rolled on. Suddenly, from the front of the room came the loud and clear command, delivered I presume by some wayward aviator, who bellowed forth, "Launch Aircraft."

In response and on cue, everyone with a pitcher of beer proceeded rapidly to the nearest commercial fan. Because of the afternoon heat, there were numerous units scattered around the room. Each fan received the remaining contents of the beer pitchers, which were tossed smartly into the whirling blades. To the uninitiated standing awkwardly nearby, it was indeed a memorable experience. To the regulars, this was a common occurrence and one to avoid if you were able to assess (in time) the beer cloud's airborne trajectory. "Down Winds," now it all made sense to me.

## CHAPTER 2

# SERE: SURVIVAL TRAINING

During the whirlwind social schedule that Bob, Ed and I were compelled to maintain during Boat School, there was one sobering element of the robust curriculum that remained outstanding. It was the training that was usually discussed in hushed tones—the notorious off-base SERE course. This stood for Survival, Evasion, Resistance, and Escape. It was one of those events that you knew was going to take place, but you mentally kept it somewhere out there in the future not really wanting to deal with it. Crews returning from SERE gave you some insight into the rigors of the course, but basically all of us chose to ignore it as long as possible.

For obvious reasons, SERE was scheduled to take place right before you went into the final phase of Boat School. After SERE, there were two final weeks of busy boat operations and then you shipped out. It occurred to me that this scheduling was all part of a nefarious plot, designed by the Navy or at least the Swift Boat School, to close out our twelve-week educational sabbatical with a very sobering dose of reality.

The intent of the SERE course was to train Navy personnel, individuals, and crews of all types, who were going into combat, how to deal with being captured by the enemy. It began focusing just on pilots and then expanded to include all types of special warfare personnel, which included Swifts. It was five days long and started with three days of wilderness survival training and then you were put in a prisoner-of-war camp for the remainder. It sounds unpleasant because it was. The Marines ran another facility for the Navy in the hills near San Diego, but our class drew the short straw and was sent to Whidbey Island Naval Air Station in the state of Washington, in February, no less.

Guidelines were provided beforehand—each boat went together as a crew, no contraband or liquids, bring warm clothing, none would be provided. However, they didn't mention weapons so a group of us, led by Ed the experienced hunter/outdoorsman, got in the spirit of the things and brought guitar strings at a music store in downtown Coronado to use as garrotes. A somewhat dramatic choice of a weapon but the price was right and it was easily concealed. Later one evening after class, at Ed's suggestion, we painstakingly hid each garrote by weaving them into the laces of our boots.

Being from Boston, home of the Gillette razor, I came up with the idea of somehow concealing razor blades. At the time, Gillette had a new product called the "Techmatic" razor. It was a plastic cartridge containing a short coil of thin but continuous razor blade that the shaver unwound as needed. I brought the razor, broke the device, removed the blade, cut it into pieces and hid it under two band aids on my fingers. Not quite as good as a James Bond multipurpose wristwatch, but at the time, I felt this was very creative. Ed was impressed.

After a miserable three-hour flight bouncing through turbulence all the way from San Diego on an overheated relic of a plane left over from the Korean conflict, we arrived at the Whidbey Island Naval Air Station. Perhaps I was reacting to my considerable apprehension about the coming week ahead, but I wondered whether our delivery flight had been designed as an introductory and integral component of the SERE experience.

My analysis was cut short as survival classes started immediately upon our arrival. Never let the troops settle in or acclimate. Each crew was provided with a huge green-colored Air Force cargo parachute. We quickly learned how to construct a four-bedroom ranch house from this silk monster. The fact that a Swift Boat would never have a para-chute on board, let alone one this big, appeared to have been lost on the course designers. However, we did learn to make a great shelter, insulate it with pine needles and utilize mutual bodily warmth. Vietnam and pine needles was another discrepancy, but what the hell, we were committed.

We learned how to make fish gill nets and then place them in waist-deep water, which was delightful in February. However, anything we caught was off limits under the no-food guidelines. We set rabbit traps and caught one, but the instructors were concerned about the health of the wild rabbits so they gave us a domestic one and we made soup for forty men. That night, the domestic rabbit soup made all forty of us sick. This, as you can imagine, had a somewhat negative impact on the ongoing student/teacher relationship. Washington was Bob's home state so we thought he would have some local pull or perhaps know a good take-out restaurant. Regretfully he did not.

After three days and some incredibly valuable experience such as freezing at night, fishing in cold water and eating tainted rabbit, we were informed that we would enter the POW Phase in the morning. During this component of the exercise, crews did not stay together and each person was on his own. If you were captured right away, so be it, if not you could stay out until 1100 and then the rules required that you to turn yourself in to join the festivities.

I am a firm believer that society arrives late and I was shooting for that 1100 arrival time. Once again, the instructors lied and in the middle of the night before the POW Phase was to begin, the "enemy" invaded our peaceful campsite, stood on our hands and feet shooting off automatic weapons (blanks only), while letting the hot brass casings fall on our heads. They concluded this "welcome aboard" introduction after about thirty minutes and left it to our own imaginations what was to take place over the next two days.

The next day at dawn, we were released and with my best sprint I took off up the dirt road and after about fifty yards dove in head-first into a thick bramble bush, hoping to hide. While painful, it worked, as the bad guys started to sweep the roadside for us, the good guys. At one point, they were standing alongside my hiding place, but fortunately I had a dark green jacket and khaki pants that blended in with the muted winter color scheme in Washington State.

You could not physically leave the base, but there were acres to roam, so my goal was to keep on the move undetected. In a crouched position with the occasional drop to the deck, I worked along the edge of another dirt road where there appeared to be some legitimate excavation work taking place. Much to my dismay and bad luck, I then rounded a blind corner and ran smack into a three-man armed enemy patrol complete with their Chinese communist uniforms topped off with fur hats and red stars.

The design of the POW Phase appeared to be a bit more theatrical than the Survival Phase. They stopped me and then stuck rifles in my face shouting their version of twentieth-century bad-guy pig Latin. In response, I dug deep, referencing some high school drama training and a couple of summer sales jobs and confidently yelled back, "Cut the crap." I told them I was the foreman of the nearby construction crew and I had a disabled bulldozer up the road and had to get to a phone fast.

My ruse worked and frankly I was quite impressed with my performance. I followed their directions, heading up the road toward their headquarters, supposedly to find a phone, but I bailed out at the next turn and gained another ninety minutes of freedom. The drawback was, when I did turn myself in at the mandatory 1100, the same three enemy troops I had encountered previously were standing nearby. Immediately recognizing me, they displayed a total absence of any sense of humor by pushing my head face down into a pool of muddy water in the middle of the road. No question, these three had not been active members of Harvard's Hasty Pudding Theatricals.

By this time all the crews had been "captured." We were organized into random groups in the middle of a small grassy meadow and told by the guards not to move. Suddenly without another word, we were left alone as our captors disappeared into the surrounding woods. This time on our own, as well as being unguarded, was undoubtedly structured to allow our imaginations to run wild, which they certainly did.

After about ten minutes, stepping silently out of the nearby tree line was what could only be described as a giant of a man, who was at least part bear. I was 6' 3" and this guy had at least two inches and seventy-five pounds on me. All this bulk was wrapped up in a massive black woolen coat. His face was covered with a full and bushy black beard and eyes of a similar color peered out from beneath a huge fur hat adorned with the big red star on the upturned front flap.

Complete with polished knee-high leather boots, surrounded on three sides by his guards, he strutted into the campsite as if he owned the place. For all practical purposes, I guess he did. In a guttural and booming tone he announced that he was Major Barkov and that we were all his prisoners. Mission accomplished, pal. You got our attention.

My jacket was open and I had no doubt my rapid heartbeat was clearly showing through the sweater beneath. Quite relevant at the time was the distinct possibility of my having a heart attack, thereby ending the training session right then and there. My only solace was a quick look to the side which revealed that my fellow crew members were equally aghast.

He asked all the officers to step forward, which we did. Even ever-so-cool Ed Bergin had lost that suave patina. The major then proceeded to walk up to each of us, whisper something in our ear and then slap each of us in the face calling us all "American Pigs and Warmongers." If you were lucky, he returned a moment later with a second slap.

Without a pause in the script, he then turned his head left, then right and yelled, "Would the two American girls step forward?" On this one we were all at a loss. He continued, "Shirley and Carroll, where are you girls?"

Bob Shirley and Dennis Carroll were both boat skippers who were part of our class. This meant that Major Barkov had spent time reviewing our personnel records beforehand, a very nice touch on his part. After his henchman dragged "the girls" around the meadow feet first, he then turned to the minority component of our group, roughing up three black crew members, one of whom was my engineman, Oscar Wells.

We knew from previous training that their goal was to provoke some action from the crews. They hoped to find out who was a potential leader or, in their eyes, a future troublemaker who required additional control. So far, nothing they had done was significantly grave; therefore any action on our part would be a foolhardy move, which was just what they wanted.

However, at the time, there were several officers (not from Swift Boats) taking the course with us. One was from the Naval Academy and had delusions of grandeur or had misread the "capture" chapter in the book. During these welcoming festivities, he stepped forward and formally identified himself as a United States Naval officer. They were so impressed with that they hung him by his arms from a tree branch with only his toes touching the ground for support. "Point made, Major Barkov."

The day quickly went downhill from this Welcome Aboard Phase. We were interviewed and interrogated for hours on end in a wooden hut, while sitting beneath the hanging single lightbulb in an uncomfortable chair with one short leg. This was followed by a session outside in your underwear (again Washington State, in February), where they took a woolen watch cap, soaked it in water, then put it over your nose and mouth. For good measure, they then held your head back and poured more water onto the hat while asking you various questions to which you responded with name, rank, and serial number. Overall, this was a most unpleasant experience, later to be known as waterboarding. In this case, they just held you on the ground while you groaned, choked and threw up. No actual board was involved.

In between these fun-time sessions, we received reprogramming education. We marched to classrooms, in a single line, our right arms extended and placed on the shoulder of the man in front with canvas bags over our heads. Before we started this session, I laid out a plan with Boats to walk in front of me and when I squeezed his shoulder he would dramatically fall to the ground and, in the confusion, I would attempt to run off. For good measure, I told Bob Mack to provide additional cover by yelling when he heard Boats fall. It worked like a charm. Boats went down like a ton of bricks and actually pulled the guy in front down with him. On cue, Bob started yelling, bringing more attention to Boats.

Meanwhile in the confusion, I sprinted for the cover of a nearby small wooden shed off to my right that I had seen while previously lifting the corner of my hood. However, the best-laid plans can indeed go askew. I had carefully planned the front component of my escape and that execution was flawless. However, to my rear was a young man who

I had not included in my plan. When I ran off, his hand obviously no longer rested on my shoulder, which caused him distress, and he started calling, "Mr. Daly, Mr. Daly, where are you?"

The guards could now clearly see the gap I had left in the line and soon surrounded the shed, which unfortunately was the only structure nearby providing any cover. Regretfully, my freedom was very short-lived, but the slaps and shoves were not excessive and the message was sent to the troops that we need not be totally passive.

The rules said you could escape, but only for a limited time and under no circumstances could a weapon be taken from the guards. Several weeks before, the SEALs had come to the course and, based on their team training, had done some significant damage to the real estate, the curriculum, and a couple of the guards. As a result, the new rules changed the playing field decisively in favor of the bad guys.

Considering these changes, before the major's initial arrival and the commencement of fun, we were standing at attention in that bucolic meadow and were instructed to turn in any weapons. Therefore, the guitar string garrotes entwined in our bootlaces were gone. In consideration of good sportsmanship and full disclosure, I peeled back my band aids revealing my "Techmatic" razor blades. Somewhat surprised, the guards stated this was a first, but since there was currently no award for creativity, I should get my ass back in formation.

The classroom sessions were unbelievably boring, with the instructor in the front of the room preaching from Mao's little book on revolution. It was all part of a master plan—exhaust you, then hit you on the head with a book every time you nodded off. All the while, you were sitting in old wooden theater chairs that were screwed to the floor so close front to back that you could not sit straight and constantly had to squirm, causing even more discomfort.

Ed Bergin was nearby with his bos'n Bobby Don Carver who was beside Boats (Fielder), all of them off to my right. Boats was about 5' 10" but the rest of us were over 6'. I decided we needed some emotional relief or at least some distraction, so I gave Ed the high sign and got his attention.

We started to cough during the presentation and this soon rolled across the room. The instructor was no fool. He saw what was developing, and immediately called for assistance and the head whackers all joined in to provide the appropriate cough remedy. Although short-lived, our coughing had resulted in maximum disruption at the cost of just a few head whacks in return. Score one point for the good guys.

The various types of harassment continued all night. We were corralled in a compound surrounded by a chain-link fence with a wood and dirt hut in the middle with a charming out-house off to the side. Not exactly the Bachelor Officer Quarters (BOQ) but this was not their intent. It became obvious that their goal was to deprive us of sleep to render us exhausted, while constantly harassing us, both verbally and physically. It was definitely working.

During the night, we were pulled out of the compound for more one-on-one interrogation, with the single lightbulb and the tilting chair routine. If you were in the compound and sat down with the idea of a little shut-eye, some armed gorilla was in your face. Major Barkov would make the occasional guest appearances with his appropriate inspirational comments about America, our basic intellect and other items of personal interest. This guy was good cop, bad cop, all rolled into one oversized, black-bearded reign of terror.

The next day was somewhat like a field day. They put us in boxes, approximating the size of dog houses, for about four hours. You could not stretch out, but you could kneel if you bent over. The day before, I had gathered a fist full of brass machine-gun casings from the blanks they were constantly firing at us as background music. I worked on the premise of being a good collector and felt everything might be of future use. In the dog house, I took one of the shell casings and began to carve various clever sayings like "Fuck You" in the wooden wall planks.

Not to be outdone, Ed was in the unit next door and saw through the cracks that our Annapolis friend had been dragged out for some infraction and slapped around, then tossed back in. Whenever the guards went away, Ed would cause a ruckus yelling and the guards would assume it was our neighbor acting up again. All done in good fun.

All these adventures were truly character-building and helped to pass the hours. The only saving grace was we knew this was only two days long. God help the real POWs. After the Dog House Phase, there was a trade down in the real estate category to what I could only describe as a cheaply built coffin. It was your basic pine box made of loose fitting planks, so airflow was not a factor. However, to make the occupant more comfortable, they put in short wooden cross pieces of 2x4s. This meant you had to bend your torso and twist your legs to fit.

I started out in the horizontal version of a coffin, but the top would not close because there was simply too much of me. The guard's solution was to stand on the top to close the lid. I had previously noticed that there were monitors walking around dressed as guards, but merely watching so that the troops' enthusiasm for reality did not get out of control. I yelled to the guy on top of me that the lid was not going to close and in the process he was going to break my back. My message got through, so I was then dragged unceremoniously to the upright version.

The upright design was basically the same, somewhat roomier but still with the extra pieces of wood to cram you in and bend you over. As I was going in, I took out my trusty brass shell casings and shoved a couple into the door frame to provide some extra airflow. Unfortunately, the coffin construction was somewhat shoddy and the extra pressure broke the latch. The wooden door flew open catching the guard smartly in the ass. Understandably, this did not sit well with him and probably cost me some extra time in the box.

I did not have claustrophobia at the time and there was light and air, so the situation was certainly unpleasant but bearable. However several feet away, I could tell by the yelling that someone was not in the least enjoying this segment of the training exercise. I couldn't see who it was but he was removed and led off the premises protesting all the way. I suspect this marked the end of the program for him. Certainly this would be the result if he was a member of a Swift Boat crew. However, I don't think this was the case because that was the last any of us heard of the incident.

After about an hour in the coffin, my lower extremities were vacillating between pain and numbness, neither one very pleasant. It appears the camp management had this exercise timed to perfection because along came the guards who opened the lids, or in my case the door, and let you fall smartly on your face. Then you crawled along the ground or were dragged away from the area. All these actions, especially if you were an officer, were carefully meant to enhance your image in front of the troops, along with building your own personal esteem.

Nightfall was coming and we were taken back to the compound after that full day of fun field exercises. It was quickly becoming obvious to all of us that this POW routine was a no-win situation. We were beat up, hungry and exhausted, the last element probably being the most dangerous. Major Barkov dropped by to ask, "Did we need anything and how was everything going?" In my opinion, this guy was watching way too many old war flicks and might soon be up for an Oscar himself. With his toothy grin, he informed us that because some of our troops had been so cooperative and forthcoming, he might authorize a small feast of beef stew for all of us. I saw that this was definitely the old divide and conquer play.

After his announcement, he turned smartly on his shiny boot heel and departed. Several of us were so pissed off we decided to make one more try at rebellion. Bob and Ed had earlier tried the tunnel under the fence routine, only to come up outside the fence right at the feet of two guards. This was followed by the usual screaming and face slaps. We then decided on something more cerebral and tried a tactic Bob said he had previously seen in a movie. We all had coffee mugs; no coffee was served but they were used for water. We discussed the fact that the government had spent considerable money training us, so in the last analysis we calculated that they couldn't let us die or be permanently damaged.

Therefore, we took all the mugs and hung them on the fence spelling "USA" backwards. Then we took rocks from the dirt in the compound and placed them in the slanted dirt wall of the hut spelling, again backwards, "Fuck You." The word was passed to our troops and these two efforts provided them a small motivational uplift as they walked around the compound. This effect only increased as time went by, without our handiwork being discovered by the guards.

About 0300, the major came back into the compound. It was obvious this guy did not keep bankers' hours. In that booming voice that no one could ignore, he announced that the "People's Republic of Wherever" was going to provide us with a feast. On cue, two of the guards brought in firewood and we were ordered to build a fire. One of the boat skippers, Bruce Wentworth, had been an Eagle Scout and volunteered to start and manage the fire. We were not certain but guessed that we were down to about three or four hours left in this horror show. Bruce's woodland expertise got high votes all around and considerable support.

After thirty minutes, the fire was roaring and the guards brought in a large pot, complete with vegetables and previously chopped meat. They were smart enough, at this point, not to let us near a knife. The aroma was outstanding. In five days each of us had eaten one clam, a Chunky candy bar (why Chunky, I don't know), and the rabbit stew that had made everyone sick. Next, the stew bowls were brought in and we stood around waiting to dig in. At that moment, we all began feeling somewhat positive toward our captors, especially with the end of SERE in sight.

In strutted Major Barkov. Circling slowly, he smiled at each of us as he paraded around the hut, finally stopping beside the smoking pot. He approached it slowly, scanning his audience from left to right, ensuring he had all our attention. Still watching us, a smile on his face, he waited one more poignant moment. Pivoting smartly to his right, he kicked the smoking stewpot over with a single but powerful swing of his big black boot. Then with one more sneering look around the hut, he triumphantly strolled out, surrounded by his armed guards, all of whom were walking backward with their weapons drawn.

The moment just hung there, as we stared at the stew flowing along the ground with the aroma wafting toward us from the massive over-turned pot. A couple of minutes went by, maybe five, then in walked a U.S. Navy lieutenant commander in his working khakis uniform and announced to all that this session of the SERE training camp was over. He told us that hot showers were available and breakfast would begin in one hour in the mess hall. Then he waved and yelled, "Follow me." I did a quick inventory to make sure my crew was in one piece and saw that Ed and Bob were doing likewise. We didn't need a second invitation.

Coffee was available, located just outside the showers, probably to make sure no one fell asleep and drowned. We all made our own way to the mess hall, officers and enlisted all in the same line. We were told to eat with some reserve and go back for seconds if we felt good enough. There was no hurry. The bus to our plane would be leaving in three hours.

Dressed now in my working khakis uniform, I started through the line again for a second cup of coffee when I saw a young sailor, who I guessed was part of the SERE school, and asked him if he was a member of the staff. He emphatically replied "Yes," and stated that he was part of the enemy team and been here about eighteen months. Just making conversation, I said that the week had been a very demanding one but certainly educational. In response, he then looked me straight in the eye and described how he had recently come up with what he felt was a great idea for the Prisoner Capture Phase that the school should definitely use.

He then described a scenario that when we were all finally captured they would force us to march down the dirt road to the prison camp while their girlfriends and wives would all throw rocks at us. I nodded blankly, attempting to conceal my reaction while I digested his suggestion, not knowing quite how to respond. As I left the food line, I saw standing nearby a Navy lieutenant who was an M.D. as indicated by the medical insignia on his collar. Introducing myself, I described my prior conversation with Seaman Hicks, having read the name on his shirt. My suggestion was that the "Doc" spend a little one-on-one time with Seaman Hicks doing a reality check and discussing some of his training ideas.

Now that everyone was back in Navy uniforms, it was hard to tell the guards from the inmates, except for Major Barkov. Ed and I immediately spotted him; it wasn't that difficult, based on his size and the black beard. We approached him and introduced ourselves. Unlike young Seaman Hicks, he was most pleasant and outgoing. We learned he was an American Indian from Colorado and was a first class bos'n mate. He had previously served on an aircraft carrier and had been recruited to this assignment a year ago, but his tour was up and he was leaving shortly.

Despite the past grueling five days, we congratulated him on the quality of the job he had done and the message he had sent. The message in our opinion was simple: "Being captured should be avoided at all costs." Ed, the ever inquisitive, wanted to know where the idea of kicking over the stewpot had come from. Major Barkov smiled and said that most components of the program were understandably scripted by a training staff, but he had introduced that stewpot scenario because he had seen it in a cowboy movie. He asked the staff if he could do it one time and now it was the crescendo component of the curriculum.

We wished him good luck in his career and, with some qualifiers, thanked him. Along with a handshake, this again brought out the booming laugh of Major Barkov. Despite the fact that Ed and I were once again officers dressed in U.S. Navy uniforms, the major's goodbye was still very disconcerting.

Goodbye SERE and Major Barkov. Goodbye Whidbey Island, Washington. Next stop—Coronado.

## CHAPTER 3

# SHIPPING OUT FROM CORONADO

We returned to Coronado from SERE training late on Sunday afternoon; it was early March 1967. Ed, Bob, and I joined all the other boat skippers for a couple of drinks and dinner together at the base O'Club. We decided to call it an early night to catch up on some much-needed rack time, despite Ed's best effort to coordinate a downtown recon. Besides, we knew the following morning at 0730 we would commence the boat operations training phase. The past week in SERE had resulted in each of us more clearly understanding the realities of the combat mission on which we were soon to embark.

Bob had gotten married two weekends before in Seattle, but his new wife Connie was a school teacher and had remained there working because Bob was off to SERE. This was one of the more sobering examples of the sacrifices military families make. No two-week honeymoon in Hawaii for the Macks, maybe a weekend at the Hotel Del but the departure clock was ticking.

At 0800, all crews and officers mustered on the pier. Spirits remained high but there was an added sense of seriousness regarding the tasks at hand. We were assigned an instructor, usually a chief petty officer, one for two boats. We spent the next hour individually and as a team checking out all systems, equipment, weapons, and engines on our assigned boat. Then we fired up the engines and let them warm up for the recommended five minutes.

Those specific GM diesels had a very distinctive sound, especially when they first started and were warming up. At idle, it was a hesitating deep-throated, rolling rumble accompanied in the background by a higher pitch mechanical sound, almost but not quite musical. At full speed the sound became more like roaring thunder. You felt it in your feet and it pulsated in your ears. Definitely not an engineer, I learned later that this had something to do with the way the valve lifters and fuel injector system worked together. Anyway, it was a distinctive sound, one you could quickly recognize and, for most of us, one you just plain grew to love.

Three boats were tied up "portside to" the pier with another three boats outboard of them. The lead instructor on the outboard boat, which was located third in line, instructed the boat officer to get under way. Lines were taken in and the boat was twisted with the starboard engine ahead and the port engine astern with the helm turned hard to port. The result was the bow of the boat turned to port, hopefully clearing the boat ahead, while its stern twisted out to starboard away from the pier.

Most of the officers had experience driving destroyers, but there was a significant difference between having the conn (physical control) of a ship 400 feet long giving orders to the helm compared to maneuvering a fifty-foot boat with your own hands on the throttles and wheel. During this first training sortie there were a couple of close calls, but slow and steady in most cases worked effectively. Like Ed Bergin, I had a fair amount of boat experience, although not with a boat this size with big twin diesel engines. Some basics applied: "Don't overpower the situation and observe what the wind is doing to you." This basic ship-handling technique was somewhat of an art form and it was never acquired by some individuals, despite doing it day after day for over a year in Vietnam.

Being at the wheel, in this instance, at the aft helm located portside at the rear of the main cabin, was something I had thought about and visualized from the first day I arrived at the base and saw the boats. This was my crew and we were finally, after almost ten weeks, under way. I know Ed and Bob felt just as I did as their crews cast off. When all boats had left the pier the lead instructor told us to fall into a column formation following at fifty-yard intervals and maintain radio communication.

We proceeded slowly out of the small Coronado harbor where the Swift base was located and commenced a wide left turn into the middle of the huge San Diego Bay. We then headed north past the main Navy base with its massive piers off to our right where aircraft carriers, destroyers and cruisers, as well as various amphibious ships, were all berthed. Years later, when the bridge was built connecting San Diego to Coronado, the carriers were berthed farther out at North Island on the Coronado side. This was a security measure so that if an enemy ever sabotaged the bridge, the carriers would not be trapped inside, unable to sortie.

Boats took over the helm in the pilothouse after I disengaged the aft wheel and I walked forward to join him there. The rest of the crew were scattered about the boat: Muller and Buck at the weapons positions, Newcomer was below at the main radio, or in Oscar Well's (Snipe's) case, down with his big diesels with the engine hatches wide open.

Proceeding at a conservative 10 kts out of the harbor was not quite the dramatic white water picture I had visualized. However, this was our first day on the boats and as that old Navy saying goes, "A collision at sea can ruin your whole day." Without question, despite our slow speed, a column of six Swift Boats still looked, at least in our humble opinion, "pretty impressive." This was especially true as we passed several large Navy ships transiting the harbor, as well as when we waved to some of the local San Diego tour boats.

Following the main channel, passing the North Island Airbase on our left, we turned to port heading west by the promontory Point Loma out to the harbor mouth and open water. Once outside, we increased speed to about 20 kts, again maintaining a column formation. In this case, the primary training goal was avoiding a collision with the boat just in front or the one close behind. This was a relatively basic maneuver but in the military one always keeps in mind that "Shit does indeed happen."

Even though it was mid-March, the day was sunny and clear with the seas calm so we moved from a column formation to what is defined in Navy parlance as a line abreast. Basically, this maneuver encompassed all six boats traveling in the same direction alongside each other about 100 feet apart. This maneuver was executed by radio commands and repeated several times without incident.

The next training evolution was to stop and come alongside another Swift Boat without the gnashing of teeth or the bending of aluminum. The Navy cared more about the latter, so some yelling was acceptable. Being able to execute this docking maneuver was critical because it was going to be a common procedure in Vietnam. Therefore the drill was a first step in learning how to approach, land alongside, board and inspect a Vietnamese junk or cargo vessel.

The next day was more of the same in terms of boat handling, but we started some navigational training, plotting and laying out courses to various points in and outside the harbor. If you had been serving on board a ship in the United States Navy for two to three years and couldn't do this basic type of navigation you had a serious problem, so this section was basically check off the boxes.

A full afternoon was spent on learning positioning and targeting as it related to the 81mm mortar on the afterdeck of the boat. Our machine guns were basically a line-of-sight weapon. If you could see or had some general idea where the enemy was, then you pointed the gun at him and pulled the trigger. With the mortar everything was more complex. This was a standoff weapon that required two elements, the first being that you knew on a map where the target was and second, you could determine an accurate position (fix) for your own vessel. *Without* both inputs there was a damn good chance you would drop a mortar round on some friendly forces or at a minimum miss your target.

Locating your own position at sea was the tricky part. While there were numerous buoys to reference in San Diego Bay, there would be none along the coast or the rivers of Vietnam. Therefore you had to sight multiple positions that you could actually see onshore at various angles that would lead you to your position known as a "fix." To do this, you could use a small handheld sighting compass, pick a point on land, read its direction from your compass, and then reverse that direction by 180°. The next step was to draw a line on a chart from that position onshore, out to the water in the vicinity of where you thought you were located. This was known as a "line of position" or LOP. Doing that type of measurement three times generated three lines from three *different* onshore locations. Then, hopefully, you had a small triangle on the chart and your boat's position was in the middle of that triangle.

If the compass method was not available because of darkness or bad weather then you could do something similar with three radar ranges that would give you not a direction (line of position), but three distances (ranges) to the object. Then you took a basic elementary school mathematical compass, (pencil and pointer), open it to the appropriate distance which was the radar range, place the pointed end on the chart at the onshore position and swing an arc with the pencil again approximately at your position on the chart. Do this three times and you had your position in the center of the arcs.

Now that you had the position of your boat, you knew where the target was located and you could measure the distance between the two from the chart. This result gave you range and bearing to the target. Next, you would adjust the mortar so that the fired round traveled that distance by setting the elevation for the proper range (distance) and turning the mortar on its swivel mount for the bearing (direction) to the target.

Sounds simple until you do it in the middle of a windswept rainy night while the boat beneath you tosses and turns, with no lights on, just two hundred yards off an enemy-held beach, with somebody on the other end of the radio yelling at you to "Shoot the goddamn mortar, they're coming over the hill." Therefore, the time doing this exercise in sunny California was certainly time well spent. We did this without firing the weapon because there were few, if any, enemy targets in the San Diego area and one misfired round from an 81mm mortar could definitely ruin someone's afternoon garden party.

The next day was spent without instructors, basically more of the same but with the individual boat officers in charge. On the way out of the harbor Bob Mack had to go into the upscale Shelter Island Marina because the compass on his boat was being repaired there and he was scheduled to pick it up. We felt Bob needed some protection on this risky mission so Ed and I volunteered to go along in our boats.

With the big diesels on all three boats rolling and rumbling, we proceeded into the Shelter Island Marina maneuvering amongst beautiful motor yachts and sleek sailboats. Although we had no ammunition on board we decided to uncover all the weapons to demonstrate to the nearby taxpayers where their hard-earned money was being spent. However, we were smart enough to elevate all weapons skyward lest any Nervous Nellie on the piers felt they'd be taken under friendly fire.

As expected, the trip made for great theater, especially as we tied up all three boats alongside the pier while we waited for Bob to retrieve his compass. Answering questions about Swift Boats from nearby civilians was a demanding task, but one we felt was truly owed to those less fortunate.

Later in the afternoon, after several hours of operating independently, we rendezvoused with the other boats and all six of us headed back into San Diego Bay returning to the base at Coronado. The main harbor was several miles long and maybe a mile or two across in certain sections. Based on this expanse, we saw no reason to proceed at a conservative 10 kts but felt a line abreast of six boats cranked up to 20 kts was much more appropriate. Since there were no instructors on board, we decided to initiate another boat-handling exercise by closing the side-by-side interval between the boats to approximately 100 feet. Each boat was generating its own rolling bow wave while we left six foaming white wakes straight astern. This maneuver looked a lot more impressive and we all agreed it was very relevant skill training.

As we approached the San Diego Navy piers, Bob Mack on PCF 27, on the east side of our formation, spotted an admiral's barge (aka his personal Navy yacht) with the admiral's personal flag unfurled as he proceeded across the harbor heading in our direction. Most likely, the admiral resided in Coronado and was returning home for the evening.

Bob had spent six months on an admiral's staff, so he felt it was most appropriate that we as juniors render honors to this senior officer in accordance with long-standing naval etiquette. Therefore, he picked up the radio, identified himself in PCF 27, and transmitted to the rest of us, "Maneuvering message to follow, all units stand by." Shortly thereafter he continued, "Fall back in sequence forming a column behind PCF 27, stand by, execute."

This was done quite professionally as each boat slowed in an orderly fashion and fell in behind the boat immediately to her left. Soon we had a crisp column of six Swift Boats still standing into the harbor at 20 kts.

As we passed in front of the Admiral's barge approximately 200 feet away, Bob again came on the radio with the order, "Attention to port, hand salute."

At that moment each officer stepped out of the pilothouse and, along with any crewmember on deck, rendered a hand salute to the admiral as our six boats passed his bow, all churning white water.

Arriving at the Coronado piers shortly thereafter, we discussed what an outstanding maneuver this had been and this opinion was heartily seconded by all of our crews. In a professional way, we felt that indeed we had arrived.

Our self-generated enthusiasm was somewhat mitigated the next day when we were called to an "all hands" meeting at 0800. The Commanding Officer of the School read a personal message from the Admiral which read as follows: "Reference your recent Swift Boat maneuver, indeed you looked very sharp, well done men, don't ever do it again." Certainly a mixed message, but nonetheless very well received.

One night, when I called home to Boston, my father informed me that he was going to be in the San Diego area in a matter of days and asked if we could get together. While I was growing up, my father traveled a great deal around the country on business. As a family, we were very close and I knew that, in fact, my father had most likely rearranged a West Coast business trip just to visit me. At this point in time, we had several more days of boat training and then school would be closing out shortly thereafter. I asked the CO of the school, a salty Lieutenant Commander who had previously been an enlisted man, if my father could visit the boats. He looked at me with a somewhat questioning expression on his face and said, "Well, why doesn't he come out with us for the day, we're going to be conducting a night patrol with a live fire-gunnery mission?"

Frankly, I was flabbergasted at even the possibility of my dad going out on the boats, but then I realized that this was a very different part of the Navy. I thanked Commander Cook and told him that I would try to contact my father and let him know immediately. He said fine, "If he can join us, I will send an UNODIR letter. Do you know what that is, Mr. Daly?"

In fact I did. It stood for the most efficient piece of military communications ever conceived. It was basically, "Unless otherwise directed (UNODIR), I intend to do the following blank, blank." It was based on the principle that the recipient of the message might well be too lazy or not sufficiently interested enough to respond. Think of it as kind of a one-way self-permission slip.

I was able to reach my father by phone in Texas. He said he could be out the next day and would make a reservation at the Hotel Del Coronado opposite the base. He arrived on schedule and we took a brief tour of the landmark hotel because I had never been inside. We shared several bourbon old fashioneds in the ocean view bar and this was followed up by an enjoyable meal in the main dining room under its remarkable three-story-high vaulted wooden ceiling. I told him about our next day schedule and that we would be under way at 0800, out overnight and return early the next morning.

Time and accommodations were never a factor with Dad but he was concerned about his attire. I think on business trips my father slept in a dark blue suit with a white shirt and striped tie. I told him I had a casual shirt and some appropriate shoes but his suit pants would be fine and we would get him a foul-weather jacket. The next morning I picked him up at 0630 at the Hotel Del so that he would have no trouble getting onto the base. We had breakfast at the O'Club and walked together down to the Swift pier.

This was going to be an overnight training mission and because we were going to fire the weapons with live ammunition, there was an instructor present on each boat. On this trip, we had Chief Harrington on board, who had been with us on several other occasions. I introduced my father to the Chief who said, "Welcome to Swift Boats, Mr. Daly."

*Dad, Boats, and me with San Diego in the background.*

My father was in the investment business and dealt on a regular basis with wealthy and powerful individuals. However, he had a wonderful trait that I have always admired which was that he was totally comfortable with the man on the street and thoroughly enjoyed being with them. Therefore, I was not the least bit surprised when my father responded, "Please, Chief, call me Bill."

From that point on, I knew we were in good shape and I proceeded to work with the crew to get the boat started and under way. I took control at the aft helm to maneuver away from the pier. Once we had cleared the base, I gave the helm to the Chief who was in the pilothouse because I wanted to discuss the day's events with the crew. I figured my father could entertain himself for the next fifteen or twenty minutes but I needn't have worried.

When I was finished my meeting with the crew, I walked to the pilothouse and looked inside. Seated at the helm was my father, looking very content driving with his left hand firmly positioned on the top of the big stainless-steel wheel and a cup of coffee resting on the dash nearby. He was getting the fifteen-minute verbal tour from Chief Harrington.

Along the way, we went through a series of maneuvering drills with the other boats. This demonstrated to my father that both my crew and I could actually drive a Swift Boat.

All the boats arrived at an offshore firing zone by early afternoon and each of us carefully took turns firing the aft-mounted .50 caliber machine gun at an oil drum that had been carried out by one of the other boats. For the first time, I heard the repetitive racket this gun made when it fired, combined with the smell of burnt gunpowder and the sound of the spent brass cartridges jumping from the breech, and then rolling about on the deck below the gun.

This brought a new sense of reality to our training and where we were going. The goal of the exercise was relatively basic: learn how to load, fire the weapon, and subsequently clean it. No one could really become skilled at its use in such a short period of time. At best, we learned that it was a difficult weapon to effectively shoot because of its significant recoil and its tendency to climb up and away from the target with the ongoing firing of each round. More rounds, more climbing. Therefore, you learned to fire in short, repetitive four-round bursts. That day, the end result was that the oil drum target was returned to the base with minimal damage inflicted.

We did not fire the mortar, I presume, due to the size of the explosive round and restrictions in the firing zone. For me, the highlight of the firing exercise was when I was standing aft just observing, while Chief Harrington supervised each crewmember as they took their turn firing the aft .50 caliber. He then casually turned to my father and said much to my horror, "Bill, would you like to take a turn at the .50?" I have always respected Dad's judgment and he wisely took a pass saying, "Thanks anyway, Chief, more important that the boys do it."

We spent the remainder of the evening on night operations that were basically navigational and, finally, some docking maneuvers, all without lights which made both more challenging. Dinner was canned and unheated C-rations, which I was convinced were surplus from the Korean War. In his usual fashion, Dad was standing on the after deck leaning casually against the cabin with a C–Rat can and a plastic fork and said, "You know, Dan, these ham and beans are really not all that bad." As much as I loved and respected him, my only response had to be a simple, "Get serious, Dad!"

During the night, we remained a decent distance offshore. I suspect at least forty to fifty miles, well out of any shipping lanes to allow for the gunfire exercise. As the stars faded and first light began to appear on the horizon to the east, we all rendezvoused and commenced our trip back to the base.

The transit was uneventful and we cruised in no particular formation at 20 kts. However, when we were about ten miles north of the harbor mouth, we spotted four or five destroyers steaming ahead of us. We assumed they were part of a squadron returning from a deployment to Vietnam heading back toward their home port of San Diego. As we approached them from astern, Bob got on our radio circuit and, again assuming the role of operations officer, suggested we line up in a column formation and overtake the destroyers at full speed.

The instructors on board by this time felt we were ready to graduate and either we knew what we were doing or we were never going to learn. God help us all! On Bob's command we formed up in a column and cranked up the diesels to about 30 kts making our approach down the starboard side of the destroyers, while standing off about seventy-five yards.

The "tin cans" were steaming at about 25 kts so overtaking them was gradual. As we came abreast of the formation, the lead destroyer, which I assumed had the senior officer embarked, suddenly belched heavy black smoke out of both of her stacks. Being a former engineer, I knew that meant just one thing—they were adding more boilers generating more heat, more steam and *more speed*. Basically, they were putting the pedal to the metal and the race was on. Soon after the other destroyers behind followed suit and now there was no question about what was taking place.

Bob, with his innate sense of fairness, pulled our formation back to 27 or 28 kts, while the destroyers caught up to us. This went on for about thirty minutes with a lot of white water being churned up and

*Destroyers and Swifts drag racing to San Diego.*

tossed about on all sides. We looked somewhat like little brother, big brother in a drag race. Up ahead about three miles was the San Diego harbor mouth that would require a relatively sharp turn to port. Bob put out the order "all ahead full" and because our boats were light on fuel we climbed quickly to 30 kts and pulled away from the destroyers, albeit at a respectful pace.

We pulled into the harbor mouth and slowed down, looking astern, anticipating that the destroyers would also make the turn just behind us. Instead, they steamed beyond the harbor mouth missing the turn. Again, putting on my engineering hat, I remembered that steam boilers with that much heat needed some time to cool before they could slowdown. In an emergency, they could do it but it put significant physical strain on the engineering plant.

We had won the race but there was no question these destroyers and their crews were our "brothers in arms," returning from battle, and we should pay them the appropriate respect. Once again, Bob, calling on his admiral's staff experience, directed us to assemble approximately a mile inside the harbor mouth in a column formation, proceeding at idle speed as we waited for the destroyers to cool down, turn around and proceed into the harbor.

As they approached, we had every member of our crews lined up along the starboard side of the Swift Boats and rendered honors with a hand salute as the destroyers steamed by. Not to be outdone by us, we heard the on-deck speakers on the destroyers bark out with: "Attention to port, hand salute," followed by "Two," then "Carry on, carry on." The latter command was appropriate for the senior vessel responding to honors rendered to her by the junior.

To quote a hackneyed old phrase, we all thought this was pretty much "the greatest thing since sliced bread." My father was standing aft on my boat and was totally enjoying the festivities. Then, with a smile, Chief Harrington shook his head and said, "Bill, you've got to love the spirit of these young men."

*The crew ready for graduation.*

With respect for the destroyers' seniority, the Swift Boats all fell in line behind them, entering port at their pace. We felt that we had sufficiently pushed the envelope with our high-speed antics over the past two days.

As we were tying up, Dad shook hands and said goodbye to each of my crew. He then asked me if he could take the other boat officers to dinner. Not even needing to ask, I accepted his invitation and said I would meet him later in the afternoon back at the hotel. He and the Chief climbed off the boat leaving us to do the cleanup and wash down. With a sense of pride, I watched them walk together down the pier and up the roadway, deep in conversation, discussing who-knows-what topic.

Late that afternoon, I picked Dad up at the hotel and he was back in the uniform of the day: blue suit, white shirt, and striped tie. We met my other partners in crime at the Coronado base O'Club and after a drink in the bar proceeded upstairs for dinner, once again with Bob Mack in the lead. Bob approached the maître d' and without missing a beat announced, "Admiral Daly's party of seven is here."

My father, serenely confident in that blue suit, never said a word in response but politely played host for one of the most enjoyable evenings in my memory and I hope in his.

Dad and I said our goodbyes that evening, which were not easy considering we would be flying out in about forty-eight hours and most likely, I would not see him again for a year.

The next day Ed Bergin, ever the social director, took us for a brief farewell visit with our instructors who wished us well. In turn, we thanked each of them for their guidance and good wishes.

The other highlight of the last two days was the chance to meet Bob's new wife, Connie Mack. Ed and I shared a most enjoyable lunch on base with the two of them. She was a delightful girl, a short blonde, most attractive, with the unbridled energy of a firecracker. Ed and I both felt Bob was an incredibly lucky guy, but certainly we did not envy the burden of his departure from his new and loving wife.

Bob had been assigned to the southernmost Swift base at An Thoi, near the Cambodian border, and therefore he was taking a different flight. Ed was joining me on the Da Nang flight, but one of his crew had a minor medical emergency and they would catch a flight most likely the following day.

The remainder of the afternoon was devoted to packing, paperwork and ensuring our crews were equally prepared and squared away. My notorious unopened trunk of dress uniforms, which had been stored under my bunk, had been shipped back to Boston the previous week, thereby greatly simplifying my wardrobe. Later in the evening, my day ended with several emotional goodbye phone calls home. In 1967, any calls home from Vietnam were radio based and difficult to schedule, so most everyone in Swift Boats never called home but depended on letters that had at least a seven-day airmail transit time. Early in the morning next day, we left behind the palm trees of sunny Coronado and took a short hop to Travis Air Force Base. Touching down, we immediately grabbed our gear and climbed aboard a large C-141 cargo transport. Facing backward, all together in our web seats, we began our twenty-four-hour multi-stop odyssey to Vietnam.

# Section II
# Da Nang Arrival, Coastal Div. 12

## CHAPTER 4

# MOVING INTO THE APPLE

The final leg of our twenty-four-hour airborne odyssey thankfully ended as we touched down midday at the large U.S. Air Force Base at Camh Ranh Bay, Republic of South Vietnam. Stepping off the plane, *WHAM*, we were hit with heat, humidity and a big-time culture shock. Next step, we spent the bulk of the afternoon involved in personnel processing and inane meetings. This included my testimony, I presume under penalty of death, that I was, as my military ID indicated, LTJG Daniel W. Daly and that the five people accompanying me were in fact my Swift Boat crew, designator 68A.

I thought to myself that when Ed Bergin arrived the next day, he was really going to enjoy all this paperwork along with the Q&A. Bob Mack, arriving down south at a smaller facility, hopefully would have an easier time. In the military, big facility usually meant big bureaucracy. However, we were committed and there was no turning back.

This exercise was followed up by a sumptuous "Welcome to Vietnam" dinner composed of mystery meat residing on a bed of rock-hard carrots served in the mess hall and followed up by a one-night stay in the nearby barracks. Descriptions like "big," "too noisy," and "cement floors," were all applicable.

At 0800 the next day, with each of us manhandling our own gear—two bags for 12 months—we were more than happy to climb on board a twin-engine prop plane, courtesy of the USAF, for the short hop north to Da Nang. At least the weather was good. Blue sky was everywhere without a cloud in sight. Despite it being a March morning the temperature was in the 70s and climbing as we flew slowly northward along the coast of South Vietnam. We were cruising along the coast at an altitude of about 3,000 feet, and I was looking casually out the port side window. Below us was the shoreline, precisely defined by gently rolling white surf, which broke peacefully onto a seemingly endless sandy beach that stretched miles to the north and miles to the south. I could see that the actual beach rose at a gentle rate of climb, reaching inland about 100 yards, where it blended into grass-covered dunes. Those dunes eventually melted into a dense jungle canopy with a backdrop of rolling green hills farther off in the distance with the mountains of Laos behind. At the time, I thought to myself that the panorama stretched out below resembled more of a vacation postcard scene than a war zone.

The pitch of the engines changed and they began to roar as I felt our plane tilt upward and aggressively climb for altitude, interrupting my survey of the local real estate. Five heads turned to me for a response. Seat belt straining, I twisted to face the dusty window full on. Now I could see the reason for the pilot's abrupt maneuver. Two F-4 Phantom fighter-bombers raced below us, north to south, their ordinance of high explosive bombs and napalm falling in deadly slow motion on a jungle hillside just below our left wingtip.

This was the real thing, live combat. We were close enough to the action that we could clearly see each of the first two 500-pound high-explosive bombs falling as the pilot released them from where they hung beneath the wing of his plane. Compared to the speed of the aircraft, the bombs seemed to glide slowly downward as we watched each of them detonate almost simultaneously when they struck the ground below. The shockwave from the explosions was clearly visible from above. I watched as it flowed through the tree line like a wall of water being pushed by an invisible hand. This was trailed close behind by a rising cloud of smoke full of dust and debris. Seconds later as the first jet rocketed skyward to avoid possible enemy fire, his wingman rolled in dropping the next deadly cargo of napalm. This, for practical purposes, was jellied gasoline that instantly ignited on impact. In this case, there was no shockwave but instead a roaring fireball that rolled ferociously across the target leaving an oily black cloud in its wake. This one/two method was designed to first blow the roof off the enemy bunker or collapse a cave, leaving the enemy exposed in the open as the napalm finished the job.

It had started first with Boats, but in seconds every member of our crew had turned in their seats and was locked on, staring below, out the plane's windows, each one with a front-row seat for his first view of the realities of deadly combat. It was over in less than two minutes and then our crew, sitting in silence, continued the journey north. Until this moment, our Vietnam experience had been either answering inane questions or filling out redundant forms.

Within an hour, we were circling wide around the acres of real estate that made up the Da Nang airbase. On final approach into the wind, we touched down smoothly on the long east–west runway that ended at the edge of the harbor. This body of water was a huge expanse, beautiful from the air, but as we were soon to learn, it had parts that were friendly and parts that were treacherous. Either way, this was to be our home for at least part of the next twelve months.

As we rolled onto the taxi strip, we could see waiting nearby six Air Force McDonnell F-4 Phantom fighter-bombers lined up for takeoff on the main runway. Their wings were fully laden with bombs, hung below in groups of three, as they roared down the runway in afterburner, this time heading toward enemy targets in North Vietnam. "Afterburner" was when the pilot dumped raw fuel into the plane's exhaust leaving behind a ten-foot stream of flame that gave him about thirty percent more emergency power. On takeoff, these planes were basically empty of fuel which allowed them to carry a heavier bomb load and then they refueled from a tanker aircraft circling nearby overhead.

We were unquestionably small change and quickly moved off the taxi strip to a parking area. As our plane braked to a halt the Air Force loadmaster (he was hardly a stewardess) came aft, opened the door and said, "Welcome to Da Nang, gentlemen."

Parked nearby on the tarmac, I quickly spotted a large open military truck that was painted in the omnipresent olive drab and called a six-by. The name, I am told, had something to do with its six-wheel drive capability. Later I was informed that this particular vehicle had recently been acquired (stolen) from our Marine Corps brothers. On board was a sailor seated at the wheel accompanied by an officer in tropical khakis wearing dark sunglasses and a blue baseball cap.

Immediately swinging open the door, he jumped from the shotgun seat, walked over to me, stuck out his hand displaying a big grin and said, "Thompson, Eldon Thompson, Swift Boats. You must be Dan Daly."

Not bothering to wait for my answer, he yelled to my crew to load up, toss their sea bags into the open back of the truck and climb on board. Boats, ever squared away, snapped a salute and responded with a "Aye, Aye, Sir," catching my eye at the same time.

Eldon was somewhat of a bear of a guy about 6' 3", I guess in the vicinity of 220 pounds and balding with blond hair. He had an infectious grin combined with the enthusiasm of a hand grenade, all of which was carried along by his rolling gait. Then Eldon pushed, perhaps it would be better described as shoved, me into the middle of the front and only seat of the truck.

"Officers' Country," he said with a laugh. By now, my troops were loaded in the back of the truck, sitting on benches that ran along the side and leaning against the horizontal wooden slats, surrounded by their gear.

Exiting the massive airbase, we merged onto a paved two-lane road that soon took us by native shacks or huts. These were randomly located on either side of the road, each shelter topped with roofs made of tin or palm fronds. In most cases, the sides were built of cement blocks placed on the sand. Scattered about were children, cows, goats and a few unpenned and meandering chickens, with the only vegetation to be seen an occasional stunted palm tree. Tropical, but definitely not paradise.

Eldon, who I now realized was the "Greeter in Residence," waved to some of the children along the way; they smiled and held up their index finger implying, "You're number one." This was a positive Vietnamese message rather than the more offensive American middle finger.

Then without a pause, Eldon turned to me and said, "You're from Boston and you went to Harvard. What was that like?"

*Eldon Thompson and APL-5 management.*

Flattered by his research but somewhat taken aback by his question, my slow-witted response was an innocuous but dumb-sounding, "You know, small town, small college."

Eldon went on to explain that he had grown up in Oregon where he had gone to Linfield College and that he had recently served on the helicopter carrier USS *Princeton,* which was a West-Coast ship based out of San Diego.

Fortunately for me, there was a pause in the conversation as we approached a Marine security check post where they waved us through, saluting us as we passed. This led us onto a steel-framed bridge crossing the Da Nang River which had all the earmarks of fast but sturdy combat construction. Eldon informed me that this bridge was always a prime target for enemy sappers (literally, bomb throwers) and that was the reason for the well-armed guards. He continued describing this bridge as the vital link along the route that started at the Deep-Water piers where ammunition, fuel and supplies were offloaded from cargo ships and then transported by truck to both the airbase and the Marines staging area.

As we crossed the bridge, I looked on the north side of the river toward the harbor beyond and saw two small U.S. military installations located across from each other on either side of the river. Eldon, continuing the tour, informed me that on the left was the Navy headquarters and on the right was the Marines'. He did emphasize quite clearly that the Officers' Club was located on the Navy side and it was called the Stone Elephant. Further upriver were stucco-covered light industrial buildings, probably used as warehouses dating back to the days of the French occupancy. In contrast, looking downriver on the south side there were no signs of civilization, just marshland covered by swaying reeds and the much smaller, meandering river. It was as if the bridge was some historical marker between today and yesterday.

Departing the bridge, we soon returned to viewing a landscape that could be best described as "humble residential" and this continued for the next mile or two. Up ahead, I could see that the road turned gradually left, winding back toward the harbor as Eldon lifted his arm to point out "Home Sweet Home."

In this case, "Home" was two large rectangular barges with grey hulls about 200 feet long topped with three-story white superstructures. They were tied up side by side to a pier in the midst of nowhere at the edge of what appeared to be several acres of plain flat sandy fields spotted with some dried-out scrub grass. Located in front of them were three more barges, in this case painted all grey and tied up end to end. The complex had more of an industrial than residential look.

As we bounced to a halt in the soft sand near the ramp that led on board (parking was not a problem), Eldon announced that this was the "Apple." Seeing a somewhat confused look on my face, he informed me that the official Navy designator for this vessel was Auxiliary Personnel Living (APL-5) therefore the "Apple." The grey barges tied up forward of these were ARs, Auxiliary Repair. In small steps, I was indeed getting up to speed.

As we unloaded our gear from the truck, other sailors nearby quickly joined in to help my crew, and I recognized this as a positive sign. Eldon gave me a hand as we climbed the outside stairway to the second deck where the officers lived. By now my "in-country" wardrobe had

*New guy gets THE BOOT AWARD.*

fortunately shrunk to only the basics, so a duffel bag and suitcase were the extent of my luggage.

Arriving on the second deck and somewhat out of breath, Eldon led the charge through the screen door announcing with his booming voice, "Daly has arrived. He's from Boston and a Harvard graduate." Eldon was great with the one liners.

Seated along a long table were about ten Boat officers just finishing lunch, working on a last cup of coffee or a cigarette. Fortunately for me, Eldon did not seek my grade point average. With this crowd and this mission, I suspected it was not a significant factor. I remember, to a man, they each stood up and introduced themselves with a hearty handshake and a "Welcome Aboard." All in all, a good start and much appreciated.

I did notice that several of the boat officers were full LTs not LTJGs as I was. Later, I learned that Swift Boats were considered prime career duty for graduates of the Naval Academy, who in most cases had graduated a year or two ahead of me. Years later, there were numerous admirals, two-, three-, and four-star, that had seen Swift Boat duty earlier in their careers. However, there was minimal consideration of rank in the Swift program and first name or call sign among the boat officers was SOP—standard operating procedure.

Eldon, with a sweep of the arm, gave me the quick, very quick tour. We were standing in a large open room with a table that would hold about thirty people. The color scheme was standard Navy issue, light green table tops, grey painted legs and metal chairs to match, all equally uncomfortable, no discrimination. At the near end of the room was a cafeteria food line and on the left side, dividing the big room in half, were a series of tall vertical lockers.

I was informed that there was more than enough space so everyone was assigned two lockers. Luggage was placed on top and boxes were scattered about with various purchases, such as stereo equipment from the Base Exchange and what appeared to be *objets d'art* from the local economy.

Down a short passageway was the bunk room which was huge and looked like it could easily sleep sixty people. The setup throughout the room was three tiers of bunks, four to a tier, hung by chain from the overhead. Eldon informed me this was not originally "Officers' Country" but was built for chief petty officers. Regardless, it worked just fine because there were never more than twenty people there at the same time. As a result, it was highly unlikely that the traditional toe-to-toe sleeping arrangement would ever be necessary. The equally large head and showers were nearby. Overall, adding in the powerful air-conditioning, our surroundings while quite impersonal were, in fact, comfortable; except for the damn chairs.

During this brief tour, it occurred to me that my shipmate Ed Bergin, who was scheduled to join us in Da Nang the next day, would not be happy with these living accommodations. Ed was an outdoor guy, a hunter and a camper, and this was without question institutional living, however, one day at a time. It took me a total of ten minutes to stow my gear in my lockers. I then joined the others at the table and was informed that the cooks were still serving lunch.

Eldon, now morphing from "Greeter in Residence" to "Social Director," pointed me to an open seat beside him and introduced me to

*Larry Meyer outside APL-5.*

Jay Fleming and Lou Masterson. Jay had arrived a week or two earlier and was Southern California born and bred—the classic blonde surfer. Lou already had about four months in-country making him senior. He was from the Midwest, had attended Notre Dame and actually knew several of my friends from the Boston area who had been his classmates.

Early on, I noticed that Lou, on occasion, would exhibit that somewhat detached look where you suspected his mind was not presently with you but locked onto some other time and place. That said, he had a Hollywood smile and a matching great set of teeth that lit up the conversation. Eldon informed me that Lou's assigned radio call sign was

*Swifts alongside APL-5 including Killer Lou's 75.*

"Hootenanny Six," but on occasion he was referred to simply as "Killer Lou." The whole concept of personal call signs was totally new to me, so I smiled and simply shook my head in a knowing fashion.

Lou told me that he actually was operating out of Da Nang's smaller sub base, which was located at Chu Lai about 25 miles to the south, but he had brought his boat PCF 75 up to Da Nang to have one of the engines replaced. As a result, his crew had a day or two off, but he said he would be happy to take me and my crew out on our mandatory training mission the next day.

Eldon chimed in, "You couldn't have a better instructor than Lou, providing of course he doesn't get you killed."

Knowing smiles appeared all around.

## CHAPTER 5

# FIRST PATROL

After lunch, I checked in with Boats to ensure that our crew was okay and had settled in. I informed him that we would be conducting our first patrol the next day with LTJG Masterson. He would be our training officer using his boat PCF 75 but his crew would not be with us because they were on two-day in-country R&R. Boats said he would meet shortly with our crew and discuss their individual responsibilities. We agreed to meet portside at 0630 on the main deck of the Apple where the boats were tied up. Later that night, I confirmed with Lou that his boat was going to be available and that we would be using PCF 75.

We were scheduled to shove off at 0730, but I wanted my crew to have at least an hour to do a complete pre-mission check out of PCF 75 before Lou's arrival. No surprise, the boat looked in great shape, spotlessly clean, with all weapons oiled and stowed appropriately. Engineman Wells (Snipe) climbed on board, opened the engine hatches and spent the entire time below checking out both engines, especially the newly installed one. He yelled up for me to start them, as well as the generator, so he could check them out with a load on.

"Engines look good, Skipper," came the response from below. Newcomer reported satisfactory on all electronics, while Muller and Buck gave similar thumbs-up on weapons and ammunition. Boats double-checked each of their reports and confirmed it to me,

"Ready to get under way, Skipper."

Now, we were just waiting for "Killer Lou" to arrive.

With several minutes to spare, I looked around the boat once again and saw that there were several small square patches in the aluminum hull and cabin superstructure. I knew these could only be bullet holes. Just aft of the pilothouse door I noticed colored battle ribbons painted on Plexiglas, not unlike the ones seen on the bridge of a larger warship. On the top row was a Purple Heart ribbon with several stars in the middle. I had no doubt that Boats had made a similar observation.

At 0730 sharp, Lou showed up, complete with his blue ball cap with the officer's emblem embroidered on the front. Over that was written "Officer-in-Charge" and below the emblem was "PCF 75." I introduced him to my crew, who Boats had lined up side by side on the fantail. They looked sharp and Boats rendered the appropriate salute. This "squared away" message was not lost on Lou. Out of respect, he asked Boats if he wanted to get the boat under way and his response was a succinct, "Aye, Aye, Sir."

Boats was an at-sea sailor and he was ready to go. Lou's boat was tied up solo alongside the Apple, so taking the lines in and making a simple twist with the engines opposed got us smoothly under way. I had not heard the rumble of the big diesels since we left school and it was a welcome sound.

Lou explained to me that we had to first check in with the Coastal Surveillance Center (CSC, call sign "Article"), which was our operational control. It was located on a small peninsula that jutted out into the harbor about two miles away. Lou then opened his briefcase that he had carried on board and explained that each Swift Boat, while on patrol, carried two days of code that was used for any type of confidential radio communication.

Arriving at the CSC, I was introduced to the watch officer who updated us on the friendly activity along the coast and specifically in our assigned patrol area. At the same time, we received the latest intelligence gathered from all sources on any nearby enemy activity. Today, we would be assigned to the Charlie patrol area that ran from just south of the Hue River mouth, approximately twelve miles north and ended two miles south of the Cua Viet River. Our call sign on station would be "Enfield Cobra Charlie." Despite the hour being 0800, I noticed Lou added his aviator sunglasses to the blue baseball cap as we departed Article's location.

We left the pier and proceeded across the harbor at 20 kts to the mouth, which at its opening stretched almost three miles across. Turning left we headed north varying our speed to break in the new engine, while still averaging about 20 kts. Actually, these were rebuilt engines but this process was so effective that the engines would last another 3,000 to 4,000 hours and could be rebuilt multiple times.

As we approached the southern border of the patrol area, using his binoculars, Lou saw a cargo junk two miles ahead of us, approaching the Hue River mouth. He instructed me to call the crew to General Quarters and proceed at full speed to close the junk. "Guns" (Muller) uncovered the twin mount above the pilothouse and aft Boats removed the cover from the single .50 caliber. Everyone else broke out small arms—.38 caliber pistols and M-16s. Helmets and flak gear were worn all around.

I informed Lou that I would be taking the helm and wanted to drive from the aft station and he concurred. Walking aft, with my right hand I pulled out the lever on the backside of the main cabin that engaged the steering wheel and pushed the throttles forward with my left. I felt the boat smoothly lift up as the big engines increased speed and watched its bow wave roll aside, eventually blending into our foaming white wake that was now stretched straight astern. Lou walked into the pilothouse and sounded the siren, which was located on the cabin top. This signaled to the junk that we wanted them to stop and go DIW (dead in the water).

Lou explained to the crew that he had ordered General Quarters because this was a larger cargo junk and therefore posed a greater potential risk. This would absolutely be our method of operation at night. A smaller open vessel inspected during the day would not present as great a risk and therefore did not require going to General Quarters. This was real life, key information that was not covered in the book but passed on between boat crews. In fact, there was no book.

As we approached the junk, I noticed that Lou established eye contact with "Guns" up in the gun tub and then nodded to Boats at the aft mount, basically saying, "Are you ready and do you have any questions?" I had an M-16 resting in a bracket on the cabin top near me, Lou had one, Buck and Newcomer each had one at their positions alongside the main cabin but near the pilothouse. I heard Lou yell loud and clear, "safeties on." Any change in that status would require his command to "release safeties" or for the enemy to fire first. I was quickly appreciating the value of having a pro as our first mission instructor, someone who took his responsibilities very seriously.

I knew the crew's adrenalin was starting to flow because mine was well under way. It was their first mission and we were closing in to come alongside a good-sized cargo junk. Until you climbed on board, you had no idea what cargo was below decks—the fish sauce "nouc mam," bicycles, or munitions? Was the crew friendly or just waiting for the right time to make their move?

Approaching the junk on its rear starboard quarter, I slowed to idle speed giving us a chance to visually observe what the crew of the junk was doing before we came alongside and became more exposed. In this case, they all appeared to be out of the cabin on deck watching us approach, each with the omnipresent cigarette dangling from their mouth. White t-shirts, shorts and the ever-present Ho Chi Minh sandals made from automobile tires was their attire.

Lou turned to me and said, "Dan, with your permission, I want to take Boats on board and conduct the inspection; you keep us covered." I gave him the appropriate "Roger that."

The two of them then boarded the junk and Lou motioned to someone, who appeared to be in charge of the cargo junk, to lead the inspection below. Back on PCF 75, without yelling, I instructed Snipe who had taken over at the after .50 caliber to grab an M-16 and told Muller to do the same. The big .50s firing at this close range would most likely kill everyone including Lou and Boats, so small arms coverage was the best way to go.

After approximately fifteen minutes on board, they emerged topside. Lou took some papers from someone, who I now assumed was the captain, and walked over to me. The papers included IDs of the crew but also a cargo manifest that stated what they were carrying, where they were coming from and where they were going to, in this case the city of Hue. In a quiet voice, Lou explained to me that reviewing this documentation was anything but an exact science; you had to look for significant exceptions as possible indicators of trouble. These could include people on board who did not have papers or a cargo or destination that did not match the manifest. To make matters more complicated everything was written in Vietnamese.

Lou was satisfied that there was no problem. He then reached over, returned the papers to the captain, thanked him for his time and waved them off. We delayed our departure on purpose so that we remained behind the junk, never becoming a target "stern to" a potential enemy. I also noted Muller was back on his twin .50s in the gun tub, just in case. This was a heads-up move on his part, which got a knowing nod from Lou. We had been in-country about forty-eight hours.

This was an aggressive and good start to the patrol, which I'm sure was Lou's intent. We decided it was now the appropriate time for a quick lunch which I soon learned was "the usual," white bread, hand-cut baloney with yellow mustard and iceberg lettuce. While you never learned to love it, it was edible, tasty, and perhaps, most importantly, could be eaten in all weather conditions. The latter, I was to appreciate over time.

After our brief but delicious repast, Lou set up driving drills, patrolling at various distances off the shoreline utilizing the radar and best-guess visual. He explained the importance of knowing where you were, especially at night, so that you didn't wander into a dangerous surf line or become an easy target for the enemy by traveling too close to shore. Worst case, you unknowingly drove the boat up on the beach. Not often, but it had been done. Now, I began to better understand the critical importance of knowing where you were, as well as where the enemy was.

Next, Lou spent considerable time with Boats and me using the binoculars and explaining what we should be looking for along the shoreline that could be an indicator of trouble. Often this could be as simple as seeing no people near a village or someone suddenly disappearing behind a sand dune as they saw us approaching.

*Coastal cargo junk.*

Dark was setting in and Lou wanted to know how the watch sections were going to be set up. Boats and I had discussed this previously on numerous occasions and had decided that my watch would have the two most junior members of the crew, Muller and Buck, and he would have the more senior, Wells and Newcomer. This gave each of us a blend of capabilities, but on a fifty-foot boat the rest of the crew was never far away.

I had already heard a Swift Boat horror story where one watch section at night had unknowingly approached close in to a Chinese Communist trawler that was smuggling weapons. The crew then proceeded to illuminate the trawler with their spotlight. All of this took place while the other watch section remained asleep. The results were almost deadly. During the ensuing battle, adding a touch of humor, the Officer-in-Charge got shot in the ass. The senior powers that be reviewed these events and saw them in a somewhat more critical light, not exactly career enhancing.

Lou seemed satisfied with my watch assignments, so he decided to turn in as I took the first watch. He said he would join Boats for the second watch. I began our sector patrol heading north along the coast about 500 yards off the beach using our radar as a guideline. Routine night patrols such as this were usually conducted at a speed of 10–12 kts.

I was stationed at the wheel in the pilothouse and just before midnight a radio call came in on the boat's secondary radio set, which was located immediately to the right of the driver's seat. Lou had informed me that this radio was tuned to specifically monitor local Marine Corps operations. They were calling "Navy Patrol Boat" not knowing our designated call sign but figuring that call sign was good enough for government work.

Before I even had time to acknowledge the call, the Notre Dame sprinter was in the pilothouse with the radio microphone in his hand answering, "This Is Enfield Cobra Charlie, Navy Patrol Boat at your service, over."

"This is Tiger Four (USMC), we are presently located in a small village about one klick inland and suspect enemy activity probing our perimeter, can you assist, over?"

Lou responded, "That's affirmative, we have 81 mike mike capability both illumination and HE (high explosive) backed up by multiple .50 caliber."

I detected a slight touch of the warrior braggadocio on Lou's part. Then he turned toward me winding his finger in the air as a signal to get all hands up and set GQ. Having heard the radio broadcast, Boats was one step ahead of me yelling for Wells and Newcomer to rise and shine, get out of the lower cabin and set battle stations.

Even though this was their first patrol, I knew I could count on Boats to quickly get everyone to their assigned positions. In the meantime, I wanted to be available to help Lou plot the position of Tiger Four which would be critical if we were going to conduct gunfire on his behalf. As expected, they were soon back on the net with position coordinates for the village they were in, as well as the coordinates that they suspected the enemy was at that time.

I wrote them down on the ever-present pad of paper using the (hopefully) ever-present red flashlight with which to see. All night patrols were conducted at "darken ship" with no exceptions. Any sniper onshore would certainly hear our engines even at low speed and then he would be looking for the slightest flash of light to confirm the position of his target.

Lou read the coordinates back to the Marines to confirm them as correct, which they did. He continued, "This is Enfield Cobra Charlie. Interrogative, illumination or HE?"

The response was "This is Tiger Four. Request you start with illumination."

Lou radioed back, "This is Enfield Cobra Charlie. Roger that, understand illumination, 5 minutes to commence fire. Will advise, out."

Radio communications such as these might appear repetitive or even cumbersome, but the goal was to ensure that there was absolutely no confusion and that both parties understood who was talking and exactly what they were saying. Specific words were used because they were more likely to be understood over the radio when the actual transmissions might be weak and garbled.

Just then, Fielder stuck his head in the pilothouse door and reported, "General Quarters is set, all hands on station."

Lou's response was succinct, "Very well, go to the ammunition locker and break out four rounds of illumination, secure them on the deck and I'll join you shortly."

"Dan, plot on the chart the enemy position, then get a radar fix for our location and calculate a range and bearing to the target. When we have all that laid out, I'll show you how to calculate elevation and bearing on the mortar and how many rounds of propellant we will leave on each mortar round to carry it the distance to the target." No Q&A in this training, just do it!

"I'm going aft to show Boats how to set the mortar rounds for an airburst without dropping a lot of hot metal on the heads of our Marine Corps friends."

School was over, this was the real thing and the clock was ticking. The enemy position was easy to plot based on the two north–south, east–west coordinates we received from the Marines. A location was designated in letters and numbers which referenced a land map set up in square grids. We had a copy of a coastal map on board that included these grids and you simply marked the position where the lines intersected.

Determining our own location was more of a challenge, especially at night. We couldn't see visual points of reference on shore so we had to use three radar ranges, specifically the distance from us to three points onshore. This was further complicated by the fact that the shoreline in this area was basically a straight line of beach with few notable geographic exceptions.

Newcomer was now at the helm and I told him to slow the boat, maintaining minimal headway so that our basic position did not change. The first range was easy; we were 500 yards perpendicular to the beach. The second mark I used was the northern edge of the Hue River mouth south of us, about two miles away. The third was a challenge, so I referenced the paper chart in the pilothouse to see if there was any feature along the shoreline that might appear clearly enough on the radar to provide me my third radar range.

I saw a mark on the chart north of us that said "Tower," but little else, so I didn't know if it meant radio tower, church tower or whatever. Turning to look at the radar scope, I was relieved to see that there was a bright spot painting north of us about a mile and a half, maybe a quarter-mile inland. Because of the brightness of the target it had to be the tower and it became my third radar range.

With three radar ranges I could get a decent fix on our location. Using the scale on the chart, I measured each radar range, and then took a basic mathematical compass with a pencil on one end and stuck the other pointed end at the onshore reference. I opened it to the correct distance and drew an arc on the chart. The hope was that the three arcs would intersect, and we would be located in the middle. The next step was to draw a line from our position at sea to the enemy position onshore, measuring the range (distance) and the compass bearing from us to them.

Lou returned with a simple, "Whatcha got?" He checked my marking of the enemy location, reviewed my radar fix and, lastly, my line from us to the target, specifically 1800 yards, compass bearing 300°, both measured from the chart.

The next step was to reference a firing manual that told us for a round to go 1800 yards the mortar had to be elevated a certain number of degrees and each round had to contain a certain number of propellant elements. In this case the calculation was 30° of elevation and all

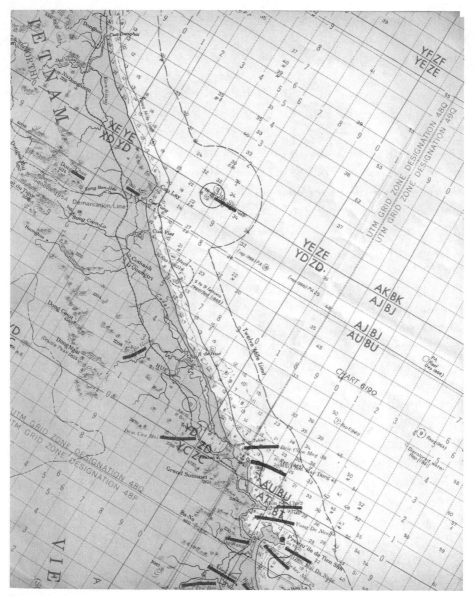

*Grid coordinate chart, Da Nang North (Author's collection).*

eight elements would remain on each round; more elements meant longer range.

All of this required the boat maintain its current position at sea as well as the same compass heading. The boat was maintaining a compass course of about 340° while running slowly parallel to the shoreline. If the mortar were facing forward along the bow-to-stern axis of the boat it would then have a relative bearing of 360°/0°. From this we could calculate that a relative bearing of 320° on the mortar would result in the correct 300° compass bearing to the target. Any twist or movement of our boat would change the firing solution and conceivably illuminate the Marines or worse drop a high-explosive round on their heads. All that grammar school geometry was finally paying off.

Understandably Lou said, "Walk me through the entire calculation one more time just to confirm." At the moment, his Notre Dame degree far exceeded my Ivy League credentials. "Confirmed," was his response, then, "Let's go aft and give Boats the calculations."

I told Newcomer to remain on the helm and carefully maintain our position parallel to the beach holding the compass course 340°.

At the aft gun mount, Fielder elevated the mortar to 30° and set the relative bearing at 320° which was slightly forward of our port beam (270°). We then checked each mortar round and removed no propellant increments. These were the explosive charges attached to the base of the mortar round. The more propellant packages you left on, the further the range of the mortar round. Lou pulled the mortar trigger back and locked it open. Most mortars were drop-fired, but the mortar on a Swift Boat could also be trigger-fired, which I now realized was a tremendous advantage. Lou told Snipe to drop in the first round and Boats to wait for his firing command.

Quickly, we moved back to the pilothouse and radioed, "Tiger Four, this is Enfield Cobra Charlie. Ready to commence fire, one illumination round."

Their response was immediate and I detected some urgency in the voice: "This is Tiger Four. Commence fire, will adjust." Considerably less formally Lou leaned out the door and yelled aft to Boats, "Commence fire, one round."

The muzzle flash and the deep-throated *whaaa wump* that followed was almost instantaneous as Boats pulled the trigger. This first-time evolution from start to finish, which included plotting positions, radio communications, loading and firing, had taken less than ten minutes.

In a matter of seconds, we saw the first round burst in the air as the parachute deployed and the phosphorus illumination round burned brightly swinging below.

Tiger Four was immediately back on the radio, "This is Tiger Four. No adjustment, repeat, no adjustment. Request 2 more illumination rounds followed by 5; repeat 5 high-explosive rounds VT fuses rapid-fire."

I was closest to the pilothouse and turned to Lou who gave me the thumbs-up as he returned aft to execute the firing request. I reached behind Newcomer who was carefully running slowly parallel to the coast utilizing the radar picture. I grabbed the radio microphone:

"Tiger Four, this is Enfield Cobra Charlie. Roger wilco, I say again, 2 illumination rounds, followed by 5 high-explosive rounds, VT fuses, rapid-fire, OUT."

VT fuses were variable time fuses that caused the round to go off above the ground, perhaps at a height of 200 feet, functioning very effectively as an anti-personnel weapon.

In the radio transmission, my "Roger" told them that we understood; the "Wilco" said we would comply and, lastly, my repeating their request was simply for safety purposes.

Leaving the pilothouse, I went aft just as Boats trigger-fired the second illumination round. Snipe then loaded the third round which they fired after a one-minute delay. I saw that Lou was standing at the ammunition box adjusting the timing fuses on the five high-explosive rounds. There was a sensor in each fuse that determined proximity to the ground and exploded the round at a preset height.

After passing the first HE round to Snipe, Lou turned to me and said, "Looks like we got those fuckers out in the open."

As we stood nearby, Boats and Snipe continued a rapid tempo of: "Load"—pause—"Trigger fire"—"Load"—pause—"Trigger fire."

*Killer Lou and friend.*

This verbal sequence of events was critical and the best way to avoid the deadly mistake of a double load. This was a tragic mistake that had occurred two months before on a boat farther south killing several people surrounding the mortar.

The night was calm, without any wind, so the smoke from the muzzle of the mortar soon formed a grey cloud over the fantail of the boat which quickly mixed with the pungent smell of gunpowder. While this was distracting, I was thankful for the lack of wind because I knew that maintaining our critical firing position was much easier when there were no waves and wind to contend with.

After firing the five rounds of HE, Lou called cease-fire and gave a thumbs-up to Boats and Snipe and told them to stand by. Flashing his white toothy grin as we walked to the pilothouse, he turned to me and said, "Let's get some customer feedback."

"Tiger Four, Cobra Charlie fire mission complete. Interrogative SitRep (situation report), over?"

"Cobra this is Tiger. Wait, out."

I noted that the communication procedure on both sides had suddenly become more casual, hopefully because the stress level had dropped somewhat. Lou mentioned that based on his experience the illumination rounds may well have surprised the enemy out in the open as they were approaching the village, which was why Tiger wanted the rapid firing of the follow-on HE rounds.

After approximately ten minutes, Tiger returned to the net.

"Cobra Charlie, this is Tiger Four. Be advised, based on our recon of the perimeter, 3 enemy KIA, bad guys appear to have departed, many thanks Navy."

"This is Cobra Charlie. Glad to be of service, any other assignments, over?"

"This is Tiger Four. Any possibility of you remaining in the area and shooting a random single illumination round perhaps once an hour just to keep everybody honest? We should have land reinforcements shortly after dawn."

"This is Cobra Charlie. Let me check with my HQ and callback, out."

This would alter our patrol schedule but Lou felt we probably would get the okay from Article. A quick radio call to Da Nang and Article gave us the green light. This was not a surprise because Tiger's request for one round per hour would still allow us to conduct a high-speed sweep of our assigned patrol area.

Lou's follow-up was, "Tiger Four, this is Enfield Cobra Charlie. We have permission to conduct H and I (Harassment and Interdiction) fire at your target. That is, various rounds at various times at our discretion. Do you understand and grant permission, over?"

There was a pause on the radio and the next transmission came with a somewhat deeper tone, "Enfield Cobra Charlie, this is Tiger Four. Understand your latest transmission. Permission granted for H and I, my location, thanks again, Navy."

"This is Cobra Charlie. Roger that, Semper Fi, out."

Sensing my confusion at the last several minutes of radio transmissions, Lou explained that radio transmissions such as these could easily be intercepted by the enemy. We knew that there were North Vietnamese regulars in this area as well as Viet Cong troops and they could well have an English translator with them.

Therefore, if they knew a single illumination round was going to be fired by us on a scheduled basis this would provide absolutely no deterrent to the enemy's movement. They could easily launch an attack between our firing times. Therefore Lou's radio message had clearly included *firing at random times, random rounds* which could and would include the more deadly high-explosive rounds. The individual we last heard on the radio was obviously senior and in charge of the Marine detachment and clearly understood our intent. Heads up, all around.

During the night, we remained at General Quarters, which was standard procedure for firing the mortar. The time intervals between firing ranged anywhere from thirty to ninety minutes, carried out with a variety of illumination and high-explosive mortar rounds. In total we expended fifteen more rounds along with the two pots of coffee we drank.

As the Pacific morning's red glow started to creep up above the eastern horizon we received a call again from the deeper voice: "Cobra Charlie, this is Tiger Four. The cavalry has arrived, situation secure, your support much appreciated, Semper Fi."

Lou gave me the nod and I transmitted, "This is Enfield Cobra Charlie. A pleasure to be of service to the Corps, Semper Fi, out."

Leaning out of the pilothouse door, Lou yelled, "Secure from General Quarters, let's head for the barn."

I was at the helm, so I slowly turned to starboard and brought the engines up to half speed about 15 kts. Lou called my crew aft to demonstrate the procedure for cleaning the mortar and re-securing all the ammunition. After that, he had both Boats and Snipe demonstrate to the other three the procedures for setting the fuses, loading and firing the mortar. Like me, he was a firm believer in cross-training. Sleep time—zero.

At around 0800, halfway through the Delta patrol area, we saw our relief boat charging north to rendezvous with us. Coming alongside us was PCF 22 with Eldon and his crew looking well rested and clean-shaven. As expected, Eldon greeted us with a smile and asked, "How did the training mission go?" This was followed by his quick glance at my crew, "You guys look like shit." "Lou, what did you do to the Harvard guy?"

Lou putting on his sunglasses and carefully adjusting his blue ball cap replied, "Just the usual drills, nothing special."

After a brief patrol update, Eldon, with a chuckle, shoved off and headed north. My crew was on the fantail so it was easy for Lou to turn and say, "Men, a good night's work and welcome to Swift Boats."

Our running time to the base was just about an hour so there was little point in trying to get any rack time. I instructed the crew to give the "white-glove once over" to PCF 75. Boats came back with a hearty, "Aye, Aye, Skipper." Again a response not lost on Lou.

Lou and I poured ourselves another cup of black and retired to the pilothouse where I took over the helm. I sincerely thanked him for his considerable effort and for all the experience that he had imparted to us in the past twenty-six hours. He switched his coffee mug to his left hand, stuck out his right to me and said, "Dan, it looks to me like you got a good crew. Push 'em hard and make sure you take care of them."

Time in-country—98 hours.

## CHAPTER 6

# TAKING OVER PCF 76

We had been in-country just over two weeks when I was informed that we would be receiving our own boat. It was PCF 76 and we would be the second crew to be assigned that boat. Lieutenant David Dawson was the current OINC and he and his crew were heading home. The boat itself had been in-country slightly over a year.

Patrolling out of Da Nang, eventually every crew had its own boat but some crews had to share boats and wait several months for their own boat, so we considered ourselves lucky to get our own boat so soon. I had not been on this boat before but knew Dave and his crew to be squared away, so I assumed the condition of the boat would reflect that.

The first step in the transfer process was for the leading enlisted man of the departing crew to give the incoming crew a thorough tour, with the departing members standing nearby to answer any questions regarding equipment. Standing on the pier, I could see Boats on board leading our crew. This was the moment each of them had waited for. Hatches were opened, weapons broken down, electronics tested. At the same time Snipe seemed to disappear for hours, laying claim to his engine room. I had anticipated this type of diligence from our crew and was glad not to be disappointed.

During the transfer process, Dave soon appeared with a black, four-inch loose-leaf binder filled with official-looking documentation covering all the onboard equipment indexed by serial number. The Navy wanted to ensure that no one left Vietnam with a .50 caliber machine gun, or perhaps, more realistically, one of the boat's .38 caliber revolvers or M-16s. Yelling back and forth from the pier to the boat, with Muller and Buck in the loop, we cross-referenced weapons to numbers and I signed on the appropriate line. As expected, this took the bulk of the transfer time.

Dave and I both agreed that it was highly unlikely that he or his crew would be shipping a two-ton diesel engine back home but the Navy took no chances, so I signed on the line even for the big Jimmies. Electronics took a minimum of effort; they were not likely to disappear because they were bolted into frames, were well-worn and readily available on the commercial market. The two pairs of binoculars on the other hand were great souvenir items and thus their physical presence was individually and visually verified.

The sign-over and instruction process took almost three hours. It gave my crew an opportunity to really get a hands-on understanding of the boat for which they would be responsible, but this would also be a vessel that our lives would depend on.

At the end, Boats swung out of the pilothouse and gave me the thumbs-up with a big smile. "She looks good, Skipper."

I thanked Dave and his crew for their cooperation. We shook hands all around and wished each other well.

As the new OINC, I had some solo paperwork to do, so I remained seated on the pier and spread out on some wooden shipping crates. Out of the corner of my eye, I saw Boats already had our troops beginning the white-glove clean up. A fresh water hose, mops, brushes, and rags had suddenly appeared. Snipe remained in his engine room, shirt off, appearing occasionally to request additional rags or a temporary set of hands.

Wading through the paper bureaucracy, I saw that I needed several signatures from the senior enlisted member of the crew, which would be Boats. I yelled to get his attention and got a muffled response from inside the main cabin, where I could see him diligently involved in some project.

PCF 76 was floating almost level with the pier so it was easy to climb on board while still clutching the big black four-inch loose-leaf binder.

This was in definite conflict with the John Wayne image I was trying to project, but I had no choice for the time being.

Boats was below kneeling on top of the counter that ran along the starboard side of the boat, right below the sliding windows of the main cabin. The counter was capped as one would expect with Navy-grey vinyl tiles. This surface area was assigned multiple purposes including small arms maintenance, message decrypting, chart plotting and, on occasion, food preparation. Today, however, none of these seem to justify Boat's total concentration, ass in the air, armed with a power drill, screwdrivers and what appeared to be several pieces of L-shaped light aluminum.

His intensity for this project caused me to stand by until its completion, which took another five minutes.

"Sorry Skipper, if these weren't installed with just the right amount of tension they wouldn't work."

I nodded my head, attempting to understand what had just taken place until my curiosity won out.

"Boats, they look terrific, but—?" With a respectful but querulous look he responded, "Skipper, heavy weather coffeepot holder, after the guns and engines, nothing is more important."

Shaking my head in absolute agreement to his priorities, I told Boats to call me when he felt the boat was cleaned to his standards and that I wanted to have a brief celebration with the crew. About an hour later he found me on the APL and said, "PCF 76 ready for your inspection, Skipper."

This degree of formality was not my intent, but I knew they would be proud of their work and I wanted to recognize their efforts. They were lined up on the aft deck and saluted as I climbed on board.

The results were impressive. All weapons were laid out, cleaned and broken down, the decks were spotless and Snipe had his engine room clean enough for a formal dinner party.

It was late afternoon and I knew the boat was going to be tied up for the remainder of the day. Therefore, I reached into my upscale gym bag and pulled out two bottles of Dom Pérignon champagne circa 1955, along with plastic cups. I had left the crystal flutes back in Boston.

*Christening PCF 76 with champagne.*

*PCF 76. (Courtesy of* Stars & Stripes*)*

*The crew of PCF 76, spring of 1967.*

*Engineman Second Class Oscar Wells.*

*Radioman Third Class Michael Newcomer.*

*Gunner's mate John Muller.*

*Seaman Bob Buck.*

*The management team.*

Boats and Snipe were the only two over twenty-one and I suspected they were more inclined to beer than wine, so I gave them a brief history of the acquisition and the background of the champagne. Not wanting to appear a pompous ass, I simply stated that I had a good friend by the name of Joe Santos who owned a fancy restaurant in New York City called "The Sign of the Dove" and he had given me these bottles as a gift to share with my crew.

If they were so inclined, they could determine the value of the gift on their own at a later time. I had no doubt that Boats, who was always looking for the good story, would have full details within thirty-six hours or fill in the blanks on his own.

I asked him to rig a light line so that I could break one bottle over the bow of PCF 76, while the crew drank the other bottle in a toast to "smooth seas and fair winds." Standing on the pier, they raised their glasses high. With the bottle securely tied by its neck, I swung the line in a slow six-foot arc in the air, ensuring that when the bottle fell it burst smartly on the stem of the bow. As I looked the other way, the bottle burst with a mild explosion, the champagne sparkled and in the finest naval tradition, we christened PCF 76.

To quote John Paul Jones, "Give me a fast ship for I intend to go in Harm's Way." At that moment, I had little idea how well this quote described what lay ahead for our crew in the months that followed.

## CHAPTER 7

# TOP SECRET CALL SIGNS

One of the things I fondly recall about being a member of the Swift Boat program was the refreshing lack of many burdensome military regulations. Not that we were rebels, because we were not. There were definitely operating policies and procedures we adhered to, especially those regarding combat patrols and the welfare of our crew. However, when it came to certain items of military formality and bureaucracy, as a group, we concluded that following them was basically a waste of our valuable time and, in fact, could be hazardous to our health.

As a boat officer, I ran our boat, managed our crew, and was held responsible for their welfare and the completion of our mission. Any commitment to multilayered bureaucracy, incomprehensible rules and regs, along with general Navy B.S., was noticeably absent from the program. My friend and classmate Ed Bergin, now ensconced at our more casual sub-base at Chu Lai, had fine-tuned this approach to an art form.

Most likely our attitude was a direct result of the Swift Boat program being a totally volunteer organization, both officer and enlisted, made up of competent people assigned to a relatively demanding combat mission. Each crew member was a part of a small team that was critically dependent on each other and then each of those teams learned to depend on their Swift Boat peers.

On patrol, radio communications that were both efficient and effective were a key component of everything we did. Often lives could depend on this. Whether you were communicating with other ships, aircraft or troops on shore, identifying who you were, what you were doing or where you were located, in a clear and concise manner, was critical. In Swift Boats, for example, while transiting to or from the northern patrol sectors a Swift Boat's call sign was Newsboy India plus an individual boat's hull number such as "Newsboy India 76." When you arrived on station and began your patrol you then utilized a sector call sign that, up north, carried the prefix Enfield Cobra plus a letter designate for the specific area in which you were patrolling. This began at the most northern point with "Enfield Cobra Alpha," then changing to Bravo, Charlie, etc. as you proceeded south.

I don't know anyone in the Swift program who had the vaguest idea of the origin of all these various call signs or whose brainchild they might have been. Who came up with a designator such as Enfield Cobra, Newsboy India, or Same Drink? However, "Same Drink" might provide some clue as to their source. Most Navy call signs were listed in available communications publications. Marine and Air Force call signs were more of a challenge and you picked them up along the way at various social occasions and passed them on to your peers.

In the end, the only thing that really mattered was that you could be heard clearly in your radio transmission without any confusion or misinterpretation. If you sent a message such as "We are taking fire," or even worse, "We've been hit," and the response was, "Who's calling, please?" then you had a real problem.

The quality of your short-range radio transmissions could be affected by weather, time of day, time of year, air temperature or your distance from the other unit. Stick a hill or a mountain in between and that added to the problem. Lastly, sprinkle a touch of enemy gunfire in the background, and then diction and pronunciation could go to hell relatively quickly.

Early on, we concluded that the official military call signs that had been assigned to Swift Boats were neither clever nor cool. To rectify this problem, early in our tour but after an appropriate period of observation, each officer was assigned a personal call sign by his fellow boat drivers.

Pilots had followed this personal call sign tradition for years, but in the case of Swift Boats it was more likely based on the fact that larger warships had official individual and often unique call signs. One of my favorites was the official ship's call sign *Mauler*, which belonged to the heavy cruiser USS *Boston*. Whenever the *Boston* returned to resume patrol along the coast of Vietnam it was with great drama that the Officer of the Deck radioed to inform all those within several hundred miles, "This is *Mauler*, I repeat *Mauler*, checking into the net." Very cool. Of course, when you are the first cousin of a battleship, that factor alone carries a certain cachet.

My personal call sign was significantly less impressive and happened to be "Megaphone Bravo." While you were never sure of the precise origins of your assigned personal call sign, I was told mine was Megaphone for loudness and Bravo (from the phonetic alphabet) B for Big. Regardless of the source or what it referenced, your call sign designation usually was non-negotiable and it was hung on you as an understated badge of honor.

I was accepting of mine because there was no call sign appeals court, but certainly there were far more clever ones such as "Big Ben" (Ben Wagner), "Mortimer Sierra" (Edward Bergin), "Mary Poppins" (Eldon Thompson) and one of the best was "Moll Flanders" (Tom Jones). Moll was the ravenous prostitute from the eating scene in the book/movie *Tom Jones*.

In Swift Boats, too much of a good thing was never the case, so in addition to our personal call signs we assigned code words to various points of land. Actually, this had a very practical purpose because we were constantly referencing points of land relative to where we were going or identifying our current location. Messages of this type, specifically *who* and *where*, for security reasons were supposed to be put into code or encrypted, before they were sent. The reason for this was to prevent the Viet Cong or North Vietnamese from taking this information and setting up an ambush, then waiting patiently for your arrival. On the flip side, the enemy could commence some action if they knew you were at a position a distant five to ten miles away from them.

Because Swift Boats were purchased commercially, ninety-five percent of the gear on board was off the shelf. We had no secure government-issued or government-designed communication equipment similar to that found on a larger ship or at a shore installation. Therefore, to send an encrypted message, we had an 8 × 11 paper code book that changed each day. In it were a series of three letter groups of which hundreds were listed on a sheet of paper. On top of this sheet of paper, you placed a small piece of black plastic with multiple holes punched in different locations. You then took the device and, depending on whether you were encrypting or decrypting a message, three letters would equal one single letter so the word "dog" on a particular day might represent nine random letters.

It sounds much more confusing than it was, but in fact it did require some manual dexterity. The bottom line was that this process took way too much time. Add to that the fact that the boat was often rocking and rolling, the paper could get wet, and the process might need to be undertaken at night using the red lens flashlight, and then it became next to impossible.

Therefore, we (Swift Boats) concluded that this complex encryption procedure was far too burdensome when often all we wanted to do was meet another Swift Boat, perhaps in the next patrol area to discuss some operational issue or more importantly get some ice cream, additional coffee or a new jar of the all-important yellow mustard.

Having been provided with this extensive background on the official secure radio procedures for Swift Boats, we had little choice but to develop our own more efficient method of communicating. After extensive deliberations, which were enhanced by a bottle of scotch, the "In Port Communications Committee" brought forth a new and very sophisticated communications protocol.

The unanimous decision was made that the northern points of land would be assigned Disneyland names. So a rendezvous or meeting place could very well sound like this: "Moll Flanders, this is Megaphone Bravo. Request Romeo Romeo two klicks south of Minnie Mouse at figures 1830."

Translated: Daly wants Jones to rendezvous one mile south of the Hue River mouth at 1830 (6:30 P.M.).

To totally comprehend the force-wide impact of our innovative radio procedures, you had to understand that there were these U.S. listening entities called Naval Communication Security Groups located through-out Vietnam. Their task was to monitor both friendly and enemy radio traffic attempting to acquire any useful type of intelligence. For some strange reason, which was totally lost on us, they felt that the Swift Boat mission should involve some level of security. Unfortunately, most of the time, we did not agree with this premise.

Whenever we used our new improvised and clandestine security transmissions, a day or two later we would receive an official-looking report on yellow paper via our control Article. This informed us (Swift Boats) that we had been involved in a radio communications security violation; furthermore, it was to cease immediately.

We might have considered complying, if the security people had even the foggiest idea who Moll Flanders was or even better the location of Minnie Mouse. Since the Security Group was never able to link these transmissions any closer than in general to Swift Boats, active enforcement became extremely difficult.

On one occasion, when we were on a quiet patrol north of Da Nang enjoying our yacht and the glass-like seas of the southern Pacific, we pulled alongside to greet a newly arrived U.S. Navy oceangoing minesweeper (MSO). This larger vessel, perhaps 150 feet in length, was assigned to patrol ten to fifteen miles off the coast of Vietnam and it was considered the outer barrier for our Market Time Operation. This was the Navy's operational order for Swift Boats and other Navy vessels outlining their responsibilities along the coast of South Vietnam. In fact, we never saw this op. order or read it, but I am sure it was very well written.

All of us in Swift Boats, led by Eldon Thompson (Mary Poppins), felt quite strongly that we were the unofficial but very qualified "Ambassadors and Welcoming Committee" for the arrival of any new U.S. Navy vessel. In truth, we usually had the simultaneous goal of picking up some fresh food but we also felt it was appropriate that we reinforce the image of just how cool we were, at least in our own minds. This was an ongoing responsibility and one that all of us took quite seriously.

This day, we closed on the newly arrived MSO with our traditional high-speed, one-full-circle-around-white-water approach, which concluded with a rapid deceleration alongside. All this was smartly executed with Boats driving at the aft helm. We were soon greeted near the stern of the MSO by a young and newly minted Navy ensign (bright eyed and bushy tailed), who came to the rail to speak with us. In our usual humble fashion, we had expected the commanding officer but perhaps he had a prior Vietnam tour under his belt and was underwhelmed by our arrival.

"Ensign New Guy" explained to us that one of his duties included being the ship's communications officer. He described, in a most sincere fashion, how he had spent considerable time reviewing the naval communications procedures for the locale and had identified all the relevant call signs except for a select few. He then proceeded to recite a list of all the boat driver call signs that he heard on the radio during his first week, along with our assigned designators for the various points of land.

He had concluded that the Disneyland call signs were probably specific geographic locations. For that, I gave him A+ and told him that I felt he had a real future in this man's Navy. Still frustrated, he stated he could not locate the other call signs or what they represented in any formal listing of naval ships.

I felt it was my duty to inform him that he was about to become privy to a critical piece of information pertaining to the operations of the U.S. Navy surface fleet patrolling off the coast of Vietnam. These names, I told him, were in fact personal call signs used by a group of misguided souls, most experiencing delusions of grandeur, like myself.

As expected, he was extremely grateful for this sensitive information and in exchange rewarded us with a carton of fresh fruit and a stack of current magazines. Upon review, we concluded that our movies back at the base were in fact better than his onboard inventory.

Panhandling and freeloading were part of our operational creed, so we had no guilt, but in reality we also had little to complain about. Food, equipment, and ammunition, even way up north at the DMZ, were supplied from Da Nang. The all-important mail from home was frequent and flown in from the U.S. with a travel time of under a week.

On the other side of the ledger, our visit had made this young naval officer, who was embarked on his first combat tour, a little more salty.

Now, he was a true insider who had been confidentially briefed on some of the really important things that were going on. Last on the list, we may have recruited another Swift Boat volunteer when his current tour of duty was completed.

The bitches and moans from the Naval Communications Security Group about our call signs continued. Their notes were always good for a laugh, especially when the operational people, the Coastal Surveillance Center, CSC (call sign Article), with whom we worked, were the first individuals who received these chastising missives. They in turn, playing by the book, were duty bound to ask us if we could be somewhat more professional in our communications procedures.

In no way did we even remotely report to these mysterious Naval Communications Security Groups. Therefore, because they had no idea of our real identity and their complaints were based on solely our personal call signs, the practice continued along with their yellow admonitions the entire year I was in-country and I'm sure well after my departure.

To avoid any confusion of names, a brief word on the Coastal Surveillance Centers is in order. Each CSC would monitor all maritime activities along the coast of South Vietnam from their six shore-based locations. They would coordinate all U.S. Navy surface activity and often aircraft along the coast, as well as operations near the river mouths including the Vietnamese junk bases with their U.S. Navy advisors. They did, in fact, bring a semblance of order to operations that could, on occasion, involve large Navy ships conducting naval shore bombardment, Marine Corps operations and related air strikes—all underway at the same time.

Standard procedure while on a patrol was for every Swift Boat to check in on an hourly basis with your control. In our case this was Article and the basic hourly message was "Ops normal." This informed Article that we were alive and well, operating in our assigned area and nothing of specific concern was going on. When a significant event was taking place, which could range from investigating a suspicious maritime contact, firing at onshore target, or a knock-down firefight, Article could coordinate support or whatever else was needed.

Frankly, not every night on patrol was exciting and some nights were downright boring. At the top of each hour, the five or six patrol areas checked in "Article, ops normal," each with their individual sector call signs and then we all knew that things were generally peaceful. However, when things were too quiet, before long, creativity could creep into play.

One evening, when the seas were pancake flat and no action was taking place anywhere, Killer Lou Masterson, decided that the 0200 "Ops Normal" check-in to Article was not what was called for. Lou decided that he would inject a sense of drama into this otherwise mundane radio report.

Slightly after 0200, with an urgent tone and a raised voice, Lou radioed for all to hear, "ARTICLE, ARTICLE, this is Same Drink Delta." No further message was transmitted. All the while in the background, there was the unmistakable clattering of Lou's twin .50 caliber machine guns being fired. This was accompanied by a great deal of muffled background yelling on the part of his crew. All this action took place while the "transmit" button on Lou's radio remained fully depressed.

Naturally, this got the attention of Article along with every other boat on the circuit. If the first short transmission was good theater, it certainly justified the second equally dramatic one which was transmitted immediately after.

Before Article could respond to either radio message, the thundering machine-gun fire suddenly ceased along with screams from the crew. After a prolonged ten-second pause, with silence across the entire net, a somewhat breathless but simple transmission was heard by all as Killer Lou announced, "Article, this is Same Drink Delta. Operations normal, out." Without question, a vignette worthy of an Oscar nomination.

On another ink-dark night in early February, with no moon above as the winter monsoon season was beginning to wane, the California surfer Jay Fleming (call sign Malibu Foxtrot, in PCF 13), was patrolling in the sector just south of Da Nang. While in that specific sector, PCF 13's assigned call sign was Enfield Cobra Foxtrot. The crew was proceeding north along the coast, approximately a thousand yards off the beach, when they detected on their radar scope a well-defined steel-hulled contact transiting along what appeared to be a southerly course several miles to their east out at sea.

Jay was well aware of the fact that in the last twelve months there had been several prior reported instances of possible enemy trawlers traveling south from China or North Vietnam. One had been captured farther south. The enemy's tactic was to run slowly south parallel to the coast but well offshore, appearing to be an innocent cargo ship. Then they would suddenly turn 90° toward land making a full-speed sprint onto the beach. There the cargo of weapons would be delivered to the waiting enemy troops and the ship abandoned or blown up.

Therefore, standard procedure was to immediately investigate any unidentified radar contact that appeared to be of steel construction that appeared to be of steel construction and so might well be an enemy trawler.

Jay and his crew cranked it up and proceeded to close the target at max speed having set General Quarters with all weapons manned. When approaching any potential enemy target, you wanted to close at high speed to maintain some element of surprise. Regretfully, in this case, Jay soon visually identified the contact as a newly arrived 400-foot U.S. Navy destroyer. For some reason, this ship had not followed the mandatory communications protocol and had failed to announce its arrival on station over the Market Time radio circuit, which we all monitored.

Having confirmed at about 1,000 yards that it was indeed a U.S. Navy destroyer (we knew the Viet Cong did not have any destroyers), Jay, without slowing, did a quick circle around the ship and headed back to shore to resume close-in patrol.

Suddenly, a booming voice came dramatically over the radio circuit, "This is Plymouth Rock, identify yourself immediately."

Jay's Swift Boat response was prompt and succinct, "This is Enfield Cobra Foxtrot, out."

Jay assumed that his succinct response provided enough information because our ongoing relationship with the larger Navy ships in the area had always been outstanding, cordial and supportive.

However, in this instance, "Plymouth Rock" immediately radioed back and commenced some on-air diatribe stating that his security zone had been violated, etc., etc. Jay decided his best response was a short and simple one and transmitted: "Plymouth Rock, this is Enfield Cobra Foxtrot. Hear you Lima Charlie (Loud and Clear). Roger, out."

To Plymouth Rock, this professional but succinct response was totally unacceptable and the next transmission was from "Plymouth Rock Actual." This indicated that it was the ship's commanding officer present on the radio.

The transmission that followed went along the lines of, "The next time you pull a stunt like that you'll be looking down the barrel of a 5-inch 38 cannon." The item described was the main armament of a destroyer of this type.

This ill-timed, poorly phrased harangue of our friend Jay was not acceptable and more than enough to gain the attention of any Swift Boat within 100 miles, especially on a boring and quiet night. Numerous anonymous calls to Article quickly commenced such as, "ARTICLE, ARTICLE, did you hear Plymouth Rock threaten to blow Enfield Cobra Foxtrot *out of the water*?" This was followed up by numerous exhortations transmitted by other Swift Boats for Cobra Foxtrot to simply run for his life.

On this type of radio, unless you identify yourself there is no way for anyone to know who is making the transmission or from what location it is coming from without special locating equipment. As a result, the follow-on radio cacophony was good for least another thirty minutes nonstop. Eventually, the Swift troops quieted down. Perhaps, by then, the newly arrived CO of Plymouth Rock had finally realized that he had slightly overreacted to the perceived threat presented by Jay and his crew.

Swift Boats were never ones to abandon a good thing. After waiting approximately two hours, at 0300, from some unidentified source, a pearl of wisdom radio message was transmitted to all U.S. Naval units—large and small—along the coast of Vietnam for at least several hundred miles.

"Attention All Units, Attention All Units" and then a five-second pause, "If I were a dog, I wouldn't piss on Plymouth Rock, OUT."

Sophistication and maturity were never in short supply.

## CHAPTER 8

# BEAUTY SLEEP

It was about 1815 and with my usual trace of awkwardness, I swung my right leg carefully over the metal railing that enclosed the entire main deck of APL-5. I then proceeded to climb slowly down the short steel ladder, which was one of two attached to the side of the APL's hull. This was no simple task because I was carrying my trusty gym bag that contained a host of critical items: my foul-weather jacket, bathing suit (I was ready for any weather contingency) and my personal pistol—a Smith and Wesson .357 Magnum—along with 500 rounds of ammunition.

The gun had been nicknamed by some of the other boat drivers, "The Cannon." They often borrowed it when they took the duty truck and were assigned to do the weekly pickup of Swift Boat ammunition. This pickup included 81mm mortar rounds, belts of .50 caliber, grenades and small arms, all of which were stockpiled at the nearby Marine base. We all felt that climbing down from the truck while wearing the leather shoulder holster, complete with its small bandolier of extra rounds, helped to mitigate the delivery-boy image.

Tonight, heading out on patrol, the ammunition in my bag served a secondary purpose because it provided the weight required in whatever bag you carried the confidential daily KAC-135 communication codes. On each patrol, most of which were thirty hours long, the Officer-in-Charge was required to carry two days of radio communication codes because each day started and ended at midnight. It was mandatory that whatever container the codes were carried in had to have adequate weight to ensure that if the boat sank, or they were dropped overboard, they would not remain afloat. My 500 rounds of ammunition would be more than adequate.

I was the first on board PCF 76, so I dumped my gear below and walked forward to the pilothouse to start the engines and let them warm up while the rest of the crew finished evening chow. We had cleaned, fueled and armed the boat the day before when we returned to port, so we were set to go. It was a night patrol, so food for dinner or breakfast was not required. Boats (Fielder), in the finest naval tradition, always kept enough coffee on board for the entire Pacific Fleet just in case they dropped by for a mug, all at the same time. Therefore, our coffee supply was never a concern, providing of course, you drank it black. If you didn't drink it black, you were looked upon with a suspicious eye and the welcome mat was the somewhat smaller version.

The Delta patrol was the only nighttime patrol out of Da Nang and generally was a no-brainer. We called it the "out-at-seven in-at-seven" patrol. Geographically, the patrol area itself began just outside of Da Nang harbor and was defined by a long curving shoreline that wound north for about seven to ten miles. On the west side, along the water, there was a bluff high above where you could see the edge of the infamous Route 1—the road described in the war-torn book, *A Street Without Joy* by Bernard Fall.

In contrast to the road of sadness above, the bay below was defined by beautiful long unbroken stretches of smooth sandy beach. Directly behind these narrow contours grew a dense and menacing backdrop of thick green jungle growth. Here and there was the occasional tall palm tree bent by the winds but still determined to break through in its reach for the sun. Scattered at the edge of the tree line were several simple shacks belonging to the local fishermen, each with a roof and sides made of palm fronds. Beyond them was nothing more significant until you reached the northern rim of the bay. At that location, there was a fishing village located at the mouth of a small river that ran several miles north where it merged with the larger Hue River, which in turn flowed inland to the Imperial City of Hue. This smaller stretch of water was where Killer Lou set his long-distance record for slalom waterskiing. It was a beautiful area, where in another life it would have been delightful to take a tranquil stroll barefoot in the sand.

In the pilothouse, I swung into the driver's seat, facing the big, spoked aluminum wheel, then reached over and pressed the starter button located on the port side of the dashboard. Immediately, I heard the engine starter engage, driven by that powerful 24-volt kick from the bank of truck batteries located back in Snipe's engine room. After a short cranking, the big engine turned over and began that uneven rumbling roll accompanied by the slight hesitation that was the trademark of the 12-71 Detroit Diesels when they were cold. I reached over to the other side of the dashboard and repeated the procedure for the starboard engine.

These engines put out a sound that for some odd reason gave you the simultaneous feeling of security and control, of course neither of which was true. However, to the Swift Boat crews that engine rumble had become something akin to their theme song.

The troops arrived well fed, reasonably alert and in good spirits. The last several days had been grueling patrols—one all-night fire mission, another way up north to the DMZ, followed by a six-hour return trip in a teeth-shattering, fast-moving tropical storm. In between there was no time to get a decent night's sleep so tonight's Delta patrol would be a chance to grab at least five hours, albeit in a couple of shorter stretches.

The sun had almost set by the time we stopped by Article, our onshore control, to pick up and discuss the night's operational orders. Article's briefing contained nothing of significance. Shoving off, we put on our running lights as we moved across and out the wide mouth of Da Nang harbor. Outside the harbor, on patrol, we only ran "darkened ship." However, in the harbor with warships and cargo ships of all sizes coming and going, plus the chance of being targeted by one of the small harbor patrol boats, "lights on" was the policy. As any sailor knows, a collision at sea or friendly fire can ruin your whole day, let alone your night.

Related to friendly fire, I thought back to an incident the week before that had taken place early in the afternoon as we were heading north back to the base at Da Nang from one of the southern patrol areas. We were peacefully running a mile off the coast, turning about 28 kts, when we passed a U.S. Navy LST on our port side travelling closer to shore. LSTs were about 300 hundred feet long, hardly graceful with a high bow made up of two big clam-like doors that open to reveal a ramp that allows the roll on, roll off of equipment. This was not an unusual sight because the U.S. Navy used these ships to bring supplies in and out of Da Nang on occasion, as did our South Korean allies (the ROKs). However, this vessel suddenly began to flash us "Alpha, Alpha" (dot dash, dot dash) using her signal light. This signal was basically an interrogative challenge, "Who are you?"

"Alpha, Alpha" was a signal I could read, but it represented the full extent of my flashing-light communication skills. Boats was no better qualified than I was to read flashing lights and I was pretty sure he represented the rest of the crew's capability. On other occasions, our successful solution to this problem had been a very basic one: turn toward the signaling vessel, approach it at high speed, and establish close-in voice communications. Usually the message was a simple one, such as: did we need any supplies, what was the status of any local enemy activity or could we transport someone to the beach for them?

Regretfully, as we closed this particular LST at high-speed, it became obvious to me that something was definitely wrong with our standard response to the flashing light challenge. The ship's entire crew appeared to be at General Quarters, specifically helmets donned and all guns manned. Upon closer inspection as we continued our high-speed approach, using my binoculars, I saw that all their weapons were unfortunately aimed directly at PCF 76. Their warlike countenance was in stark contrast to our somewhat more casual fashion statement, which included ball caps, sunglasses, no shirts and cut-off shorts. It was obvious that what we had here was a definite failure to communicate.

Being the Officer-in-Charge, I immediately made a command decision to reduce the threat envelope and rapidly slowed 76 to a conservative 5 kts. As we continued our approach, a khaki-clad officer complete with helmet and flak vest hastily emerged from the bridge holding a bull horn. Even to the casual observer, it was obvious this was the captain of the LST. Loudly, and in no uncertain terms, he informed us that we were extremely lucky that he had not ordered his ship to open fire on what he had interpreted as an enemy patrol boat beginning a high-speed attack run.

Rather than point out to him the fact that we were proudly and clearly flying the American flag (approximately three feet by four feet) from our radar mast, I decided it was more prudent, because he was senior, to just apologize for the confusion and instead welcomed him to Vietnam.

Closing to about 100 feet, I did take a moment to inform him that the risk of running so close to shore might expose his vessel to gunfire from any lost and lonely enemy sniper. However, other than that risk, the local real estate was pretty much controlled by the United States Marine Corps. In my comments, I carefully selected what I hoped was just the right blend of risk assessment and security evaluation. On the bright side, I have no doubt that our apparently provocative visit would provide his crew with some preliminary combat stories for tomorrow's mail home.

Having completed our very effective "people-to-people" mission, we turned the boat slowly to starboard waving as we pulled away from our new friends. Boats was at the helm aft, and when we had separated about 200 feet from the LST, I gave him the twirling finger "wind 'em up" sign. I knew my signal would provide him with all the motivation he needed. Full forward went his hands on the throttles, quickly followed by the rumble and then the roar of the diesels as our bow lifted out of water with the big white wake streaming out astern. We did after all, have our Swift Boat image to maintain.

About twenty minutes later we approached the middle of the wide Da Nang harbor mouth (three miles) and began our gradual turn to port. I was below in our spacious and gracious main cabin completing some critical operational paperwork. Newcomer was in the pilothouse on radio watch, Snipe was with his engines cleaning who knows what, Muller and Buck were either oiling the guns or were stowing gear prior to entering port. Boats was still driving at the aft helm, out in the sunshine, as usual enjoying his yacht. He was reaching for the mug of black coffee he had strategically placed nearby on the cabin top, when suddenly he yelled, "Skipper, come topside."

As I stuck my head out of the stern cabin door, he pointed to port and I saw that for some reason, the LST, having completed her turn to port, was still hugging the shoreline along the southern rim of Da Nang harbor. We both knew that this was a very bad idea because there was a large rock unmarked on the charts about a quarter-mile off the beach dead ahead. Usually, no one paid much attention to this because the harbor was so wide there was no reason to transit that close to shore.

I had no idea of our new friend's radio call sign but he was definitely heading into "Harm's Way" and I felt it my duty to warn him. Perhaps he was monitoring our Market Time radio frequency, so I quickly turned and climbed the two steps to the pilothouse, picked up the radio microphone and transmitted, "U.S. Navy LST, U.S. Navy LST, entering Da Nang harbor from the south. Be advised you are heading into dangerous and obstructed waters." ... Nothing heard.

Then I repeated my first transmission again with no response. Boats had the binoculars out and said he could see that the LST was still at General Quarters and appeared to be making about 8 to 10 kts. This was definitely not the speed at which you wanted to kiss a large and immoveable object, i.e. the rock. However, there was no way I was going to warn him by repeating this morning's high-speed approach, especially considering the fact that the crew of the LST still remained at General Quarters.

Failing to establish radio contact, my only remaining solution was to fire a series of small handheld parachute flares and at least try to get their attention. I decided not to use the large illumination rounds fired from the 81mm mortar because the last thing I needed was for this captain to hear the *thump* of our mortar firing and see an explosion overhead as the parachute flare fell toward him. However, our small hand-held flares were pretty effective even in the daytime and might carry close enough to at least attract his attention. Boats and I each fired one apiece about thirty seconds apart. Meanwhile, I instructed the rest of the crew to stand on the cabin top waving their arms back and forth.

This sophisticated signaling method appeared to work and at least the LST slowed and eventually stopped. Then, I decided I would risk one more very slow approach. I figured by then that even this captain must have come to the conclusion that we were "friendly forces." Due to our slow speed and a lack of any wind, Snipe offered to stand on the cabin top and display our drooping U.S. flag, holding it out by hand. I declined, fearing this gesture might somehow be misinterpreted.

As we closed to about fifty yards, I stopped the boat and simply shouted: "Captain, there is an unmarked rock dead ahead. I would recommend you turn 90° to starboard and proceed into the harbor at least one mile off the beach."

Rather than wait for any response, or encourage any drawn out awkward discussion, I simply gave a full wave of my arm, which I hoped was interpreted as a friendly gesture. Then, we proceeded in the recommended direction, sincerely hoping "Captain New Guy" would follow us. Slowly making his turn, this time to starboard, he did indeed follow our recommendation.

Once again this evolution demonstrated that while it is important to be serious about combat risks, not keeping things in the proper perspective can also be a great way to get your ass handed to you. I made a mental note that this guy owed me a drink at the O'Club if the occasion ever presented itself.

With a smile, I returned that story to my memory file and shifted my thinking back to our current night patrol and the business at hand. By now, we had cleared the harbor mouth and had entered the Delta patrol sector. As we headed north, no traffic showed on the radar scope so we killed the running lights and set the standard underway watch: three men up and three asleep, with me taking the first watch: 2000 to midnight.

I knew tonight was the "dark of the moon" on the calendar. This always presented some cause for concern because the Viet Cong and the NVA both had demonstrated that they preferred and were quite effective operating in total darkness. However, the seas tonight were almost flat calm, which gave us good visibility with binoculars and also allowed the radar to paint a clear and crisp picture without any distracting sea clutter. Therefore, we were unlikely to miss any suspicious movement, at least on the water.

My first watch was uneventful and I woke Boats about 2345 to make sure he had his mug of black coffee before we discussed everything relevant from my watch. This time, it took longer to pour his coffee than it did to brief him and then I turned in. I had tremendous confidence in Boats that had developed over the past six months, starting with Boat School in Coronado. He was good with the men, took outstanding care of PCF 76 and could be counted on in combat when things went to hell. However tonight, I doubted that was going to be the case.

With peaceful thoughts in mind, I climbed up onto the top bunk in the main cabin because the lower bunk was usually covered with gear, and quite often several loaded M-16s were laid out there at the ready. The upper bunk was also level with the main deck and I could open the sliding window, which gave me an eye-to-eye view if Boats and his watch section came alongside to inspect a smaller junk. Many an unsuspecting fishermen was shocked to look up and see my face looking straight at him, accompanied by the .357 in my right hand.

Tonight, I grabbed our Navy-issue grey woolen blanket and picked up the life jacket that we used as a pillow and pushed it under my head. On Swift Boats regular pillows, because of the night dampness, ended up being very efficient sponges, so the Navy decided to put them in plastic bags which were even worse unless you were partial to sweat. The life jacket, however, seemed to work just fine. Also, one never knew when it might come in handy.

About 0130, Boats came into the main cabin where I was out cold ensconced with my blanket and life jacket. When he woke me there was an unusual tone of urgency in his voice which immediately caught my attention.

"Skipper, you're not going to believe this."

When I asked "believe what?" he simply repeated his original statement. After his second rendition, I was becoming somewhat irritated as a result of having my *beauty sleep* interrupted. I asked him, "Boats, what the hell am I not going to believe?"

His rapid response began with the fact that he had picked up a small radar contact, but one that painted clearly about two miles away. Then he described how he drove slowly, approaching the contact, put the spotlight on it and saw what he felt was definitely the periscope of a submarine.

He had one thing right—I wasn't about to believe him, but we had to determine just what was going on. I then swung around, jumped down from the bunk, landing with both my feet firmly on the deck. Somehow I hoped that this jolt might bring some clarity to the current situation. Regretfully, it did not.

Our highly skilled engineman Snipe was at the helm with Buck on lookout in the gun tub and he had seen the same thing. Boats and I went forward to the pilothouse to watch the radar and see if the small contact reappeared on the scope. It did about five minutes later, about half a mile ahead. I reached over and jammed the throttles full forward and told Snipe to follow the electronic bearing marker on the radar scope toward the contact. We would close the distance in less than a minute at 30 kts. Frankly, I fully expected to find a bamboo fishing stake weighted at the bottom with stones, which the Vietnamese fisherman often deployed and anchored to at night.

As we approached at full speed, the radar contact simply disappeared off the scope. I ordered Snipe to drop to idle speed and soon felt our four-foot wake catch up to us and roll under the boat lifting the stern as it went by. From the leather case on the dashboard, I grabbed the second pair of binoculars, which were top-quality Navy-issue Bausch & Lomb 7 × 50s that were very effective at night. Stepping out of the pilothouse, I gave the area a quick visual scan. Nothing seen, nothing heard except the rumble of our own engines.

"Boats, anything showing on the scope?"

"Negative, Skipper."

Good, bad, or indifferent, this situation now had my full attention. If this was an enemy submarine we would not be torpedoed because the draft of a Swift Boat was way too shallow and any weapon launched underwater would most likely pass harmlessly below us, just like in the movies. So I hoped.

On the other hand, if they surfaced for a gunfight that would be a very big mistake on their part considering we had three .50 caliber machine guns, an 81mm mortar and we were highly maneuverable. This analysis left me with several options: they were laying mines, but they would have done that in Da Nang harbor, not this peaceful basin with no ship traffic. However, they could be infiltrating enemy troops or the most likely case was that they were delivering weapons and munitions. This last one made the most sense and that meant that onshore there would be a well-armed reception party of enemy troops waiting to meet them and offload the cargo.

Reviewing these scenarios, it occurred to me that despite it being the "dark of the moon" which provided us visual cover, the racket of our engines with no wind made us an easy target for any enemy onshore who could pinpoint us based solely on sound. I thought back to the events of several months ago when our classmate Ed Bergin and PCF 79 had captured the Chinese Communist trawler south of Chu Lai loaded with weapons and explosives, after a running and deadly gun battle. All that took place during the "dark of the moon."

Immediately, I called Article, our Da Nang shore-based control, and questioned them about any friendly activity in the Delta area including the possible transit of a submarine. They assured me nothing was going on in the Delta but answered me with a tone that seemed to inquire "Just what's happening on your end?"

The last thing I needed at this moment was a long, drawn-out radio conversation about my list of wacky submarine scenarios with someone sitting back in Da Nang with his feet up on the desk. When I got some answers and had some facts, then I could make decisions about possible support. Even though they would be friendly, combat aircraft and Huey helicopters with rockets and Gatling guns providing close-in air-support in a confined area on a very dark night was a risk I wanted no part of. I also recalled that Ed mentioned, after capturing his trawler, the greatest risk to his crew's survival was friendly fire from units joining in the activities.

"Roger, Article. Thank you, out" was my response.

Article now knew my status, present location, and that was all I was going to convey to him at the moment.

Just as I closed out my radio transmission to Article, we saw machine-gun fire with blue tracers streaming along the beach about 700 yards off our port side. I knew this could only mean that nearby were enemy troops, VC, or more likely NVA, because U.S. forces used red tracers.

Several months ago, we had installed a separate radio on board all the boats dedicated just to monitoring the Marine Corps radio channels. Leaning behind Snipe, I reached below the driver's seat on the right side, where that radio was located, grabbed the microphone and gave them a call utilizing our patrol area call sign "Enfield Cobra Delta," which fortunately they immediately recognized.

Their response was, "Go-ahead Navy," and then came the good news. They informed me that there was a full-strength North Vietnamese company operating in the area which they anticipated engaging later in the evening. This explained the blue tracer fire on the beach.

Thanking them for the update, now my cardiac rate had picked up substantially. I told Boats to wake up the rest of the crew on the double and set General Quarters. At the same time our mysterious radar contact reappeared on the scope about a mile away. Rather than simply making another high-speed run to its location, I came up with the clever idea of using the 81mm mortar to lob an illumination round up and over our pilothouse in the direction of the contact. Hopefully, this would give us a quick visual under the bright light of the illumination round which the submarine would not be expecting. At the same time, we would combine this with another high-speed approach.

The danger in this procedure was when the fired mortar round left the barrel, it might hit and blow off the top of our radar mast. This would result in a host of other explosive consequences none of which would be career enhancing. However, luck was on our side. When Boats and Snipe fired the round, it cleared the radar mast. We had calculated the range to target correctly and the round went off perfectly. The parachute flare deployed and everything within half a mile was illuminated almost like daylight.

Buck yelled from the gun tub above that he could see nothing. After about thirty seconds of burning, the parachute illumination was gone. During this time, I had been standing on the bow forward of the pilothouse locked onto the rail with one hand, the other holding the binoculars trying to scan below the falling parachute, all the while charging ahead at 30 kts. Our contact was nowhere to be seen as we slowed.

The flip side of all this noise and activity was that now there could be little doubt on the part of the enemy onshore as to our presence and who we were. Boats remained with Snipe on the stern having recently fired the mortar. Newcomer was at the wheel during this evolution and had one eye on the radar scope as he drove. Suddenly, he yelled for me to come back inside the pilothouse. Once again, he made my day, or in this case my night, by jabbing his finger at the radar screen and showing me that we now had two additional small contacts off our port stern quarter in the surf line, about half a mile behind.

Keeping my voice somewhat modulated, I told the crew that we had been unable to confirm the periscope contact but now had two additional radar contacts close to shore and we were heading in. The night was dead black with no moon and no stars and the water was without even a surface ripple. Add to that, there was absolutely no wind and my once-favorite sounds, our Detroit Diesels, were gloriously trumpeting our approach to anyone within a country mile. Even at idle speed, there was no disguising our less than subtle arrival.

As officer-in-charge ("Skipper" to the crew) my "General Quarters policy" had always been that any individual could ready his weapon by simply announcing "round in the chamber." The result being, you simply had to flick off the safety, pull the trigger and you were in business—the battle was on.

Soon, I heard the metallic *ca-chunk … ca-chunk* of the twin .50 calibers as Muller in the gun tub above loaded the first round into the breach of each gun. Boats remained aft and loaded the .50 caliber with a single *ca-chunk*, while Snipe prepared to feed him the belted ammunition. The 81mm mortar mounted underneath was the wrong weapon for close-in fighting but we might need it if we received sniper fire from the shoreline. Buck broke out and loaded the M-16s, safeties on—two in the pilothouse, two in brackets on top of the main cabin top. Perhaps, I should have been concerned about all of the other small arms being loaded by my crew but at this point in time I was focused on the noise and havoc the three .50 calibers would make if they started tearing up the night.

I told Newcomer I was going to drive at the after helm where I felt I had the fullest view, except for a small sector directly ahead. The helm in the pilothouse had some advantages in terms of viewing straight ahead plus the radio and the radar, but to me it was like operating in a closet where you peeked through the slats in the door. Communicating with the crew, no matter what was going on, was never a problem, as my call sign was "Megaphone Bravo." Now, I saw that our radioman Newcomer was crouched in the doorway of the pilothouse with his M-16 and the radio nearby if we needed it. Buck was in position in the other doorway.

At the after helm, scattered around me on the main cabin top, was an M-16, an M-79 grenade launcher and my personal .357 Magnum pistol. In terms of hardware, the only weapon that appeared to be missing was the "M-1 Brick" for me to throw at the enemy when all else failed.

Straining through the darkness with one hand on the wheel and the other on the throttles, I looked out over the port bow as we closed the contact. About seventy-five yards ahead, I saw what appeared to be two large rubber rafts sitting low and squat in the water. From this distance, in total darkness, I could not be sure if anyone was on board or if they were empty. I purposely stopped and kept the target at a 45° angle to ensure that all our guns could be brought to bear if any firing started.

I soon realized that this put us at a disadvantage if we received sniper fire from the shore and had to shift guns to the starboard side. However, the big .50s could pivot in that direction in a matter of seconds. With that in mind, I kept shifting my eyes from our port side approach to the rafts to conducting a quick scan across the starboard side, along the beachfront looking for any muzzle flash. Unfortunately, by now we had closed the beach to about 100 yards, making us a very easy target for the enemy that might be hiding in the dune line or concealed in the jungle behind. There would be no long-range firefight tonight.

I could have given the order, "Guns Tight," but had enough confidence in my crew that they would not fire without provocation. As we approached, I thanked God nobody in the rafts moved and for our part the big .50s did not commence their recognizable and deadly *baa-baa-baa-bap—baa-baa-baa-bap.*

Suddenly on one of the rafts, I saw a red light waving back and forth. This was definitely some sort of signal, but not one that meant anything to me. However, it did confirm that there were people on the rafts. Thank God, no one on board PCF 76 had misinterpreted the moving red light as a muzzle flash and commenced fire; once again the advantage of a well-trained and disciplined crew.

After another very tense minute or two, it became obvious to me that this Hollywood standoff was going nowhere and the risk of someone opening fire, friend or foe, was increasing by the minute. All this time, I was concerned that that we were still conducting our rumbling diesel engine symphony. This made us a no-brainer target for any enemy that might be setting up camp onshore.

I knew Boats was standing aft of me manning the single stern .50 and I yelled over my shoulder, "Turn your .50 to starboard, cover the beach and if you see any muzzle flash hose it down."

Then in horror it occurred to me, that if he did this, it might be misinterpreted and cause whoever was in the rafts to open fire on us.

The stalemate was over. Without further thought, I yelled in the general direction of the targets, "Both rafts paddle slowly, very slowly towards us."

At the same time, I lifted my left hand from the steering wheel waving my arm in a motion to come alongside, hoping they could see me in the darkness.

At this point, I had no idea who I was yelling at, or whether they could understand my command. I decided that my two-week Berlitz Vietnamese course was not going to cut it, so English was my choice. At least by speaking and waving, in what I hoped was an authoritative manner, I projected some image that I was in charge. It appeared to work, at least for the moment.

After a very long and stressful two minutes watching these two dark objects move slowly through the flat water and hearing the splashes as their paddles broke the surface, the first raft finally came alongside. Looking down from our deck there appeared to be five people on each raft and everyone on board was rock still, dressed totally in black with camouflaged faces.

A series of events like these had definitely not been covered in our Coronado training. I was somewhat reassured by the fact that up to now

I had not been shot, my crew had not committed mass murder and as the Officer-in-Charge my stampeding pulse had not led to cardiac arrest. My quick assessment was that the situation had advanced, but frankly not improved.

Building on what I evaluated to be my successful handling of the situation so far, once again in my best command voice I said, "One person and one person only stand up, climb on board and no one else move." This was accompanied with the appropriate hand motion, I hoped.

Utilizing my peripheral vision, it suddenly occurred to me that our advantage in weaponry, specifically the .50 caliber machine guns had in fact disappeared. The truth was that the .50s could not be depressed far enough down toward the two rafts now alongside us because the rafts sat so low in the water. This basically rendered our big guns useless. This could well mean that we were equally matched from a small arms standpoint. Conceivably, they could gain an advantage by simply tossing a hand grenade on board PCF 76, providing they were willing to take some of the hit themselves. I hoped the troops in the raft had not figured this one out and I had to assume that they were as terrified as we were.

My analysis aside, one person slowly stood up in the raft and climbed onto the bow of PCF 76. He slowly but very clearly introduced himself as "LTJG Robert Harrington, United States Navy."

At that moment, I felt there was now a remote possibility that my world was not about to end in a flash of gunfire and cordite. Some of my confidence slowly began to return along with the blood flow to my lower extremities. Still, I did not understand all the events that were taking place and there remained a great many unanswered questions.

Perhaps based on a somewhat overactive imagination, I did contemplate the remote possibility that our camouflaged visitor was in fact an English-speaking Caucasian working with the enemy.

Standing in the pitch dark with disaster just a trigger pull away, I did a quick mental review of the events. We suspected that the rafts came from an unidentified submarine and we knew from the Marines that there was significant enemy activity in the jungle along the beach. Once again, I returned to my vision of Ed Bergin and PCF 79 several months ago when they captured that Chinese Communist trawler filled with weapons and explosives as it raced for the beach where the enemy lay in wait.

Contemplating this possibility and perhaps recalling some World War II John Wayne movie scene, I responded again in my best command voice to the introduction from our mystery guest.

"So what?"

He quickly mumbled something in response to my "So what?" about being a member of Team Three. I fortunately recognized Team Three as a frogman unit from the base at Coronado. For some unknown reason, I felt it best to continue with the John Wayne scenario a bit longer and challenged him again with "Why, should I believe you?" It did occur to me that perhaps I was beginning to stretch my Caucasian enemy commando theory just a bit too far.

Realizing our discussion was not progressing toward any satisfactory conclusion, I made one more effort, again utilizing the movie scenario by questioning him about a famous person to demonstrate his true American roots. In this case, I was able to personalize it a bit with the question, "Who has the most famous name among the West Coast Frogs?"

I felt this was a very clever challenge on my part and should bring us to some conclusion. After several blank looks and a few very difficult swallows, he burst forth with the answer: "Teddy Roosevelt the Fourth."

I responded, "That is indeed the correct answer." I knew this because TR IV was a college classmate of mine and he was an active-duty frogman. Those four years at Harvard had finally paid off.

My response was immediately followed by numerous sighs of relief on both rafts as well as on PCF 76. I gave the immediate order "Secure all weapons" because there was no question when tensions were this high, mistakes could be made. It was very comforting to hear the *clunk* and the *clank* all around as weapons were cleared and secured. As I had expected, the frogs were also well armed, locked and loaded.

As the emotional dust settled further, LTJG Harrington informed me that we had in fact detected a top-secret submarine-based operation, which now had been compromised. As a courtesy, I reviewed for him the chain of events that had taken place as well as the action we had undertaken in response. In summary, and in a reasonably pleasant way, I said, "While I regret compromising your top-secret mission, this is my real estate and the bottom line is, you and your team are trespassing."

After some secret handshakes and smiles all around the frogs departed and began to paddle away, I presume back to their submarine. For some strange reason, I felt we should give them a semblance of privacy, so we turned slowly away from shoreline and proceeded north just as subtly as we had arrived. There was no doubt in my mind this was only act one and the events of the evening had not completely played out.

Approximately one hour later a call came over the radio to "Enfield Cobra Delta" from "Beauty Sleep." My keen intellect suggested that this might well be our new submarine "comrade in arms." A brief message was then sent in code which we carefully copied and proceeded to decrypt with our onboard decryption Ouija board device. This was the piece of plastic with holes that you placed over a page full of letters that changed each day. One group of letters led you to another, so on any given day the letters DEF might decrypt to mean the letter "T," etc. You can see why this procedure was used for short messages only. Communication between large Navy ships and shore facilities used much more sophisticated online electronic equipment. Swift Boats were pretty basic. We did short messages only and liked it that way.

In this case, the message from "Beauty Sleep" would not break (decrypt). I requested that it be transmitted to us again and I tried to make it sound like we had screwed up in copying the message the first time. Believe me, this was not the case, we had not miscopied it! The follow-on transmission was the same coded message with the same garbled result.

Then much to my dismay, a deeper voice came on the circuit declaring that, "This is Beauty Sleep Actual, what is the problem?"

"Actual," while not quite official Navy parlance said quite clearly that he was "the man." This could only be the boss himself.

Regretfully, the only response I could make after his two transmissions had failed to decrypt was a simple, "Beauty Sleep, Your message does not decrypt, Suggest you check day and date." This basically said it was after midnight and you are using the wrong day's code book. While I was correct, I am quite sure this did little to win friends and enhance my reputation with our submerged friend.

The next message was straightforward and did decrypt "Rendezvous at position XYZ (about three miles east) at 0300."

Despite the hour and my worn state of mind, both Boats and I clearly noticed the absence of any friendly "Request you" at the beginning of their message. Our obvious conclusion was that this was not their invitation for a predawn mug of coffee.

At 0300, we were at position XYZ, no question. We triple-checked our position, triangulating with multiple radar ranges. "Beauty Sleep" was nowhere to be seen visually using the binoculars or on the radar scope. Then the radio calls began in the clear, "Enfield, Cobra Delta, this is Beauty Sleep. Where are you?"

My response was again straightforward. "This is Enfield, Cobra Delta. We are at rendezvous."

Then casting aside any attempt at a clandestine rendezvous while at "darken ship" we were instructed that both vessels should put on red, green, and white navigation lights. This effort also yielded negative results. After some ongoing and terse communications, our submarine friend, who we now assumed was on the surface, informed us that he was turning on his yellow strobe light. This brilliant and sweeping light was used by submarines operating on the surface to clearly identify their position and avoid collision. Within a minute, we located their flashing light. They were several miles away, nowhere near the requested rendezvous site. We later learned that their radar had been malfunctioning and they were unable to get an accurate position fix. In a word, they were "Lost."

Picking up the radio microphone, I transmitted, "Beauty Sleep, this is Enfield Cobra Delta. We have identified you both visually and electronically. Your flashing light is no longer required. We are proceeding to your location at 30 kts and anticipate ETA alongside Beauty Sleep

5 minutes, over." When you lived on the radio you could make these transmissions sound pretty professional.

They were unimpressed and their response was prompt and terse. "This is Beauty Sleep. Roger out."

It was now around 0345. After my "right-between-the-eyes" radio transmission, I decided to cast caution to the wind and I instructed Boats to make a traditional high-speed Swift Boat approach. I was determined to arrive at my questionable destiny at least in style.

A submarine on the surface, under any circumstances, is a strange and menacing sight, with its long thin black hull and strange cigar shape. Take away any moon and stars and the result is a pitch-black night. Now, we had the submarine sitting silently in flat water without a ripple, not a breath of wind, and the image as we approached was downright Captain Nemo/Jules Verne *Twenty Thousand Leagues* creepy.

Any submarine, because its design is basically tubular in nature, is difficult to come alongside when it is on the surface. Boats made the final approach, regretfully coming to rest alongside the pressure hull a bit too aggressively, resulting in a resounding *BOOONG* despite our fenders being out. In this case, the cause was aluminum hitting steel. Undoubtedly, this clearly announced our arrival to all those below decks.

My jumping onto the submarine was somewhat of a track-star challenge based on the different hull shapes, which also prevented us from mooring evenly alongside. Landing on deck, I was greeted by the captain of the boat who was quite friendly but informed me that the commodore was waiting for me below in the officers' wardroom.

To me, this operation appeared to be somewhat top heavy in the brass area with a captain for the sub and a commodore for the mission. Swift Boat skippers have always been criticized for their lack of naval decorum but I decided this was a good time to keep those opinions to myself. I descended the ladder (there are no stairs) and at the bottom I was greeted by several of my new frogman friends whose looks implied that I was in "deep shit." Upon my entering the wardroom, their prediction proved amazingly accurate. I stood at attention and introduced myself as LTJG Dan Daly, Officer-in-Charge PCF 76. Commodore "Actual" responded by beginning a diatribe that insulted my naval competence, core intellect, Swift Boat training and numerous other deficiencies. Basically, he chewed me up one side and down the other. While painful, I stood my ground until he crossed the line and said,

"You Swift Boats are a disgrace to the United States Navy."

Applying that somewhat questionable football logic that states "the best defense is a good offense," or something to that effect, I responded, "Commodore, with all due respect, Sir, you are pissed off at me because I found your submarine and detected your frogmen before they hit the beach."

Without a pause, I continued on this path of self-destruction and stated that after we had detected his periscope on radar, I immediately checked in with my control Article inquiring about any friendly maritime activity, including submarines in the area. Their response had been negative. I also told him I had seen tracer fire on the beach and as a result I had had direct radio communications with the Marines on shore, who informed me that they were pursuing a North Vietnamese company in the area.

"Immediately thereafter, we detected what appeared to be two rubber rafts in the surf line proceeding toward shore. I set General Quarters and we commenced our approach toward a target that at the time was designated possible enemy."

I thought saying that I had "set General Quarters" gave my ranting some flavor of big-time Navy.

At this point, I had little to lose and decided to go for the extra point by saying, "Commodore, this was my patrol area of responsibility and your people should have informed me of their intended activity."

Take note that I carefully used the possessive "your people" while avoiding the nominative second singular "you."

Then, just to put a neat close on the morning's enjoyable conversation I said, "Commodore, *unless otherwise directed*, I intend to return to my Swift Boat and resume my assigned patrol."

This was my modification of a somewhat questionable military course of action called (UNODIR), "unless otherwise directed." I somehow felt that it fit the moment at hand. I waited a maximum of five seconds, maintaining eyeball-to-eyeball contact with the commodore, then pivoted and left the ward room. No salute was rendered because in the Navy you don't salute when uncovered which I was at the time, holding my blue ball cap in hand. Opening the wardroom door and passing my frogman audience gathered outside, all with their jaws somewhat lowered, I gave them a knowing nod of the head. I made my way up the ladder at full speed never looking back and, without stopping, made a successful leap onto PCF 76, while giving Boats the "wind 'em up" order, all in less than sixty seconds.

Swift Rules!

## CHAPTER 9

# BALL CAP SMITHSON

For some strange reason the Navy felt that Swift Boats in Vietnam should retain some semblance of the real blue water Navy and therefore designated that the officers wear wash khakis and the enlisted men dungarees, which were normal shipboard working uniforms. This was in definite contrast to the uniforms worn at the large Naval Support Activity (NSAD) in Da Nang. There, all personnel, officers and enlisted, dressed in jungle greens, which were basically baggy pants and a loose-fitting over blouse.

Never at a loss to make a strong statement, especially in the fashion arena, some Swift Boat crews began to wear blue baseball caps purchased in Hong Kong and embroidered with their individual boat numbers, rank or rating. Quickly, this became a status symbol worn by most Swift Boat crews, and worn with significant pride and an appropriate swagger. Over time, many of the officers had their assigned individual radio call signs added to the back of their hats. We felt this was adequate compensation for our inability to walk around in green utilities (work uniforms) disguised as a palm tree with a .45 caliber pistol slung on our hip. While each boat had a significant inventory of weapons, none of us were issued personal sidearms. By way of compensation, the Navy did provide us with two pairs of really cool Bausch & Lomb aviator sunglasses.

Where we lived on the APL 5, with the boats birthed alongside, was about four miles from downtime Da Nang. Downtown was a bit of an urban myth. It was better described as several paved streets and numerous open-front local shops selling every conceivable item, contraband included. The architecture, although war-torn, did retain a slight European flavor left over from the French Colonial days.

Walking along the tree-lined streets the more sophisticated Vietnamese women wore the attractive *ao dai*, a fitted garment with both front and back panels extending to the ground, worn over loose-fitting long pants of a similar material. I presumed, in most cases, it was silk. Usually the colors were soft pastels enhanced by decorative stitching, especially on the top part of the garment. The overall effect was attractive. The women seemed to glide along rather than walk. In stark contrast, the peasants of both sexes wore the traditional black pajamas and peaked straw hats. Unfortunately, this was also the uniform of choice for the enemy, the Viet Cong. Along the eastern edge of the city flowed the Da Nang River that began or ended, I was never quite sure, at the point where it intersected with the massive

*Vietnamese women in* ao dais.

deepwater Da Nang harbor. The river was bordered on both sides by fishing and light industrial activities.

About a mile downriver from the harbor on the left side was the Marine Corps headquarters III MAF (Third Marine Amphibious Force).This faced the Navy headquarters located directly across on the other side of the river about an eighth-mile across. Nearby, the Navy headquarters at the edge of the river was a small club called the Stone Elephant, appropriately located in one of the remaining French structures. The origin of the name Stone Elephant remained a mystery to me over the next twelve months. However, despite the wartime setting and undoubtedly with some reconstruction by the Seabees, the building displayed some semblance of sophistication. With our heavy patrol schedules often resulting in minimal sleep, our social jaunts downtown for a cold one at the Stone Elephant were sporadic at best. Whether or not it was legal, we kept hard liquor on board the APL in our individual lockers. Ice was always at hand but cold beer was not.

There was an Enlisted Men's Club nearby and a somewhat less glamorous Officers' Club at the large Naval Support Activity. Therefore the trip to the Stone Elephant was more for a social occasion or celebration than just a convenient local watering hole. Since there was only one truck assigned to support the entire Swift Boat Division, and this I believe had been stolen from the Marines, transportation was at a premium and the trip downtown was too far to walk. A one-way boat trip to the Club was a fallback position, which usually meant thumbing back to the base later in the evening. Besides, there were usually senior officers in attendance at the Club and on occasion they could put a real damper on our Swift Boat comradeship.

Attached to NSAD (Naval Support Activity Da Nang) was one Commander Smithson, who was relatively senior and had some position of importance on the Admiral's staff. Because we reported operationally to the Marines and from an administrative standpoint to the Navy, in Saigon we paid minimal attention to NSAD's chain of command. I assume, actually *I absolutely know*, some of the NSAD officers, especially Commander Smithson, were irritated by our non-traditional naval reporting structure.

Early on, our blue baseball caps and especially those worn by the boat officers became a target of Commander Smithson's keen sense of naval etiquette, eventually evolving into his personal obsession. On a regular basis, whether downtown or on the grounds of the NSAD, any Swift Boat skipper sighted by him wearing a blue baseball cap was deemed to be out of uniform and was immediately ordered back to our base for the appropriate headgear.

Most likely, he would have threatened to send us to Vietnam, but since we were already there and had volunteered for this, it was not an option available to him. We found his adherence to Navy uniform regs somewhat incongruous, especially coming from a group we described as "walking palm trees in their baggy jungle greens." Based on his tireless effort to instill both naval discipline and tradition among the Swift Boat officers, Commander Smithson was soon classified as a pain in the ass and assigned the moniker "Ball Cap Smithson."

On numerous occasions, as we approached the Stone Elephant in anticipation of that delightful and well-deserved first "cold one," Ball Cap would appear out of nowhere intent on playing the role of fashion police. In a confined environment he was tough to avoid, but this became somewhat easier on the downtown streets where a quick "Yes, Sir" and a salute followed by four right turns around the block usually solved the problem. While the "Ball Cap conflict" was not really an issue of strategic military significance, it soon became a great source of discussion leading to exaggerated reports of numerous Ball Cap encounters.

Early in the winter of 1968, the historic enemy Tet Offensive took place. This involved a major aggressive thrust throughout South Vietnam by the North Vietnamese. For months prior, they had infiltrated large numbers of troops and supplies down the Ho Chi Minh Trail. Major cities were the targets, Saigon to the south and to the north the historical capital Hue, and also Da Nang with its major airbase.

At this time in Da Nang, Swift Boats and the local UDT detachment (frogman and SEALS, our nearby neighbors) were the U.S. Navy's only onshore combat units. To some of those officers stationed at the Naval Support Activity (NSAD) navigating those mahogany desks armed only

*Side street in downtown Da Nang.*

with pencil and paper, we were a constant reminder of their support status. Naturally, as you would expect, whenever possible, we demonstrated that we were quite sympathetic to their plight.

However, during the Tet Offensive it was their combat chance to shine and in short order every officer in his jungle greens was seen resplendent with his trusty .45 pistol slung smartly at his hip. In contrast, a Swift Boat skipper was protected only by the aura of his personalized non-regulation blue baseball cap.

One evening, a group of us were stuck in port due to bad weather because the monsoon season was well under way with its heavy winds, high seas and horizontal rain, all beneath a blanket of multicolored and streaking clouds. We decided that despite the significant risk in the midst of the enemy offensive, we would "retreat to" the Stone Elephant. We knew Da Nang was defended by several thousand well-armed Marines and that there were many more attractive targets for the enemy, such as the nearby airbase. Regardless, we agreed that we should arm ourselves as appropriately as possible.

As I mentioned, we did not have personal weapons except for my .357 Magnum. It was now emblazoned with a fluorescent pink gun sight, carried in a soft leather shoulder holster complete with a bandolier of twelve rounds of extra ammunition.

With our boats in port, we felt that this trip definitely justified the removal and utilization of appropriate weapons and munitions from on board the boats. For good measure, on a mission of this importance, we felt we should invite our frogman neighbors, especially considering that they had a remarkable inventory of unique foreign weapons that could only add to the glamour of our expedition.

From the boats, we were able to bring what would best be described as a cornucopia of military hardware. I had matching shotguns with a bandolier of shells across my chest, resembling an outlaw from some Pancho Villa movie. Eldon Thompson chose a form-fitting vest of grenades with matching survival knives. Jay Fleming had two shoulder holsters with .38 pistols and a matching hip-mounted M-79 grenade launcher. The result was a kind of an overdone "Gunfight at the OK Corral" look.

Without question, the ultimate statement belonged to Larry Myers and Doug Smith who were carrying, draped over their shoulders, a linked belt of 1000 rounds of .50 caliber machine-gun ammunition. This was at least six feet in length and probably weighed over sixty pounds. We decided to leave the actual .50 caliber machine gun behind on the boat because the ammunition was heavy enough and most likely we couldn't locate the correct wrench to remove it.

We climbed into the open back of the duty truck with all our gear for the four-mile ride to the O'Club. Joining us were our frog friends, a group that was always game for some action, complete with their "armory of weapons." Along the way, our enthusiasm for the cleverness of this brilliant adventure only increased.

Upon arrival, we entered the foyer of the Club. Off to the right, outside of a coat closet for rain gear and covers (hats), there was a sign that specified: "All weapons must be removed and hung on the hooks provided." The visual effect was not unlike some Olde West saloon. While we fully intended to comply with these regulations, the bulk of our assorted armament was not really hook compatible. Calling on our military leadership skills, in short order, all of us made a command decision. That was to pile everything in an unobtrusive corner of the lobby in what would best be described as a large heap. This included knives, pistols, grenades, shotguns, the frogman weapons, with the "piece de resistance" being the 1,000 rounds of belted .50 caliber ammunition draped casually over the top of the pile.

Then in an orderly fashion, we proceeded onward into the bar area. During the first round of drinks we were happily joined by a solo Marine Corps major. He informed us that he had just returned from three weeks in the field and judging by the mud and dust on his boots and utilities, there was little doubt about the veracity of his story.

Swift Boats and the Marines, especially their smaller independent units, had worked effectively together since our arrival. The "grunts" never seemed to have enough firepower in the right place at the right time. Swift Boats were mobile and provided a platform for gunfire support, and, if necessary, we were available for extraction. Both these factors formed the foundation for one of those unique battlefield relationships.

From an alcoholic consumption standpoint, the major had a head start on us but soon we were close behind, all the while exchanging stories of mutual admiration. "Semper Fi."

Much to our surprise and ultimate chagrin, who should appear, this time resplendent in his tropical white uniform, but one Commander Ball Cap Smithson. From the Navy blue brassard on his arm, which read in gold block letters CDO, it was obvious he was indeed the Command Duty Officer. Loosely translated that meant that, at the moment, he ran downtown Da Nang. His remarks began as expected with some disparaging remarks about the basic intellectual caliber of Swift Boat drivers and advanced to how we were a threat to national security and other relevant American ideals. Somewhere, I had heard all this before.

At the time, because our blue ball caps were nowhere in sight, we assumed his comments could only be based on his prior observation of the stockpile of weaponry that he had just passed in the outer lobby. Even considering his hurtful and very personal accusations, it soon became obvious that Ball Cap felt quite strongly that we had overreacted to the perceived threat to our personal security presented by the current Tet Offensive.

Our Marine Corps major immediately came to defend the honor of Swift Boats and any other issue that occurred to him, albeit in a somewhat halting prose. Regretfully, at that time, on either side of Ball Cap were two rather large official-looking armed guards.

There were some additional remarks made by Ball Cap, most likely in jest, about putting us on report, or words to that effect. Although somewhat put off by these remarks, we were convinced that once again our friend Ball Cap had simply failed to see the subtle humor in our activities. The decision was made by our team that we would protest no more but leave the O'Club peacefully under his escorts and "Take your Marine Corps friend with you."

As best we could, while we removed our assorted weaponry, we were able to generate a maximum amount of noise and confusion to the delight of all the other officers present at the Club. We were then escorted, again under guard, out the door to our waiting truck. Climbing into the truck, Eldon, ever the Social Director, started ranting about my Ivy League sensitivity being offended by this turn of events but, fortunately, he quickly abandoned that tactic.

Outside, Ball Cap, with a pointed finger and an arm extended somewhat menacingly in our direction informed us, "The Club is off limits to you thugs for thirty days."

However, once again, in the good spirit of the evening, we simply attributed these comments to combat stress and Ball Cap's somewhat awkward attempt to participate in the festivities.

The ride back to the base was a joyous one, full of shouts of comradeship, at least that's how it was described the next morning. Major Robert Henderson, United States Marine Corps (according to the name on his uniform patch), spent the evening with us and shared a final nightcap on board. His somewhat slurred descriptions of the APL 5 as a "fine naval vessel" were testimony to his current state of mind. Regardless, he was our comrade-in-arms and that was all that mattered.

In the morning, over very black coffee, analyzing and reflecting upon the prior evening's events, we were all able to agree on three significant factors. To the best of our knowledge, we had not shot ourselves or accidentally pulled the pin on a grenade, and that was an outstanding testimony to the safety designs of all U.S. weapons manufacturers.

Ed Bergin (Mortimer Sierra) was at the time only thirty miles to the south, at our Chu Lai base so he would receive this story of our highly successful adventure within a day. Bob Mack, on the other hand, was about 500-plus miles away at An Thoi and he might not be aware of this historical event for some time to come. So, we took pictures outside the Apple as we loaded our gear prior to the mission. Film developing took about ten days, sending it to the States and back, but it was well worth it when I sent the pictures off to Bob.

This image of our crack fighting forces armed and prepared for any contingency during a dangerous night on the town was indeed a memorable moment in military history.

CHAPTER 10

# THE HOSPITAL SHIP
# USS *REPOSE*

The transit to the Alpha patrol area, which was our northernmost responsibility and included the DMZ (demilitarized zone), was always a tedious one. It was ninety miles north of Da Nang, taking over three hours travel time each way, and that's when the weather was decent. This time the mission had been longer than usual because we had been up all night firing illumination rounds interspersed with high explosives.

The target was the real estate between the rivers Ben Hai to the north and Cua Viet to the south. All of this was a no-man's-land designated as the DMZ. What this meant was that anybody who moved through that area was fair game to be shot at by the other side. Our goal that night was to discourage enemy troops, suspected of operating in the area, from being able to fire mobile rockets at the Marine base located at the southern river mouth. The official term for this was harassment and interdiction fire (H&I). Basically, you move, you lose.

On the northern side of the DMZ, located just above the Ben Hai River, were rocky cliffs with caves that contained North Vietnamese artillery. These guns would, on occasion, lob a friendly round or two into the U.S. Marine base at Cua Viet, just to keep everyone honest. These same radar-controlled weapons could also detect a Swift Boat that wandered too close to the shoreline and proceed to take it under fire.

To add to the nighttime enjoyment, during a patrol this far north you wanted to keep a sharp radar lookout for any small vessel that might be the enemy sneaking south hugging close to the coast, hoping to avoid detection.

Between our gunfire mission and these other considerations, the crew had been up most of the night with each of us unable to grab more than an hour of sleep on the off watch.

However, the coffee was hot, fresh and as usual Navy outstanding. With a boatswain's mate as your senior petty officer, you were assured of a squared-away boat with good hot coffee at the top of the list. Fortunately on this patrol, the seas had remained calm and after rendezvousing with our relief boat, we were able to maintain 28 kts the entire trip back to base.

As we approached the turn for the wide harbor mouth to Da Nang, off our starboard bow I could see the hospital ship USS *Repose* was anchored inside. With her white hull she looked somewhat like a cruise ship until you saw the large red crosses painted on her sides. The doctors and nurses on the *Repose,* along with her sister ship the USS *Sanctuary*, did great work and it never hurt to have friends in the stitch and patch department.

As a result, an unwritten Swift policy was to always swing by the hospital ship and pick up anyone waiting to go ashore. I mentioned this to Boats and without further direction he commenced his now standard "premier Swift Boat approach." In this case, it encompassed a full-speed approach followed by a tight half-circle around the ship's stern with a hard stop at the small barge tied up alongside the *Repose.* The barge was basically a floating heavy wooden platform secured alongside the ship when she was at anchor. A ladder from topside descended down to the barge often called a camel, allowing for easier and safer offloading of personnel and supplies. However, when the ship was under way wounded personnel were almost always brought on board by helicopter.

Boats made his usual first-class landing, coming tightly alongside with a minimum of helm turns. This ended with a last-minute back down with both engines growling in reverse while their big propellers generated the appropriate display of white water at the stern. By now, he had turned this approach into a thing of beauty.

*USS* Repose *anchored in Da Nang harbor.*

*Boats' high-speed approach, note the sampan.*

PCF 76 was already squared away and ready to enter port, which at this point in the patrol meant her weapons were stowed and the crew was at least fully dressed. As far as appearances went the thirty-six-hour patrol hardly left us prepared for any white-glove inspection. I was the second oldest on board and, along with Boats I definitely needed a shave, and the entire crew needed a fresh water wash down. Tropical weather, humidity and salt spray took its toll on personal hygiene, but with a slight breeze blowing we were acceptable.

As we tied up, the *Repose*'s topside speakers announced: "Transportation is currently alongside and available for anyone going ashore."

While we waited for any passengers, I leaned against the back of the aft cabin with my brain pretty much in neutral, listening to the roll and rumble of our idling "Jimmie" diesel engines. Refocusing, I went below to get myself a second cup of coffee and thought about my upcoming shower, clean clothes and some time in "horizontal plot" (the Naval term for the rack). It is amazing in combat situations how much awake time is actually spent thinking about sleep time.

Out of the corner of my eye I saw three Navy nurses, two LTJGs and what appeared to be a more salty LCDR at the top of the ladder, just starting their descent,. I gave the subtle nod to Boats who sprang to life, always the ready showman, complete with the appropriate tattoos for full naval effect. He then helped each of them on board accompanied by a snappy salute that reflected well on his previous Navy experience, which had been on more formal cruisers and destroyers.

The younger two returned his salute looking like they probably had executed this procedure less than ten times in their short naval careers. This, however, was not the case with the more senior member of the team. I had moved toward the bow of the boat but was carefully observing Boats' intricate execution of this maneuver. With coffee mug in hand, I walked aft, saluted the lieutenant commander, welcomed her aboard and offered her a cup of black coffee. Boats served nothing else.

Giving them a quick look, the junior twosome appeared to be sufficiently impressed just being on a Swift Boat, or at least that was my humble opinion.

The senior member of the squad introduced herself as Kate Hancock, although her name tag said Katherine. Being from Boston, I made mental note of the historical significance of her last name. John Hancock was the famous rolling and eye-catching signatory, top center on the Declaration of Independence.

She politely refused any coffee but thanked me for the offer. She was tall, thin, and quite attractive, probably in her late twenties and without question had her act together. Boats yelled to Muller and Buck to take in the lines while Snipe had the helm in the pilothouse. She quickly sized up that her two younger charges were reasonably safe with Boats, who had commenced his usual tour. Most versions usually included some time spent driving at the forward helm during the trip to shore. As skipper, I completely approved of this educational theme. After all, we worked for the same Navy and understood the importance of creative cross-training.

I was always respectful of rank, but it did not overwhelm me because in the last analysis this was my Boat and as the book said, for better or for worse I was the "Officer-in-Charge." As we moved away from the ship, Hancock changed her mind on the coffee. She casually mentioned that she had just worked the four-to-eight watch, but had eight hours of down time before the ship got under way and returned to the line. I knew this was a heavy time for Marine operations and the *Repose* was the first line of medical support while it steamed back and forth at sea several miles off the combat zone. Theirs was a serious business; they were not fixing hangnails and treating cases of the clap.

The two of us stood on top of the aft engine covers leaning against the main cabin top and did those two-minute mini resumes you do at times like this. She was from the D.C. area, had lost her husband while working at John Hopkins and joined the Navy about three years ago. Because she was an emergency room professional, she had moved up fast and was the leader of a team of eight on board *Repose*. I suspected she wasn't really buying my act, but then again I wasn't really selling it. Rather, I was just maintaining the required persona of a Swift Boat skipper being appropriately cool.

In reality, what they really wanted from us was a lift down the river to the Officers' Club (which we could provide), a couple of drinks and lunch, followed by a short walk around downtown Da Nang. "Short" was the operative word for two reasons: The first being the area was not large and somewhat battle scarred and the second was that the back streets, despite the Marines' control of the city, could be dangerous. During the day, it was relatively safe if you didn't wander, but recently there had been several attacks at the nearby airbase and an enemy rocket attack or an explosive satchel charge could bring an abrupt end to your shore leave.

However, I'm not sure this threesome really wanted to hear my risk assessment. For them anything was a change of pace from white paint, antiseptics, wounded and sometimes dying Marines.

Even though our crew was tired and the nurses were officers and therefore off-limits, they were female, clean, young and all three were easy on the eyes. Refueling and rearming PCF 76 at the base could wait. Also a brief diversion downriver to the Navy O'Club at the Stone Elephant was not an unpleasant side trip. Hancock did her wash-khaki uniform ample justice and had a set of hazel and blue eyes that simply said, "Been there done that." As we picked up speed, she remained the mother hen and watched her two charges out of the corner of her eye. Perhaps out of politeness, she asked for the quick five-minute tour and in response I explained that it could actually take up to ten.

Snipe was still on the forward helm and the other three were below cleaning weapons and stowing gear. Meanwhile, Boats had guided the two junior nurses aft where they both lit cigarettes and sat down for a comfortable cruise across the harbor and down the Da Nang River. Boats was a salty twenty-nine-year-old sailor with all that implied, in contrast to the two younger nurses who were brand new to the Navy and had not yet seen twenty-two.

I could see the next scene playing out as I moved forward with LCDR Hancock. "You can't sit there while you smoke," Boats counseled.

The next few lines in the script were predictable. "Oh, we just want to have a cigarette, enjoy the ride and see the view from your boat."

Boats didn't disappoint me with his standard response which was artfully delivered.

"Oh we certainly want you to enjoy the ride but it might be cut real short because you're sitting on the ammunition locker and it's filled with high explosives."

From a safety standpoint he was correct. Regardless, it still made for great theater as they leaped up and looked at the locker as if it was a time bomb with five seconds left on the clock.

Hancock had seen this vignette play out, turned to me and casually asked, "Dangerous?" "No, not really," was my response. She just rolled those big eyes and gave me a knowing Navy smile that said, "It never changes."

Fifteen minutes later, we slowly approached the O'Club pier to drop off our three VIP guests and Boats made his perfect ten-point landing. This was usually conducted with a little more flourish whenever there was an audience nearby. The rest of the crew smartly handled the lines and secured PCF 76 alongside. With Boats there were no excuses for not landing in a top-notch fashion. On the pier, Buck stood by the bow line and Muller manned the stern line, waiting for any fine-tuning instructions from Boats.

I asked LCDR Hancock how they were getting back to the ship and she said a launch from the *Repose* would come by the O'Club pier to pick anyone up at 1500 hours. For some reason, I said that we might be able to return and could give them the full harbor tour, if they were interested. Making a weak attempt at covering my too rapid response, I referenced her earlier comment that they didn't have to be back on board until 1700. To my pleasant surprise, she tentatively accepted my invitation but politely said they would take the *Repose* launch at 1500, unless I showed up beforehand.

Just as they were about to step off PCF 76, down the gangway came Rear Admiral Russell Planitzer, Commander of the Naval Support Activity. We didn't work directly for him (we worked under his Marine general counterpart on the other side of the river), but he was still a two-star admiral. "He had the stars and we had the bars" and that said it all. I had heard Planitzer was a tough nut, but fair. More relevant was the story that he had somehow been involved with Swift Boats early in his career and thus we all felt he was a definite comer. Boats, ever the hawk eye, called, "Attention on Deck!"

We all snapped to, although the junior nurses were a little slow off the mark facing in the wrong direction.

Planitzer gave me the once over as I stood there with thirty-six hours of beard and a shirt that looked like I had slept in it, well, because I had.

"Tough patrol, Lieutenant?'

"No sir, just a long one, DMZ and back," was my response.

"Keep up the good work." Then he turned to Hancock and said, "Commander you're in bad company, but I presume you know that?"

She gave him a million-dollar smile and said, "Just hitching a ride, Admiral."

He laughed and as he walked by Boats, who was standing at the aft helm, Planitzer stopped, turned and said, "Bos'n, you take care of this crew. That's an order."

"Aye, Aye, Sir" was Boat's response with a sharp salute that was returned in kind. All this transpired in under two minutes, real life, no bullshit allowed.

Having delivered our cargo, now my mission was a more complex one—return to the Apple where we lived and recruit a couple of our more adventuresome boat captains. I preferred someone who had a sense of style with some decent moves who could reinforce the positive first impression that I assumed we had just made.

Our crew was happy to facilitate this adventure, so they serviced, washed and rearmed the boat, tied it alongside the Apple and then headed off to get themselves a decent meal and a cold beer. Meanwhile, I took a quick shower and returned to complete the mission.

Swift Boats, in general, were a casual organization certainly not one top-heavy with bureaucracy and command. If your boat was not being used by another crew, within reason, we could do what we wanted with it from a time and usage standpoint. This attitude became more prevalent the longer time you spent in-country, especially if you were not planning on a long-term naval career. The bottom line was do your job, do it well, take care of your men and nobody gave you a hard time. If they did, unless they were an Admiral or in your direct chain of command you simply said, "Yes, Sir," gave them a quick salute and that fuck-you smile that came with driving Swift Boats.

I recruited two experienced boat captains: Eldon Thompson (Mary Poppins) and Jay Fleming (Malibu Foxtrot). Both of them had become good friends over the last several months. Of course with Eldon, it started with our airport pick up and greeting when we first arrived at the Da Nang Airbase. They were a couple of unattached studs who felt their "wow them" sales pitch from their last R&R was getting a little rusty. Listening to my social dilemma, they volunteered to come along as tour guides. My ongoing exposure to Eldon as the self-appointed Chairman of the Social Committee gave me great confidence in his ability to carry out this upcoming role. Jay, on the other hand, was a Californian surfer with a high-risk profile willing to take on any new challenge.

The two of them set out to locate a bottle of good champagne, while I grabbed an hour or two of rack time. At 1430, the three of us, clean-shaven, starched, and all wearing our personalized blue baseball caps, boarded PCF 76 and headed down the river toward the O'Club.

Off our starboard side, we steamed past a row of small fishing huts, and some occupied one-story stucco commercial buildings left over from the French Colonial era. This section of the river shoreline was quite active and considered safe from possible enemy fire. It was unlikely that any NVA (North Vietnamese Army) troops would waste a rocket on a suicide mission for targets like this that were surrounded by thousands of Marines.

Below the Da Nang Bridge was a very different story. This was no-man's-land pockmarked with marshes, tall reeds, and tricky estuaries where the enemy could easily hide with a rocket or machine gun, but that was not our destination.

We three musketeers, especially the two new members, were up for some time center stage. I gave them a quick brief on the two younger nurses who, I felt, would buy their act, especially if the duration of our mission was only two hours. Hancock was a different story. She definitely had more time in the chow line, but I was still looking forward to some female company and continuing our earlier conversation.

I brought PCF 76 alongside the Stone Elephant pier, I thought, in a most respectable fashion. Jay and Eldon, as expected, smartly tied off the lines while several bystanders looked on, most likely in awe of how "with it" Swift Boat guys really were.

We were, indeed, legends in our own minds. Who really cared, especially when we looked up and saw those three nurses strutting down the pier, full of smiles from a little well-deserved shore leave. They were helped on board by Eldon and Jay who introduced themselves and quickly took in the lines.

As we departed the pier, there was a slightly larger audience viewing our guests, which put me under some performance pressure. I twisted the boat smartly away from the dock, backing out into the river and then with a quick port engine ahead and starboard astern we pivoted into the channel. As usual, I was driving at the aft helm where I felt most comfortable when maneuvering in tight quarters. In my opinion, the sight lines in the Swift Boat pilothouse were so limited they presented an accident waiting to happen, unless you were going straight ahead.

I was hoping Eldon and Jay would start with some small talk because immediately popping the champagne would not play well as we moved away from the pier where the Admiral's barge (his personal boat) was tied up. However, my concerns were unjustified, the two charmers rose

*Leaving the O'Club heading east on the river.*

to the occasion, standing nearby on the fantail jawboning and delivering who knows what lines of trash.

Hancock stayed aft with me, standing on the starboard engine hatch, and thanked us for returning to pick them up. She looked over at me as I spun the big wheel with my right hand and with my left adjusted both of the nearby throttles to the forward position. With a knowing smile and a friendly aside she said, "You really love to drive this thing, don't you?"

Perhaps my "Yes, I do" response was a bit too revealing.

As we cleared the river mouth out came the champagne with a pop of the cork and was served all around in coffee mugs. I explained that our crystal champagne flutes were still on order but we felt this combat camouflage made good sense.

The harbor made for an interesting tour and could be described as "commercial scenic." We started on the southeast side, with the massive deepwater piers where the huge cargo ships from around the world tied up unloading day and night. Their cargo could include anything from bulldozers to explosives, electronics and clothing to pretzels and beer.

Next along the shoreline was the Vietnamese Navy junk base and just beyond that the "Nasty PTF" base which was some kind of Top Secret CIA operations headquarters. Supposedly, these boats infiltrated South Vietnamese frogmen into North Vietnam. I always suspected that they simply charged north, shot up the enemy shoreline at night and returned to Da Nang for breakfast. Over time, you cynically learned that inserting "secret" into any story, let alone "top secret," always made for a taller tale.

About two miles across, on the other side of the harbor, was the mammoth Da Nang Air Force Base. This facility started several miles inland and extended to the water ending literally at the harbor's sandy beaches. There you could see firsthand the ongoing conflict that most of us could never completely resolve—the picture of bomb-laden fighter-bombers streaking down the runway taking off over peaceful white sandy beaches and rolling surf.

The beaches then merged into the curving tropical coastline which made up the northern rim of the harbor. Although this area was beautiful, it was not secure so we kept offshore well out of range of any small arms or rockets. However, from that distance our panoramic view was like a picture postcard, as it was a cloudless day with brilliant blue skies and bright sunshine, unusual for the monsoon season.

The standard script called for each of the younger nurses to once again have a longer turn at the wheel, which was well received. Despite the laughter and champagne we were careful to continue our tour far enough offshore to be safe. Jay or Eldon, who I completely trusted as boat skippers, were with the nurses at the helm in the pilothouse. I sat aft with LCDR Hancock on the big ammo box with its white top and PCF 76 painted in large black letters. This was to specifically identify us and facilitate communications with any aircraft.

Neither of us smoked, so I wasn't required to give her my safety lecture. She obviously got a kick out of our Swift Boat pageant and eventually asked me,

"How many times before have you done this?"

I responded that we had done the pickup and delivery routine numerous times, but the longer harbor tour and champagne component was brand new. She smiled and laughed at my comment in one of those knowing but honest ways that you can't help but remember.

Underway time for the *Repose* was fast approaching so we had to end the harbor tour and head for their ship. I saw that Eldon and Jay were fast compiling information for their respective black books. Between the two of them, along with the nurses, they had polished off not just one but the second, magically appearing bottle of champagne. Our senior-ranking guest and I each were nursing a half-full mug. With safety a consideration, I assumed command of PCF 76 and announced that our traditional high-speed approach to the *Repose* would be conducted with me at the helm, so hold on.

Driving from the aft station, I pulled the lever that engaged the big wheel, pushed the throttles forward and the twin diesels started to wind up with their throaty rumble. The boat quickly accelerated and climbed up on her plane generating that rolling bow wave that rapidly flowed aft leaving behind a crisp, white wake. At full speed, I had to admit PCF 76 looked pretty impressive and definitely businesslike with all the

*Top-secret "Nasty PTFs" heading to North Vietnam.*

guns uncovered and our big American flag snapping smartly from the masthead.

LCDR Hancock remained standing opposite me on the other engine hatch. She had a firm two-handed grip on the rear end of the life raft, her hair was blowing in the wind with a real down to earth "this-ain't-bad" smile on her face. In between glances ahead, I looked quickly across at her and I thought to myself, she was probably five years my senior and most likely this was going nowhere, however.... Sometimes in life you briefly meet someone, man or woman, and they make a significant impression on you, but it goes no further though you always remember them. I refer to these as "those special people moments." Upon reflection, I suspect they take place more often in wartime with its sense of urgency and compressed timeframe.

Between concentrating on my driving, along with an occasional quick glance at Hancock, I was still concerned that Eldon and Jay were attempting to set their own new speed record and possibly turn PCF 76 into the Love Boat.

My fears were in fact unfounded and time was on my side. Alongside the *Repose* was a small supply ship that had just finished unloading and was starting to pull away. As a result, some of the ship's crew was still topside along with several of the hospital staff. All of them were looking down from the rail, which mandated we approach on our best behavior.

By this time Jay and Eldon had undoubtedly acquired more than enough tracking data, the girls had had a great afternoon with first-class champagne and, hopefully, a memorable ride on a Navy combat patrol boat. Lastly, they were returning to the *Repose* with a decent-size audience in attendance. After we tied up alongside the camel, my fellow Swift Boat skippers once more rose to execute the closing scene. Posing as officers and gentlemen, they assisted the two younger nurses onto the barge as if they were porcelain dolls, albeit slightly unsteady from the champagne.

Hancock was the last to leave the boat and I helped her step up from our aft deck onto the barge. Perhaps, it was my imagination, but I thought she held my hand a bit longer than the physics of the situation required. She then bent down as if she was going to pick up something off the deck of the barge. She looked me right at me and whispered a simple,

"Thanks, my friend, and I truly pray that you or any of your crew will never have need of our ship."

She then stood up, we locked on, eye to eye with an intensity I can still recall. Then I saluted, not in a way that said Junior to Senior, but rather goodbye to a new but respected friend. This time, with All Hands waving on both vessels, PCF 76 pulled away from the *Repose* at a most uncharacteristic slow speed. It seemed the right thing to do.

# Section III
# Relocating South to Chu Lai

## CHAPTER 11

# CHU LAI, THE BASE, COS. DIV. 16

In the late spring, they asked for volunteers to move south and man our smaller sub-base in Chu Lai, soon to be named Coastal Division 16. My heretofore partner in crime, Ed Bergin, along with his crew, were first in line. The next day, with their boat PCF 79 armed and fueled, they departed, leaving me behind to hold court with curmudgeons such as Eldon Thompson, Jay Fleming and Larry Meyer at our larger base in Da Nang, Coastal Division 12. However, in a month or two we would also rotate south to rejoin Ed.

Chu Lai had recently been established as a smaller Swift base and was located about forty miles south of Da Nang. It was set up with the goal of giving better patrol coverage to that area with reduced travel time to station. In the summer of 1967, Chu Lai and especially the real estate to the south had become a hot bed of active VC operations. It was suspected that the enemy in that area was being heavily supported with weapons from the North and possibly regular NVA troops as well. Much of the material and men were transported via the Ho Chi Minh Trail located inland to the northeast, extending through Laos. Possible infiltration from the sea by enemy cargo ships had become a significant concern.

The Chu Lai Swift Boat base itself was situated within a small harbor about half a mile inland, a short transit to open water. This location provided more than enough shelter from the frequent Pacific storms, especially those that raged during the rugged winter months. The harbor opening was wide enough and the channel deep enough that it usually presented no access problems in clear weather. However, shifting sandbars always presented a challenge. As testimony to that, on the left side of the channel as you approached from seaward, there was the rusting hulk of a tugboat that obviously had made a serious wrong turn. As a result, it was now enshrined permanently high and dry on the sandbar, clear testimony to the need to stay alert while transiting these river mouths.

Inside the harbor on the south side there was one floating dock that allowed for the birthing "stern to" of the Swifts. About 100 yards further along the sandy shoreline was an off-loading ramp for the omnipresent Navy LSTs. These were the Navy's workhorses with their two large clam-like bow doors and interior ramp that could deliver anything to the nearby Marines. Their cargo could include anything from pallets of beer, ammunition and bombs to a tank or bulldozer. The strategic purpose of this smaller Navy base was to provide logistical support to the large Marine airfield nearby and it operated under the banner of Naval Support Activity headquartered in Da Nang (NSAD). In turn, the primary mission of the airfield was to provide fighter/bomber aircraft for close-in air support for Marine combat operations. In addition, the base housed a significant number of helos for troop transport and gunfire support.

Without question this was "grunt" country and Swifts were just a small tenant. This arrangement was fine with the Swifts because our size and manpower did not allow us to provide any base security. As a result, the presence of Swift Boats was simply a small add-on to the Chu Lai base with about eight boats and twelve crews. Actually, we got along better with the Marines with whom we operated than we did with some members of the Naval Support Group.

A negative first impression was not all that difficult to establish, but to fully enhance and solidify our reputation did take some time and creative thought. With that goal in mind, Coastal Division 16 was formed as another Patrol Craft Fast (PCF) Division. The legal legitimacy of this self-established entity was certainly in question but in wartime, there were greater concerns than these, even for the most diligent of paper pushers. About this time, some wayward scholar in Swifts, most likely an aspiring attorney, concluded that Swifts operationally reported to the Marines because they controlled all of "I Corps," the northern part of South Vietnam.

Whether the Marines realized this fact or even cared about it was not really relevant to us. However, what it did do, in our opinion, was to grant Swift Boats a declaration of independence from a good part of the Navy bureaucracy and its command structure. We only had to report to the Navy hierarchy from an administrative standpoint that included primarily personnel matters rather than all operational matters. For us, this was a very big deal and made life significantly more simple and enjoyable, especially for the Ed Bergins of the world.

The result was a group of crews and boat captains who were LTJGs with a smattering of LTs reporting to a senior LT as Division 16 Commander. Often, this individual had previously been a boat driver but in most cases remained a team player. His job was to keep the trains running but if he was smart he didn't try to run the place as if he was Commander of the Pacific Fleet. Most individuals who held the Swift Division Commander position saw it is as good independent duty, charged with overseeing some competent and independent officers albeit some with big egos. Most importantly, we were a group who could be counted on to maintain a well-stocked liquor cabinet and provide a good poker game.

With this independent structure in mind, several of the boat drivers, most likely led by Ed, decided that their new group needed some product branding along with physical identification. Therefore, they designed a Division logo that would eventually appear on all the boats operating out of the Chu Lai base. As is often the case, alcohol formed the basis for these bursts of creativity. After much discussion and extensive research, they settled on a motto of "No Quarter" with the yellow flag of South Vietnam as its background and the flag's three red stripes signifying "tested under fire." A black spade playing card was adorned with a human skull. This symbolized bad luck to the Viet Cong and thus completed the Division plaque. With this momentous decision made, all of the troops were anxious to get the Division insignia painted on their pilothouse doors, much like the nose art of war planes during WWII.

Ed Bergin, being a natural leader and a definite showman, was quick to paint the new insignia on the doors of PCF 79 and for good measure added three-foot-long eyes to the bow of his boat. All the Vietnamese Navy junks that patrolled along the coast were equipped with these "eyes" so they could see safely through fog and inclement weather, especially during the monsoons. Ed concluded that his boat absolutely needed this non-electronic, all-weather capability. The Vietnamese fisherman they stopped and searched always got a kick out of their "nose art." This type of boat customization was unauthorized by existing Navy regulations, but if that proved to be a problem, grey paint was near at hand. All in all, it enhanced the *esprit de corps* of Swift Boats.

Occasionally, a senior officer passing through Chu Lai on some vague mission would visit the Swift base and find this type of artistic display "not in the finest tradition of the United States Navy." Depending on where that individual stood in our chain of command, the offending

*Ed's place at Chu Lai.*

non-regulation item might disappear for a day only to reappear again shortly after the visitor's departure.

This temporary response could apply to decorative art in the bar room, the Vietnamese eyes on the bow of Ed's boat, or his utilization of unauthorized weapons. My boat PCF 76, when we operated out of Chu Lai, carried a twelve-foot mini-sampan on our fantail made of woven bamboo bark. On a patrol, we had found it drifting at sea upside down with the bottom definitely in need of repair. We negotiated a repair contract with a local fisherman, compensating him with several steaks, and the vessel was returned to an acceptable state of watertight integrity. The craft was utilized for "nighttime, close-in and clandestine coastal surveillance" (aka beach visits).

Our sampan was always a prime acquisition target for any visiting souvenir-hunting paper-pushing senior officer who cast his eyes upon it. However, during my time in-country, I knew of no successful trophy grabs by transiting higher ups. Most likely, this was the result of our fine-tuned instant removal program. Correspondingly, there were many senior officers who thought our creative ideas were terrific, great morale and team builders. Obviously, we voted with this latter group.

Ed's boat, PCF 79, was painted almost black (darker than any of the other Swift boats) and maintained that way by his boatswain mate, Bobby Don Carver. On a monthly basis, Carver would wash the boat completely down with diesel fuel. As a result, she was more difficult to see on a dark night and Ed wanted to keep her just that way. I often wondered if that darker color, based on the diesel fuel rubdown, would cause the boat to have a higher ignition signature, especially if it was ever hit with tracers and incendiary shells. Fortunately, it never ignited and in fact, the fuel may have evaporated soon after it dried and the paint darkened, or so they hoped.

Bos'n Mate Bobby Don Carver was one of the more senior enlisted in Swifts (he was a first-class petty officer). He was about 6' 3" and 220 pounds with a British Navy handlebar mustache and the sailor's swagger to match. Whenever they were together, he was a mentor to my bos'n mate Bill Fielder (Boats), who was several years younger and

*Boats and Buck doing a little people-to-people.*

a second–class petty officer but with every bit as much style, especially if tattoos were factored in.

Some of the more seasoned and salty sailors assigned to Swift Boats, especially the deck types, i.e. bos'n mates, knew little tricks of the trade that you just didn't learn in school ... any school. Most possessed an uncanny ability to acquire things ... almost anything. They frequently avoided the official Naval supply system by utilizing a time-honored Navy procurement procedure called "cumshaw." This technique would be best described as very effective bartering, accompanied by a touch of thievery. It could be implemented anywhere regardless of geographic location and, for some sailors, it had evolved into the ultimate job skill. Both Carver and Fielder had achieved that elite status. Many of the more successful Swift Boats crews had a senior bos'n mate on board.

Enemy activity both underway and onshore near the base had continued almost nonstop since Ed and PCF 79 moved from Da Nang to Chu Lai in the spring. Firefights on patrol were almost a daily occurrence.

The small base was mortared and rocketed on several occasions and the boats while in port were shot at from the small island across the river. Somehow this particular location continued to remain an active VC hideout despite the heavy U.S. military presence nearby. On one occasion, even the old washing machine located on the dock was hit by shrapnel. In an appropriate recognition of its service, it received a Purple Heart painted proudly on the side of the tub.

After my arrival in Chu Lai, I found out why Ed had originally joined several other skippers, all of whom had eagerly volunteered to move to Chu Lai. Their rapid departure from Da Nang had taken place after they had been involved in a social altercation with some pilots from the Air Force "Gunfighters" at their own officers' club. Their behavior as guests of the Air Force Club was considered poor social form and most likely it was. So to prevent any chance of a repeat performance, at the first opportunity Ed and the gang simply left town.

As it turned out, Chu Lai was much more to their liking, no more hard covers (hats) along with khaki uniforms and the other traditional accoutrements of a naval officer. Desert boots, khaki shorts, a green t-shirt, and a blue baseball cap with your rank embroidered on it, completed the Coastal 16's uniform of the day.

Prior to my move to Chu Lai, Ed and I did meet face to face in overlapping patrol areas. In a weak moment, he confessed that he did on occasion miss the air-conditioning of APL-5 (the Apple) along with the well-prepared meals served on china with cloth napkins and real silver. However, Ed was quick to point out that freedom from many of the more burdensome Navy regulations (I believe "bullshit" was the term he actually used) made the sacrifices at Chu Lai all worthwhile. By now, he was well aware of the Ball Cap Smithson incidents which I am sure he regretted not being part of. I had no doubt that Eldon Thompson had filled him in on all of the details with appropriate enhancements.

It would be incorrect to assume that any of us were outright rebels, because we were not. Everyone in the program that I knew, both officers and enlisted, were volunteers, which gave us a slightly different attitude regarding military protocol. The entire Swift operation was a new activity for the Navy. It entailed independent combat operations conducted on small boats, commanded by junior officers. From this standpoint, Swift Boat duty was not dissimilar to the PT Boats of World War II. As a result, it attracted and encouraged individuals who were not "by the book"-type leaders. Interestingly enough, over time the Swift program generated a disproportional number of flag officers (admirals). Our enlisted crews were of similar high caliber, courageous, hard-working, and dedicated.

Onshore in Chu Lai, everyone lived in hooches, which were small wooden buildings built on a cement slab with screened-in sides. Louvers were installed to keep out the rain and the structure was topped with an overhanging metal roof that had rows of sandbags placed on top. The actual purpose of the sandbags remained a mystery to most of us. Whether they held the roof down in high winds or served the same function in the event of an artillery attack, either way, it gave home a touch of the dramatic.

Ed's hooch was set up when I arrived and like most it was divided into a bunkroom sleeping area with a head and shower, while the front half

*Topping off at the fuel pier.*

was turned into a social lounge. Ed and his roommates, one of whom was Killer Lou Masterson, had given it what they felt was the tasteful look of an English pub with stained dark wood. As I recall, mahogany may have been the only tone available and most likely someone's mother had sent the stain. Regardless, it provided a perfect contrast with the whitewash trim.

The mandatory octagonal card table was covered with an off-green army blanket; real felt for the top was not available although they certainly tried. The overhead light was a large green industrial electric light fixture cumshawed from an army utility pole which provided just the right masculine touch. All the latest *Playboy* centerfolds competed for wall space, alongside two Viet Cong battle flags and captured weapons. Understandably, the bar was the social focus of their decorating effort and was constantly in use. The crews played volleyball in the sand just outside the front door and there was more than adequate real estate for a vigorous touch football game. The latter was both demanding and exhausting due to the fine sand which made any sprint to the goal line a significant challenge.

On occasion, although he was not involved in Swift Boats, Roger Staubach would play with us. He had recently been a star quarterback at the U.S. Naval Academy and went on to attain equal fame with the Dallas Cowboys. Roger was friendly even then, but did not recognize the nuances of touch football and usually required two hands or a take-down tackle. Much to my regret, on two occasions I was somehow able to catch his passes and remember to this day the significant pain those receptions inflicted on me.

One of the more relevant Chu Lai stories was when Ed had just returned from patrol and was told by the Division 16 Commander, call sign "Senator Claghorn," to prepare the lounge for a visitor. Following orders, the beer cans and cigar butts were thrown out and the girlie magazines were placed temporarily in a neat stack on the deck. The brass magazine rack had yet to arrive. The cards and chips were secured behind the bar, the booze bottles were strategically arranged to demonstrate not only our good taste but as a testimony to our ample logistical and acquisition skills. About half the officers and crews were in port so we completed a reasonable effort to clean up our act and awaited the arrival of the visiting brass.

It turned out the guest was our new overall Swift Boat boss. The commodore, although he was officially by rank a Navy commander, was responsible for all the Swift Boats and crews in Vietnam. He was being daisy chained (boat transferred) between Swift Boats starting in Da Nang, which was then our most northern base, all the way down south to the base at An Thoi in the Gulf of Siam. The base was located on Phu Quoc Island, where Bob Mack was stationed. Along the way, he was visiting all of his six coastal divisions.

The commodore arrived in the early afternoon and gave everyone a pep talk regarding Swifts' important role in inspecting local junks possibly transporting weapons for the VC. The other mission was intercepting larger enemy trawlers from North Vietnam and China that were supplying significant quantities of arms to the VC and NVA troops in the south. Along with the core mission that the commodore was describing, we knew that the Swift Boats operating out of the Chu Lai

*PCF 76 and the fleet in port.*

and Da Nang bases were providing extensive gunfire support for smaller Marines units along the coast. However, this was a local operational fine point that we felt was best left for another discussion.

He continued his presentation, outlining that U.S. intelligence sources had determined that replenishment from the sea was a major means of enemy resupply. Trawlers or small steel-hulled cargo ships (around 100 feet long) would be loaded with weapons and explosives in North Vietnam or China. Then they would head east, go far out to sea and then transit south, appearing to be normal vessels with the destination of delivering their cargo to ports in Southeast Asia. In his presentation, the commodore stressed that it was imperative to stop them at sea and he promised Silver Star medals to those boats that were successful.

If awards and citations sound like a ridiculous motivation, they were. Remarks like this usually indicated that the individual making the statement had spent very little time on Swift Boat patrols. The job, the crew and a basic sense of duty were the driving forces and the reasons we had all volunteered for this assignment. If you got a medal, that was fine, but medal hunters were not well received by any of us and could be very dangerous people to be on patrol with.

Shortly after I arrived in Chu Lai, Ed told me he had his crew practicing running their boat, PCF 79, at full speed while simultaneously trigger firing the 81mm mortar located on the fantail. The other method of firing was the traditional drop fire method with its up-and-over trajectory to the target. This was adjusted by a spotter located on the ground or in an aircraft. The trigger-firing method, providing you had a clear line of sight, was very much like sighting a rifle. It took some practice, a steady eye, combined with calm seas, but in this trigger-fire mode it could be a very effective weapon indeed. Anything out to 500 yards became easy pickings for a skilled gun crew. Correspondingly, if the seas were rough, the danger to the crew (it was very real) was that a fired round might explode when it hit a nearby wave, having armed itself early in its flight.

Another plus for the Chu Lai location was that about five miles off the coast was an unoccupied island which was classified "a free-fire zone" (no clearance required) that Swifts could use for target practice.

*Proudly displaying Killer Lou's slalom ski.*

The ability to see where your rounds landed from both the 81mm mortar and .50 caliber machine guns was a tremendous help to the crew in gunfire training. As a result, over time, most Swift Boats became quite proficient in utilizing their weapons. These weapon skills became valuable, especially as our original mission evolved well beyond just inspecting junks for smuggling.

## CHAPTER 12

# THE FIREFIGHT AT CAP BATANGAN

By early summer, we had several months of patrolling out of Da Nang under our belts, and we volunteered to transfer with PCF 76 to Chu Lai for a change of scenery and perhaps a little more action. Upon arrival, over a fresh mug of coffee (in Chu Lai there were no cups and saucers like there were at the Apple), Ed and a couple of other drivers updated us on the patrol areas that were historical enemy trouble spots, specifically Cap Batangan and the Sa Ky River. Reflecting back, those locations were bad news before I arrived, bad news the entire time I was there, and were still bad news after I left.

On our second patrol we were in the Delta area south of the Chu Lai base where we were scheduled to meet up with PCF 75 and Killer Lou, who had done an outstanding job on our training patrol when we first arrived in country. We joined Lou and at his instruction we followed him about 100 yards astern making about 15 kts. He led us into a large open-mouth cove on the rocky southern shoreline of Cap Batangan close to where the peninsula joined the mainland. This area was consistently hot with enemy activity so both crews were at General Quarters (GQ), which meant helmets, flak gear and every weapon manned—safeties off.

We crossed in front of what appeared to be an abandoned village on our port side, running about fifty to seventy-five yards off the beach with PCF 75 still in the lead. This distance was damn near eyeball to eyeball with the enemy and certainly within rock-throwing range. On our boat GQ usually meant that I was the driver and I usually chose the aft steering station because of the visibility it offered. I would prefer to see who was shooting at me and from where, rather than be able to send out a couple of radio messages. Besides, Newcomer was stationed near the door in the pilothouse; he was our radioman and a good one.

By definition, a firefight that involved a Swift Boat was not a long, drawn-out affair simply because the enemy could easily hide while you were riding on a noisy grey boat close offshore and very visible. Therefore, the best solution for survival was a massive return of fire, if necessary combined with a high-speed departure.

Standard operations in enemy territory like this was to travel close into the beach at a speed of 10 kts plus, seeing what you could observe taking place along the shoreline or perhaps detect hidden in the sand dunes, all the while showing the American flag. Clandestine was not the operative word. The white water of the rolling wake would catch the eye or the sound of the diesels would cover the audio spectrum. Some more cynical observers might refer to this as drawing fire, which frankly was a comment that did have certain validity.

The first indication of trouble was when I saw several small puffs of sand along the beach. These soon lead to splashes in the shallow water working their way directly toward me. Keep in mind, the Navy felt that Swift Boat officers should wear traditional khaki uniforms with the enlisted men in dungarees. As a result, my uniform announced, "I'm the man, hit me."

Obviously, this was an enemy machine gun, most likely fixed on a tripod with someone at that the trigger who had enough experience to walk his rounds toward the target for better accuracy. Before the rounds even hit the water, I knew we were in trouble. Obviously, they had let Lou's boat pass by first and opened up on PCF 76 as the second boat. This was a classic ambush technique used to minimize return fire.

I yelled for the crew to open fire and jammed the throttles forward. The big Detroit diesels roared to life in response but not before multiple rounds hit our boat just forward of my position at the aft steering station. The first bullets shattered the glass in the portside cabin windows continuing out the starboard side. The next rounds screamed by me

*Air Force "Bird Dog" assessing the target below.*

and, with a metal-to-metal squeal, drilled holes into the aluminum cabin side.

Boats was stationed at the aft .50 caliber, legs solidly spread on the deck, hands locked on the handles and trigger, as he sighted down the barrel and pumped out four rounds at a time with that *ba-ba-ba-bab* ... *ba-ba-ba-bab* sound that only a .50 caliber can make. This firing discipline kept the recoil of the big gun from climbing up in the air off the target. His controlled-fire approach soon lost out to the locked-trigger method with the result of rapidly emptying the ammo bin. I was a firm believer in the theory that the more lead you threw at the enemy the less likely they were to keep their head up and continue to shoot at you.

PCF 76 started to accelerate and we moved north of the target. Lou had seen and heard the incoming rounds, so he circled hard back at full speed and immediately turned his guns to starboard and opened fire with his twin .50 caliber forward mount. As he approached the suspected target location he fired an 81mm round in the trigger-fire mode from his after mount toward the dune line. The round went off prematurely because it was fired too low, hit a nearby wave and exploded but fortunately far enough away from the boat to avoid any red hot shrapnel hitting his own crew.

After a high-speed turn we completed a similar firing run in Lou's wake with all guns blasting. Clearing the firing area, I did a quick survey and confirmed that we had taken some hits but no one was injured.

Considering that this was well-known enemy-held territory, namely the notorious Cap Batangan, combined with the fact that now we knew they were using at least one crew-served weapon (machine gun), we decided the next logical step was to call in an airstrike. Lou and I moved PCFs 75 and 76 about 300 yards off the beach, but still in the vicinity of where the enemy had been firing at us. We felt this was an adequate safety buffer but at the same time this position would allow us to scan the beach and dune line with our binoculars for any enemy movement out of the area.

In this sector, air operations came under Air Force control and they were a crowd that knew how to conduct close-in air support. Using our area call sign Same Drink Delta, Lou called our operational control in Da Nang (call sign Article) and requested the air support. Within minutes, a small USAF single engine spotter plane appeared approaching from the west at an altitude of not much more than 1500 feet. The pilot immediately made radio contact with us by name and identified himself.

"Same Drink Delta, This is Red Devil 45. Interrogative your mission, voer?"

Lou responded, "Red Devil 45, this is Same Drink Delta. We are two Navy Swift Boats presently located offshore approximately 300 yards from the beach. We recently took heavy machine-gun fire from a location onshore from our present position. We have remained in the area and have observed no enemy movement onshore, over."

"This is Red Devil 45. Are there injuries on board requiring medevac?"

Lou responded, "This is Same Drink Delta. Negative on your last, minor damages to one boat."

"Roger that Same Drink. Stand by, I will mark possible target with smoke and you adjust." Again, Lou radioed, "Red Devil 45, roger that, Same Drink standing by, out."

This FAC (forward air controller) was an experienced pilot who was constantly updated as to what aircraft were airborne at the time as well as the status of their fuel and weapons on board. Why any experienced pilot would choose to fly around in a slow propeller-driven two-seater aircraft over enemy territory was lost on me. Undoubtedly, his view was better at a low altitude while traveling at a slow speed, but so was his exposure to even enemy small-arms fire. Regardless, these guys were pros and we were glad to have their support. With pilots from any service, radio communications soon became a casual procedure, usually conducted in a flat monotone voice with a slight western twang, regardless of the surrounding combat chaos.

Red Devil 45 fired a small white smoke rocket at the suspected target location from the launchers located beneath his wing. Lou and I did our best to recall the exact position of the original gunfire, but sand dunes and sea grass along a straight beach line all look the same and are not the best navigational aids to reference.

Lou's boat was nearby so I gave him a visual thumbs-up and he radioed, "Red Devil 45, this is Same Drink Delta. Your smoke looks good to us, if it does to you." All we got in response was a laconic, "Roger that, maintain your present position, stand by."

Red Devil 45 fired another smoke round and in less than a minute two jet fighter-bombers approached from the north coming out of the sun, screaming downward toward the target below. Obviously, the spotter and these aircraft had been communicating with each other on a radio frequency that we could not receive on the Swift Boats. There was no approaching black speck in the sky, no sound of their engines, until we heard the roar as they flattened out and were on their final low-level run to the target.

From an altitude of no more than 400 feet the first aircraft, traveling at least 300 mph, dropped two high-explosive bombs that you could easily see tumble from the bomb racks below each wing. As they hit the ground below, we saw the red-orange blast of the explosions and then we watched as the shockwave marched along and bowed over a row of palm trees, leaving behind a whirlwind of dust and debris. Shortly thereafter, we could hear the sound of the massive concussion as it rolled out to our position offshore.

The second aircraft rolled in, not much more than thirty seconds later, dropping incendiary bombs. There was less noise, a much smaller

*The high-explosive bombs find their mark.*

shockwave but a huge rolling fireball accompanied by oily black smoke that hung over the bomb site. This was napalm, jellied gasoline. A terrifying thing to watch close up, let alone imagine what it would be like to be on the receiving end. The airstrike procedure had been straightforward: if the enemy was dug in, demolish his roof and then kill him exposed in the open.

"Same Drink Delta, this is Red Devil 45, mission complete, evaluate your target destroyed." Lou responded, "Red Devil 45, this is Same Drink Delta, thank you for your assistance, you have a nice day, out."

Regretfully, we all knew that there was a definite possibility that the enemy was hiding safe below ground deep in a tunnel with the only damage being temporary hearing loss. The suddenness and intensity of our own firefight combined with the ferocity of the follow-on air strike brought home to me, in the clearest fashion, the incredible violence of combat. This was not an emotion you casually dismissed or an experience you would ever forget.

I moved PCF 76 slowly offshore and after a more thorough inspection, I saw that the boat had taken about eight hits. The cabin side had four holes in the aluminum and four additional rounds had blown out the port side cabin windows and then carried across inside the cabin doing a repeat performance on the starboard side windows. However, the glass fragments were held in place by overlapping rows of olive drab cloth tape, basic but still effective.

We put out the fenders and had just maneuvered alongside Lou's PCF 75 to debrief the operation. Boats and I were standing by the starboard rear cabin window when suddenly, without warning, there was a violent explosion. Both of us felt the heat and smelled the cordite powder spread across our faces.

Lou's gunner's mate had committed two cardinal sins of omission. He had not cleared his guns in the forward twin .50 calibers after the firefight. This was always done to ensure there was no live round of ammunition remaining in the breach of the gun. Second, he had not elevated his guns straight up for safety purposes but instead had left them depressed downward, literally pointing at our boat. The result was a "cook-off." This could occur when a gun was hot and it caused a round to fire without the trigger being pulled. A .50 caliber round about the size of your thumb blasted between Boats and me, burying itself in the heavy Styrofoam of the life raft located just behind us. At this distance, with a round this size, no one would be wounded, it simply blew your head off.

Total travel distance was about ten feet, missing our heads by less than six inches. Within two seconds, Boats had leaped onto PCF 75 and charged up to the gun tub. The result being that the life of Lou's gunner's mate was now at significant risk. While my leadership position demanded that I intervene, I chose to move with some appropriate deliberation.

Both boat crews had heard and seen the incident and were still in total shock at what had happened and what might have been the deadly and tragic result of this accidental cook-off. With guns and ammunition, certain rules and procedures are ironclad for a reason and this certainly demonstrated that reason. Fortunately for all of us. the lesson that day was a cheap one.

The firefight, the air strike and the subsequent cook-off had drained all of us emotionally, so Lou and I decided it was best to shove off and return to our separate patrol areas. We would debrief at a later time...

Later, as I reflected on the initial firefight, I was not satisfied that our crew had returned the enemy fire fast enough. My criticism included Muller on the twin .50s forward, our principal weapon, but also Buck and Newcomer, who were armed with M-16s. Boats and Snipe, both of whom were older, were on the after .50 and they immediately commenced fire until they ran out of ammunition. Upon inspection, their gun barrel had literally acquired a small bend from the heat of nonstop firing and had to be unscrewed and replaced with our spare.

My crew was well on its way to becoming top-notch but this was their first close-in firefight with an enemy less than 100 yards away, so there were definitely lessons to be learned. Comments were made to me that they didn't return fire because they couldn't actually see the enemy and Gunner's Mate Muller said he was adjusting his helmet and flak vest.

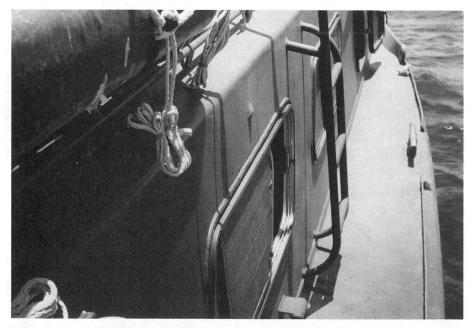

*PCF 76 after the firefight at Cap Batangan: two holes in the life raft; one from the sniper, one from the cook-off (top left); three holes in the starboard window and cabin side above.*

In a low-key manner, this was not the time for yelling, I shared with them my combat theory of "the more lead you fire at the enemy the less lead he was likely to fire back at you." After this training discussion, for good measure, we had a high-output nonstop hour of combat drills, including sprint to the weapon, load it, cock it, turn it toward the target area and, most important, commence firing the weapon. The result, at the conclusion of our drills, was that when fired upon we could return fire from all stations in under twelve seconds, whether or not we saw the enemy or were in fact fully dressed for the occasion.

The rest of the patrol was uneventful and we had not expended so much ammo that we had to return to base to rearm. The baptism by fire had been quite real and we were a far better crew for it. We had indeed paid a very small price to be combat seasoned. Regretfully, PCF 76 looked a lot worse at the end of the day then she had at the beginning when we left the pier at Chu Lai.

We crisscrossed wooden braces that Snipe had found below into the window frames to support the glass which the tape held and kept from completely shattering and falling out. The bullet holes elsewhere were in the cabin sides, not through the hull, so watertight integrity was not an issue.

Later, Boats went to dig the .50 caliber round fired from Killer Lou's boat out of our life raft as a souvenir. I heard him yell, "Skipper, come here," with a sense of urgency that made me very uncomfortable despite the fact we were now well offshore.

When I joined him, it took me a moment to identify the source of his concern. The hole from the .50 caliber round cook-off was quite recognizable and Boats had removed the actual slug from the life raft and he now held it in his hand. About a foot away, he was digging with his knife at another hole in the raft. We knew the cook-off round had been a single shot but to our mutual horror he pulled another round similar in size to the first .50 caliber, but this one was not U.S. made.

We had never heard this other enemy round being fired nor had we seen any activity onshore. We came to the realization that while we were coordinating the air strike with Red Devil 45, PCF 76 was starboard side to the shore with the life raft facing the beach. This was *the only time* it had faced the beach. At the time we had both felt we were well out of enemy gunfire range, as had Lou. Seeing this second slug, it became obvious that a sniper onshore, with the NVA equivalent of a single-shot long-range .50 caliber, had hit us without our even suspecting it. Who on board PCF 76 had been his target we would never know, because we had heard nothing, seen nothing, and felt nothing when that long-distance round hit the life raft.

There could be no other explanation for the second round. So despite the heavy fire from two Swift Boats and the subsequent arrival of an air strike, there was a sniper well dug in somewhere on that beach who took his single shot at us. Fortunately for us, that day, his aim was off the mark.

For each of us, this short two-hour segment of the day had been an incredibly draining one. Each of us knew well that there had been multiple occasions that could have ended in tragedy or death. Fortunately, that had not been the case, and that was something for which we were all truly thankful.

CHAPTER 13

# PICKING UP SUPPLIES

It had been two days since the firefight and cook-off incident. We were again patrolling south of Cap Batangan but there appeared to be little activity in terms of coastal cargo traffic or fisherman from the Sa Ky River mouth south. To be safe, we stayed about 500 yards off the beach with all guns fully manned and the crew stationed at General Quarters, just in case. Thinking back, I hoped the volume of return fire from our boat and Lou's during the firefight, followed up by the massive air-strike, had either killed the enemy or certainly lowered their risk profile. However, that single .50 caliber round fired by that well-concealed and dug-in enemy sniper onshore remained forefront in my thoughts.

The day turned out to be a quiet one, so as evening approached Boats mentioned that he wanted to get some supplies and suggested that we contact one of the U.S. Navy destroyers patrolling about five miles offshore. The larger ships carried out a north/south barrier patrol as they waited for any requests from the Marines for shore bombardment. We radioed one of the destroyers we had seen the day before, call sign *Collarbone*, and requested a rendezvous around 1930 hrs. We figured that would be after their evening meal was finished and before the movie.

*Collarbone* responded in the affirmative and gave us an approximate rendezvous location. An accurate position was not really required because we could see their steel hull paint clearly on our radar scope. Out of curiosity, I asked Boats what was on his shopping list because supplies in Chu Lai were not as good as Da Nang but certainly satisfactory.

He mentioned perhaps a couple of steaks would be of interest and possibly ice cream which was at best sporadic on the menu at Chu Lai. Also he wanted some canvas and white cord line.

With this last item, he had lost me completely. In best bos'n mate jargon, he explained that his intent was to put fancy work on the steering wheel and supporting poles in the main cabin. As he described it, the canvas was stitched onto the wheel or the pole and then on either end fancy "Turks heads" were braided with the white cord line. When that was completed the entire display would be varnished.

I had seen this done on larger ships but suspected it would be a first on a Swift Boat. He had previously asked me if we could call our crew the *Vikings*, which was fine with me. The next day, the inside of the forward hatch cover was resplendent with our new name and bloody crossed battle axes. To complete the image Boats felt we needed a pennant with the Vikings name to fly below the ensign on the radar mast. My father, having met Boats in Coronado, understood the importance of this matter and it arrived two weeks later.

I had a great deal of professional respect for Boats and PCF 76 was one of the sharpest looking boats in the division. This was confirmed by the fact that everyone wanted to use our boat whenever we were not patrolling. Related to that, without any encouragement from me, Boats made it quite clear that only God could save the crew that returned PCF 76 damaged or with a spot of dirt on board, let alone unclean or unoiled weapons.

At about 1730, we received a radio call saying that *Collarbone* was proceeding to seaward for a refueling rendezvous with a tanker. Obviously, this evolution took priority over our shopping spree but she stated that upon completion she would contact us and reschedule. That was fine with us, so we continued our uneventful north/south patrol watching the day's bright sun start to set in the west, slowly falling behind that deceivingly peaceful shoreline.

This was followed by a sumptuous dinner of turkey cold cuts and iceberg lettuce with yellow mustard on what I suspect was either Wonder Bread or its generic first cousin. Regardless, it filled the hole. Boats made a fresh pot of coffee and by 2130 we had set the first night watch.

I took it along with my section composed of Gunner's Mate Muller and Radioman Third Class Newcomer. Boats' watch section had the next most senior person onboard, Snipe, who was an engineman second class and Seaman Buck, who was the most junior of our crew but even he had matured quickly and was an integral member of the team.

I put Newcomer on the wheel and Muller above in the gun tub as lookout but also to keep his twin .50 calibers company. Newcomer was seasoned enough that he could monitor the radar for any targets and also use it to follow the coastline, staying offshore 1000-plus yards. I sat on the port side of the pilothouse leaning against the chart table in a raised and quite comfortable chair that Boats had built.

This non-regulation piece of furniture comprised an aircraft pilot's seat that somehow he had cumshawed from the Air Force base, supported in a wooden frame he had designed. Originally, the pilothouse had only a helm seat for the driver, which meant the second individual had to stand and hang onto the small chart table, which made for a very long four-hour watch. As a result, most boats in some fashion had built a seat or used the less creative solution of simply stealing a bar stool from somewhere. Once again, a little local creativity supplemented the Navy's crew comfort design process.

From my portside position, I could lean over behind the driver to see the radar scope and I was also able to see the fathometer mounted forward on the dashboard. These instruments provided a double check to see that we were not veering toward shore or proceeding into shallow water. Both these actions reflected poor seamanship on the part of the helmsman or even worse could ruin your whole day. Most important to me was the ability to swing off the seat and quickly step out the pilothouse door. Here, with a pair of binoculars, I could do a clear scan of the shoreline as well as get a visual on any target that appeared on the radar scope. Guns in the tub above also had a pair of binoculars.

I can never visualize stepping out the port door of the pilothouse without thinking of another boat driver, Walter Doblecki, who did it one night in rough weather. Just as the boat rolled unexpectedly, out the door went Walt. A good athlete in college, he was able to grab the top of the door frame. He swung overboard and quickly lost his grip, falling into the briny deep. Whoever was at the wheel was most likely watching the radar scope and had missed this entire rapid evolution. He turned to speak to his officer-in-charge only to be greeted by an open door with the wind whistling in. Since the pilothouse was less than forty square feet in size, he immediately assessed what had happened, stopped the boat and yelled for help from the rest of the crew. Walt was approximately five boat lengths astern unhurt and clearly announcing his location, which was quickly confirmed with the spotlight. No damage done and a great story for the archives, but one which could have been a tragedy if you added fifteen or twenty minutes to the recovery. "Man Overboard," at night in rough weather, has been and will always continue to be serious business.

While I had great faith in my crew, I felt strongly it was the responsibility of the officer-in-charge to double check what was going on, even if it was to confirm that nothing was going on. In Swift Boats surprises were not a welcome event. "Darken ship," which in our case was defined as absolutely no lights showing, was standard operating procedure. Even a brief moment of white light could provide a target for the patient and watchful enemy on shore. Therefore, I checked to make sure that the red lens flashlight was secured in front of me, along with the duty pad of paper and a fist full of pencils for any incoming radio message. The radio was located below in the main cabin and over the driver's head was a small speaker and a microphone attached to a coiled cord that stretched so that it could be used anywhere in the pilothouse. You ran some risk of strangling the person at the helm, but these were the compromises that you endured on a fifty-foot boat.

The night, without any moon, was dark but clear with plenty of stars overhead and a breeze blowing down from the north at about 5 kts. As a result, it looked like we would have a quiet evening based on no current intelligence reports of nearby enemy activity. Pouring myself a fresh cup of black coffee, I did another mental inventory of the damage to the boat from the firefight two days before. We found that the hull, well above the waterline, had two additional small bullet holes in the vicinity of the engine room. After we arrived in port and the engines were cool, we climbed all over the blocks and found no damage to any hose or critical engine component. With broken windows held in by tape and wooden slats along with bent window frames we looked a lot more battle scarred than we were in fact. The two large bullet holes in the life raft were an item I was still mentally dealing with and would be for quite a while.

At midnight, Boats relieved my watch section and the three of us headed below. At 0200, I was awoken by a radio call from *Collarbone*. She had completed her refueling and notified us that she was leaving her normal patrol pattern to rendezvous with us about five miles off the beach. I was always amazed how I could sleep through standard radio messages but anything out of the ordinary usually woke me up. During the year, I realized this was a common trait among those boat officers and senior enlisted that I had grown to respect.

I jumped down from the upper rack in the main cabin and told Boats to send a Roger Wilco (will comply). I was not too happy about bringing a destroyer off their normal patrol pattern for what I evaluated was a less-than-routine supply pickup. We had good relationships with the "tin cans" so I decided to leave well enough alone. We could not yet detect the destroyer on our radar scope, which meant she was probably more than twelve miles away. I told Boats to put the shoreline 90° astern and bring the boat up to 25 kts. After about ten minutes we saw *Collarbone* on our scope due east at about fourteen miles. This distance was stretching our radar range but she was a large metal target and the sea state was calm with no clutter or sea return. I estimated that she would be closing us at 15 kts and combining that with our 25 kts that would be almost fifty miles an hour or about 75 seconds per mile. I picked up the radio and transmitted,

"*Collarbone*, this is Newsboy India 76 (our in-transit call sign), ETA *Collarbone* figures 18."

If my calculation was off, I could have Fielder pour on a little more coal and we would arrive on schedule. At fifteen minutes out, her silhouette was clearly recognizable even by starlight. I told Boats to crank it up to 30 kts for the approach. This lifted our bow farther out of the water and increased that rolling white wave, which formed at the pilot-house and carried aft into our wake leaving a phosphorous glow behind.

From a safety standpoint, I wanted to ensure that they clearly saw our approach. Well, in all honesty, even at 0230 style was important. Due to the hour, I did tell Boats to forget his usual 360° high-speed circle approach. As we closed to 500 yards, I took the helm in the pilothouse so that he could handle the ensuing delicate trade negotiations.

I approached the destroyer on her port quarter coming slowly alongside just aft of amidships. Boats was outside the door on our starboard side and we had bow and stern lines ready to toss to the mother ship. Actually, *Collarbone* had come dead in the water (DIW) and without any wind the lines might not be needed. As we came to rest alongside, I noticed that there was an officer at the rail along with two sailors. Then much to my dismay I heard him announce, "I'm Captain Cunningham, how can we help?" I thought to myself, *Shit, the old man himself.* With some trepidation, I quickly recalled Boats' non-critical shopping list. I fully expected the captain to take a large bite out of Boats' ass for pulling him off station and then gradually work over to me. During our time alongside, I was doing my very best to keep my 200-pound frame away from the starboard door carefully balancing on the left side of the driver seat without falling off. With any luck the captain, who was on the main deck of his ship and approximately three feet above the top of our pilothouse, would not have the correct angle to see me inside.

I needn't have worried. Without a pause Boats responded that we needed some canvas to do some additional patchwork on the broken windows and perhaps some light line to secure it in place. To add an additional touch of drama and to fill in the blanks he requested several more pieces of unneeded wooden strapping. The captain sent one of the two sailors standing nearby in pursuit of our requests, "on the double."

"Boats, it looks like you were in quite a firefight."

"Yes, Sir, they blew out most of the windows in the main cabin with machine-gun fire but I think we can hold them in place unless the weather turns nasty. They also put a fair number of holes in the hull on the port side and a couple snipers hit us in the life raft over here as you can see."

All of this was clearly pointed out with a casual matter-of-fact wave of the right arm. Boats obviously had his audience well under control but the next remark was a somewhat of a shocker.

"Where's your boat officer?" Never missing a beat, Boats responded "Captain, the Skipper's below working on the pumps."

This led to another offer of pumping assistance from Captain Cunningham, which fortunately Boats declined. Listening to this repartee, one should understand on a Swift Boat, there was no real "below" and any pumps were located in the engine room compartment aft and at about the same level as the main cabin.

"Boats, what's next?"

"Captain, by any chance do you have any beef on board? We eat with the Marines and shoe leather, or actually boot leather, is their specialty." Fortunately, that brought a laugh from the captain who turned to the other sailor and told him to get a box of steaks from the freezer and a quart of ice cream while he was at it. Within five minutes the shopping list was filled and, much to my amazement, with every item required. The two sailors reached down and passed the all-important decorative canvas and cord line along with the steaks and ice cream to Boats who handed them off to Snipe, who was standing nearby.

"Boats, anything else we can help you with tonight?"

"Negative, Captain, many thanks, we all appreciate it."

"Take care men and give my best to your Skipper."

Boats' response was a simple and straightforward "Aye, Aye, Sir," followed by a smart salute, which was seconded by Snipe.

At this time, I saw very little advantage in entering stage left and introducing myself, so I slowly moved both throttles forward. Gradually, I turned the wheel to port pulling away from the ship, all the while careful to remain in the shadows.

During our departure, leaning casually against the open pilothouse door, undoubtedly appearing as the hardened warrior, Boats lit one of his ever-present Marlboros. With a long and somewhat dramatic exhale which he blew skyward into the warm air of the South China Sea, he slowly turned toward me and with a mischievous smile and a nod of the head said, "Skipper, that's the way we do it in the real Navy."

Returning his smile, I couldn't have agreed more.

## CHAPTER 14

# THE TRAWLER, SKUNK ALPHA

During his early days at Chu Lai, Ed shared a hooch with Killer Lou, Red Ryder and the Phantom, all good skippers; to a man they were fearless, competent, and aggressive. Obviously, self-promotion was freely encouraged. Killer Lou in the 75 boat while on a recent patrol had seen a good-sized explosion on the southeast side of Cap Batangan, known to all of us as a long-time VC stronghold. This was in the patrol area designated Same Drink Delta, which was located several miles south of our base. Waste no time trying to determine the logic behind the naming of these patrol areas because after a brief time in-country you realized there was none. By comparison, our personal call signs, which were assigned by the senior boat drivers, usually referenced some personal trait (ideally a negative one) but at a minimum reflected a great deal of research and intellectual peer review.

Killer Lou felt because the explosion he had seen was in the water and not on land, VC sappers might possibly be blowing up the reef located at the river mouth. This particular reef was a significant obstruction because it made any transit into the Sa Ky River south of Batangan quite difficult.

Later that day in a knock-down firefight, he killed three VC near the same spot. The next day Ed, who was always the explorer and carried a mask and snorkel aboard PCF 79, dove nearby the explosion site recovering some weapons, TNT, grenades, and blasting caps. Ed was always a safety-first advocate.

Adding up these various bits of information and combining them with Cap Batangan's ongoing bad-guy reputation, Lou and Ed speculated that this might well be the ideal place to intercept the next enemy trawler.

Real life intelligence on enemy activity was often based on interpreting what appeared to be a series of related events combined with some previously known facts all mixed together with a little black magic. Often this unsophisticated approach was just as likely to generate worthwhile information as that based on some lengthy analytical process undertaken by the intelligence professionals. Even today with massive computers and unlimited data acquisition, the competent hunch still plays a role.

We knew from stories of past trawler encounters that the enemy trawlers usually started in China, liked to steam down the coast, maybe fifty-plus miles offshore, well away from any sea patrols. Arriving off Vietnam, they would aggressively alter their course turning 90° to the west and crank up full speed running for the coast through the "free-fire zone." This extended from the land offshore for twelve miles. This activity always took place at night usually during the dark of the moon phase. Combining these two tactics minimized their exposure to radar detection or being visually sighted. The policy was that the Navy could not fire on them outside the twelve-mile contiguous zone. Therefore, we had a limited amount of time and real estate to detect, identify, and attack any trawler before it reached the shore.

The next month was significant with Killer Lou completing his Swift Boat tour and flying the "freedom bird" home. He left behind his fearsome combat reputation and just as important his unbroken Swift Boat water skiing (single ski) endurance record, all in enemy territory, but then sport records are not attained by the faint of heart.

The arrival of the good weather signaled the breaking of the South Pacific monsoon season with its seemingly endless days of streaking grey clouds, biting horizontal rain driven by high winds and accompanying white-capped seas. All of this rotten weather had made for rugged patrols, demanding on both the crews and boats. However, better weather meant that there was the definite possibility of increased enemy coastal activity and more Swift Boat encounters.

In the weeks that followed, there were major Swift Boat firefights around Mui Batangan at places with names like Co Lay (gunfight at Co Lay corral; 5 WIA), and all across the Batangan peninsula. It was perennial home to the 48th Main Force Viet Cong Battalion. That crowd had fought the Japanese, the French and now they were fighting us.

Located at Chu Lai, the resident Naval Intelligence Liaison Officer (NILO) was LT Charlie Crigler, who was affectionately named "Charlie Nilo" by the local Marines. Around May, he informed us at a briefing that recently a long-range P2V Naval patrol aircraft had reported sighting a suspicious trawler transiting in a southerly direction, very possibly with a cargo of weapons. At that time, the trawler was located far to the north near the Paracel Islands off the coast of China. This tidbit of information was our first indication that possibly a trawler was headed our way.

Charlie Crigler was a Chu Lai neighbor and, while part of the Naval Support Activity, he had become a good friend. On a weekly basis, Charlie used to drive by jeep to Tam Ky (about twenty miles inland from our base), to attend intelligence briefings. Often, he would ask if we wanted to join him on these trips. However, the Swifts felt these intelligence sessions were usually long on maybes and short on facts. Instead, we preferred a first-class observation seat; actually it was a backseat, choosing to fly with the pilots of the Army "Bird Dogs" and "Cat Killers." They flew small single-engine light observation aircraft often along the coast looking for enemy troop movements or suspicious construction such as bunkers or possible weapons emplacements. On other occasions, we would upgrade and ride as a door gunner on a Huey helicopter. At the time this all made good sense.

These flights gave us the opportunity to broaden our social skills beyond just our membership in the Navy's Vietnam Yacht Club. At the same time, they allowed us to observe the coastline from several hundred feet in the air. From this low altitude, we could see what lay behind those peaceful rolling sand dunes dotted with sea grass that we saw every day on patrol. We knew from experience that the enemy was more likely to open fire on us concealed behind a sand dune or undercover in a bunker than he was to shoot at a Swift Boat from a small sampan in open

THE TRAWLER, SKUNK ALPHA • 173

water. While these airborne reviews of enemy real estate were definitely valuable, the flying interludes were also an enjoyable change of pace from our patrol schedule. In most cases, a low-level flight could provide more than enough material to be woven into a good cocktail story.

One day, Charlie Nilo roared into the base at full throttle, returning from his weekly briefing with a bullet hole clean through the passenger side of his jeep's windshield. Arriving at our hooches with wheels spinning and sand flying he hit the brakes, jumped from the jeep and sprinted to the bar for a couple of quick ones. We assumed he needed some liquid assistance to mentally regroup before he briefed us on his recent enemy encounter. Considering we were good friends and understanding his state of mind, we certainly wanted to help in some small way. With that goal in mind, Ed and a couple of other boat drivers took the opportunity to paint a six-inch-wide fire-engine-red racing stripe down the entire length of Charlie's jeep to memorialize his recent combat baptism. Somewhat surprising, at least to us, he was not completely enthralled with Ed's artwork. There was some muttering by Charlie to the effect that we had just painted a bull's-eye on his ass.

We did find out later, and frankly much to our relief, that our "Red Badge of Courage" did not present a major risk factor to Charlie Nilo from Charlie Cong. From that time forward, Charlie Nilo's preferred method of transportation to the weekly intel briefing was by helo leaving behind his faithful but wounded jeep.

On the positive side it became a simple exercise to locate Charlie Nilo around the base there, due to his sporty paint job. Over time, we concluded that Charlie began to feel that his unique red racing stripe, combined with the still unrepaired bullet hole in the shattered spider web windshield, was a statement that definitely qualified him a combat player.

Ed remembered Charlie Nilo's remarks a week or two later when he saw that the calendar indicated that the next dark of the moon was scheduled to occur in two days. That night Ed and the crew of PCF 79 agreed to volunteer for patrol in the Same Drink Delta area. He figured if a trawler was going to make a run to the coast, it would be during the dark of the moon with low visibility and that the area around Batangan would be their logical destination. Sometimes these enemy trawler reports, like the one that we had received earlier, were nothing more than legitimate cargo ships heading south with a destination beyond Vietnam. At other times the long-range patrol planes simply lost track of their suspected contact in a storm. This time, PCF 79 was taking no chances.

As they transited to their patrol area, Ed's crew broke out three rounds of Willie Peter (White Phosphorous, anti-personnel) and three rounds of HE (high explosive) for the stern-mounted 81mm mortar. The mortar rounds were carefully removed from the ready service magazine (ammo box) which was located on the fantail of the boat. The magazine was basically a large, secure and watertight box welded to the deck with internal brackets built to hold seventy-five to one hundred various types of mortar rounds. These mortar rounds were not the type of items you wanted rolling around the deck, so Ed's crew positioned and secured them carefully near the gun mount with all the fuses set for short-distance firing.

In addition to the mortar, the three .50 caliber machine guns, two located in the gun tub over the pilothouse and the single .50 caliber aft were each loaded with ammo belts composed of hundreds of individual rounds linked together by brass fittings. This allowed the firing of short bursts of multiple rounds or even nonstop firing. On many of the boats, the aft .50 caliber had a larger ammo box attached which held close to 1,000 belted rounds rather than the usual 450. Naturally, Ed's boat had this non-regulation modification. We were well aware that this modification most likely violated some Naval weapons policy but when it came to ammunition most of us subscribed to the more-is-better philosophy. The Navy's restriction was probably based on the fact that if the full belt of ammunition was fired without stopping, it would usually generate enough heat to warp the gun barrel. Therefore, someone in the government figured that if you did not fire at the enemy too rapidly, you might be dead, but your gun was still going to be in good working order.

Tonight on PCF 79 all other small arms on the boat were laid out with additional magazines of ammunition close at hand. Ed had placed the M-79 grenade launcher in the pilothouse with a bandolier of grenades, all within easy reach of the wheel. The M-79 was a good weapon because at close range it was easy to aim; you just pointed it at the target and pulled the trigger. It packed a good-sized 40mm high-explosive round maybe two inches in diameter. Anyone who has ever fired one would remember its unique firing sound which was a hollow *thonk*, somewhat like hitting the bottom of an empty paint (not beer) can. This was the reason that the Marines and Army nicknamed it "Thumper."

That night, all spare flak jackets that were not being worn by the crew were secured to the vertical stanchions and life lines around the stern and aft sides of the boat. This gave the aft gunner and loader some protection. I emphasize *some* because the height of these wire railings was about thigh high. Ed's boat, like all the Swifts, had no armor and was made of quarter-inch aluminum. All of us were realistic about the impact of receiving a direct hit, but sometimes the equally deadly pieces of exploding red-hot shrapnel would ricochet. They didn't call a Swift Boat "The Reynolds Wrap Wonder" out of deep respect for its armor credentials.

While the night was still calm, before any change of weather, cruising safely offshore Ed's crew cooked a real dinner (cumshawed steaks). The grill was their modified 25-gallon oil drum barbeque located on the aft deck but a safe distance away from the ammunition.

During dinner the sky overhead remained cloudless, and the crew was able to enjoy firsthand one of those magnificent South China Sea sunsets that could only be viewed at sea. Seated on the ammo box or on the top of the main cabin, each man looked to the west and followed that special light show of changing colors. First came the broad background of fiery reds, and then the few clouds resting low on the horizon changed into slender streaks becoming a horizontal blend of blues and pinks. From their first-class seats they watched this entire display across the radiant silver water as the sun gradually set. First it sank behind the jungle green hills, and then it silhouetted each darkened hill radiating from its location just below the horizon. To be expected, each member of the crew spent some time with his own thoughts, but as a team they were confident and ready for combat, if tonight was in fact the night.

As PCF 79 commenced a routine north–south patrol, the wind began picking up at about 2100. The sea state was gradually increasing so the waves were cresting in the four- to five-foot range. Now with each wave, they were taking water over the boat's stubby bow with heavy spray up and over the pilothouse carrying aft with each increasing wind gust. Anything that wasn't lashed down was shifting and rolling with the waves and was soon secured. Small arms were laid out but kept dry inside.

PCF 79 continued to run slowly back and forth between the boundaries of their patrol area maintaining about 7 kts. Bow on or stern to, depending on the direction travelled, the boat pitched and rolled over each wave. The weather alone began to put additional demands on the crew to just hold on and stay on course. Added to this was the very real possibility of unknown combat in the hours just ahead. Eyes were on the radar scope and ears locked onto the radio. Every member of the crew was focused and sharp. Ed's gunner's mate was on lookout located in the gun tub above the pilothouse in the worst and wettest seat, but he had donned his foul-weather jacket and had the official cleaning rag to constantly wipe the spray from his binoculars.

The single side-band radio, which was our longer-range unit, suddenly burst to life with someone using the call sign "Impair" calling Ed's boat. They were utilizing the "Same Drink Delta" call sign, assigned to Ed's current patrol area. This meant they had some reasonable knowledge of the Swift Op. Order. "Impair" however, was a call sign that Ed didn't recognize. It was not another patrol area nor was it another Swift Boat skipper's personal call sign.

Naturally, the op. order that could provide Ed with the caller's identity was stored safely below in some drawer. This was logical because it was hardly ever used and frankly, it was something we ignored. As skipper under these weather conditions, Ed was not about to leave the wheel, go below and search for it. Ed made a command decision and took the action that was close at hand and was the most common procedure in Swift Boat operations. Get an answer and get it fast! He grabbed the microphone and called on the PRC 46 (our short-range FM radio) to the other Swift Boats, all of whom monitored this radio.

"All units, this is Same Drink Delta, who the hell is Impair?"

He was greeted with an immediate response and verbal chewing out for compromising radio security. This radio call came from none other than "Impair Actual." The owner of the mystery call sign "Impair" was obviously also monitoring this short-range frequency. "Actual," when used in less formal radio communications, meant it represented an individual commander rather than a vessel. Based on this rapid response, Ed knew that Impair must be physically close by and most likely was someone in a position of authority. His radioman, the ever-competent Raul Herrara (call sign Bean) went below and was able in short order to find and retrieve the op. order, which as expected was safe and dry nestled in the drawer below the main radio.

Within seconds, Bean yelled up to the pilothouse that the call sign Impair belonged to the Commander of the CSC (Coastal Surveillance Center), our local operational boss. The Commander was in fact afloat (on a ship, not onshore) but on what type of vessel, Ed still didn't know. Call signs often can change when an individual is afloat versus onshore which is why he didn't recognize it. If he had been chewing Ed's ass from a shore location, he would have probably introduced himself as "Article Actual," somewhat of a phonetic mouthful. While these nuances of U.S. Navy radio etiquette were usually ignored by us, tonight they had Ed's full attention.

CSCs were the onshore Navy groups that all Swift Boats reported to on an hourly basis when we were on patrol. We notified them regarding our current status and what if any unusual activities we were involved in. They in turn coordinated joint operations between the various at-sea units and occasionally aircraft. However, this linkage did not usually extend to our Marine Corps friends. On the whole, they were good guys located at various shore stations along the coast, but most important they tolerated our idiosyncrasies. However, their officers were infrequently or never at sea. None of us had ever heard of one of their commanders going to sea, let alone at night in rotten weather. Ed concluded, something very big had to be up. The question was, what?

Again, the radio came alive, this time with messages transmitted in groups of three letters in the format of KAC 135 security codes. This type of encryption presented several challenges: first just holding on and trying to copy the messages onto paper; then the task of decoding it while holding the red flashlight because at night "darken ship" was mandatory; all on board a 50-foot boat rolling and pitching, while climbing through the building seas.

Ed quickly realized when he heard the number of call signs addressed in the message that there must be a task force of ships headed his way. Bean later identified the group by their call signs. It included a destroyer escort DER (Impair embarked), a mine sweeper, a jet-turbine-powered fast motor patrol gunboat (PGM) and a Coast Guard patrol boat (WPB). It was never quite clear how these letter designations related to the name of the vessel itself but tonight this was not a high priority for Ed. On the other hand, the designator PCF was pretty basic—Patrol Craft Fast.

Now Ed understood how Impair was able to transmit his encrypted radio messages in this armpit weather; he was riding high and dry with the big boys on a destroyer. As was often the case, the people in charge had not felt the need to brief the Swifts on the operation beforehand. That night, this armada had just appeared on the scene. This was a factor that constantly pissed off the Swift Boat skippers and tonight Ed was a charter member of the "pissed off club." Of course, the big boys were located ten miles or more off shore while Ed was 500 yards off the beach, so it all made good sense that Swifts were the last to know.

Despite the noise, weather, and confusion, Bean worked on the KAC codes, slowly decoding them one word at a time under very unpleasant conditions: wet paper, flashlights, and disappearing pencils. Ed became increasingly furious as he visualized his superiors ensconced aboard larger ships with air-conditioned spaces, good lighting, high-powered radars, phone talkers complete with charts laid out and plotters keeping track of the surface picture. Ed and his crew meanwhile were getting slammed around and tossed about by the building seas which had just passed the quite unpleasant level.

When Impair next sent the "Execute" order, radioman Bean had only half of it decoded. This was slightly better than nothing, he hoped. He yelled to Ed that PCF 79 was to take a position 1,000 yards (half a mile) astern on the port quarter of a radar contact currently believed to be a North Vietnamese trawler. The Coast Guard WPB would be on the opposite starboard quarter. This result would be an upside-down V with the enemy trawler at the top of the intersection. Ed told Bean not to worry about the rest of the radio message; their mission was simply evolving way too fast.

Ed grabbed the throttles in his left hand and pushed them both full ahead. The big GM diesels responded with their usual confidence-instilling, deep-throated roar. Now, as the boat climbed over the waves they were headed at flank speed to take up their assigned position on the stern quarter of the target. Out of pure habit, Ed yelled for everyone to "Hold on." In reality, after just one day riding on a Swift Boat, especially in heavy weather, everyone made sure a firm handhold was always nearby.

Moving rapidly south away from the task force, they swung briefly offshore then circled back to the east. Ed eased up on the throttles and smoothly slid in 1,000 yards behind the radar contact now designated "Skunk Alpha." "Skunk" for enemy contact, "Alpha" for first contact.

His crew now had identified what they hoped was the enemy trawler painting clearly as a greenish-yellow mark on the upper half of their radar scope. The brightness of the contact indicated it was most likely a steel-hulled vessel. Straining his eyes through the spray-spattered windshield Ed thought he could see some vague outline of the contact. Alpha was definitely headed due west, currently landward of them preparing to make his high-speed run towards shore. The Coastie (Coast Guard) in the 80-foot WPB was also painting on the radar screen. He was 200 yards abreast to starboard of PCF 79 about the same distance astern of the trawler. Both units radio signaled Impair when they were on station.

The other Navy ships showed up as large illuminated targets on the radar screen and were spread out much further astern of Ed and further offshore. There was an unusual amount of sea return (reflected electronic clutter) around these more distant radar contacts due to the heavy sea state. At the same time, Skunk Alpha kept popping in and out of the radar clutter on Ed's scope due to its close proximity and the cresting sea state nearer shore. It was now becoming increasingly difficult to visually follow Alpha's sinister black outline because of no moon and both boats rising then falling with each wave.

Both the Coast Guard WPB and PCF 79 were ordered to fire their mortar-illumination rounds over Skunk Alpha. Ed told Impair that at his current speed and the short distance to the target, most likely he would be driving under his own illumination round, not a good idea. On a Swift Boat, the illumination round was a 30-second phosphorus flare descending with a parachute providing visibility over 200-plus yards. Ignoring Ed's concerns, both boats were ordered by Impair to fire the illumination rounds. Not a surprising directive from a "desk jockey."

The rounds went off overhead and were so bright that the entire crew of PCF 79 was immediately blinded and couldn't see anything. As a result of the illumination rounds, the enemy trawler would now be keenly alert to not only their presence, but probably that of all the other ships located behind Ed. This also confirmed that at least one Swift Boat was in the hunt.

Visually and on radar it was now obvious that the trawler had started its full-speed run to shore. PCF 79 and the Coastie were ordered by Impair to fire across its bow. This was indeed a textbook attack, circa the War of 1812. Climbing again to full throttle, Ed moved his boat from its position astern of the trawler. A Swift Boat was much faster and he rapidly pulled ahead of the Coastie, now running briefly up the trawler's port side. Passing the trawler's bow, Ed's gunner opened up with his twin .50s mounted in the gun tub. There was no mistaking the gun's familiar firing sound of *ba-ba-ba-bab* as the spent brass casings cascaded down behind Ed's seat and rattled into the pilothouse below.

The muzzle flashes from the enemy machine guns at multiple locations were immediate; they were returning fire. No element of surprise existed; instead the enemy was well prepared for Ed's attack. The chase was on.

The Coast Guard WPB had fallen back in position as the Swift's greater speed allowed it to close the trawler. This action was a heads-up move on the Coastie's part and was critical to preventing a deadly crossfire situation that could have taken place between two friendly units. That risk appears to have been missed by those directing the operation, several miles behind out to sea.

The trawler passed a small rock and coral island off its starboard side continuing its full-speed run towards shore. Not far ahead, Ed saw the white foam as the breakers crashed onto the rocks as well as the dark silhouette of the island, but once again he had lost visual contact with the trawler. Making matters worse, at the same time, the target had also disappeared in the electronic clutter and sea return on the radar. As they maneuvered around the island, the radio buzzed with nonstop confusion suggesting the larger ships behind had also lost radar contact with the trawler. Next, Impair announced that they were turning north to pursue a contact they felt was in fact Skunk Alpha.

Ed was committed and decided to stick to the original plan he had developed days before with Killer Lou. He continued heading west toward the Sa Ky River mouth because this was the most logical place for the trawler to beach itself and unload its cargo of weapons. His knowledge of the area told him the trawler could unload in shallow water while an enemy stronghold on onshore provided cover. A return trip for the trawler was never a consideration. Ed's goal was to cut him off.

A faint green dot reappeared on the radar; it had to be Skunk Alpha. Ed yelled to Guns sitting above him that his goal was a simple one, "Kill him first, before he gets us."

His first burst had to be deadly accurate. Guns knew that, as he heard the diesels roaring to life below while their twin screws churned their frothy wake astern. At full speed PCF 79 was now literally plowing head first into the crest of the wave. The entire boat shuddered then climbed up and crashed over each foaming crest. Solid sheets of white spray were being thrown off the bow at least fifty feet to each side as the 20-ton boat surged into the eight-foot seas at close to 30 kts. Ed described it as riding a bucking bronco with a bag over your head.

The telltale phosphorous bow wave of Skunk Alpha suddenly glowed into sight off their bow, and Gunner started the deadly tattoo of 800 rounds a minute from the twin .50s. Four rapid rounds at a time, fired simultaneously from each gun. This firing discipline, though difficult to maintain in the chaos of a firefight, insured the most accuracy. Gunner knew his accuracy was critical in close-quarters combat like this.

He was on his game and the return fire from the enemy ship was brief and silenced in mere seconds. The relief the crew felt along with the brief silence was soon ended. Two major explosions resounded nearby accompanied by brilliant flashes of light just abeam of them as they pressed forward racing past the trawler.

Speed was a key advantage in a Swift Boat and Ed kept his at full throttle preparing for his second run. Later he told me when they inspected the trawler, they determined the sound had been the enemy firing two 37mm recoilless rifle rounds at them from a mid-ships position.

Fortunately for Ed's crew, with the confused sea state the enemy shooters were unsteady and their aim was off target. One decent hit on a Swift Boat from this type of weapon would have ended the battle and not in their favor.

Ed yelled for the crew to once again commence fire. Never slowing, he swung his wheel hard to port positioning for a run back along the trawler's port side. The twin .50s forward and all the small arms were now aimed at the amidships gunner on the trawler. At the aft mount, Bos'n Mate Bobby Don Carver trigger-fired a WP round from the mortar directly at the trawler's pilothouse but missed his mark.

The Swift Boat again raced along the trawler's side, hopefully exiting the enemy's zone of effective fire. With a sweeping glance, Ed now saw, almost dead ahead, the rocks dripping with white foam as the waves crashed over them. Because of the multiple turns and high-speed runs they were close to entering the river mouth itself. This was definitely not where he wanted to be; the water was treacherous, rocky and shallow with the enemy waiting on shore. Again, without slowing or touching the throttles, he spun the wheel left full. PCF 79 heeled hard into a port turn and they headed back to the target once again with all guns blazing.

Despite the continual volley of enemy fire it appeared that PCF 79 had taken no substantial hits and no crewmember had reported being wounded. Now that they had passed the target once again, Ed decided that it would be a good idea to seek partial cover in a position slightly astern of the trawler. He was confident that the stern gunner had been eliminated. In this position his crew could take time to regroup, assess what had taken place and plan their next move.

Meanwhile the aft gun crew, with Carver still in charge, hastily readied and fused another mortar round. This was no easy task in the pitch dark with water from the churning seas washing over the stern and around their feet. While this task was completed in seconds, it appeared to drag on more like minutes because of their charging adrenalin. The enemy was waiting for them, only yards ahead, slightly off Ed's bow. They had their own game plan and were ready to respond to his next move.

The trawler meanwhile continued its rush toward shore and the safety of the enemy river mouth. Ed heard Carver yell from the stern, "Skipper, loaded ready to fire."

In response, with a forward thrust of his hand once again, Ed drove both throttles hard against the stop blocks. As the boat emerged from behind the partial cover of the trawler's stern, it rapidly built up speed leaving its telltale wake to clearly mark their location and close-in approach.

With his long legs spread apart for stability, Carver braced himself and locked onto the frame of the mortar mount with both hands, carefully taking his aim, his right index finger closing slowly on the trigger below. Knowing the risk of any delay at this speed, seconds later he fired.

This time, he had targeted the enemy with deadly accuracy despite the total darkness and tumultuous seas. His round hit cleanly, crashing through the open door of the pilothouse. The white phosphorous mortar round exploded, generating a burst of blinding white light illuminating both the inside and outside of the pilothouse. In seconds, it incinerated the rifleman, who they briefly saw was armed with an AK-47. He was the one who had previously been firing at them from behind the cover of the now-blazing pilothouse door.

In the next moment, other sections toward the bow of the trawler suddenly burst into flames as the Swift's twin .50s with their incendiary tracer rounds raked the hull and topsides along with the other small arms that were being firing. The crew of PCF 79 continued hitting it with everything they had. The pilothouse and bridge were now fully engulfed in flames. In a matter of just minutes, the trawler was now fully out of control with its crew either dead or injured. Not slowing, it drove hard aground in the nearby shallows missing the safety of the deeper river mouth.

Ed concluded that the entire trawler crew had been killed because any return fire from the trawler had ceased. The main deck and pilothouse continued to burn out of control. The towering flames reached skyward and were now a brilliant orange and yellow as they reflected off the surrounding waves. This cast a dancing but eerie shadow across PCF 79 and beyond to the nearby shoreline. At the moment, Ed and his crew were far enough off-shore so that gunfire from the beach was not a major concern but they knew that the enemy unloading party on shore was fully armed and waiting for any approach on their part.

With events around him still evolving at full speed, Ed contemplated how to deal with the potential threat from the enemy on shore while at the same time considering how they might go aboard their capture.

For the past several minutes the primary radio on PCF 79 had been deathly silent with no transmissions—in contrast to the nonstop messages from Impair prior to the attack. For a moment, life appeared to have been suspended and all parties were running in neutral.

Seated in the helm seat with his hands still locked on the wheel, Ed felt he could now grab some reflection time and a little welcome silence. This ended abruptly when the secondary radio located under the helm seat burst into life loud and clear. It was an urgent call from a U.S. Marine advisor attached to an allied foreign force (in this case, Korean) with the task of providing liaison with the U.S. forces. In no uncertain terms, he told Ed, "Be advised, you are currently located in the Republic of Korea (ROK Marine Corps) Blue Dragoon Division TAOR (Territorial Area of Responsibility)."

This warning, because it had been sent in the clear (no encryption), had Ed's complete attention. The ROKs, despite being allies, were well known for their "shoot-first, ask-questions-later" policy. The Marine advisor informed Ed that the ROKs were about to start a heavy artillery bombardment of the trawler as well as the surrounding enemy shore area. Most likely they would be firing 105mm howitzers or even worse the larger 155mm set for airbursts, both very serious weapons. Ed was well aware that they could not stop them from firing because the ROKs were not known for being team players.

The U.S. Marine's concern for their safety was definitely appreciated. His message was pull back, exit the area, and *fast*. It briefly occurred to Ed what a wise decision it had been when Swift Boats installed that second radio dedicated to communicating solely with the Marine Corps. Chalk one up in the "we owe you" column to the grunts. The Marines had either observed what was going on, or figured out from previous radio transmissions that Swifts were involved in the attack and knew the ROKs wanted their part of the action regardless of the risk to friendlies, in this case PCF 79. Knowing that they may not have heard the radio message Ed screamed to his crew, "Hold on, grab anything, we're leaving town."

One more time, he jammed the throttles full forward just as an air burst of VT frag (anti-personnel) exploded from the first ROK round about 1,000 yards away. Half a mile, but Ed assumed that they would immediately begin to walk the rounds closer to the trawler, observing and correcting with each successive burst. This was standard artillery procedure and hopefully it would give Ed enough time to safely clear the target area. If the ROKs adjusted their range more quickly with larger increments or utilized the firing technique of bracketing the target, Ed had a real problem.

Once again, those big Jimmie diesels answered the call and carried their butts out of "Harm's Way." With their unplanned and high-speed exit there had been little time for the crew to reflect or savor the victory. In fact, combat adrenalin was still running high throughout the boat as they cleared the risk area and Ed pulled back the throttles. With the engines at idle, all hands turned aft as they watched the incoming ROK artillery rounds air burst astern over the blazing trawler hulk.

Ed finally grabbed a series of deep breaths and sensed his pulse rate was finally slowing down enough to allow him to reflect on the past supersonic fifteen to twenty minutes. The end result and rapid departure had not been a bad turn of events for PCF 79. Thinking back he had not relished the idea of crawling around on a burning ship full of ammunition and explosives ready to blow up and take them with it. He realized this might have been the next order given to him by the on-site commander, "Board, assess and report."

No surprise, they later found out that the enemy had placed at various locations throughout the trawler several hundred pounds of C-4 plastic high explosive rigged with enough detonation cord to blow up the vessel rather than allow it to be captured. Fortunately, during the firefight, Carver's second round of "Willie Peter" had hit the bridge dead on, killing the crew before they had time to set the charges to detonate. An explosive cook-off caused by the intense heat of the fire alone could have definitely taken place, thereby ruining their day and that of anyone nearby.

A short time after the ROKs ceased their artillery fire and with PCF 79 well clear of the area, friendly aircraft, both helicopter and fixed wing, arrived on scene for a few shots at the target. This capture was a significant enemy combat action and everyone wanted in on it. In the coming weeks a couple of well-written battle reports would most likely lead to some battlefield citations. This could be a definite "moment-of-fame" opportunity for some senior types who usually commanded a mahogany desk. Actually in Vietnam, the aforementioned desk was more likely to be painted grey metal with a green Formica top.

Now that PCF 79 was safely out of range of both enemy and so-called friendly fire, Ed did a post-battle inventory. The boat had only sustained a handful of hits, including a couple of holes in the hull and a cracked cabin window. They were incredibly thankful there had been no personnel casualties. This was a significant blessing considering the volume and caliber of fire that had been exchanged. It had all taken place at incredibly close range (less than 100 yards) with an open field of fire—no trees, no hills, no cover, just eyeball to eyeball with the enemy.

It became crystal clear to Ed that there had been absolutely no element of surprise in their attack. The enemy knew they were coming, most likely they had seen the approaching naval armada on their radar. They had definitely been ready, fully armed, and well prepared. But it was the dark of night; the speed of the Swift Boat carrying a well-trained and seasoned crew in the end had given PCF 79 that all-important winning edge.

The pace of the action had slowed and now the combat rush had almost completely dissipated. Ed could feel it himself and see it clearly as his crew moved slowly about the boat and this was a good thing. They had accomplished an amazing feat of capturing a much larger, more heavily armed enemy ship without casualties. Now, they were basically out of ammunition except for some small arms ammo and it was a long run back to Chu Lai.

Ed radioed the onsite commander Impair, who he assumed was still in operational control. He requested permission as Same Drink Delta to leave the combat area and return to base. Someone quickly responded to his request on the primary radio circuit with a succinct, "Same Drink Delta, this is Impair, permission granted, roger out."

With the volume of radio transmissions that had been taking place in the last hour or two, it occurred to Ed that this release from station might very well have come from someone who was completely unaware who they were.

"Heading Home" was Ed's simple radio response.

In keeping with a long-standing naval tradition, Ed's crew located PCF 79's long-handled straw broom, most likely their only piece of cleaning equipment. They tied it smartly to the radar mast (submariners in WWII did this to signify a clean sweep or a good patrol). Next, he told Carver to "splice the main brace," another old naval term which he knew Bos'n Carver would relate to. In response from somewhere, Carver pulled out a hidden and equally forbidden bottle of Crown Royal. He poured a generous measure into six coffee mugs (unwashed). They then toasted each other, their success, giving thanks for their safety all while celebrating in the best tradition of the British and Australian navies.

At that moment, it did occur to Ed that perhaps he had been reading too many historical seafaring novels. Carver drank radioman Bean's grog allotment, carefully explaining that he was way too young to drink, despite the occasion. Rank does have its privileges.

The trip to Chu Lai took about two hours at half speed because they all needed to fully wind down and comprehend what had actually taken place. As was often the case in the South China Sea, the wind of the previous night had abated and the seas were settling down as dawn approached from the east.

As they closed on the river mouth leading to the entrance of the base, the sun had risen just above the horizon, indicating a very good day. Turning a sharp left just past the sandbar, Ed told Carver who was at the helm to "crank it up." On this occasion as skipper, he felt they should definitely arrive in traditional Swift Boat fashion—full speed and foaming white water. As they approached the docks, Carver slowed down, swung her around, pulled back the throttles and smartly backed her down, stern to the pier.

Ed looked aft and saw the corners of the deck were still littered with spent brass shell casings from the machine guns along with the empty plastic containers that previously had held the mortar rounds. No post-combat cleanup on PCF 79 had taken place. Later, Ed was to swear that this bit of theatre had not been planned. However, when he saw the size of the crowd on the dock awaiting their arrival, he thought perhaps a little drama might be acceptable.

Good news and success travels fast and the welcoming committee, despite the early hour, included all the Swift crews in port, the Naval Support types and some of the local Marines. The conquering heroes stepped off PCF 79 greeted by hearty cheers, calls of congratulations, and a choice of fresh hot coffee or cold beer. To offend no one they chose both.

Later that night, after Ed learned the trawler Skunk Alpha had been towed to the Chu Lai base, he rounded up his crew and went down to the docks to inspect the enemy vessel they had fought to the death less than twenty-four hours earlier. The trawler had been the target of a massive artillery barrage conducted by the Koreans and follow-on strikes by US aircraft. Except for the fire-scorched hull and burnt-out interior, it looked much the same as when Ed and his crew had left it. So much for the accuracy and destructive effectiveness of our allies in combat.

Ed admitted later he had been on a definite roll that night, enhanced by his new interest in naval history and tradition. As a result, another brilliant idea occurred to him. He felt his crew was obligated to memorialize their personal involvement in the previous night's attack. After a brief search, they located a small Boston whaler, albeit with no motor but two oars. Next, they rounded up some yellow zinc chromate primer paint along with several brushes. All this was no small task operating in total darkness at 2230. His crew then approached the trawler with their fearless leader dramatically standing in the bow of the boat looking very much like George Washington as he crossed the Delaware.

Fortunately for all, the congratulatory toasts had stopped much earlier in the evening because their floating artist's platform was far from stable especially with all six of them on board. Carver and Ed were not only the senior members on this clandestine mission but more important, they were the tallest. Therefore, they were able to reach higher up on to the side of the trawler's hull. Proper placement was a critical factor as was the size of the lettering. They painted "Mort" (a truncated version of Ed's call sign) along with PCF 79 and to avoid any historical confusion, "Crew 74A" which was their crew number assigned in Boat School back in Coronado. Letters four feet high seemed appropriate as did the location, halfway up the trawler's already rusting side.

Upon completion, ever so delicately, they pushed off from alongside the hulk of Skunk Alpha to fully review their handiwork. It was deemed by this somewhat self-serving group of judges to be right on, the appropriate signature. The personal victory of PCF 79 and her crew was now immortalized in large yellow letters against the background provided by the trawler's burnt and blistered hull plates.

Earlier in the day, another Swift Boat skipper Bob Shirley on PCF 45 who had been escorting Skunk Alpha as it was being towed into port had wisely boarded the trawler. Without fanfare, he removed the Chicom (Chinese Communist) flag that had been flying from the ship's stern. There was no doubt in Bob's mind that if the flag remained in place, it was soon going to be someone else's combat trophy. Bob's selfless gesture of giving Ed that bullet-riddled and burnt flag meant a great deal. His action was typical of the *esprit de corps* that existed in Swift Boats.

During the days that followed, to the crew's delight and some relief, there were no other units claiming recognition for the capture. Equally gratifying to all was the fact that no one had mentioned or attempted to remove their four-foot-high yellow zinc chromate signature from the trawler's side. The likely conclusion was that the senior officers who had been involved in the incident probably didn't understand the significance of the message. Those people that really mattered, they knew the meaning.

As a result of the crew's new-found fame several significant events took place. First, Ed's personal call sign when he relocated to Chu Lai had been derived from his legal name Edward Bergin, which was similar to the puppeteer and comedian Edgar Bergin. One of his lower intellect puppets was Mortimer Snerd and this seemed to be an appropriate handle for Ed. This had been modified to "Mortimer Sierra" for radio transmission clarity.

With his enhanced warrior status Ed's call sign was significantly upgraded to "Lord Mort." Understandably, Ed felt his new call sign was far more appropriate, and technically much more suitable to crisp transmissions. With this final call sign update, Ed joined an infamous list of other notorious call signs, "Minute Sierra" (for little shit), "Sweet Pea" (nasty disposition), "Boy Scout" (he was one), "Non-Dancing Ray" (Bolger) and on to "Megaphone Bravo," "Sandy Bottom," "Baby Huey," "Senator Clag Horn," "MoTac," "Mary Poppins," and of course, "Killer Lou."

About a week after the trawler capture, our boss received a message that Ed and his crew were to be honored at an awards ceremony in Da Nang. Uniform of the day was tropical whites, no skivvies and shower shoes. After some very hectic search and rescue, they all found their "whites." However, these uniforms had not been worn since their arrival in Vietnam so some quick cleaning and pressing had to take place. Two days later looking very much "real Navy," they flew to Da Nang. On the local military flight north, surrounded by the ever-present sand and dirt, the crew of PCF 79 felt and undoubtedly looked significantly out of place.

The actual ceremony was very formal and well attended, but was definitely a Vietnamese affair. The senior American military brass attended but U.S. presence was low key and in the background except for the crew of PCF 79. Each of them was presented the Vietnamese Cross of Gallantry with Palm by then Air Marshal Ky and Vietnam President Thieu. General Big Minh and many Vietnamese dignitaries were also in attendance. Ed, as the officer-in-charge, received the well-deserved U.S. Bronze Star with Combat V.

The trawler, their trawler, was very much on display anchored off the nearby quay right behind the ceremony. All the captured arms and ammunition from the trawler were spread out along the pier: machine guns, rocket launchers, and claymore mines. All laid out side by side, a deadly but impressive sight. Beautiful Vietnamese girls dressed in their traditional *ao dais* put flower wreaths over the heads of the crew, which was a nice touch. Somewhat like Honolulu but that was over six thousand miles to the east. Later, we all saw that the picture of Ed and the crew at the awards ceremony had made the front page of the *U.S. Star and Stripes*. This recognition was a great treat, especially for their families at home and other far-flung military friends.

*LTJG Ed Bergin receives the VN Cross of Gallantry from future Prime Minister Ky.*

*The captured Skunk Alpha.*

To each of them, it was a very special day, a once-in-a-lifetime experience. To a man they were proud of their success. All were thankful that they had been together to experience it, miraculously with not one crewmember wounded. As the ceremony wound down with congratulations all around, they prepared for their flight back to reality, but something very significant remained behind. Visible for all to see, clearly painted in four-foot-high, yellow zinc chromate letters on the charred hull of the rapidly rusting trawler was the signature: PCF 79, Mort, Crew 74A.

## A Closing in Ed's Own Words

In the weeks that followed "our time in the sun," I was told by someone outside of the Swift Boat community that they had heard on Radio Hanoi that Hanoi Hannah (the 60s counterpart of Tokyo Rose) announced that a bounty had been placed on PCF 79 for our role in the capture of the trawler. Never hearing the broadcast myself, we shrugged it off as a combat rumor. There was too much ongoing enemy action to allow that type of distraction. The crew of PCF 79 was to find out later that the ominous Radio Hanoi meant business.

Coastal Group 16 was a Vietnamese Navy junk base with U.S. Navy advisors located about eight miles south of the Swift base inside the Sa Ky River mouth. I had been convinced that this was the eventual destination of the trawler before we intercepted it. The entire enemy area was in the shadow of the notorious Mui Batangan. Those men who served in this area before me, as well as those that followed, Navy, Marine and Army, all knew the reputation of this enemy stronghold. The place was simply "bad news." The Batangan peninsula itself was surrounded on three sides by water; the enemy was dug in with tunnels, hidden in caves and moved about freely, especially at night. The area was well manned with seasoned troops and well fortified. It was the core base of VC operations for miles around. Over the years, artillery bombardment from ships and bombs from planes had little effect in changing the ownership.

The month after the trawler capture, the Vietnamese Navy junk base was overrun by the 48th MF-VC, a well-equipped and established enemy unit. We were told by the locals that the attack was in retaliation for the recent U.S. capture of Skunk Alpha.

The attack was fierce and well coordinated with a heavily armed and overpowering enemy force approaching from multiple directions. Several Swift Boats raced to the area in response to the urgent radio messages from the junk base but regretfully they arrived near the end of the battle. With heavy .50 caliber fire from multiple boats they were able to drive the VC away from the shoreline allowing them to pick up those survivors that had made it to the safety of the river bank. Far more significant and tragic was the fact that the U.S. Navy Coastal Group Commander located at the base was killed; this marked the third such casualty in a year. Today a guided missile destroyer, the USS *Fitzgerald* DDG 62, proudly carries his name.

The weeks that followed that Vietnamese junk base attack saw a significant increase in firefights and river ambushes for Swifts as we patrolled the coast and river mouths. During this period, we continued our boat searches especially of the larger cargo junks for possible weapons smuggling and also conducted local gunfire support for the Marines along with PsyOps. The latter was a program carried out as the Swift Boat ran parallel to the coastline, usually with a loud speaker and a tape recorder. The message was delivered in Vietnamese and encouraged the VC to cross over to the other side where they would be welcomed. It was often effective but without question it was like pouring gasoline on a roaring fire to those hardcore VC and North Vietnamese regular troops that were located along the coastline.

During one of these PsyOps operations, which were always conducted at General Quarters, meaning all hands were armed and ready, we were patrolling just offshore of Co Lay. This was an area about two klicks down the beach and south of the infamous Sa Ky River. I was back aft on the fantail for a better view of the dune line with a .30 caliber machine gun which we had illegally acquired. I had fitted it to a stanchion which was part of the aft railing structure. My Bos'n Bobby Don Carver was nearby manning the single .50 caliber. One of the other crewmen was in the pilothouse driving with strict orders to run parallel to the beach using the radar to keep out of the surf line by about 200 yards.

The air cracked and snapped when the first machine-gun rounds zipped close overhead. Soon, they sounded like a swarm of angry bees attacking the boat. It was obvious to me from the rapid rate of fire that these were automatic weapons. I was also able to detect that the sound came from several different directions and this suggested multiple firing locations. Most likely each weapon was concealed in a bunker somewhere along the dune line.

Swift Boats by definition were a sitting duck target, clearly visible in situations like this. There was no place to hide, we had no armor, nothing but our own weapons to return fire combined with the boat's speed. Firefights such as these were always short and intense with the enemy just yards away.

Immediately, I felt the big hand of Carver on my shoulder pushing me down and out of the way. Often the enemy would identify the officer by our khaki uniform rather than the dungarees the crew wore. As a result, the skipper was often the first target and Carver must have realized this. I hit the deck but even prone, I was able to commence fire with the .30 caliber. In seconds our bigger .50 caliber guns came to life and I heard that deep-throated tattoo from the twin mount located forward atop the pilothouse.

As we returned fire, I could hear the enemy rounds finding their mark as they hit the hull and cabin of the boat. First a *zing,* then a mid-level *thunk* as the slug hit the quarter-inch aluminum sides. If the round came in straight it went right through the aluminum penetrating the cabin and in certain cases heading out the opposite side. If it came in at an angle it could ricochet and shatter into shrapnel and end up anywhere. Despite our significant counter fire, the enemy hits were coming fast and hard. The compass in the pilothouse shattered with a crash after taking a direct hit through the windshield, but it fortunately deflected the actual slug away from the man at the helm. I took a quick glance around while still prone on the deck. It appeared that the boat was damaged with bullet holes through the gun tub, pilothouse, cabin sides and several of the windows were shattered or blown out.

In the midst of the gunfire, I could feel from the lack of vibration that the engines beneath me for some reason had suddenly stalled. I yelled forward and we managed to quickly get them started. I stood up, grabbed the nearby aft wheel and took control at that steering station. I pushed the throttles full ahead as fast as I dared, thinking that perhaps being too aggressive might have been the reason the engines had previously stalled. This time the big Jimmie diesels held true to form; they roared to life with their distinctive sound and the boat leapt forward quickly gaining speed. I hoped the crew was holding on as I spun the wheel hard to starboard but in reality, my sole focus was getting the hell out of that ambush and fire zone.

As we were clearing the area, I did another quick visual check, once around the boat. That's when I realized that the after .50 caliber behind me had ceased firing. I immediately saw that Carver had been hit and he was down on the deck off to my right side. Our engineman ran over to him and then cradled Carver bleeding in his arms. I yelled at Bean to get on the radio and call for "Dust-Off," which was a medevac helo. I knew there was a destroyer patrolling offshore, so I headed for it full speed.

We could do first aid as we went but it was obvious to me that we needed serious help and fast. I hoped and prayed that they would have at least a medical corpsman on board who would be better equipped than we were to handle Carver's wounds. Still driving at the aft wheel, I turned and gave a quick look at my engineman who still held Carver in his arms. I saw in his eyes that frightful truth and not moving heard him say as he looked up at me, "Skipper, Skipper, Carver is gone."

This hit me hard, very hard. Instinctively, I pulled back the throttles to idle speed and had to stop for a moment, shake my head and simply try to regain my breath. My combat adrenalin was still surging and it took me almost a minute just to focus on what was going on around me. I forced myself to review what had taken place, just minutes before. We had been caught in a brutal ambush receiving heavy machine-gun fire from several locations, the boat had been hit hard and now the worst was realized. We had wounded on board; no we had casualties. We had lost one of our own.

I struggled with all my strength just to pull it together; I was the skipper, the officer-in-charge, but nothing had prepared me for this. One step at a time was all I could do. I first determined that Carver's wounds had been fatal and that there was no heartbeat. There was no need to proceed to the destroyer offshore. Next, I evaluated that there were no other serious wounds among the crew other than a few scratches, perhaps from flying glass. Our boat was sound and still seaworthy despite a multitude of holes. I radioed the base, gave them a SitRep on what had taken place and requested permission for us to leave the patrol area and return to Chu Lai.

I gathered the men on the aft deck and together we said a short prayer. We had wrapped our shipmate in one of our Navy-issue grey blankets, and ever so gently moved the body of Bos'n Bobby Don Carver below. My decision was to proceed to the base at Chu Lai at just 10 kts out of respect to our fallen brother. I knew this could only be a slow and sad ride home. We were all together, but at the same time each of us was alone holding those thoughts and memories that we would carry for a lifetime.

## CHAPTER 15

# SAMPAN RECONNAISSANCE

Two weeks had passed since our baptism by fire, when we had been ambushed, along with Killer Lou and his crew, south of Cap Batangan. This had been followed just minutes later by the machine-gun cook-off which had almost killed both Boats and me. Afterwards we had discovered that a VC sniper hidden onshore had almost nailed us while we didn't even hear his shot. Growing up was coming fast and furious to the crew of PCF 76, myself included.

Today, we were patrolling on the northern side of the Batangan peninsula, still in the Same Drink Delta sector. This area was made up of a gently curving bay a mile or two long edged in most places by a shoreline of white sand and jungle beyond. The bay offered some protection to the fisherman on both the northern and southern ends, but still had a wide opening to the Pacific Ocean on the eastern side which was almost two miles across. On the southern end were a series of small dark-colored rocky islands, none of them were more than half an acre in size or much more than fifty feet above sea level. The fisherman in their wooden sampans would move in and around these islands, where the water was calmer and I presume the fishing better due to the rocky bottom.

We were cruising slowly among the boats just showing the flag more than anything else because no one remotely suspicious was transiting in either a northerly or southerly direction. Instead, the fisherman would just drop their handheld nets, drag them for a while alongside and pull in any catch. Despite this somewhat bucolic scene, we were still patrolling at General Quarters so I had all hands on deck and fully armed. The mirror-like surface of the blue water with the bright sunny sky above could be a deadly backdrop if you let your guard down for a moment and forgot where you were. This was unquestionably still enemy territory and another sniper could be silently tracking us onshore, less than a football field away.

I was driving at my preferred position, the after helm. I heard our main radio in the pilothouse crackle to life with the clarity and volume of a message that was most likely transmitted by our Da Nang control, Article. I couldn't make out the details, but Newcomer was in the pilothouse. He leaned out the door and gave me a thumbs-up, meaning he had received the entire transmission.

Article's message stated that they had recently received local intel for our area that the Viet Cong had planted explosives in several empty sampans which they had anchored off the beach in our vicinity and control wires had been seen being rigged back to the beach. "Investigate and report," was at the close of Article's transmission.

I thought to myself, *What planet do these people live on?* We were supposed to drive up alongside the sampans, peer over the gunwale confirming their intel as the explosions inside went off.

"Article, this is Same Drink Delta we were blown up but your intel was right on!"

Boats gave me his best get-serious look and I told him to break out the M-79 grenade launcher. This was a great weapon that looked somewhat like an oversized single-shot sawed-off shotgun. It fired a 40mm grenade several hundred yards and we had two of them on board. I'm not really sure what the rationale was for their presence on a Swift Boat but today they fit the task just fine.

Using my binoculars, I confirmed that the sampans were in fact empty and anchored relatively close to shore, which in itself was suspicious. There was no way in hell that I was taking PCF 76 anywhere close to them. I told Boats to fire one round of high explosive hoping to blow a hole in the hull of the sampan, followed up by a round of white phosphorus, which would start a fire or ignite any hidden explosives. A hundred rounds fired from our big .50 calibers would have been far more efficient, but I was concerned about friendlies being nearby and worried how far the rounds might carry beyond, possibly hitting the fisherman.

Boats had just loaded the first round into the M-79 and was adjusting his aim when our short-range FM radio started to squawk. Newcomer was still in the pilothouse and I saw him reach for that radio handset. Again, I couldn't hear all the details but I could tell from the tone of the transmission that it was urgent in nature, which usually meant trouble.

Newcomer had the handset in his left hand and was rapidly writing the message down on the omnipresent pad of paper. In less than a minute, he stuck his head out of the pilothouse door, yelling back to me that the message was from the Marines onshore. They had observed a crew-served weapon (machine gun) being loaded into a sampan at map coordinates such and such. Before I could tell him to plot the coordinates he was coming aft with the chart in his hand. A quick glance at the chart told me the position in the radio message was on the other side of the peninsula directly south and opposite of our current location. Anticipating my next action, Boats broke open the breach of the M-79 and removed his first round.

As I started to push the throttles forward and head in that direction, I immediately felt the starboard engine began to drag, misfire once and then stop. By the time I turned around, Snipe had already passed his M-16 to Buck, had lifted the engine hatch open and while it was swaying on its hinges, he jumped below. We all knew that the likely culprit was bad fuel, probably contaminated with water, which would require replacing several fuel filters on that engine.

Normally, this would not have been of concern to me especially during the day in calm weather but today we were deep into bad guy territory and now we had only one engine. This gave us a top speed of 5–8 kts and we were sitting just 100 yards off the beach. A Swift Boat running on one engine goes from being a roaring and rumbling machine to something akin to a high-powered sewing machine.

Instantly, adding to my mechanical management problems, I heard a couple of high-pitched *zings* with the accompanying cracks which sounded nearby, very nearby. We were under fire, most likely from the beach. Boats had sprinted from beside me to man the after .50 caliber and yelled to Muller in the gun tub to search the shoreline for any sign of the enemy.

I yelled to the crew, "Guns tight, guns tight!" because I saw that multiple fishing boats were in our direct line of fire back to the beach.

Undoubtedly, the enemy was aware of this situation, but they simply fired at us, shooting through the fisherman, fully knowing that we would not return fire with civilians in between. The VC standards of operation were somewhat different than from those of the U.S. forces. Collateral damage for them was not a consideration.

All this time, I was moving the port engine throttle forward, but the result in terms of decreased speed was not a drop of 50 percent but closer to 90 percent. Hearing me increase speed, Snipe poked his head up through the hatch, wondering what was going on. I yelled, "Fix the fucking fuel filters; we're taking fire from the beach."

I swung the wheel hard to starboard, intent on opening our distance from the beach and at the same time presenting our stern as the smallest target silhouette to the enemy. We were sitting ducks, our butts to the enemy, out in the open for full minute or more making a rip-roaring 7 kts, not even fast enough to leave any white water behind. I heard the snap of several more enemy rounds going overhead but saw no splashes in the water and heard no hits on the boat.

In another minute or two, Snipe had completed his magic and the starboard engine roared to life. I saw an arm appear from below giving me the hand motion to push the throttle full open. Seconds later, we had cleared the area and now we had to figure out what the hell was going on.

Anchored sampans possibly filled with explosives, machine-gun fire from the shore with a Marine Corps report of enemy action on the southern side of the peninsula. All these pieces didn't fit together. Having some prior navigation experience, I believe I had the answer.

When you are a plotting a position relative to yourself, it is possible to calculate the direction backwards or 180° off in the wrong direction. As a result, the Marines' reported position of enemy activity was indeed on a straight line from them, but they calculated it on their map to be on the opposite side of Cap Batangan from where we had just received fire. Hey, the Marines were great fighters, not navigators.

Enough with the mathematical analysis. I got on the radio and reported to Article and all units that we were taking enemy fire from the shore nearby at a position north of Cap Batangan, most likely from a heavy machine gun. I transmitted the message in the clear, without encryption knowing the enemy was well aware of what activities were going on.

Same Drink Echo and Same Drink Charlie, as expected, immediately responded, "Under way your location, ETA figures 15 to 20."

The local Coast Guard unit was offshore and responded in a similar fashion. I knew that when the cavalry arrived, three units would provide plenty of firepower in support.

Meanwhile, the VC on shore had without question gotten my attention. If I waited until reinforcements arrived, most likely they would have packed up their weapons and departed the area. Normally in a situation like this, we would initiate a high-speed run directly at the enemy position presenting a small bow on target, while firing the twin .50s fully loaded; each gun pumping out several hundred rounds per minute. Then we would quickly swing broadside to the target with all three .50s firing at the target along with our small arms. Lastly, we would turn a rapid 90° departing the area still at full speed, our stern to the enemy with the after .50 caliber continuing to fire. This much red hot lead usually meant the enemy would end up holding the losing ticket or at a minimum stop firing and keep their heads down.

Unfortunately, today that tactic was not going to work for several reasons. There would be no element of surprise, the area had several small rocky islands scattered across our approach, and most likely there were other rocks lurking just below the surface. Also, I could see that the fishing sampans, for some unknown reason, had not completely cleared the area and would block any high-speed attack and departure.

It occurred to me that while the islands presented a risk to any high-speed approach, they might be a solution in terms of coverage for us. If we came in slowly, keeping the islands between us and the enemy's last known location we would be less of a direct target. Always the tactician, I had another brilliant idea that included launching our own sampan, paddling to a nearby island where with binoculars I could do an accurate recon of the beach line assessing the enemy strength. Perhaps, there was a slight trace of General George Patton in my genetic makeup. Correspondingly, others might see my plan in a less favorable light.

One quick look at Boats and there was no question he felt the skipper had finally lost his mind. The other troops were younger and still thought most of my decisions were brilliant. We stopped PCF 76 about 100 yards off the largest island, which in turn was about 200 yards off the beach. Boats and I lowered the sampan, all 12 feet of its bamboo-woven hull. Snipe was at the after helm and I could see his hands locked onto the throttles ready for action. Muller was in the gun tub, scanning the shoreline with binoculars, Buck and Newcomer were manning the after .50. Buck, weighing in at a massive 140 pounds, was sighting down the barrel as Newcomer held up the belt of ammunition across his forearms providing a level and smooth feed into the breach of the gun. No one at the guns had yet marked his twenty-first birthday.

Sitting amidships in the sampan, I stabilized it as best I could adjusting my 200-plus pounds. Accompanying me was an M-16, my trusty .357 Magnum, a set of Bausch & Lomb Navy-issue binoculars and three grenades that Boats insisted I bring with me. No baloney sandwiches with traditional yellow mustard were on board because it was going to be a short reconnaissance. Boats' grenades were a nice touch, but they were something called thermite grenades that were used to melt things rather than blow them up. If the boat was sinking you could destroy the machine guns and the engines because these grenades burned at some absurd temperature and would melt and fuse the metal denying it to the enemy.

In terms of any encounter with enemy troops, I guess Boats felt that the hissing, smoking and brilliant white light of these grenades would basically scare the shit out of them. More realistically, anyone observing this entire procedure could only conclude that my attendance at an Ivy League school was the result of a significant admissions error.

Paddling slowly, I turned toward the island, helmet on, head down, flak vest snugly zipped. No more than halfway to the island, I heard that familiar but unfriendly *zing* and snap of bullet rounds passing overhead. I

*After the VC firefight, fishermen rescue their families.*

*More fisherman near Batangan.*

had been told that the sound is the bullet breaking the sound barrier. To my horror, I realized, the firing was coming from behind me, from my own troops. Fortunately, there was no burst of .50 caliber fire from the boat, but instead Boats had an M–16 shoulder high and was accurately firing in short bursts by me toward the beach. He bellowed at me in no uncertain terms,

"Skipper, get your head down and get the hell out of there. They're firing from the beach."

I understood that riding this low in the water, I was a tough target for the enemy to hit, but with a machine gun enough lead coming your way could reduce those favorable odds. Significantly, picking up my paddling pace, I made for the island now no more than 100 feet ahead. Hitting the rocky shoreline, I awkwardly rolled to my right out of the sampan onto the wet stones. Then crouching low, I crawled to some very welcome cover that was provided by larger rocks beyond.

With me out of the line of fire, Boats had now replaced the more accurate M–16 with the after .50 caliber and started to hose down the shoreline beyond my position. There were no fishermen nearby and I could see his big rounds clearly walking across the water then sweeping left and right, as they churned up the sandy beach into small clouds of dust. The .50 caliber machine gun was a weapon which could tear up the pea patch in short order but also was very effective in keeping the enemy in a heads down position. At the moment, either one worked for me.

In a crabbing position, I began to move slowly towards the center of the small island which was no more than a pile of rocks about thirty feet high. Suddenly, somewhere directly ahead of me, I could hear voices but saw no one. I soon realized that I was now at the rocky edge of a cave mouth about twenty feet wide and the noise was coming from within. After a quick assessment of my equipment, I determined that the binoculars at the moment were of little use, so I left them on the sand, which was probably a court martial offense. The M–16 would necessitate my charging into the cave mouth, not the best idea, so I slung that over my shoulder. The grenades if tossed into the cave might provide an element of surprise working to my distinct advantage.

*Marine and medevac rescue helos.*

It did occur to me that I had absolutely no training for this type of mission other than being a James Bond fan. At the time, I took no solace whatsoever knowing that other Swift Boat crews had engaged in similar foolhardy recons such as this—my friends Ed Bergin and Killer Lou to be specific.

Blood pressure up, cardiac rate climbing, I moved slowly in the crouched position away from my rocky cover rotating towards the darkened cave entrance now only a few feet away. A grenade canister was in my right hand, my left index finger hooked onto the pin, ready to pull. The voices inside the cave continued, apparently unaware of my approach, but now I heard shouts from another direction out across the water. Two fishing sampans were rapidly closing the island with men on board in black pajamas and straw hats waving, shouting and pointing at me.

I could see no visible weapons on board the approaching sampans and for whatever reason Boats had stopped his firing from PCF 76. I put the grenades down on the sand and lowered myself behind a nearby rock

*Coast Guard WPBs back in Da Nang.*

about three feet high, which provided me some cover. The M-16 had been strapped over my shoulder, so I brought that down into a firing position and flipped off the safety. I was hoping for the best but prepared for the worst. The fisherman continued to approach my position still yelling and waving their arms. In short order, their boats came ashore and they jumped out. Four of them started to run towards me but had their hands held high in a surrender position, clearly without weapons.

They stopped about thirty feet in front of me and pointed to the mouth of the cave, calling to someone inside. Even if I was able to understand some basic Vietnamese, I am sure their dialect was local and therefore incomprehensible to me. My decision was to hold tight, maintain my marginal position of cover while crouched behind the rock, keeping the M-16 on fully automatic with my finger on the trigger. In short order, this situation had to resolve itself in some fashion, either for me or against me.

In seconds, out of the cave came ten to twelve people; they were all women and children bunched close together. The fisherman had left their families on the island, and when the VC started firing at us, they hid in the cave for safety. I lowered my weapon but slipped my finger on to the trigger guard just in case. At the same time, I had to stop and as best I could take in three very deep breaths to fully comprehend just how close to a deadly tragedy all of us had come.

Behind me, I heard the rumble of PCF 76 as Boats approached the island with all guns directed portside aimed at the sandy beach beyond us. Seeing his arrival, the fishermen, without hesitation, loaded their families into their boats, at the same time rapidly pointing so that I knew they were going to the other side of the bay, which hopefully would be a safe haven for them. After a few quick bows between us, they made a hasty departure, for which I certainly couldn't blame them.

With 76 nearby, my return trip was a quick one. I climbed on board while Snipe and Newcomer lifted the sampan onto the stern.

Reinforcements had arrived. Lord Mort and his crew at General Quarters were making a high-speed approach, white water cascading off either side of the bow. We proceeded about 500 yards off the beach

*Another long day.*

and Ed came alongside and hopped on board 76 for an update. Our boats maneuvered broadside to the shoreline with more than enough firepower at the ready to discourage any suicidal action by the VC unless they had a very big cannon hidden nearby onshore.

Ed informed me that the situation was a complex one and had deteriorated more than I realized. The VC had shot through the fishing fleet, injuring several fishermen. The Coast Guard carried a 13-foot Boston whaler on their larger WPB, which they had launched and were rapidly going from boat to boat rendering first aid. Two badly wounded fishermen, one a young girl, had been transported to the third Swift Boat on the scene.

They had radioed for a Marine medevac helo, call sign "Dust Off," which was just approaching the third boat, located about a quarter mile north of our current position. Ed and I watched in amazement as the Huey helicopter approached the stern of the Swift Boat with its tail down and nose up as its rotors generated a surrounding blanket of saltwater mist. No more than four feet off the deck, it slowly, delicately, put the front end of its two landing runners on the Swift Boat's large ammunition magazine located at the stern. If the small high-speed vertical tail rotor even touched the water below, it would spin the aircraft out of control smashing it into the Swift Boat killing everyone. Not exactly the traditional landing pad but then again, these Dust Off pilots were the best and knew no fear. I found out later that helicopter's main large horizontal rotor blades had taken the radio antenna off the Swift Boat but fortunately had missed the more rigid radar mast, thereby avoiding a disaster.

The two wounded civilians were somehow lifted from the Swift into the open cockpit door of the balancing chopper. The racket from the whirling helicopter blades made all communications impossible and the airborne spray only added to the challenge. Sadly, despite all this teamwork, risk and heroic efforts by many, we learned later that the young girl, just a teenager, did not survive her wounds. Once again, another long sad day recorded in our logbooks.

CHAPTER 16

# HOMEMADE EXPLOSIVES

As we debriefed from a patrol two days later, I saw on the watch list that we were assigned the next day to once again patrol Same Drink Delta. Our recent encounter at Cap Batangan and all the deadly carnage carried out by the well-armed VC was really grating on me.

I met Boats for an afternoon cup of coffee on our day off and outlined another wacky idea I had conceived. Perhaps just being around Ed Bergin, who in the combat area was Mr. Creative, was starting to rub off on me. Gradually, on board his own boat PCF 79, Ed was building an unauthorized cache of additional weapons such as a recoilless rifle and various other non-nuclear armaments.

That day, my plan was somewhat more exotic. It involved planting explosives in a cave we all had observed nestled low in the rocky shoreline that opened to the northeast at the most seaward point of Cap Batangan. Many of the boat skippers felt the cave was being used by the enemy for the safe and hidden storage of weapons and munitions they could move in and out at will, transporting them in small sampans, thereby avoiding any suspicion.

A cornerstone of my plan was the fact that rounds of our 81mm mortar ammunition were shipped in a package constructed of heavy Styrofoam that provided both strength and safety insulation. My vision was to open the crate, utilize only the bottom half and surround the separate two mortar rounds with a pool of diesel fuel. Because the Styrofoam was light and waterproof, it could also be used to float the rounds into the cave. Then, we would ignite the diesel fuel with a flare from our signal gun fired from a safe distance outside the enemy cave. The mortar rounds would then cook-off, generating a decent-sized explosion in a confined space.

I could see from his querulous expression that Boats had some initial concerns, but I knew he was from Texas, liked guns and ammunition and was really getting into anything related to clandestine operations. He did, however, ask the pivotal question, "Skipper, how are we going to get the Styrofoam floats from 76 to the cave mouth?"

My answer was simple. I would paddle the distance in the *Captain's Gig*, our trusty bamboo sampan. This component of the mission took a little more reflection time on Boats' part, but he soon signed up to the plan and he, in turn, would sell it to the troops.

In Swift Boats the acquisition of ammunition, which we expended on a regular basis, was never a problem. The plan called for six mortar rounds, which meant three floats. We found a metal gas can on the Chu Lai pier and filled it with diesel fuel. We felt diesel was far safer than

*Cap Batangan viewed from a Cat Killer flight.*

gasoline, which would most likely explode way ahead of schedule. Our preparations completed, we loaded this sophisticated weapons system aboard PCF 76, which was fueled, armed and ready to depart the next morning at 0700 for a thirty-hour patrol.

The day's patrol was relatively uneventful and around 0300 we had all hands on deck to commence "Operation Cave." We had complete darkness, without moon and stars, and the weather was cooperating, at least so far. At this early hour, we calculated that the nighttime fishermen in the area had returned to shore and the early morning fishermen would not arrive until daybreak.

We maneuvered PCF 76 approximately 200 yards off the jagged mouth of the cave, which we could barely make out in the darkness ahead. We knew it opened in a northeast direction so our compass was some help. The seaward tip of Batangan itself was a flat and barren plain that dropped approximately fifty feet to the rocky water's edge below where the cave was located. Having flown over it on several occasions, I knew it was a desolate area. Therefore, we concluded that it was unlikely that any Viet Cong lived nearby or that troops would be patrolling it on a regular basis. Of course, this conclusion was based on our own "wing it" self-generated intel report.

We cut the big diesel engines along with our raucous and spitfire electrical generator. I was reluctant to do this in case we needed a rapid departure but realistically, even with the engines at idle, a Swift Boat generated a rumbling racket. On the safe side, we knew all of our guns could still fire without any external power. Now in eerie silence, we could listen for any sounds while we slowly scanned the area with binoculars searching both onshore and on the water for the slightest movement whatsoever. Tonight the weather was on our side, the seas were flat calm and there was little if any wind or tidal drift.

We decided to keep the radar on because it was powered by the boat's batteries and it might provide us an early warning of any approaching vessel, friendly or otherwise. The antenna did however make a whirring sound as it rotated, but we felt this could not be heard on shore. We shut off both radios, eliminating any possibility of an unexpected message blasting through the quiet night. Noise from a radio would quickly carry clearly inland, without any waves or wind to break up the sound along the way.

At 0330, after we completed our visual and electronic surveillance, we launched the sampan and I climbed aboard. Lowering the three floats and six mortar rounds had to be done slowly and carefully. Each had been fused beforehand because it enhanced their potential to explode in the burning diesel fuel. Once they were on board, I slowly poured the diesel from the can around each round. This was relatively straightforward since they were laid out side by side in the contoured Styrofoam containers. Next, Boats passed me the signal pistol, which was empty because it had no safety, along with five rounds of star shell ammunition.

I was wearing my .357 Magnum in its shoulder holster but this was mostly for psychological support. There would be no firefight with me sitting snugly between our homemade bombs. Loading complete, I shoved off after a casual salute from Boats as the rest of the crew manned the rail looking on in horror or admiration. It was difficult to tell which in the darkness.

Paddling slowly, my only choice in this craft, I estimated it would take me twenty minutes or more to reach the cave, and then I would slowly float the explosives inside. I figured if they remained near the mouth of the cave that would be satisfactory because an explosion in any confined area was usually quite effective. Also hitting any of the floats with the flare gun would be a lot easier at the entrance than if they were deeper inside the cave. My intent was to fire from a position set back from the side of the cave opening. I wanted to be nowhere near the mouth, where the explosion, rolling fireball and subsequent shockwave would most likely terminate my short but illustrious Navy career. Any knowledge of our clandestine mission (Operation Cave) among the more senior naval bureaucracy would probably have the same career result.

Stroke by stroke, making hardly a ripple in the water, my target drew closer. Despite the darkness, I could just begin to see the outline of the cave ahead. Kneeling amidships on the bottom of the sampan (there were no seats), I began to feel some sloshing and liquid along my legs. My first reaction was that I was sinking, but I soon eliminated that theory as the pungent smell of diesel fuel rose to my nostrils. I knew that I had left the fuel can on board 76 and during my brief journey there had been no significant odor from the fuel that was surrounding the mortar rounds in the Styrofoam floats. I had carefully placed them several feet away in the bow and stern of the sampan.

Without question, I now had some sort of an operational problem and I needed answers fast. Leaning forward, I was able to slowly reach out and grasp one of the floats moving it carefully back to my location where I could examine it more carefully. One does not move rapidly in a twelve-foot long sampan made of bamboo bark while riding no more than ten inches above the surface of the water. My size only added to my craft's instability factor.

To my horror, I immediately saw the source of the problem. The diesel fuel had eaten the thinner ends of the Styrofoam float and it was now pouring out into the bottom of the sampan around my legs. At that moment, I realized that I should have taken Chemistry 101, instead of that Fine Arts course with all the cute coeds.

Here I was, in our crappy little sampan, awash in diesel fuel, surrounded by explosives while drifting several yards away from a darkened cave mouth that we suspected was a weapons/ammunition storage site. All located well within enemy territory. Anyone with a gun who happened to look down from the overhanging ledges and see me would have a very easy target directly below.

Adding to my plight, I noticed that the horizon behind me was just starting to brighten and in less than thirty minutes the glow of sunrise would start to be a very real problem. It would also reveal that PCF 76 was sitting idle, dead in the water about 150 yards from my position. I was not a big-time card player but had enough experience that I knew "when to hold 'em and when to fold 'em." The latter got the nod and within seconds, I executed Plan Bravo, which included "Get the hell out of here and *Fast!*

Slowly, but without any hesitation, I lowered each mortar round over the side into the water letting it sink to the bottom. Obviously, none of them exploded. Next, I decided to keep the white Styrofoam floats on board lest they drift away, possibly being spotted from shore and

*Leaving the cave at sunrise.*

thereby generating an unwelcome interest on the part of the enemy. By now all the diesel fuel had basically flowed out of the containers to my amidships position. It was only a couple of gallons but not something I was anxious to kneel in during my return trip. The only solution available was cup my hands together and bail like hell. Within a minute or two, most of the liquid was gone and I would have to live (I hoped) with the remaining diesel fumes.

The entire unloading procedure, both mortar rounds and fuel had taken over ten minutes and the new day arriving was not going to be my friend. Grabbing my single paddle, I turned the bow smartly toward safety then bent forward and leaned into the stroke. Speed clearly overrode form; besides, rowing on the Charles River in Cambridge was never a sport I totally understood. As I approached PCF 76, I realized that the engines were still silent. This was a smart decision on the part of Boats, thereby avoiding detection as long as we could. Once again, I was thankful for the competence of my crew.

Coming alongside, I tossed a bowline to Boats. In one awkward motion, I stood up in the sampan (before it sank), immediately grabbed the gunwale of 76 and clawed my way on board. Snipe retrieved the stern line and the two of them with very little ceremony dragged the sampan on board. Boats pointed to Newcomer, who was already hanging out the pilothouse door, and with his two hands, gave him a rolling "start-up" signal. Forward was the only location where you could fire up the engines, other than on an emergency basis in the engine room. Starboard, then port roared to life, each engine starting with their rumbling roll. This morning it was the sound of a symphony to me.

Boats had moved to the aft helm and looking over at me, with his twirling index finger, he made the "wind 'em up" motion. I responded with a hearty thumbs-up. We all knew that we had overstayed our welcome at this garden party and it was definitely time to move on.

I could feel the big screws underneath us digging in and the bow starting to lift as we gained speed. I looked astern and saw that we were

*Time to get out of Dodge.*

building our signature large and frothy white wake. In this case, it clearly marked our high-speed departure from bad guy territory.

As we proceeded to sea and were almost a mile off the peninsula, it occurred to me that not one word had been spoken during the entire evolution. Everyone knew what to do and simply did their job. No superstars, just a seasoned combat crew all working together and this made me proud.

In a moment Buck appeared with two steaming mugs of black coffee. The second, I assumed was for Boats, delivered as usual in automatic. Taking mine first, I said to Boats, "Give me a couple of quick sips, then slow the boat down and I will update the crew."

Quick sips indeed, because I knew Boats wanted the full story as would the entire crew and they deserved it. Pulling back the throttles, in his mellifluous tone, Boats yelled, "Everybody aft, Skipper wants to talk to us."

Knowing that they could not have seen what was going on near the cave, even using binoculars because of the darkness, I gave them all the details of our scrubbed mission. My ignorance of the chemical reaction between diesel fuel and Styrofoam was readily admitted, but paled compared to my graphic description of sitting in diesel fuel, surrounded by high explosives. That picture was a winner!

As I finished their briefing, I strongly suggested that it would be wise if we kept the outcomes of this clandestine mission just within our crew, lest we be sent on some sort of medical leave, most likely not at an R&R venue. I continued that as a result of this mission, I more fully appreciated the value of our frogman friends (Underwater Demolition Teams) and their bomb-making capabilities. Unfortunately for us, during this operation, they had been residing at the base back in Da Nang. However, their high-explosive skills would absolutely be a factor in the planning and execution of any future sampan operations.

## CHAPTER 17

# THE VILLAGE ROUNDUP

The "Same Drink Charlie" patrol was the northernmost sector out of Chu Lai and it covered the areas north and south of the Swift base, a distance of about ten miles. The length of any patrol area wasn't the problem; it was the time and distance travelled to get on station, especially in bad weather. Two or three hours battling seas that could often be well above six feet, constantly working the wheel and the throttles, made for a very long day. On this day however, we exited the river mouth and there we were on station.

We had just turned around at our southern patrol boundary, which encompassed the notorious Cap Batangan. We were heading north at about 10 kts, running 500 yards off the beach.

Normal inspections were being conducted of junk traffic and local fishermen, but we expected nothing out of the ordinary. The weather was perfect, no wind, flat seas and a cloudless blue sky above. We had been under way since 0700 and by 1000 the temperature was climbing towards 90°. Shorts and t-shirts became the uniform of the day, along with shades and ball caps.

On patrol, standard procedure was to look very carefully at any larger vessel with a cabin or below-deck storage. We were at General Quarters because we were alongside a sixty-foot wooden cargo junk transiting south along the coast from Hue. The manifest said they had a full cargo of the aromatic and overpowering Vietnamese fish sauce *nuoc nam*. The Vietnamese put this delicacy on almost everything they ate. I personally had trouble just getting by its method of manufacturing which was fermenting fish, along with the subsequent odor that reflected the production process. It was transported in five-gallon tin drums that were usually stacked four or five high in the cargo hold.

It was my theory that if you're going to smuggle weapons, what better cover than a cargo that was likely to shorten the inspection process, while instilling nausea at the same time. Being a true leader, I assigned Boats to carry out this inspection as part of his training and development. He, in turn, brought along our resident chef and engineer, Snipe. This process could best be described as "misery likes company" and "rank has its privileges."

Not to be outdone, I remained on board as part of the backup team to provide topside coverage. Frankly, with three people armed with M-16s and a fourth sitting between two .50 caliber machine guns all pointing at you, it was doubtful that a potential enemy would find this an appropriate time for a shootout. Regardless of our firepower, there was always a risk that the suicide toss of a hand grenade could quickly level the playing field. It had been done before. Bottom line, on PCF 76 standard operating procedure was to rule on the side of caution, which was why even Boats and Snipe carried pistols onboard, although they were holstered during the inspection. There had been one tragedy, well before our arrival in-country, of someone on a Swift Boat conducting an inspection and accidentally tripping and firing his drawn handgun, killing an innocent civilian. Therefore, primary coverage was provided by the crew located aboard the Swift Boat.

From my vantage point, standing by the pilothouse door, our dynamic duo seemed to be enjoying themselves while conducting the inspection. I did detect a slight look of frustration on the face of Boats as he reappeared, climbing out of the cargo hold gasping for a breath of fresh air. Snipe was slower to emerge; my guess was that he had been below exchanging recipes.

Boats stepped from the rail of the junk back onto PCF 76 passing me the cargo manifests. Reviewing these documents for legitimacy was hardly an exact science, primarily because they were written in Vietnamese. We could usually recognize point of origin, trip destination, and do a rough estimate of cargo capacity and verify registration numbers on the vessel itself. A little eyeball-to-eyeball assessment with the captain and crew was often more telling than their respective IDs. Their nonstop smoking was never an indication of nervousness. Any individual moving away from the main group, which we usually gathered together on deck, could be suspicious. A person remaining below was never acceptable.

At this point, the operation appeared normal. I could read the better part of the manifest. It appeared legitimate, so Boats returned the paperwork to the junk captain and thanked him for his time. The captain saluted as they pulled away, which was not uncommon and we returned it in kind, albeit not quite Navy crisp.

We resumed patrol, remaining about 500 yards off the beach as we continued north. At this distance offshore, we still kept weapons near at hand, all loaded with safeties on. This was territory that could completely change from friendly to enemy in twenty-four hours or less. I remained outside, my back against the pilothouse for stability, using my binoculars to provide one more set of eyes to scan the beach. Muller was in the gun tub above me with another set of binoculars scanning the beach and coastline for other sampans or cargo junks. Buck had climbed up on the roof of the pilothouse to join him. Newcomer was at the wheel behind me and I could see Boats and Snipe sitting aft, quite comfortable in the folding deck chairs we had purchased from a cargo junk several weeks before.

The secondary FM radio, assigned to the Marine Corps frequencies, burst to life with Tiger Five calling us as Same Drink Charlie. The fact that they knew our specific call sign meant they were familiar with the Swift Boats' operations plan. I recognized Tiger Five as one of the small Marine CAP units that often were assigned to protect small Vietnamese villages from enemy VC attack.

CAP stood for Civilian Action Patrol and usually they were composed of five or six men led by an experienced E5 sergeant. They often operated independently, in or nearby a village, without the support of any larger unit. It could be dangerous duty, so we tried to assist them in any way we could. This might be providing gunfire support or even extraction off the beach if the going got really rough.

Today, Tiger Five informed us that the village in which they had been living and operating was going to be shelled by the South Koreans (the ROKs). Despite the fact that they were our allies and in theory, we were all in this together, they had some very different operating standards. This piece of real estate was in the ROK- assigned sector of operations and they had recently taken enemy fire and some casualties from the vicinity of the village. In response, their solution usually was a scorched-earth, take-no-prisoners policy.

Tiger Five was a little more knowledgeable about to the good guy/bad guy ratio in the village and felt the announced action of the ROKs did not pass the smell test in the morals and ethics category. This mattered little to the ROKs, especially at the senior decision-maker level.

Tiger asked if we could assist with evacuation of the village prior to the artillery attack which would most likely indiscriminately kill many of the inhabitants—women and children included. I gave Tiger a "Wait, out" because this procedure was definitely not in our operations manual.

I thought briefly about the advisability of getting some sort of clearance beforehand from our control, Article. However, this would probably require a multi-level review, which most likely would be approved just as the smoke and dust were clearing after the ROK artillery attack. Regretful, but that's how bureaucracies sometimes worked even in a war zone. The fact that this situation involved two allies Koreans and Vietnamese made it political and more complex.

An evacuation would involve closing our distance to the beach or even putting the boat in the shallows, neither one the best move in disputed territory. Briefly discussing this with the crew, we all agreed that we could not stand by and allow this carnage to take place. Expecting a heavy artillery barrage, it would be unlikely that Tiger Five could evacuate enough of the village by land in time.

"Tiger Five, this is Same Drink Charlie, interrogative, what assistance can you provide this unit during evacuation, over?"

"Charlie, this is Tiger," I detected a sense of urgency over the radio. "We can provide assistance with the loading of civilians into small boats that are located nearby. Be advised times a'wastin'."

Looking quickly around the boat and seeing my troops with all eyes locked on the skipper, I knew what they were thinking. I made the decision.

"Tiger, this is Charlie, we will assist, require ten minutes of preparation and will approach your location directly. Request you acquire small boats and prepare loading."

Tiger most likely understood that we were going to approach the beach but could not land in a boat that drew almost five feet of water because of its propellers and extended rudders. I considered the possibility of pointing the bow of the boat toward the beach and laying our anchor in deep water off the stern so that we could use it to pull us back out if we grounded. While this looked good on paper, the bottom line was we simply couldn't take the chance of being grounded in possible enemy territory. Any bow to the beach position would also mean that all our weapons could not be brought to bear on an enemy target, a very basic bad move.

It occurred to me that tied up on our after deck was the *Captain's Gig*, our 12-foot sampan made of bullet-proof bamboo strips. The seas were calm and with some careful positioning Boats and I could paddle ashore with PCF 76 idling in deeper water fifty yards away. My assessment was that if we ran into trouble onshore the rest of the crew could maneuver 76 unobstructed and provide us with significant fire support. The bureaucratic flipside was if they court-martialed somebody, it would be me and I could say that I ordered Boats to accompany me.

Snipe in terms of seniority was a second class petty officer, next in line and had proven his competence, so I put him in charge. I also had complete faith in Newcomer, Muller and Buck to support him and us if the going got rough. In the back of my mind, there was always that Swift Boat fallback position, which was swim like hell for the horizon.

Just to make sure, I called for backup, knowing that Ed Bergin was in the next area south, probably no more than ten miles away.

"Lord Mort, this is Megaphone Bravo. Request your assistance ASAP. I am two klicks north of Donald Duck. We are not under fire. I repeat, we are not under fire, over."

"Megaphone, this is Mort. Understand urgent but not under fire, is that Charlie, over."

"Mort, this is Megaphone. That's a Charlie on your last. We are working with Tiger Five and need backup."

"Megaphone, this is Mort. Roger your last, my ETA figures 20, out." At 30 kts, this put Eddie at the southern end of the Delta sector, twenty minutes would be fine providing some VC or NVA bad guys were not already dug in and waiting nearby for us somewhere in the dunes.

These radio transmissions took under two minutes and clearly showed how important and useful our own encryption system was, utilizing both our personal call signs and Disneyland names for locations. Also, Ed was a pro, with a top-notch crew, sadly now without Bos'n Bobby Don Carver, but I knew we could still count on PCF 79 providing fire cover if needed.

With Snipe in charge, Boats and I headed aft to launch the gig. It weighed less than fifty pounds, so the greater challenge was maintaining stability alongside as we slowly climbed over the rail of PCF 76. This was a homemade craft that was designed to hold two small Vietnamese fishermen, each weighing no more than 110 pounds. We maxed those load guidelines by a factor of two. Each of us brought along an M-16 just in case. Boats, as usual, had his trusty K-bar knife strapped to his belt in the unlikely event of any enemy hand-to-hand combat. In contrast, my main concern was if we sank in transit—the paperwork explaining this mission would be beyond belief.

Realistically, the greatest danger remained the ticking clock and the fast-approaching artillery barrage from our allies, the indiscriminate ROKs.

As instructed, Snipe had swung the boat port side to the beach with the three .50 calibers manned with everyone in flak gear and helmets with a scattering of other weapons nearby. This presentation was as much for show to a potential enemy as anything. In a firefight, I was not sure how our crew was going to avoid shooting us except for the fact that in the sampan we now had a target profile of only about twenty-four inches above the water. We commenced paddling aggressively toward shore using two sawed-off wooden oars that Boats had acquired somewhere in Da Nang.

Fortunately for us, as the bottom of our trusty craft gently touched the sandy beach below, there was absolutely no surf, which most likely would have rolled us over in short order. The two of us stepped smartly ashore, shoeless with rolled-up pant legs and not overly concerned about the image we presented to our Marine Corps friends.

Looking up the beach to my right was a scene straight out of some poorly cast Hollywood movie. Women and old men were walking up the beach toward our position carrying children, animals and all types of personal possessions. Most were dressed in the traditional peasant garb of black pajamas, top and bottom and on their heads the pointed straw hats. They were either barefoot or wore "Ho Chi Minh" rubber sandals, some of which were made of used tire treads.

In stark contrast, walking alongside them were six young Marines complete with full combat gear, helmets, flak vests, and weapons at the ready. All the while, they were continually scanning the sand dunes above and to their right for any sign of suspicious activity. In the shallow water nearby, heading our way, were six or eight wooden sampans, each about twenty to twenty-five feet long. The sunburnt and gnarled fishermen worked furiously as they focused only on saving their families from the deadly barrage they knew was soon to come.

Everyone reached our location at approximately the same time and almost automatically started to load the sampans. Four of the Marines, which I assumed were all part of Tiger Five, spread out and formed a semicircle back to the water providing a perimeter defense. The other two, including the sergeant in charge, helped with the loading. Introducing myself and Boats, I learned he was Conrad Hutchison from the hills of Tennessee. Understandably, he was called "Hutch." He had at least an inch on me and 30 pounds, none of which was fat. The villagers knew him and quickly followed his instructions, making the evacuation simpler and faster.

Women and children were first, grandparents second, animals third and able-bodied men were last. I soon saw that the loading procedure with the sampans resting onshore was going to present a problem when trying to get them afloat with all that additional weight on board. I pointed this out to Hutch, who promptly directed the fishermen to

*Village extraction, loading complete.*

hold the sampans offshore in two or three feet of water to avoid any grounding.

This was the correct move, but it changed the loading procedure from walk-on to carry-on. I did grandparents, children walked or ran, while Boats carried small animals, specifically chickens and pigs. The first were usually carried in straw baskets. I yelled to Boats that this scene was definitely material for a top-notch U.S. Navy recruiting poster. I was a firm believer in a little humor being used to lower the stress level, which was definitely present and growing.

Hutch and his sidekick maintained order on the beach and kept everyone moving. Any delay resulted in an instant pickup and into the sampan by Hutch, now up to his knees in the water. I knew the sand and saltwater would make for a crunchy tomorrow in his jungle boots, but they could be rinsed out and, by design, dried quickly. Besides these guys were Marines, as they were prone to remind their Navy brothers on a regular basis.

I gave a quick look to check on the status of PCF 76, ensuring the crew remained at General Quarters. There was no worry. Snipe was at the aft helm frequently scanning the beach with binoculars for any sign of trouble.

Approaching from the south at 30 kts, with a wide-open throttle generating a curling wave of white water at the bow, came Lord Mort and the crew of PCF 79, all guns manned and ready. Trumpets were missing from his arrival but the rest of the picture was complete and was not lost on the Marines. Even under demanding circumstances, maintaining style was still important.

This is what it was all about, teamwork, everybody knowing and doing their job. Looking around at the chaos, as ridiculous as the picture appeared, I was proud to be part of it. Besides, the grandparents each gave us a toothy smile as we carried them to the boats, albeit with stained teeth from their constant chewing of betel nuts. At the time, Harvard Yard seemed a long distance away.

*No one gets left behind.*

U.S. Navy Bos'n Mate Fielder, not to be outdone in the leadership area by U.S. Marine Sergeant Hutchinson, now took charge of the loaded boats and tied them in a line, bow to stern, ready for towing. I recognized that getting this wagon train secured to our boat would be a challenge but I had some ideas.

One of Hutch's troops had a radio backpack which I requested and made a call to our boat, hoping that Newcomer would hear my call. I was not disappointed. Knowing he would relay my message to Snipe, I wanted them to slowly close the beach, bow in. I told them to rig a light line they could throw to us with a longer heavier nylon towing line tied to it. During this maneuver, the risk was that the boat would hit bottom or just as bad, foul the lines in the propellers as they maneuvered. This is where cross-training came into play; all of them had basic seamanship skills that would now be required. Hutch told his Marines to move closer to the dune line to provide for faster response and better cover for all of us in case the enemy was watching our loading maneuver. At this time, we presented a much better target all bunched together tied in a line.

As Snipe slowly closed the beach at idle speed, Buck and Muller were on the bow handling the lines. Newcomer remained in the pilothouse monitoring the radios and watching the depth finder. Doing the latter was more a feel-good exercise because we knew the bottom, although sandy, was just a foot or two below the screws. As expected, Ed brought PCF 79 in close off the stern of 76, maintaining a clear line of fire to the shore. I also saw his crew breaking out their towline for a fast response if PCF 76 did go aground. No yelling, just an order or two, perhaps a nod of the head, everyone doing their job as trained.

We got the lead line and Boats and I hauled in the heavier tow line. The trick was for Snipe to twist the bow of the boat back out away from the beach without fouling the lines. No easy task with 150 feet of one-inch nylon line floating or just below the surface while the big screws rotated slowly nearby, ready to wrap around and entangle the long towline. Buck and Muller carefully guided the towline from the bow to the stern, making sure it did not go under the boat.

Now, Boats untied the light line and taking the end of the heavier towline, he immediately tied a bowline knot to the lead sampan

*The not-so-innocent get better seats.*

and gave a thumbs-up to Snipe. He acknowledged the signal and continued his slow twist away from the beach as the slack gradually went out of the towline. I radioed for 76 to proceed offshore at idle speed as we pushed each of the sampans away from the beach into a line formation.

As Boats and I prepared to paddle out in the *Captain's Gig*, I asked if Hutch and his troops were going to ride in one of the sampans. With a big grin he informed me that the Marine Corps had enough exposure to saltwater and naval operations for one day. He did say that he was comfortable that they had enough time to head south along the dune line to rendezvous with their parent company operating nearby.

He saluted with a "Semper Fi," both of which I returned but added a "Bravo Zulu," the Navy phrase for mission well done. They took off at a jog down the beach and over the dune line. Mission accomplished, so far with no shots fired.

I was not as comfortable as Hutch regarding our departure schedule and wanted to get the hell off the beach. I was not the least bit trusting of the accuracy of the ROK's artillery fire because the targeted village was just behind the nearby dune line.

Boats took the bow paddle position in our sampan. I shoved off from shore stepping on board with my usual grace, intent on not sinking the stern of our craft as we headed back to 76. Snipe meanwhile was proceeding to seaward at idle speed still driving at the aft helm where he could monitor the towline as it slowly straightened then tightened as each sampan fell in line astern. I knew our one-inch nylon towing line was more than strong enough but was concerned that any sudden shock to the bow of the wooden sampans would pull out the vertical posts that the individual lines were tied to. Reloading at sea into the other already full sampans was not an option.

Ed had maneuvered the 79 boat astern of 76, while running parallel to the towed sampans and he cast a serious eye alongside each one. Once again a smart move on Ed's part because there was no guarantee that each sampan contained only friendly folk. We had saved the village from the ROK attack but that didn't mean they all wanted to come home with us.

Boats and I soon arrived alongside 76 and climbed awkwardly aboard and quickly lifted the gig onto the fantail. I ordered him to set an armed watch on our stern overseeing the tow. He returned from below with two 12-gauge shotguns and an M-16. Boats always liked to have a selection of armament—more than enough firepower to discourage any suicide act from astern. He kept one shotgun and passed the M-16 to Buck.

Seeing the situation under control, Ed pulled up alongside to update me. He told me he had already radioed the U.S. Navy liaison officer at the Vietnamese Navy junk base several miles to the south, alerting them that we would shortly be delivering thirty or forty evacuees to their location.

In transit to our location, he had radioed Article to inform him that he was leaving his Delta patrol sector to assist me in the Charlie sector with the evacuation of a small Vietnamese village prior to an artillery attack by the ROKs.

The key to Swift Boat operational efficiency was to keep Article in the communications loop, utilizing a past or current verb rather than a future one, which might imply we were seeking their permission. The latter could result in a drawn-out multi-layered horror show. Using the term "we are" or even better, "we did" as the operational verb usually kept the onshore types comfortable.

Most of the day-to-day watch standers at Article were good guys willing to help. It was some of the more senior career types who could, on occasion, arrive and bring any operational decision to a screeching halt. Most Swift Boats subscribed to this truncated and past-tense method of communication, but frankly, Lord Mort, with some prior help from Killer Lou, had really fine-tuned the process.

Thanking Ed and his crew for providing backup, I started giving him the full debrief on our involvement. He knew Tiger Five and the other Marine CAP units and respected them all. Reflecting back, I had forgotten that the ROKs had almost taken out Ed's boat PCF 79, again with their artillery, while trying to get a piece of the action after Ed and his crew captured the Chinese trawler. When I got to the ROK section of my story Ed's response was slightly more poetic: "Fuck the ROKs, they'd shoot their own mothers if they got in the way."

As Ed and his crew departed south, I heard several large artillery rounds land and resonate nearby with that rolling rumble over the water. Next, there was a pause of about a minute while I presume the ROKs adjusted their first rounds for accuracy. Somewhere, perhaps on the ground, they had a spotter because I could see no aircraft circling in the area. Regardless, the artillery barrage soon started full force. We were safely offshore with our tow behind and we had now traveled about half a mile to the south. I could see the fiery bursts as the rounds hit and soon a swirling cloud of smoke and dust began to form over the village which would soon be obliterated.

Looking astern at the boats we were towing, I could see the families, young and old, holding their chickens and pigs, looking back at their village. Their homes were most likely straw huts, undoubtedly simple in construction, but now soon to be destroyed. I wondered to myself if they were worried about what was next, or were they so resigned to the tragedies of war that in time they would simply return and rebuild. Most likely they had no choice.

*PCF 76 at the Vietnamese Navy base delivering the villagers.*

No question, we had saved lives. We were a couple of small independent units working together, U.S. Navy and U.S. Marine Corps, with no one over the age of twenty-eight. No recognition required, we had done a good day's work and this made us proud.

## CHAPTER 18

# RETURN FROM THE SOUTHERN OUTPOST

We had now been in Chu Lai somewhat over two months for a total of five and a half months in-country. The troops had been working extremely hard and they developed into a combat crew I was extremely proud of. Around the Chu Lai base, PCF 76 and its crew was known as a crew you could count on under pressure, and this was a great source of pride for all of us.

Killer Lou had departed for home several weeks earlier and Ed Bergin and his crew understandably were still dealing with the tragic loss of Bobby Don Carver. Meanwhile, PCF 76 was still patrolling with the semi-repaired cabin windows, held in place by a combination of the olive-colored cloth tape and wooden strapping, though I had recently been notified that the replacement parts had arrived at Da Nang.

Our crew had been discussing the possibility of taking R&R at some time in the near future. They all had earned it, both from a performance standpoint and time in-country. Policy was that you could submit your individual R&R request for a specific country, but the more flexible you were in terms of date availability the better your chances of getting your first choice. Since the flights originated out of Da Nang this was a better place to not only track potential flights but respond on short notice. Buck and Muller wanted to travel together which was acceptable to me, but I put a limit on two taking R&R at the same time so we could maintain a core crew.

During this discussion, I learned that Cos Div 12 in Da Nang was planning to open a new small sub base similar to Chu Lai, but at the Cua Viet River mouth on the southern side of the DMZ. They were looking for experienced crews to volunteer. The usual suspects Jay Fleming, Tom Jones and Larry Meyer had already signed up. I knew all of these guys were top-notch skippers and would be enjoyable to work with.

Considering the boat repairs, R&Rs and the opening of the Cua Viet base, I was seriously considering a return to Da Nang. I ran this by my crew, frankly more in terms of a survey than vote format. I valued their input, but this was not a democracy. Decision made, I radioed Da Nang and told them to sign us up.

We packed our gear, loaded it on 76 and said our Chu Lai goodbyes all around. This was not that difficult because we would see our southern shipmates on patrol, or whenever they came to Da Nang for repairs or R&R. We took in the lines and shoved off the next morning after breakfast at 0730. As we exited the harbor mouth and made a gradual turn to port, the temperature was in the seventies, visibility was unlimited, winds were negligible and it was a gorgeous day for a boat ride. Boats had a second pot of fresh coffee brewing on board and we headed north at 20 kts scheduled to arrive in Da Nang by early afternoon.

We arrived at about 1430 and after refueling and some minor repairs, we prepared to move PCF 76 over to the Apple to report in.

For all of us there were greetings from a lot of familiar faces, along with a few snide remarks about our returning to civilization. Looking around at the other boats, we saw that there were several new crews whom we soon met with introductions all around. New faces were a fact of life because every month there were anywhere from two to four crew departures and arrivals. This was simply the reality of the program.

While I put on my ball cap and grabbed my gear to climb up to the Apple, I did take note that some of the new kids on the block were checking out the war wounds on PCF 76. We knew she looked a lot more battle scarred than she was in reality, but the bullet holes in the cabin and smashed windows held in place with wooden strapping made quite a picture. Out of the corner of my eye as I swung my foot on to the ladder leading to the Apple's main deck, I caught our PR director

Bos'n Mate Fielder conveying the appropriate details of our conflicts, undoubtedly bullet hole by bullet hole.

Climbing to the Apple's second deck, I swung open the still unrepaired inside screen door, as usual smashing loudly against the bulkhead behind. From across the room, I was immediately greeted with a bellowing, "Hail, Mighty Caesar Returns."

Tipping my ball cap in mock salute, I checked my watch. It was almost 1700 and Eldon had declared that cocktail hour had commenced. Smiling to myself, I was glad that certain things remained the same.

The Swift program was never one to play favorites. We had had a relaxing trip earlier in the day so we were immediately assigned the Enfield Cobra Delta night patrol, located just north of Da Nang. This should not be confused with the southern Delta patrol out of Chu Lai with its notorious bad-guy reputation. The night patrol ruled out any cocktails, so we stowed our gear on the Apple, grabbed a quick dinner and shoved off about 1830.

As was the procedure, we stopped briefly at Article's location for an operational update. The watch officer on duty looked brand new, so being a smart-ass I asked him if there was any possibility of submarine activity in the Delta area. His somewhat befuddled look confirmed my suspicion that he was a new arrival in-country, but he did respond, "Are you the guys?" Obviously, he was referencing our encounter with Beauty Sleep, the submarine, and her frogmen several months prior. Boats usually joined me for these briefings and he promptly responded, "Yes, Sir, we are indeed PCF 76."

After this brief fling with fame, we were assured that the area was quiet except for the possibility of several small Marine reconnaissance patrols taking place. I asked for the relevant radio frequencies, which Boats wrote down and we shoved off.

The seas were still calm with a light wind from the north about 5 kts. The moon had descended low in the sky providing some light along the shoreline but not enough to illuminate us, which was a good thing. One of the most dangerous situations was when the moon rose in the east as a Swift Boat was patrolling close in to shore, silhouetting the boat as a target.

We also had the Starlight Scope on board which was more effective for viewing any on-shore activity when there was less bright light. This device was based on intensifying existing light sources such as someone walking with a cigarette or people around a campfire, rather than working off thermal imaging based on body heat. It was a brand-new technology and the scope was about the size of small baseball bat and somewhat cumbersome to hold. If it fell overboard, we were informed that this would most likely mark the end of your naval career. As a result, usually the officer was the one to use the scope, hunkered down in a secure sitting position.

Tonight, I placed my butt on the lip of the port pilothouse door with the scope held securely with my arms balanced on my knees. Since I weighed 200 pounds, the narrow doorframe and my rear end were becoming way too close friends, so I kept my vigilance to short sweeps at ten-minute intervals.

Boats turned in about 2300 and told me he would start his watch early at 0300 rather than the usual 0400, which was fine with me. As we moved farther offshore, I replaced high technology with a trusty pair of Bausch & Lomb binoculars and climbed up to sit on the top of the pilothouse with Muller nearby in the gun tub. Losing a pair of Navy binoculars was not officially a court-martial offense but only slightly below that level. Therefore, neck straps were mandatory.

Newcomer was doing a competent job at the helm with double duty monitoring the radio, which was quiet, as well as the radar scope. With legs stretched out and thoroughly enjoying the evening, my yachtsmen reverie was soon interrupted by a transmission that came in on our shorter-range FM radio tuned to monitor only the Marine Corps frequencies. "Navy boat, Navy boat, come in over?"

As expected, Newcomer grabbed the radio handset and responded, "This is Navy boat, call sign Enfield Cobra Delta." This was a heads-up response on his part to avoid any communication confusion.

By this time, I had swung down from the cabin top and was in the pilothouse as Newcomer passed me the radio handset. Out of the corner of my eye, I saw Boats emerging from below. Over time, any noise out of the ordinary, especially an unexpected radio transmission, would wake either of us up, even when we were sleeping on the bunk in the main cabin below.

"This is Tiger Tracker, USMC, over."

I knew the "Tiger" designation was used for many small Marine operations and I guessed that "Tracker" implied a recon unit. Therefore, the designator USMC was overkill but I did like the "Tiger Tracker" combo.

"Tiger Tracker, this is Cobra Delta. How can we be of assistance?"

"Are you the guys with that trigger-fired 81mm mortar, and can you flat fire it?"

I responded, "Tiger, this is Delta. That's affirmative, providing we have line of sight (LOS) to the target."

I took quick note that at present our position was about 500 yards off the beach. Behind were several large hills that rolled up from the shoreline, rising to several hundred feet in height. All of them were covered with dense jungle foliage; though it was dark they were clearly visible. At various locations on the hillside, there appeared to be small flickering lights that may have been campfires. We were too far offshore to use the Starlight Scope and I did not want to approach the shore any closer before I understood Tiger's request.

"Cobra Delta, this is Tiger Tracker. I suspect significant enemy troops are approaching my position. Can you assist, over?"

"Tiger this is Delta. That's affirmative, send me best coordinates of enemy position."

No more than two minutes had passed but all of our crew was up and in motion. Boats and Snipe went aft to prepare the mortar. Buck had brought the chart up from below and laid it on the table in front of me. Then he relieved Newcomer on the helm who, with pencil and paper, was ready to copy the target coordinates. Tiger sent the enemy position, which we then plotted on the chart.

However, it quickly became obvious to me that the chart was flat and two-dimensional and we were going to fire the mortar in level flight in a real-life three-dimensional environment. For all I knew the enemy target could be on the backside of the hill. I queried Tiger whether we should fire an up-and-over round rather than flat trajectory.

*Enemy target—second hill on the left.*

Tiger was a man who knew his business and his response was, "Negative, Delta. The target is on the waterside slope of the hill and you can hit it level flight." He continued, "Start at the top of the second hill, look down about halfway and you will see several moving lights. That's your target."

"Tiger, this is Delta. Understand and will try to ID target and confirm with you."

"Delta, this is Tiger. Request minimum delay, out."

Based on that remark, the time pressure on PCF 76 had now ratcheted upward significantly. I lifted my binoculars and started to scan the hillside when Boats arrived by my side. He reached over and grabbed the second set of glasses from Newcomer.

Immediately, he said, "I've got the target and see the lights bearing about 300° relative from us (basically off our port beam) and they're moving slowly right to left in a southerly direction." Following his outstretched arm, I could see them, as Tiger had said, about halfway down the second hill from the north.

Boats went aft to prepare, as we had agreed, three mortar rounds: one white phosphorous and two high explosive, all impact fuses with all propellant increments attached for level flight. Leaning out the door I yelled, "Trigger fire only on my command!"

He repeated the mortar settings and closed with, "Aye, Aye, Sir, trigger fire only on your command!"

I figured the Willy Pete round, if fired first, would burn for several minutes and would clearly mark the target even through the jungle foliage. This would allow us to sight on that and accurately fire the second two high-explosive rounds.

Now, I had another problem to deal with. I had no idea of Tiger's current position relative to the target. Dropping three rounds of 81 mike mike on top of someone was not the way to win new friends.

"Tiger, this is Delta. We have identified the enemy position and are prepared to fire three rounds: One Willy Pete, then two HE. We will trigger fire, line of sight. Interrogative, I say again interrogative, what is Tiger;s current position relative to target, over?"

"This is Tiger. I am approximately 100 yards south of target same side of the hill, over." In combat, this was called "danger close."

"Tiger, this is Delta. I appreciate the vote of confidence but request you immediately move south another 200 yards for safety. Delta will await your confirmation, over."

"Delta, be advised, we are under way, we are under way," all transmitted in a somewhat breathless fashion. I visualized five or six men in grease paint and camouflage bent over carrying their gear, talking to me on the radio while scooting through the jungle undergrowth.

I yelled to Boats, "Load one round Willy Pete but hold guns tight, guns tight." He immediately repeated my command.

Leaning out the portside door, stretching the cord on the radio handset to its maximum, I explained the delay in the firing situation to Boats and Snipe, who both concurred.

In less than two minutes, the radio burst to life: "Delta, this is Tiger. We are clear, I say again, we are clear. Request you commence fire, commence fire."

"Tiger, this is Delta. Commencing fire, out."

I yelled to Boats to once again confirm the target visually, which he did. He was hunkered over the back of the mortar tube, legs spread apart while he sighted down its fat barrel fixed on the target with his finger ready to pull the trigger below. Then, I gave the order: "Commence fire, three rounds, rapid fire." The order was repeated back to me just before the first round left the muzzle of the mortar with a fiery belch in the still darkness.

Boats yelled "Shot" as he elevated the mortar then yelled "Load." Snipe repeated both words loud and clear and dropped in the second round. This verbal procedure minimized the possibility of a deadly double load. This was when a second round lands on top of the unfired first round causing both rounds to explode along with the barrel, sending a deadly cloud of red hot shrapnel in all directions.

Boats lowered the weapon again, visually reacquired his target, which was the still-moving lights and fired the second round. Somewhere during this process the first round exploded beneath the jungle canopy with a brilliant display of white-hot light and an echoing *wa-whomp* which rolled back across the still dark waters to our position offshore. This was followed in quick succession by rounds two and three, both high explosive. Less flash, but more concussion as each hit the target. As I had hoped, rounds two and three had landed within twenty yards of the first white phosphorous round, which still burned. Boats was definitely on his game, just when it counted.

"Delta, this is Tiger. Nice shooting, Navy. If the enemy is not all KIA, then you certainly ruined their picnic. Dead or alive, it gives us time to 'di di mau.' We're impressed with your big gun, mission accomplished. Many thanks, over."

"Tiger, this is Delta. Always a pleasure to work with the Corps. We will continue our patrol in the area until dawn and monitor your frequency. Semper Fi."

"Delta, this is Tiger. Our mission is to locate, strike and be back in time for breakfast but nice to know that you'll be on call, Semper Fi, out."

By this time, it was almost 0430 and the eastern sky was just beginning its glow below the horizon, so much for another quiet patrol in the Delta sector. I told Boats to go below with his watch section and grab

*At General Quarters, surveying the shoreline.*

an hour of shut-eye and then he could relieve my section as we headed back to base.

I took over the helm from Newcomer, who went below to put on fresh coffee. With the urgent time demands of working with Tiger Tracker, I had not informed Article of our action. They did not normally monitor the local Marine frequencies.

Picking up the radio microphone, I transmitted, "Article, this is Enfield Cobra Delta, We have just completed an urgent gunfire mission requested by Tiger Tracker—three mortar rounds expended, no friendly casualties, enemy casualties unknown this time. Tiger Tracker departing area, Delta has resumed normal patrol, over."

The delay made me wonder whether our new watch stander was still on duty. Article's response was definitely hesitant and sounded roughly like someone reading the notes he might have taken freshman year in college.

"Enfield Cobra Delta, this is Article. Understand you were firing at someone called Tiger Tracker and this was a normal patrol, over?"

*Firing the 81 mm mortar.*

At 0430 reinforced with a fresh mug of black coffee, this was a training opportunity that could not be ignored.

"Article, this is Delta, Negative on your last. We responded to an urgent gunfire request from a friendly force Uniform Sierra Mike Charlie (USMC), call sign Tiger Tracker, who was threatened by enemy troops and we took them OUT. We have resumed normal patrol. Do you copy, over?"

Without delay, "Enfield Cobra Delta, this is Article. Well done, over."

"Article, this is Delta. Many thanks. We are all on the same team, out."

A trifle pompous on my part, but I knew it would sound great when they replayed the tape back later in the day.

Section IV
Da Nang to Cua Viet

## CHAPTER 19

# DINNER ON THE USS *REPOSE*

We had just returned from a relatively uneventful patrol south of Da Nang in the Echo area and left PCF 76 tied up alongside the APL, outboard of two other boats. Upon arrival the crew had cleaned, fueled, and rearmed the boat while I did some paperwork. Every Swift Boat in port had to be ready to get under way immediately. This was a non-negotiable operating rule, which I never saw broken. I suspect any lack of adherence to it would be a serious and punishable offense. Besides, since boats were often shared, jumping aboard an unprepared boat in a "red alert" situation would bring the wrath of your shipmates down upon the skipper and his crew with justifiable and full fury.

We had been spent a good part of the night firing illumination rounds for one of the northern Marine CAP units. This involved running slowly along the beach 300 to 500 yards offshore with one of our radios tuned solely to their frequency. When we patrolled in those areas we usually loaded extra ammo on the fantail so that we would be ready to provide fire support for extended periods of time. This became more important as the better trained and more heavily armed North Vietnamese troops moved into some of these areas south of Da Nang.

One poignant memory I have of those times is of a Christmas card that was sent to Swift Boats and signed by the members of one of the southern CAP units, "Tiger Five," thanking us for our support. As we passed the card around the wardroom of the APL, where we all ate, we only recognized half the names on the card. The question that hung heavy in the air was, where were the names of the others? Had they simply been transferred home or were they in fact casualties? Regretfully, we never had an answer, as is often the case in combat.

With a final look back at 76 and a thumbs-up from Boats, I pulled my tired butt up the ladder, hung onto the side of the APL's hull, and then gracefully swung my leg over the metal railing onto the main deck. After climbing the outside ladder (in this case actually a stairway) to the second deck of the APL where we ate and slept, I swung open the door just as Eldon Thompson yelled to me, "We have just received a dinner invitation. Actually it was sent to Jay and me but let me see if it mentions you. Oh yes, here at the bottom it does include you."

Eldon had numerous responsibilities, this time as our self-appointed social director, if there was such a position in Swift Boats. He is well remembered as the first and perhaps only skipper to take several female Red Cross workers out for a night cruise and a barbeque to the Delta patrol area, just north of Da Nang harbor—also known as the "out-at-dusk, in-at-dawn" patrol.

Eldon flipped me a card from one Navy LTCDR Katherine Hancock asking to have LTJGs Eldon Thompson and Daniel Daly and Jay Fleming join her and other members of the wardroom on the USS *Repose* for dinner at 1800, on Tuesday, 12 February, two days hence. Eldon thought this was just about the best thing that had happened in months and Jay agreed. If this was not a combat zone and we didn't have just one type of uniform (working tropical khaki), I think the two of them would have been laying out their prom dresses for the occasion.

To RSVP, we did have some minor preparations to undertake, specifically, work out the patrol schedules so we would be available and get the OK to use a boat that night. Mike Tackney (MoTac) was then the acting Ops Boss and a former Swift Boat skipper, so he gave us the go ahead and we were on. The one exception was in the case of a "red alert," all bets were off because all boats would be manned and under way. Not likely, but still a possibility with the regular attacks that were taking place at the airport and the increased VC activity downriver. We could use Article to handle our RSVP.

The *Repose* entered the harbor at 1200 and dropped her anchor in the deepwater section of the harbor, well away from any potential shore fire.

She could be a potential target despite the huge Red Cross hospital ship markings on her hull. Also, enemy zappers and frogman were a concern, but that was the responsibility of the harbor patrol which was part of the Naval Support Activity. To date, their track record in the harbor defense and detection department had been a good one. Besides, Da Nang was such a large and busy harbor, between warships and commercial ships coming and going, an enemy swimmer stood a decent chance of simply being run over. Also, most vessels especially at night had a deck patrol to augment the waterborne patrols.

These security matters were of little concern to us relative to our upcoming and pressing social commitments. Making the right impression on our hosts was of the utmost importance, along with informing the other boat officers of our social good fortune. Even our crews got a kick out of the story and I am sure they added a few elements for their ears only. We took Eldon's PCF 27 for the occasion as his crew had either just painted it or certainly gave it the ultimate wash-down and scrubbing.

Naturally, all weapons were uncovered and ammunition was belted and laid out nearby for full effect. We needed one of our crew to come along to maintain a radio watch, which had been part of our deal with Mike Tackney for his permission to use the boat. Boats volunteered to drive and keep the radio watch on board PCF 27 while we were at dinner. A task for which he would be handsomely compensated. He also had the best sense of theater and high drama—critical ingredients for the occasion.

We arrived smartly alongside the *Repose* at 1745, with Boats conducting a perfect 10-point landing with a decent-size audience in attendance. As the three of us climbed onto the camel float tied up alongside the ship, Boats, rising to the occasion, formally saluted us as if we were admirals departing a battleship. We continued on, climbing the gangway ladder up to the main deck. It was better described as a stairway that was lowered down along the ship's side, well built and heavy duty.

As was Navy custom, we crossed the quarterdeck that marks the formal entrance of a ship when anchored or tied to a pier. Eldon then turned aft, saluted the colors flying at the stern and bellowed out, "Request permission to come aboard."

The Chief Petty Officer who had the duty was salty enough to see this act play out, returned the salute and joined in. "Gentlemen, I assume you are on board to join us for dinner."

Eldon responded, "We are indeed, Senior Chief," subtly recognizing his seniority. Eldon was on a roll—a dangerous thing in itself.

The Chief called out, "Messenger of the watch, take these Swift Boat commanders to the wardroom."

I thought to myself, *we had just arrived and already we had received a promotion to commanders*. The Senior Chief had obviously been picked for this role, perhaps indicating that the ship's captain had a sense of humor. We turned to the young sailor who saluted and said "Follow me, sir," singular because Eldon was now definitely in the lead. Looking at the sailor, I thought he seemed unbelievably young compared to some of our crew who were probably the same age but had grown up fast with some hard miles under them.

As we walked along the main deck, we noticed the ship was spotless and well maintained, despite its demanding assignment. This was a tribute to a squared-away ship's company. We continued forward along the starboard side and closer to the bow entered through a bulkhead door into a small foyer and seating area, which lead to the officers' wardroom and eating area. We had in good taste worn our blue ball caps with names and boat numbers embroidered on them. In the foyer was a shelf for covers and we tossed them there. Landing on the shelf, I thought, with just the right touch of aplomb.

Off to my right, I heard a somewhat familiar and deep voice and turned to see LTCDR Kate Hancock greet us with a, "Welcome aboard, gentlemen."

This whole event seemed indeed to be perfectly orchestrated. Kate used all of our first names and that set the tone for the dinner. We were introduced first to the *Repose's* commanding officer and executive office, both of whom extended a truly warm greeting to us as fellow Naval officers. This happened quite often in Swift Boats where, totally undeserved, we received a high level of respect from senior officers. Frequently, when we came alongside a warship, especially a destroyer, the CO or XO introduced themselves by their first names. I, for one, always responded to them as captain, etc., but it happened often enough that I remembered it.

We then met several of the senior medical staff, both doctors and nurses who had "overworked" written all over them. Then the ship's captain, whom I presume was a senior four striper because of the size of the *Repose,* excused himself. He did inform us that we would be eating by ourselves in a smaller room just off the main dining area, which he hoped would be suitable. Eldon chimed in with something along the lines of "Delightful! Hopefully, we are not intruding."

The captain responded, "Not at all. Please make yourselves at home."

With that, Kate led us to the alcove saying this was where the medical staff ate when they were under way and in an operating mode. That took a little of the shine off the private room concept but we were still most appreciative of their invitation. Inside the smaller room were Emily Parent and Betsey Hill, the two younger nurses who were warmly greeted and well remembered by Jay and Eldon. I knew before our departure they had referenced their black books from our harbor tour of three months ago and hoped their level of background information wouldn't terrify the younger girls.

I had no need to worry. Kate was the perfect host, explaining how happy they were that we could join them as a thank you for our previous tour-guide hospitality. "Horny sailors" was a term that kept coming to mind, but I was able to suppress the thought. The girls, rather the ladies, served us off a sideboard, which was a nice break from the cafeteria style that we had on the APL. Jay commented that all that was missing was a fine wine, as he threw a knowing glance my way.

On shore we had liquor on the APL and when we lived at other locations in hooches, but on board ships it was definitely against U.S. Navy regulations. The only time I knew when this regulation was flaunted on a regular basis was on aircraft carriers in the pilots' staterooms. These guys, right or wrong, flew and lived in their own special world. Of course, it didn't hurt that the captain of most carriers was a former airdale. Anyway, I thought Jay's remark was said with a little too much enthusiasm, considering that ice tea was being served.

Navy food, both officer and enlisted, is above average and superior compared to the fare we occasionally got from our Marine brothers. It seemed the Marines felt bad chow should be part of their "hang-tough, can-do" attitude. Tonight the menu was in a word, "terrific," with roasted chicken in a delicious white sauce and fresh, yes fresh, vegetables. Rolls from the oven accompanied by a salad of iceberg lettuce and real tomatoes rather than that infamous red rock variety. This was followed by fresh apple pie with vanilla ice cream. It was obvious that the captain took good care of his crew and that definitely extended to the embarked medical detachment. Good food started at the top. Bad captains almost always meant bad food. Also, I suspect this meal was a tribute to the high esteem in which these nurses were held by their medical brethren, as well as the ship's company.

In truth, we were honored to be invited. The conversation certainly flowed easily with Eldon and Jay supplying an adequate number of war stories, mostly true, and the remainder of which could remotely be attributed to close friends. The younger girls asked the appropriate questions while Kate, with a little more sea time, simply took it all in. She and I discussed her profession and prior experience at John Hopkins because I had several friends who were currently in medical school. We learned about where each of us had grown up. She was from Virginia and I was from Massachusetts. She passed quickly over her husband's death, which was fine with me. I doubt it would have added much to the evening.

After dinner, we took a brief tour of the ship including the medical faculties, which were sobering, to say the least. Patients received first-rate emergency trauma treatment and were stabilized on board the *Repose*. Then they were sent ashore when they were healthy enough for transport and longer rehabilitation. That said, the operating rooms were impressive just to walk through, as I am sure were the attending staffs. All three women were pros when they described their duties to us.

We ended up with a stroll around the deck which, unlike the warships that the three of us had previously served on, was laid out somewhat like a cruise ship. There was very little grey paint and no weapons platforms along with brackets and braces for handling equipment that you could stumble over.

Overhead the Pacific night was remarkably clear with a small moon and a sky full of stars, all marking the welcome passing of the winter storm season. This was accompanied by a light west wind blowing in from the harbor mouth. In Swift Boats, especially patrolling in the northern sectors where the weather could be so miserable, you tended to become a junior weather analyst. We had our blue ball caps on, so we looked somewhat professional but everyone still knew we were "the visitors" from the Swift Boat tied up alongside. This was a U.S. Navy ship and there are no secrets on board.

Eldon and Jay, Emily and Betsey seemed to be charmed by each other's company and I found myself quite comfortable being with Kate. She had an outgoing personality and over the evening a good sense of humor emerged. Still, she was serious and in a serious business, as were we. The age deferential between us seemed a minor factor to me and I learned it was just four years. I was, however, still respectful of her rank because we were guests on her duty station. We stood by the rail and she was close by, arms lightly touching, a fact I chose not to ignore. I looked down at PCF 27 tied up below and could see Boats on the bunk in the main cabin reading a book but still able to hear the radio if we were called. I mentioned that I doubted it was a current best seller which brought a smile from Kate, having met Boats on our previous trip.

In life, timing is everything and I guessed it was time to head back to the base. The other foursome was jawboning away up near the bow of the ship with accompanying bursts of laughter, no doubt brought forth by some clever remarks from my two sidekicks. I thanked Kate for her kindness but said we really had to return our rental car, which instantly brought forth a laugh that capped off the evening.

We looked at each other waiting for the follow-on comment. I thought perhaps, *"Maybe we can do this again sometime,"* but fortunately didn't say it. This was Vietnam, we were in a war zone, she was a trauma nurse on a hospital ship and I drove a Swift Boat. *"Get serious."*

I decided to take a big, big flyer and said, "Kate, would you consider doing something on R&R?"

A little vague and open ended, but still a possible next step. Long silence, eyes meeting for an instant, *"Boats, fire up the diesels,"* was going to be my next move as I regretfully realized I had probably misspoken.

"I would like that," was the response I thought I heard, but I wanted it confirmed in her eyes. The sparkle was there. I had first seen it over dinner and now it showed itself once more.

She said the *Repose* was going to either the Philippines or Japan for pier-side maintenance. She thought she could most likely get some leave time and book a flight to Hawaii. Hawaii ... I had been there before and considered it as close to paradise as I knew on this man's planet. A great choice.

In-country troops could get R&R to multiple locations in the Far East, including Hawaii. Swift Boats stationed up north got their R&Rs through the Marines not the Navy and they seemed to have more flexibility. I said I could probably adjust to her calendar and would need a week or two lead time to schedule things in the patrol department.

We set up some very tentative dates and agreed we would communicate by mail, which for both of us was about five days' transit time. The military had these R&R trips well organized so we would not have to worry about every detail. Action man that I am, I was about to fill in the blanks, most likely spoiling the moment with some moronic operations plan. Fortunately, Kate took control and simply said in a low voice, "I think Boats has finished his book."

I took the comment as intended and looked toward the bow to retrieve my shipmates before they became an embarrassment to Swift Boats and Naval tradition in general. Whether you believe it or not, there is that tagline "an officer and a gentleman."

The six of us walked amidships to the quarterdeck and said our thank yous and goodbyes. We shook hands all around and smiles were the order of the evening. I did notice a level of frivolity among the foursome that I found amusing but also somewhat surprising.

I stated to the watch officer that we would appreciate his conveying to the captain our personal appreciation for his hospitality. The watch officer was so junior that he might have thought we were somebody important and in fact deliver my message. Then according to U.S. Navy tradition, I announced to him, "We have permission to leave the ship."

Then we all in turn returned the salute of the watch officer. We did not face the stern because the colors were down. It was 2130 and the sun had set.

Boats, whether his book was complete or not, had seen our departure from the quarterdeck. He had the engines fired up and saluted as we stepped off the camel on to the boat's fantail. We pulled away considerably more slowly than our high-speed arrival and waved to all above.

As we headed across the harbor, Boats was at the helm in the pilothouse so he could utilize the radar. The three of us were aft, standing on the engine hatches, when Eldon reached into a bag I hadn't seen before and said, "Outstanding night, yes indeed, and superb ice tea," as he tossed an empty bottle of vodka over the side.

## CHAPTER 20

# HEADING NORTH TO CUA VIET

It was late October 1967 and the powers that be had finally decided that we should open a small detachment at Cua Viet to patrol more extensively the area around the DMZ. Previously, we had serviced that area out of Da Nang, a ninety-mile trip each way that took over three hours running pretty much at full speed.

This distance presented two problems: the first being, if there was any bad weather the transit time could be doubled with the boat arriving on station with a beat-up and exhausted crew to carry out their patrol. Also, a round trip of 180 miles consumed a great deal of fuel. At first, this problem was dealt with by taking on fuel from one of the nearby destroyers, usually on station several miles off the DMZ. That solution was short-lived because scheduling/making the rendezvous and often the quality of the diesel fuel we received did not work effectively in the Swift Boat engines. As a result it fouled the fuel filters, shutting down the engines, requiring filter replacement. Filter replacement was no big deal tied up at the pier, but under way in heavy weather or in a dangerous enemy area was a very different matter.

Another solution to the fuel problem was the relieving boat coming from Da Nang would carry a rubber fuel bladder on its fantail. Think of a big fat heavy black rubber balloon. The new boat would meet and transfer the fuel to the returning boat, which would carry the empty fuel bladder back to Da Nang. Transferring the fuel between two rolling Swift Boats, without pumps, became an unworkable solution and was soon abandoned. Visualize, for a moment, several of us marching back and forth across the rubber fuel bladder attempting to push the fuel across to the other boat by foot stomping. Not exactly Cal Tech engineering efficiency.

As a result, the concept of physically stationing several Swift Boats at the mouth of the Cua Viet, downriver east of Dong Ha, became the most realistic option. There were already several hundred Marines at that location and they used it as a base of operations to patrol the DMZ. Crossing the river and roaming around the DMZ, their method of transport was called an "amtrac." These were amphibious vehicles that looked roughly similar to a lightly armored tank that could carry ten or fifteen men inside. In the water, to me, they looked like a large square floating metal container with only about eighteen inches of freeboard showing above the surface. Most Marines felt similarly and as a result they chose to ride on top rather than inside whenever the amphibious component came into play. Traveling onshore, it looked slightly more credible with tank tracks and a rear loading ramp for the troops. In addition to the amtracs, the Marines had numerous 105mm artillery pieces scattered throughout the compound capable of delivering fire into the DMZ, thereby reducing the possibility of any direct frontal attack by the enemy on the base itself. This was a serious base where you knew the enemy was watching you just a few short miles away across a stretch of wide open sand dotted with a few combat-weary trees.

The Swift Boat mission was to patrol the coastline and contribute to the effort to make the DMZ a no-man's-land by prohibiting any water transport south of troops or equipment from North Vietnam into Northern I Corps. North Vietnam itself was located just four miles away at the northern border of the DMZ that was defined by another river called the Ben Hai, controlled by the bad guys.

PCF 76 volunteered to head north along with Tom Jones (call sign Moll Flanders) in PCF 80, Larry Meyer (Surf Rider) in PCF 16 and Jay Fleming (Malibu Foxtrot) in PCF 13. Each of us had our own boat plus experienced crews, so together we packed our basic belongings and headed north, anticipating that the Marines would provide us with food, fuel and ammunition. We did focus on certain essentials; my boat carried a pallet of beer on the fantail (approximately sixty cases) and the other boats carried four cases of scotch, gin, and bourbon, respectively. The load was divided between boats for security reasons. I learned later that Larry had also packed a decorator's assortment of tasteful bar signs. As usual, our sense of military and historical priorities was very much in order.

The trip north was uneventful, table-top seas with a brilliant sun above which made for some great boat and crew pictures, plus a few hours sitting on the fantail just reading a book. On PCF 76 our new folding folding deck chairs provided an element of yachting comfort. The chairs could hardly be considered contraband, so we had negotiated a fair price with a cargo junk and now they had become part of our onboard critical equipment list. Overall, the trip was somewhat like the New York Yacht Club's summer cruise, albeit heavy on the grey paint motif.

We arrived at the river mouth late morning and tied up at a small floating pier attached onshore to a larger stone and concrete structure. This arrangement could easily hold several Swift Boats and a couple of smaller work boats. The loading/unloading ramp for the larger LSTs was upriver about 500 yards and was used for delivering the bulk of the supplies for the Marines. All in all, this was a pretty basic base that had a definite frontier image.

Securing the boats stern-to we then took a stroll down Main Street. This could best be described as a sandy beach lined on either side with wooden hooches for living and operations. I was quick to notice that scattered throughout the base were large bunkers built of multiple layers of sandbags supported by huge timbers that measured 12 × 12 inches in diameter. These were affectionately referred to as "12 × 12s." Very clever, these Marine types.

The Marine amtracs and artillery pieces were scattered about, accompanied by the occasional palm tree. I assumed this deployment was made to present less of a target to the North Vietnamese artillery. I later learned that the enemy artillery was located several miles away along the Ben Hai River. The guns were actually situated within caves on a rocky cliff above and there immune to air attack. They still had a clear line of

*Traveling north to Cua Viet.*

*Boats riding an aircraft wing tank—a little en route R&R.*

*Charter member, New York Yacht Club.*

*Boats at the helm, Marlboro only, no black coffee.*

*Swifts at the Cua Viet pier, the DMZ dead ahead.*

*Main Street, Cua Viet.*

258 • White Water Red Hot Lead

fire as well as the range to fire at will into the DMZ and the Marine compound. Welcome to Cua Viet.

As we trudged through the sand, it became obvious that it was so fine that long-distance walking, or more importantly, fast running, was very difficult. No tag football games like we had enjoyed in Chu Lai. Therefore, the Seabees who had built the compound had put small wooden boardwalks in front of the hooches giving the area somewhat of a seaside ambiance. This vacation effect was complemented by the metal roofs with their strategically placed sandbags on top. This was the same design feature we had seen in Chu Lai. I still did not have an accurate answer as to whether their purpose was to hold down the roof in heavy weather or protect against the concussion of an artillery attack. I suspect this was a function of who was telling the story.

On the left side of Main Street resting on the sand were several massive black rubber bladders similar to the smaller ones we had used while trying to refuel the Swift Boats, but in this case they were twenty times bigger. Delivered by tankers from Da Nang, they held the fuel and water supply for the base.

On the edge of the compound were several burnt-out and rusted amtrac hulks. We were told these had been hit by artillery and because some were gasoline-not diesel-powered, they exploded when hit. I made a mental note of this and put amtracs high on my list of vehicles to avoid riding in or riding on. I guess the Marines might say the same thing about Swift Boats, but we still maintained a fairly high rating in the tourist-ride attraction category.

We checked into our accommodations—screen door, small living area in front and large bunkroom in the rear. The sides were floor-to-ceiling screens to keep out the bugs, but near the water there were not many because of the wind. Horizontal wooden slats were placed at 45° to keep out the rain, which could be a significant problem depending on the season.

Home is what you make it, so we unloaded our personal effects. The liquor was still on the boats absolutely under guard—naïve we were not—so now we settled in. First thing, we roughed out the bar location and design. It was quickly noted that we definitely needed a card table and a couple of comfortable chairs, other than the Navy-issue grey metal model. These could leave you either crippled or with incurable hemorrhoids. The good thing about Swift Boats was that you could buy things in Da Nang and have them transported north by another boat with whom you could rendezvous on patrol. In reality, this type of self-controlled logistics, or black-market acquisition, was far superior to anything the military managed. The Navy did do a fine job with food, fuel, and ammo; it was the acquisition of those personal creature comforts that were a problem, especially chairs.

We immediately started our patrol rotation but the off-duty crews were responsible for setting up housekeeping. In the officers' hooch this entailed the primary task of building the bar. Lumber was no real problem and we quickly located the necessary plywood and 2 × 4s. Tools were more of a challenge but one bottle of Johnnie Walker filled that equipment void. After four hours of design and installation we were open for business complete with the various beer signs hung, but not yet lit—it was decided that we would have only one sign lit because electrical outlets were scarce and the refrigerator for the beer and ice took priority. We all clearly understood that such were the sacrifices demanded of the combat soldier.

Our first cocktail party was a social success with our Marine neighbors in attendance, albeit with helmets, flak gear and rifles. This attire was somewhat of a regulatory Marine Corps fashion statement, which did make some sense considering the surrounding locale. Our dress code was more casual, with all the appropriate combat gear located on the boats as per Navy regs. However, t-shirts, shorts, our infamous blue ball caps, along with shower shoes, did provide a somewhat tropical ambience that was most likely envied by the grunts.

From our new-found friends, we did get the combat lowdown on those large bunkers located throughout the compound. We were informed that these structures were often twenty sandbags thick, all supported by those mighty 12 × 12 inch timbers that we had spotted upon our arrival. These bunkers could survive a direct hit from a 105mm round, which was the artillery weapon of choice of the North Vietnamese, fired from the other side of the DMZ. By comparison, our small open fox holes situated just outside the door of each Swift hooch looked tragically inadequate. They were just a rough circle of above-ground sand bags, one bag thick and four bags high with no roof and none of those 12 × 12s to be seen. I presume this was the result of the Sea Bees' mission, which had been to construct the living accommodations but leave survival protection to the actual tenants.

Despite the comradeship established and the night's enjoyable social occasion we did make specific note of this bunker issue and placed it on our mental "to-do" list. Dinnertime rolled around so we headed back down Main Street toward the operations area of the compound where the Marine mess tent was located. Walking in the fine sand was even more a challenge as a result of our successful cocktail party. The mess tent served both officers and enlisted, all eating together in a cafeteria format. It was similar in construction to the resident hooches, but significantly larger in scale.

Rifles were left outside, stacked vertically, barrels up, leaning together to prevent the ever-present sand from getting in the weapons. Every

*First-rate Marine bunker.*

*Third-rate Swift Boat bunker.*

*"We are proud to claim the title of United States Marine!"*

Marine knew that a jammed weapon could ruin your whole day. This procedure reminded me again of an old western movie when the fort came under attack and all the soldiers ran outside and grabbed their rifles from the stack.

The food was prepared in a trailer adjacent to the mess hall that was actually a self-contained turnkey kitchen that had been delivered by helicopter. It soon became obvious to any diner that this kitchen did little to facilitate the preparation or enhance the quality of the food.

Meat was overcooked and other accompanying items were either over-steamed or over-baked, depending on their molecular structure. I presume the quality of food was at least acceptable before cooking but after this preparation, it was definitely borderline edible. Cordon Bleu was definitely not in the Marine Corps lexicon but perhaps it had something to do with a "feed 'em tough, keep 'em tough" mentality. Our Thursday night steak on the Apple in Da Nang was an occasion that was definitely going to be missed.

The reality of the situation was that this was a combat area; the base was very much on the frontline and the mission a serious one. All in all, we concluded that it had been an enjoyable afternoon and evening just sharing some time with our new Marine Corps "brothers in combat." This was often the type of memorable bonding very difficult to describe to those who have not experienced it.

I decided to turn in around ten because we had the patrol duty the next day which meant a 0700 departure. My crew was located in the hooch next door, and they seemed to be of similar mind. This did not surprise me because they were now real pros after seven months in-country. The term "in-country" seemed to be a time definition or an accreditation applied to all persons in Vietnam. It could convey a positive or negative message depending on the individual and circumstances.

Sleeping at Cua Viet was not a problem—the hooches had two high metal-frame bunks with decent mattresses, not unlike a college dorm. Being near the water, there was often a cool breeze at night that could be supplemented by the ever-present oscillating fan purchased at the big Base Exchange in Da Nang. I never quite figured out why all the fans in Vietnam seemed to have blue plastic blades, never white, never clear, just blue. My theory was that must have been something cultural in Japan, where all the fans were made.

At around midnight, I was blasted awake by the explosive sound of nearby artillery. Never had I been located near artillery, let alone slept near it. I immediately surmised we were under attack with enemy troops soon to be charging through our perimeter defenses. Ever the warrior, I leapt out of bed and grabbed my .357 magnum (The Cannon), which dangled in its shoulder holster hung on the edge of my bed frame. At least now, I was prepared to defend myself against the oncoming enemy onslaught.

As the fog in my mind cleared slightly, I was informed in the calmest of tones by Tom Jones sleeping in the next bunk that this was in fact friendly fire, not enemy fire. I knew Tom to be a bright fellow and asked him the basis of his analysis. His response was immediate, although I did detect a slight touch of condescension in his voice. He informed me that an incoming round was whistle first, than an explosion, while an outgoing round was explosion first, then a whistle.

I was duly impressed by this and upon further investigation was informed that there was a group of Marine Amtracs located nearby equipped with artillery pieces, which fired H&I fire on an unscheduled basis on many nights. This harassment and interdiction fire was meant to prevent enemy troop movement in the DMZ and therefore it was totally unscheduled, hoping to catch the enemy by surprise and out in the open. I could understand the good part of our location, but the bad part was having the artillery directly behind our hooch. This was made worse by their random nighttime firing schedule. So much for the market value of our beachfront real estate and the surrounding neighborhood.

Most of the men involved in Swift Boats, because of the inherent up and down nature of our nighttime patrols, had developed the ability to quickly return to sleep. Within ten minutes, I was back in "horizontal plot," and sound asleep.

Several nights later, I was again awakened by artillery explosions. This time, they were accompanied by loud voices nearby yelling, "Incoming, Incoming."

Tom had been absolutely correct. It was indeed a whistle followed by an explosion, just like in the movies. Once again, I jumped from the upper rack but this time made the decision that under the circumstances my trusty pistol would be of minimum use. For some unknown reason I decided I needed my shower shoes to complete my wardrobe along with my t-shirt and shorts. By now, the rounds were landing close nearby with that *wa-whomp* sound visibly shaking our hooch. Way too close!

I bolted for the front door which fortunately had no lock because most likely I would have run through the screen. The boardwalk slats just outside caught the front of my sandals, almost resulting in the removal of my large right toe.

The *wa-whomp wa-whomp* sound and the concussion of the rounds landing nearby were rapidly increasing. They were exploding in the sand all around me and the dust they tossed into the air gave the night a gritty and brownish haze.

Getting my bearings, I suddenly felt something warm hit the side of my face. This was motivation enough for me to jump the remaining five feet headfirst into our Navy-issue foxhole. Boats was already in the foxhole with an M-14 rifle. Naturally, he was holding it barrel up to protect it against the sand. As a result of my high-speed headfirst approach I connected smartly with the barrel of a gun which added to the burning sensation already present on my cheek. Where Boats had gotten the Marine M-14 rifle was beyond me but he was the best barter and trade "cumshaw" sailor I had ever met.

By keeping my head down below the top row of sandbags of our definitely inadequate foxhole, I hoped to avoid any red-hot shrapnel ripping overhead. Catching my breath, I asked Boats how badly I had been hit in the face. Expecting the worst, he told me that he couldn't see anything. At the time, there was little light in our foxhole to see by other than the sporadic white flashes emitted by the explosive artillery bursts overhead.

The whistle and explosions continued for a very long ten minutes, landing all around the base. You soon realized that the length of the whistle determined how close to you the round was going to land; a long whistle probably went next door. Listening to this and wondering if your number was up was very tough on the head, especially while being crammed into a small open foxhole. It was becoming painfully obvious to me that the Marine Corps had the right design with their massive bunkers twenty sandbags thick. Looking above, because we had no roof, I could see that throughout the attack, the airborne sand was getting thicker and thicker as it drifted slowly overhead.

The next day, someone explained to me why all the surrounding sand was a real plus during an artillery attack. When a round hit the ground and exploded in the soft sand it buried itself thereby minimizing the explosion and the spread of shrapnel. Fortunately for us, at least that night, the North Vietnamese were not using anti-personnel rounds that exploded overhead. The firing finally stopped and we slowly rose on our knees peering over the top of our little foxhole. The smell of the explosive rounds was still very much in the air as was that airborne sand, but slowly this cleared and was carried inland by the gentle breeze coming off the nearby ocean.

Standing up, Boats gave my face another look in a better light. We concluded that I had not been hit by a piece of shrapnel but instead a round had landed nearby as I was charging out of the hooch. It had propelled at high speed what amounted to a fistful of sand by my face, not unlike a quick shave with abrasive sandpaper. The next day nothing remained other than a bright red circle on my cheek which was a lot better than having part of my head torn off by a piece of jagged shrapnel.

With the attack over for the moment, we swung our legs over the top of the sandbags and saw that the rest of the Swift crews nearby were also in good shape. Continuing to look around, we noticed significant activity outside of the hooch two doors down from ours. Obviously, it had taken a direct hit.

It was easy to see the impact of the exploding rounds. Wood splinters were everywhere and the roof had been partially blown off. A nearby bridge over a small creek constructed of boards and oil drums was peppered with shrapnel holes.

Sadly, we soon learned that one of the night's casualties from a direct hit had been a dentist with whom we had been sharing a drink less than twelve hours before. He had come up to Cua Viet on a rotational basis to do routine dental work for the troops stationed there. Tragically, the trip had cost him his life.

The next day, I learned the North Vietnamese often had spies or sympathizers working in the base, mostly as housekeepers, who would identify potential targets. They did this by walking and measuring distances to a target from the river's edge. Simple geometry. These targets would be sent to NVA gunners located just miles away sitting in their caves. This night of brutal reality brought an end to the concept of our peaceful seaside existence surrounded by all those tough Marines.

## CHAPTER 21

# PROJECT ECHO

After our baptism by enemy artillery fire the previous night, we decided that we most definitely had to upgrade our basic foxhole to Marine Corps' bunker standards. The Navy Seabees who had built our facility had long since departed and we were without heavy construction capability. In one way, however, we did have the keys to the kingdom or the coin of the realm—liquor.

For five cases of beer and three bottles of scotch we had one large Caterpillar bulldozer and five to ten of the famous 12 × 12 timbers now under contract. Filling the sandbags ourselves would be a U.S. Navy self-help exercise but we would utilize "all hands," both officers and enlisted. After a conclave of the great minds present at Cua Viet, it was decided that along with all of this effort for security there should be some pleasurable result. We concluded that atop the bunker there should be a patio of sorts for entertaining. This would allow us, along with our guests, to gaze out across the sand dunes and palm trees onto the magnificent shoreline just beyond.

*Project Echo* (for *Extravaganza*) was the code name assigned and we immediately constructed an appropriate 3 by 4 foot sign and stenciled on it "Project E." This was placed off to the side of the construction site firmly attached to a long 2 × 4 timber driven into the sand.

The Marine working the bulldozer was obviously well qualified and certainly needed no supervision from us as he dug the hole. As we contemplated the best angle of view for the placement of the patio we were approached from behind and heard the call, "Gentlemen."

We all turned to see the approach of what appeared to be a somewhat grizzly and real live Marine Corps Bird Colonel. The name tag said "Zak" but the look said "in charge."

Appropriate because of his seniority and also because of his august position as our landlord, we smartly saluted and stated, "Welcome, Colonel."

"Men, what exactly is Project E?" was his response as he approached the sign.

Without so much as a reflective pause and much to our horror, Larry Myers informed him that Project Echo was in fact top secret. The Colonel, without missing a beat, closed the ten-foot gap between us, removed his sunglasses and looked each of us dead in the eye. There was a pause as he moved his glance slowly from left to right without uttering a sound. Then with a slight nod of his head he clearly informed us, "Gentlemen, I am a full Colonel in the United States Marine Corps as you can see by these silver birds on my shoulders."

Because he had on combat utilities, we noted that his Eagles were in fact located not on his shoulders but sewn on his lapels. This was a minor fashion transgression and one which we decided warranted no comment on our part.

He continued, "More important, all these Marines work for me, and you Navy freeloaders are on my property." This was a hurtful but very true statement. "So, Gentlemen, once again what is Project Echo?"

Jay Fleming, without a moment of hesitation, made the critical decision to grab the verbal football from Larry Meyer and quickly informed the Colonel of our good intentions. There was a pause which seemed to be of a deadly duration while we waited for the Colonel's response.

He smiled and commented, "All makes sense to me. I trust you are adequately compensating my men for their time as well as for that material that you've stolen from the Corps?"

Now, I felt it was my time to chime in and added, "Yes, Sir, five cases of beer and three bottles of scotch."

*Site of Project Echo with the Cua Viet River behind.*

*USMC bulldozer—yours for a bottle of scotch.*

He turned to me, definitely senior to junior, and in no uncertain terms responded, "Lieutenant, why don't you make it seven cases of beer and add two bottles of scotch for the senior management?"

In an instant my comeback was, "Aye, Aye, Sir that will be seven cases of beer and five bottles of scotch."

He smiled, turned away and called, "And I'll be looking forward to seeing the invitation to the grand opening of Project Echo, as well as your next cocktail party. Semper Fi, men."

## CHAPTER 22

# FAREWELL GOOD FRIEND

We had been living with the Marines for almost a month with four boats and six crews at the Cua Viet River mouth. Across the DMZ, the enemy were still safely ensconced in their caves beyond the reach of bombs from aircraft or gunfire from ships, and their artillery was still aimed at us. This entire situation was one of those untouchable idioms, where the politicians sitting in D.C. said that no one could cross the river to take out the enemy caves because we would be invading North Vietnam. So instead, we tried to kill them by geometry, lobbing bombs into the mouth of the caves, which didn't work. Perhaps, if we had invited some of the bureaucrats to a Swift Boat/Marine Corps cocktail party and arranged for some "incoming" they might have got the point. We couldn't really do that because we were constantly short of scotch. Regardless, this was early November and we were heading into the beginning of the winter storm season or perhaps it was the end of the summer storm season. In Vietnam, especially up north, it was often difficult to tell when one ended and the other began.

There had been a heavy storm that kept us tied up in port for most of two days reading and playing cards because the neighborhood was not one that encouraged long contemplative walks along the beach. As the weather modified, our standard operating procedure was that one of the boats designated to patrol that day would conduct an early morning weather probe into the river. This was to determine if the river mouth was navigable and the condition of the open water beyond. If the report was satisfactory that boat would radio back to base and the other boats would get under way for their respective patrol areas and the weather boat would continue on patrol. This was our turn for the weather probe.

The wind was still up from the storm blowing out of the northeast and the sky was a pallet of multicolored grey with some light drizzle mixed in. We had fully prepared PCF 76 for patrol with food, fuel and ammunition and were expecting to continue on after the weather probe. After we let the big diesels warm up, we took in the mooring lines, left the Swift Boat pier and headed out into the river itself.

Along our port side was the DMZ, a no-man's-land of sand and scrub pines with the cliffs of North Vietnam in the hazy distance. Off to starboard was the Marine base with its bunkers and artillery emplacements. On the beach by the water's edge was the single burnt-out and rusting hulk of an amtrac. I guess they left the wreck there to emphasize that despite the sandy beaches this was very much a combat zone where uninvited enemy artillery could drop in at any time.

The actual mouth of the Cua Viet River was approached through a series of winding turns defined by the constantly shifting sandbars. As a result, you could not get a clear visual beforehand of the actual river mouth. On your way out, you had to enter the river mouth right after a turn and make your observations and decisions at that time.

River mouths are always a challenge, but more so when they are narrow with numerous sandbars. In this case, the sandbars shifted on a regular basis and as a result there were multiple surf lines to proceed through, rather than just a simple shot straight out. Add to this the fact that current came from several different directions depending on the tide, wind and the depth of the water at that location. The depth changed with the constantly shifting sands. Therefore, you could not always approach the waves head on but had to take them at an angle then often aggressively turn to take on the next set of waves coming from a different direction. The weather probe was not a walk in the park.

There was no question that the two days of the storm had left their mark. The first surf line soon appeared dead ahead with eight to ten feet of churning and twisting white water. If we were going to get to the calmer and deeper water offshore, we had to blast through this section.

With all waves there was another element to consider beyond just size and how they were breaking. The period of the swell is equally important. "Period" is defined as the time frame in seconds from trough to trough or crest to crest. Simply stated, it is how much time you have to recover from the first wave before the next one hits you. If you had a long period between waves, say ten seconds, that would let you, within reason, climb a big wave, ride down the other side and begin to climb the next one. A short period between waves, five seconds or less, will allow the second wave to catch you with your bow heading down before it can start to lift to meet the next oncoming wave. Somewhat like a boxer getting hit with punch number two before he recovers from number one.

In this case, we were able to turn the bow directly into the surf at a relatively slow speed with plenty of power available if we had to drive up and over. Without adequate power you can literally fall backward down the waves and if the waves are big enough, they can lift a boat and flip it over.

Driving in the pilothouse, my right hand was locked on the top of the wheel, with my left hand on the throttles located off to the port side on the dashboard. In Swift Boats the throttles and the gear shifts were integrated into one lever for each engine. Straight up, the engine was idling in neutral, move the lever forward, the engine went into forward gear and power increased as you continued to move the lever forward. The same applied in reverse. This made maneuvering and adjustment faster and simpler.

My eyes were rapidly scanning left and right trying to spot any change or perhaps an opening in that foaming wall of white water that was rolling and crashing toward us. After muscling our way through three or four waves, it became obvious to me that the period between waves was extremely short, just four to five seconds, and this presented a major problem.

Specifically, PCF 76 climbed up and over the first wave and I gave the engines some power to blast through the crest, climbing up, then over while not being pushed back down into the trough, which would be a disaster. But when the second wave arrived the bow was still heading down. The angle of the climb up the front of the wave and the subsequent drop down its back side was over 45° each way and this made just holding on, let alone steering, a significant challenge. This was all taking place not in minutes but in seconds.

I had made the decision to drive at the wheel in the pilothouse because it was the best location to evaluate the seas and judge our angle of approach. Boats was beside me crammed into the starboard corner of the pilothouse, while the rest of the crew was aft in the main cabin or out on the fantail. Everyone was experienced enough to hold on with two hands and the boat had plenty of rails, handles and poles scattered about inside and out.

The mounting risk quickly became all too clear to me. The boat was not "recovering" or rising to meet the next wave. The period was so short between waves that the bow of the boat could not rise to meet the next wave. Instead, the next wave slammed full force into the vertical front of the pilothouse structure. This was constructed of quarter-inch aluminum plate plus three front windows, hardly a battering ram against tons of crashing, churning water. The bow of a boat (or ship) is usually long and pointed for a reason—to cut through the waves and provide lift for the vessel to meet the oncoming waves.

Initially, we climbed up the first wave with the big propellers driving the boat up to the white foam atop each wave. For a brief moment, we balanced at the top before we fell downward. I used the wheel and rudders to fight the twisting action of our slide, but the angle of our fall was so steep that the stern, with the rudders and propellers below, was lifted out of the water eliminating any control.

This was rapidly becoming an untenable situation. The high seas and foaming surf, combined with a short period, was going to drive the boat underwater by the bow and hold it down as the next wave crashed upon us. To make matters worse the Swift Boat was designed such that there was a mere six feet between the tip of the bow and the pilothouse. This meant that the tons of water that crashed on the bow had nowhere to go, which further held down the bow never allowing it to rise and meet the next wave. In short order, this was going to bury the boat and probably start knocking in the windshields, thereby filling the pilothouse with water.

I could see that the surf line extended far enough out so that we could not continue and simply try to blast our way through the multiple walls of ten-foot-high raging white water just ahead.

At that moment, I made the decision to try and turn the boat rapidly around 180° and then ride "stern to" the surf line back into the river mouth. Waves crashing on the fantail, which was wide open and represented almost half the length of the boat, would be less likely to hold the boat under between waves and the engines would have enough power to drive us in.

The risk of this maneuver, once we had completed the turn, would be trying to stay in the trough between the waves with such a short period. We would try to ride the back of a specific wave without going up and over the top of the crest. If this happened the result could be deadly and was an event called "pitch poling," which is flipping forward end over end. Despite a Swift Boat weighing twenty tons this was a very real possibility.

I knew all about the potential risk of up and over, because in November of 1966, one year before, PCF 77 had been entering the Hue River mouth in surf conditions when tragically, they pitched poled, overturning the boat with a loss of three men. One year before, one river south, one number different on the boat, three men dying all flashed through my mind.

I yelled to my crew, "Hold on." I was going to spin the boat around to port. Boats was still jammed into the corner of the pilothouse with me, and the others, I hoped, were in the main cabin aft.

For a moment, the boat seemed to settle on the level in a trough as I looked up to see the next breaker, a grey and white monster, hanging above us. First, keeping my right hand on the wheel, I spun it hard left and with my left hand pushed the starboard engine ahead then quickly pulled the port into reverse. I tried to use just enough power to make a fast turn but not so much that it would drive us forward into the next oncoming wave that loomed ahead. Trying to execute this turn in that short trough between waves was my goal. With a short period this was no easy task, especially with several tons of foaming white water starting to drop down hard from above.

We moved across the trough and were starting to complete the turn when the next wave caught us square and full force on our starboard stern quarter. The foam and churning top of the wave crashed across the open fantail of the boat but the shoulders of the wave below the crest lifted up PCF 76, all twenty tons. It held us like a toy for maybe a second or two and then simply rolled us upside down, landing broadside to the oncoming seas. We had not completed the turn. It is difficult to imagine a boat that had faithfully brought you and your crew through storms and enemy firefights now being tossed around like a piece of stray driftwood.

This was not in slow motion; it just flipped. I was tossed hard to my left, losing my grip on the wheel. Out of the corner of my eye, I saw the water come crashing into the pilothouse in a grey-green wall. In seconds, the boat was completely and fully upside down. Instinctively, I lunged to my left for the side window of the pilothouse, probably because that was the direction of the turn and the boat's subsequent roll.

The pilothouse door would have made much more sense, but I wasn't sure where the handle was or whether it might be jammed. Because the boat was upside down, the port side was now the starboard side and facing out into the surf line.

Somehow, I squeezed through the side window. I don't remember whether I pushed it out or if it was already gone. The window was about twenty inches on each side and it was a tight fit. I do remember that I hit something and got stuck partway through. However, training and that basic will to survive got me out within a matter of seconds. I remember the next day looking at another Swift Boat and wondering just how I was ever able to fit through that small side window.

Now, I was about six feet underwater, getting tossed around surrounded by bubbles and foam with the shadow of the boat looming above me. Fortunately, it was about 0800 in the morning and despite the overcast there was enough sunlight that I could see which direction was up, toward the surface. This was a huge factor in correcting the physical disorientation that came as a result of having departed an upside-down boat in a very big hurry.

As I swam for the surface, which was only six or eight feet above me, I noticed the boat coming back down, driven by the surf, basically toward me. With a couple of rapid kicks and a stroke or two I was able to propel myself off to the side, just in time to avoid being crushed by the hull.

By the time I finally broke to the surface, I was incredibly short of breath. The turn, the roll over, exiting the window and my climb to the surface probably was less than three minutes but I was without air for a good part of that time.

Breaking the surface, gasping for air, unfortunately, I saw that I had ended up on the ocean side with the boat itself on the shore side of my location. PCF 76 was now fully upside down, being held captive in the surf, but at the same time being rapidly carried away from my position. Another wave, full force crashed down on top of me. In an instant, I was flipped over by its massive power, which then drove me downward about ten feet. By the time I fought my way back to the surface, the next wave was towering above me soon to crash down. All the while PCF 76, my only chance of survival, was slowly but steadily being carried away from me by each successive wave.

My present situation was rapidly deteriorating, physical strength was waning, exhaustion was setting in and in a matter of minutes I would no longer be strong enough to fight the surf. I knew enough to kick off my trusty boat sneakers, but I did not have the strength left to remove my shirt or pants, despite knowing full well this was proper procedure because now they were dangerously weighing me down.

I made several futile attempts to swim to the boat, which because of its size was slowly being carried farther away from me with each successive wave. The distance between the boat and me, I judged to be no more than a hundred and fifty feet, but I continued to be pushed down and under by the next unforgiving breaker. Each time fighting to the surface became harder and harder, as I had little breath remaining and any strength was fading fast.

My mind was starting to visualize that I was not gonna make it. This was the end. And then in a moment, my survival instinct kicked in. I don't know whether it was faith in God, training or discipline, but I was suddenly screaming to my inner self, I don't want to die, *I don't want to die,* and I dug deep one more time, swimming full out, arms driving, hands pulling, feet kicking, basically in automatic. Pushing myself—*one more stroke, one more stroke...*

I gave one last effort, fully realizing this swim would most likely be my last and then I would drown. I simply would not have the strength to try again if the boat drifted too far away.

I was near the boat gasping for air, almost there, through the splashes and the spray I briefly saw its outline. *Drive, drive, don't fail...*

And then I was there. Quickly, with my right arm extended, I reached up and grabbed onto one of the exhaust pipes protruding from the stern of the boat. I locked onto it and brought up my other arm.

Meanwhile the surf continued to pound down, slamming me against the hull, while at the same time pushing the boat relentlessly along the surf line. I was well aware that this was a huge improvement in my status and for the time being I was very much alive. I took a minute or two to gain back some strength and started to think straight again. I thanked God and tried to figure out a next step.

My current position was not tenable in the long term, simply because of the incredible force of the surf tossing the boat around and me with it. Each wave pulled and twisted my body, almost breaking my grip on the exhaust pipe. I needed to climb up onto the bottom of the boat, which was now about three to four feet above my head.

Above the exhaust ports were zincs, which were blocks of metal about 1 foot by 2 foot. They were bolted onto the hull and their purpose was to neutralize the electrical signature of the boat. I had the exhaust pipe and the zincs above, which gave me two things I could climb on. *Forget the pain, ignore the roll of the boat and its slimy bottom, just climb and climb fast*. I knew that once I was near the bottom of the boat I could reach out and grab the rudders then pull myself onto the upside down hull.

It took a moment or two for me to establish where I was. The boat was completely upside down. It was laying sideways to the surf line, which meant it was rolling heavily while being buffeted and tossed about by each successive wave crashing in, about every six or seven seconds. Just holding on with my hands was not an option, so I wrapped my legs and arms around the rudders carefully avoiding getting smashed into the sharp propeller blades, although the engines had stopped when we rolled over.

I looked around toward shore, slowly getting my bearings, and through the mist I saw my crew fifty to seventy-five yards away hanging onto the boat's life raft from PCF 76 which had broken loose. I felt a surge of joy. From this distance, it was difficult to determine what kind of physical shape they were in, but they appeared to be drifting slowly out of the surf line toward shore, while being wildly tossed around.

I began to yell to them asking about their condition and demanding that they respond to me. I was doing something that hopefully would keep their adrenalin up and maintain their will to fight and survive. Looking through the spray that was blown off each wave top, I eventually saw that one or two of them appeared to have life jackets on which they must have grabbed just as the boat rolled over. Any effective communication between us was difficult because of the wind roaring across the crest of the waves. Just knowing that they were alive was a huge boost to my mental well-being and being able to communicate, at least on some basic level, was beneficial to all of us.

Counting the four on the raft and identifying each of them, it suddenly struck me that Boats was missing. I guessed it had been ten to fifteen minutes since the boat had turned over. I looked over the foaming surf hoping, perhaps, Boats had surfaced outboard of the boat. Then reality hit me hard and everything stopped. The joy of my survival and that of the rest of the crew disappeared. Boats was probably gone and drowned.

I had to push that the painful reality out of my mind and deal with the safety of the rest of the crew and my own situation. Mine was definitely not improving because it now appeared that the boat remained stuck in the surf line and was being pushed along it. In contrast, the crew, holding onto the raft, appeared to be drifting slowly toward shore and safety. I looked up and saw through the haze what appeared to be another Swift Boat exiting the river mouth, approaching the edge of the surf line and heading our way.

I made the decision that another Swift Boat would never make it through the surf line and get to my position without encountering a similar fate. As best I could, I held on with one hand while my legs remained tightly wrapped around the rudder post and waved him off with a long slow sweeping motion, hopefully directing him toward the life raft. The raft was so small and low in the water it would be difficult to see between the crest of waves. As best I could tell, all four were still hanging onto the raft. Finally, I saw the Swift Boat start to turn and head in the direction of my crew. I learned later that day that the rescue boat was PCF 80, with Tom Jones (Moll Flanders) as skipper.

In the midst of all my waving and yelling, suddenly, right at the stern directly below me, Boats literally popped to the surface. Clad in a white t-shirt and matching boxer shorts, he was well dressed for a day at the beach. He appeared in decent shape, definitely short of breath and understandably disoriented. Immediately, I reached down with my right hand and told him to grab on and climb up using the exhaust pipe and zincs as I had done. My mind was reeling from simultaneous emotions of shock, relief, and appreciation at seeing Boats alive.

With a couple of painful slips and several motivating grunts, Boats joined me. Now, we were both wrapped securely with legs and arms around the rudders and propeller shafts. Still short of breath, but visibly relieved, Boats explained to me what he had been through.

When the boat began to roll over, he had made a lunge from the pilothouse into the main cabin with the intention of going out the rear door, but never quite made it. When the boat first turned over there was a substantial amount of air trapped in the main cabin where he could breathe. However, in the main cabin, set in the deck plates were the ammunition lockers for the machine guns. Six to eight boxes of ammo, probably weighing forty to fifty pounds apiece, must have dropped out when we rolled over, but by good fortune they appeared to have missed him. If they had fallen on him, they would certainly have injured him or possibly even trapped him on the cabin top. He said he stayed in the main cabin, utilizing the air pocket that was slowly disappearing, as the boat settled down in the water. He had the time and good sense to remove his shirt, pants and sneakers, making his movements much easier in the confined space. The ammunition boxes were now spread across the cabin top, and numerous other items such as mattresses had broken loose and were floating or strewn about the cabin.

Boats was able to manage his stress level and even though the boat was upside down, he identified his escape route as the sliding windows on either side of the main cabin. These were not watertight and would open easily and, most importantly, were large enough to swim through. Because the boat was upside down and gradually filling with water, the windows were soon below the air pocket he was breathing in. This meant he would have to dive several feet underwater thereby leaving behind that precious air pocket above him.

Realizing this, he then felt his way to the side of the cabin and found the sliding window and was able to pull it open. All the while the boat was rolling from side to side and pitching in the surf. Most likely, this would be a one- way trip with little chance of returning to the air pocket in the cabin if his first attempt was unsuccessful. Some daylight was still coming from the surface but this only marked the window's location, providing little if any illumination into the cabin itself.

He found the side window essentially by feel, using his hands and feet, was able to open it and stream to the surface, appearing just below my position at the boat's stern. His surfacing at the stern rather than alongside indicated to me that the boat was continuing to move along the surf line rather than drift toward the shore. No question, if he had remained in the water, he would have easily been swept away from the minimal safety of the upside down hull.

I was incredibly grateful—ecstatic that he was alive. I gave him the once over and he appeared to be in pretty good physical shape. My mouth was bleeding but this appeared to be from minor cuts and some broken teeth. My hips and legs were stiff, I presume from getting stuck in the window and the shock of the boat hitting or almost hitting me. Between us nothing was broken that we could ascertain and everything seemed in reasonable working order.

Now, the challenge was how were the two of us going to get off the overturned PCF 76? The crew appeared to be heading out of "Harm's Way" as PCF 80 approached them and they drifted into somewhat calmer waters. Tom was an able skipper with a competent crew and nearby was a pusher boat from Cua Viet as a possible backup. Our own problem at the moment was that we were basically stuck, locked into the surf line and not able to break clear of it.

Overhead we saw a small spotter plane which was circling, obviously aware of our situation. We hoped and assumed that they were in radio communications with other nearby units. Several minutes later this was confirmed when a Marine Huey helicopter arrived on the scene. The pilot hovered overhead which was even more encouraging. Taking no chances, we remained arms locked onto the rudders and propeller shafts of the boat.

My growing concern now was the physical integrity of the boat, which was being carried north in the direction of another surf line rather than toward calmer water. This situation most likely eliminated any chance of rescue by another boat. The violence of the slamming, rolling and twisting was so great that I felt it was eventually going to do structural damage to the boat. PCF 76 could break up and sink or might even roll over again on its own. Neither option was going to work for us.

Unfortunately, the spotter plane and Huey helicopter overhead were not capable of rescuing us. The helicopter had no lift capability and in these sea conditions, with the size of the waves and the swirling wind, he would never be able to approach the boat at a low level for a grab-on rescue. There was no question in my mind, if there was even a remote chance of success, the pilot would have gone for it. I knew their flying expertise and had seen their courage in action before.

Boats and I hung on, working to keep each other's spirits up. We fully realized that although our current circumstances were not ideal, during the last half hour we had seen a significant upgrade in our situation. Both of us kept yelling to the crew and I hoped they could see that Boats had made it out alive and we were safe for the time being. It appeared that now Tom Jones in PCF 80 was close to reaching our crew, all of whom were still hanging onto the raft as it continued to drift into calmer and workable water.

Above us, the spotter plane and the Huey were joined by a third aircraft—a U.S. Marine H 34 chopper. I had flown previously in these and knew they had lift capability to pick up wounded or move cargo.

As expected the other two aircraft backed off from circling directly overhead, but they remained nearby to provide communications or visual support.

The H 34 dropped to about 200 feet and lowered its rescue sling. This device resembled a padded yellow horse collar with the two ends closed together by a fitting joined to a lift cable attached to the winch on board the chopper. If conscious, the person slips the collar over his head and under his armpits with the lift wire rising in front of his chin. No straps, no harness—just the downward drag of your own body weight keeps you in. This is usually combined with a little touch of terror for good measure. This method of lift will even work for someone who is unconscious but it requires a little more luck. I had been lifted several times before off a ship utilizing one of these and knew they were both safe and efficient despite their somewhat simplistic limp doughnut appearance.

Boats and I still had a challenge—to not fall off the slick bottom of the boat back into the surf while trying to grab the collar. The collar was swinging wildly in the wind, definitely not in sync with the roll and twisting of the boat beneath us. The pilot was doing his best to maintain position and altitude over us despite the turbulence caused by the crashing surf below. Meanwhile, the crew chief was hanging halfway out the starboard doorway, watching us, steadying himself with one hand on the winch while relaying directions to the pilot by internal radio.

The racket from the helo so close above us was deafening and this was accompanied by shotgun-like spray pellets from the chopper's downdraft. I informed Boats of that old naval tradition that said the captain was the last one to leave the sinking ship but he should not push tradition to the limit. Instead, I suggested he get his butt in the sling. He got the message loud and clear and when the collar came close to the stern, Boats reached out.

With one hand he grabbed the harness and with the other let go of his hold on the propeller shaft. In one motion, he slipped the harness over his head with both his arms going through the same opening. Then he joined both his hands on the lift cable to make the entire rig more secure. The lift master saw this and immediately began the winch up.

They were still about 200 feet above us and Boats was soon climbing into the open door of the helicopter.

The collar was again lowered to me but not quite as close this time, requiring my moving away from my safety handholds. I slowly crawled forward, spread as best I could on all fours, feeling the wet and slippery scum on the hull bottom beneath me. If I started to slide there would be nothing to stop me and I would be back in the churning water. In the next moment, the collar swung level by me; it was no more than five feet away. I lunged for it and caught it with one hand. That was good enough to let me thrust my other hand up into the collar and pull myself upright just as my bare feet skidded and lost traction. Over the head, under the arms—a hug never felt as good. To maintain some sense of style I gave the pilot a thumbs-up, not knowing if he could even see me hanging below.

My touch of theater was most likely wasted because the pilot wanted to climb and he did so rapidly. I presume there was considerable turbulence from the surf line at this low altitude and he wanted to reach more stable air. As he turned to head upriver, I was waiting for the lift master to "crank me up," but there seemed to be some mechanical delay.

There I was dangling 100 feet below a helicopter, swinging in a rescue harness, flying along the DMZ at altitude off the deck of about 500 feet. Looking down I saw PCF 76 bottom up, still being manhandled by the foaming white water. I certainly felt a moment of sadness, but this was quickly overshadowed by the critical fact that today, November 6, 1967, all of us had safely passed by death's door. My entire crew had all been rescued and we were safe.

In under a minute, I too was safe inside the helicopter, sitting on the deck beside Boats and the lift master, who was graciously receiving our heartfelt appreciation. I wanted to personally thank the pilot, but on a combat helicopter, especially one this small, you do not simply stroll to the flight deck. The helicopter's up-and-down, side-to-side motion reminded me of where I had been just minutes before. Therefore, I crawled on all fours and headed forward. My hands and knees were somewhat bloody, my uniform was hardly parade dress, but thanks to these guys, we were survivors. The pilot was at the controls in the left-hand seat. There is a very good reason why the helicopter crew and passengers on board wear helmets with radio headsets; you cannot hear a damn thing without them.

I will never forget the image of the pilot—personalized flight helmet, sunglasses, cigar, and wad of gum all functioning simultaneously, John Wayne style. I could do no more than crawl up beside him and pat him on the leg to express my heartfelt thanks for saving our lives. His left hand never left the stick while he gave me that quick and knowing once-over look. This was followed by a simple "thumbs-up." *Semper Fi, Marine.*

I would have preferred that we be dumped at our base at the river mouth so that I could check on the status of my crew, but we were already several miles upriver heading toward the airbase at Dong Ha. The pilot quickly set the chopper down on the tarmac and the crew chief gave me a quick salute, which I returned while he pointed to the cabin door. Obviously, they were needed elsewhere and there was no time for a round of congratulatory drinks at the O'Club. On the ground, we stepped toward the front of the aircraft and gave a salute to the pilot and co-pilot. Without question, we looked Navy sharp. Boats was resplendent in his underwear and I was soggy and barefoot but in full uniform.

For my part, I wanted to get downriver and back to the base. Boats quickly found himself a pair of dry pants and in similar fashion got us on board the next landing craft that shuttled back and forth delivering supplies between Dong Ha and Cua Viet. The ride downriver took over an hour, but we were able to radio the Swift base before we left Dong Ha. We were informed that the rest of crew had been rescued by Tom Jones and his crew in PCF 80, and they were currently in the infirmary with no serious physical injuries.

We arrived at the Swift pier, both of us barefooted, disheveled and emotionally exhausted, finding no relaxation on our ride down the river. Tom Jones was near the pier and told us his crew had picked up our men. I gave him my heartfelt thanks and he walked with us over to the infirmary. The men were being checked out physically and appeared to be OK, other than a few cuts and scrapes. The mental impact of the event would only be known over time. I suspected there would be some scars but I had great faith in the crew. They were already tested in combat and hopefully no permanent damage was done. The doctor told me he wanted them to remain for several more hours just for observation.

I left Boats in charge and went back to check in at our operations shack. They informed me that several Navy frogmen were in the area and were nearby discussing the status of our boat. The frogmen were our neighbors in Da Nang, so I presume they must have flown up to Cua Viet. Together, we walked down to the beach and with binoculars were able to spot PCF 76. We saw that it was still upside down but partially submerged at the bow. It had finally drifted out of the heavy surf line but was still being tossed about. One of the frogman felt it was worth a try to swim out to the boat and try to attach a line. The theory was to attach a light line to the boat and then use that as a feeder, perhaps for a heavier cable that could pull the boat closer to shore by towing it with one of the Marine amtracs or another piece of heavy equipment.

I was in no shape nor was I qualified to make that swim, so several of us went into shallow water to help control the light line. The lead frog, Jack Darcy, put on his fins and swam out carrying the light line and soon reached the boat, but he returned to the beach in short order. He told us that the pilothouse had partially broken free from the hull. It was swinging up and down like a pair of metal jaws as the boat rose and fell each time the waves lifted the boat. There was no way, with that amount of movement and loose metal, he could approach the boat let alone secure a line to it.

I thanked them for their courage and their effort but stated my crew was safe and, under these conditions, the boat was expendable. Whether the Navy higher-ups would agree with that decision was really of no concern to me. My men had been through a torturous morning. It was still not even noon, and they were all safe. As skipper, I was incredibly thankful but also proud of the manner in which the crew had performed. For myself, I had faced death head on that morning and had been given that special strength that allowed me to make the one final effort that had saved my life. Pausing for a moment looking out to sea, I said my

*Dan Daly and all that remained of PCF 76.*

final farewell to PCF 76. Saluting, I thanked her for all her good service to our crew ... and said, "Farewell, Good Friend."

Two days later, I found out that she had never come ashore and had broken up in the surf. All that did come ashore and wash up on the beach was a wooden silverware drawer, along with the orange life ring with PCF 76 that Boats had painted on it with his best attempt at Old English script. With great pride, I later hung it on the side of my tool shed on Cape Cod.

## The Rescue of Four of PCF 76's Crew, November 6, 1967

*Tom Jones (Moll Flanders), skipper, PCF 80*

My crew and I returned to the Cua Viet base from patrol early that morning due to the heavy weather. Sea conditions were awful on the "outside," but nothing like the conditions in the channel with an outgoing tide and east/northeast wind. This was not the first time we entered the river in high surf conditions, but based on the limited experience Bos'n mate Harris or myself had, today was a major challenge. On one occasion, PCF 80 heeled over 50° driven by the seas. Looking aft, I was calling surf conditions and distance, and Gunner was reporting from the .50 caliber gun tub above. Harris had it under control and we finally made it in.

After leaving the 80 boat, I went to the skipper's hooch and then to the Ops shack to complete my patrol report. Our Engineman Vern Walters stayed with the boat for maintenance checks, and the other members of the crew, Bos'n mate Stirlin Harris, Radarman Bill Dodd, Gunner's Mates Paul Kellner and Dennis Wilson went to their hooch. I soon heard from Tom Yankura, our base O-in-C that PCF 76 was heading out on a weather probe. I told him, "That could be a big problem ... no one should be out there today."

I ran outside the Ops shack and saw that PCF 76 was already in the river, slowly heading east. I ran as fast as I could toward the boat docks,

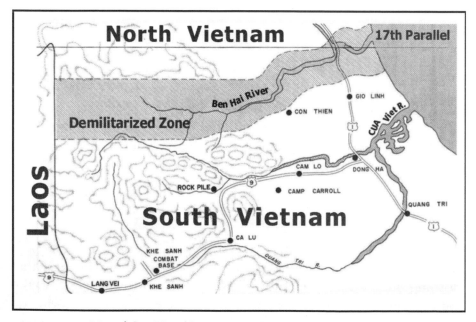

*Map of Cua Viet. (Courtesy Maritime Museum of San Diego)*

*Marine H 34 with winch located above the cargo door.*

veering off to our crew quarters and yelling to Bos'n mate Harris and the guys to get to the boat NOW! All of the PCF 80 crew made it. Walt fortunately had done nothing at this point with the engines, so I cranked them up, lines were cast off and we powered out of our slip and headed to PCF 76's location to "stand by." I was at the aft deck helm station with Walters and Kellner. Harris and Dodd were in the pilothouse and Wilson was above in the gun tub. I turned the helm over to Harris in the pilothouse as soon as we were heading east on the river and I moved forward to the pilothouse to watch the 76 boat.

By that time, PCF 76 was entering the boiling channel surf where we could see many Vietnamese fishermen had been tossed into the angry sea and were fighting to survive. In the next moment, we saw PCF 76 turn to port to reverse course, and then the fatal wave caught it broadside, followed by the rollover. Harris then powered on forward into the confused, heavy seas and churning waters, as Dodd and I went

*Crew of PCF 80, 1967–1968. Back row: (L to R) RDR3 Bill Dodd, GM3 Dennis Wilson, LTJG Tom Jones, BM2 Stirlin Harris. Front row: (L to R) EN2 Vernon Walters, GM3 Paul Kellner.*

aft to hopefully begin recovering survivors with my two other crew, Walters and Kellner. As we reached the crest of each wave, we tried to see anyone who had survived and then we finally spotted those who had surfaced. Harris moved PCF 80 thru the white water, and as we closed, I took the helm at the aft station to come alongside PCF 76's men. I cannot recall if they were still hanging onto the raft. As I maneuvered alongside each of them in the confused seas, the crew on the aft deck reached down and pulled them on board, most on the port side.

At the same time, the local fisherman nearby continued to fight for their lives as they were streaming by our 80 boat. We were able to rescue some of them and pulled them aboard. Now, we saw the 76 boat with [Daly] and Bos'n mate Fielder on top of the hull and I knew we could

*Real bad day at the river mouth (Courtesy Stirlin Harris).*

not come alongside for a pickup based on your treacherous location. By now a Marine helo had arrived and was maneuvering into rescue position. I then signaled to Harris to take the helm forward. He once again steered through the confused seas, reversed course to the west and we carefully rode on the back of the rolling waves into the calm of the river, returning to the Swift pier. The 76 crew, despite being beaten up and wet, chose to complete the ride on the aft deck of PCF 80 rather than go below ... something I could well understand considering what they had just been through.

# Section V
# Operations at An Thoi, Coastal Div. 11

## CHAPTER 23

# BOB MACK'S RIVER INSERTION

Our good friend Bob Mack, the third musketeer and Coronado class-mate, had been stationed for almost eight months at the Swift base at An Thoi, on Phu Quoc Island, just nine miles south of the Cambodian border in the Gulf of Thailand. Sandy beaches and palm trees, all of which sounded quite glamorous. Bob and I had kept in touch by letter, usually every other week. We discussed various Swift operations and traded sea stories of friends from Boat School that took place in our respective divisions. The Chu Lai adventures of our classmate Ed Bergin were often a featured story in any correspondence. He was the most colorful musketeer, and he had acquired an even more august call sign, "Lord Mort," after his Chinese trawler capture. Bob had a big news advantage over me because he had stories and pictures of the new heiress to the Mack fortune, Miss Emily.

With our patrols schedules, a phone call was never going to happen and in combat zones you didn't leave a message saying, "Call me when you have a free moment." The long-range radio worked, providing that the temperature was right, the air was clear and the signal could bounce off the stratosphere and somehow roll down the geographic center of Vietnam all at the same time. In defense of technology, Bob was about 500 miles away.

Late one night, we were both in port and I was successful raising Bob on the long-range radio and we were able to discuss the non-confidential operations that were taking place at An Thoi. I hadn't talked to him in over a month and it was good to catch up, even with the crackles and background static punctuating our conversation.

Bob mentioned that he was going north to Saigon the following week for an operational briefing and to pick up a case of electronic parts that seemed to be having trouble getting into the Navy supply system. I thought that I might be able to grab a day or two and meet him there. The Da Nang airport and the Air Force always seemed to have flights to everywhere in Vietnam, especially if you weren't concerned about first-class seating. I got the okay from our operations people and my crew would patrol on a fill-in basis for the two days I would be gone. Most boat skippers were more than happy to have someone from PCF 76 as a replacement.

Early the following week, we met together in Saigon for dinner at some nameless restaurant downtown that Bob had found. He told me it was frequented by the U.S. military and therefore was most likely safe from any bomb-throwing terrorist action. The possibility of buying the farm, during the main course, was not something I even remotely wanted to think about. This was my first trip to Saigon and to me it was a madhouse of activity—many people (not just military), riding too many vehicles, especially motorbikes and scooters with their blue-grey exhaust. The sidewalks were full and everyone was trying to sell you something along the way—bootlegged, black market, or imitation, take your pick.

I arrived first and got two seats on the restaurant's open porch facing the street, always ready for the quick getaway. It was great to see Bob when he walked in. He had lost about twenty pounds and looked fit and well, except for one item that I couldn't miss. His hand and arm seemed to be in a cast with a sling hung around his neck. His injury was news to me and had never been included in his correspondence or communications.

My first comment was, "What happened to you, my friend?"

His reply was that his boat had a run-in with Charlie and a couple of B-40 rockets about a month earlier. I recalled that Bob had always been a man of few words but this combat description was a bit of an understatement.

My next question was, "Did you lose anyone?"

His response was, "Negative, some minor injuries from flying glass but I seemed to be the preferred target, driving in the pilothouse." He continued, "The boat was another story, having been lifted out of the water by the first rocket that hit off the bow and then the second rocket that drove a hole in the engine room right on the waterline."

I immediately pictured twenty tons of Navy-gray Swift Boat rising up by the bow on a vertical column of water, driven below by a fiery explosion, just in time to take the second hit.

Bob said that his injuries were primarily caused by being blown out of the pilothouse by the first explosion and down the stairs into the main cabin, which broke his arm and wrist. I made the timeout signal forming a "T" with both hands and said we've got to get a round of drinks before I hear the complete story. Saigon being more cosmopolitan than Da Nang, I was able to order my Jack Daniels: "Two doubles, rocks, splash of water, bottled if you would."

I wanted the full story complete with background material; my flight was not scheduled to depart until early afternoon the next day and I had plenty of time. I also knew that I would be required to give a detailed report to all the boat drivers upon my return up north.

Over dinner, he started by giving me a full rundown on southern operations. Bob said that Naval Forces Vietnam (NavForV) was putting a major emphasis on Swift Boats patrolling the rivers and coast from the Mekong Delta north to the Cambodian border. This would eventually became part of Operation Sealords (SeaLords) whose goal was to shut down any enemy transport of men or materiel on the inland waterways in that area.

The Swift base itself was designated Coastal Div. 11 and was located near the small village of An Thoi, at the southern end of the mountainous Phu Quoc Island. The crews there lived on an APL with the boats tied alongside, similar to the setup we had in Da Nang, albeit with a better waterfront view.

From this location he described how the boats would transit about thirty miles to the east arriving at the mainland, nearby the coastal town of Ha Tien located four miles south of the Cambodian border. The word "town" might be a bit of a stretch—a fishing village posed a better description. At that point, the boats would start patrols in the Vinh Te Canal, which ran along the Cambodian border. Several of the estuaries off the canal were better known as Bernique's Creek, after skipper Mike Bernique, for his crusades through these treacherous backwaters.

Another major operating area for the crews of Coastal Div. 11 was located about 120 miles south of the An Thoi base, off the Ca Mau peninsula. This was the southernmost tip of Vietnam, approximately 500 miles north of the equator. Here Swifts had no onshore facility but operated off an anchored LST (Amphibious Landing Ship) several miles off the coast.

From the LST, the Swift Boats patrolled the Cua Lon River that stretched miles across the bottom of the Ca Mau peninsula from Ong Trang Cape on the southwest, through to Mai Vinh on the southeast side. Depending on the route, this could be twenty to forty miles of treacherous water. The crews often rotated off the crowded LST after four to five days of patrolling and returned to An Thoi and Coastal Div. 11, usually leaving the boats behind. As a result, there were fewer exclusive boat/crew assignments than we had up north. Out of An Thoi multiple boats would also do shorter patrols compared to the longer thirty-hour-plus single-boat patrols we were used to up north.

Another active area about thirty-five miles north of the LST was the village of Ganh Hao which lead to the river of the same name. This patrol area was also serviced off the LST and on occasion they used the large Coast Guard cutter *Wachusett* as a home base of operations. When we operated off Navy ships, I always felt a little bit like the party crasher because you often rotated bunks with the ship's crew and overcrowded their mess facilities. Also, support in terms of repair was usually minimal at best.

Since we first met in Boat School, Bob had become a good friend and by all standards he was a competent boat skipper. His leading petty officer was John Singleton who could best be described as a man of the earth: a farmer, fisherman and hunter, who had grown up in the Carolinas. He was an engineman first class and this made him a valuable crew on any diesel-driven Swift Boat. Before Vietnam, he had seen destroyer duty out of Hawaii and shore duty in the Far East. John was backed up by Gordon Wagoner, a first class bos'n mate from the Midwest. As a result, Bob's crew was a little more top heavy in terms of age and Navy experience compared to my crew, but I would still match my team against any in Vietnam.

Listening to Bob further describe operations off the LST, with its cramped living conditions and rotating crews, I decided that our setups in Cua Viet, Da Nang and Chu Lai, even considering the monsoon weather with its high seas and horizontal rain, were preferable. Home Sweet Home was always a soft spot.

I was anxious to hear about the multiple boat operations they conducted during SeaLords and the transport and insertion of Vietnamese troops. Up north, ninety percent of our ops were single-boat patrols. While we were firing gunfire support on a regular basis for the Marines, especially the small remote units, we never delivered them by Swift Boat. The one exception I knew of was when a team of Marine recon types stationed at Cua Viet wanted us to dump them well inside North Vietnam. Fortunately, the common-sense review board vetoed that project.

This background discussion took up much of the time while we enjoyed a second drink and dinner (chicken with some sort of rice dish with vegetables (*no nouc mam* sauce). The chopsticks were a challenge but we were both committed to going native. I was happy to listen because I knew Bob's injuries were part of a traumatic experience and purposely let him tell stories at his own pace.

After we finished the meal, leaving behind little but the utensils and napkins, Bob said he would be happy to share the multi-boat troop insertion story that had led to his injuries. But first we had to order cognac (VSOP) and I had to review the latest pictures of new daughter, Miss Emily. Both were most enjoyable. The last time I had cognac was almost eight months previous with my father at the Hotel Del Coronado.

Bob began his story describing a planning meeting that had taken place over a month ago with the Swift base commander who arrived with a U.S. Army major in tow. The Navy and the Army had come up with a mission whereby Swift Boats would be utilized to carry Vietnamese Special Forces along with U.S. liaison officers up the Vinh Te Canal.

The goal of the mission was straightforward: Approach fast, strike deep and hit hard well into enemy territory. The plan was that each Swift Boat would carry 10–15 troops.

This mission represented a change from the Army's other "brown water policy," under way in the rivers around Saigon. It entailed carrying troops on board slow-moving converted landing craft that had been fitted with additional armored-steel plating. These were almost like the iron-clad monitors of the Civil War. For heroism in this line of duty, my Boston friend Tom Kelley had been awarded the Medal of Honor. Sealords (SeaLords) was a new Swift mission based on surprising the enemy by utilizing a high-speed river approach and quick insertion.

The decision was made to use four Swift boats, all with experienced crews, approaching the enemy territory in the dark. Then as first light broke, they would proceed at full speed upriver, dropping the troops at a designated spot along the river bank. Swifts provided gunfire cover only, while the troops disembarked and the boats moved back downriver again. Nylon nets, not unlike the old cargo nets used to unload the U.S. Marines in the South Pacific, were hung over the bow of each boat. These would allow the troops to climb down into shallow water without our boats fully grounding. Any boat that grounded in the shallows was in serious trouble, so no anchors would be put out and both engines would be kept running—"Stop and Drop."

Bob said he carefully listened to the presentation and questions while he watched the reaction of the other three boat drivers. Mike Bernique was an experienced and cool customer who would be the lead boat. He was followed by Virg Irwin, recently transferred south from our Swift base at Cat Lo. Bill Franke, a relatively new arrival but competent skipper, was in the third position with Bob bringing up the rear. Along with Bob, they were all experienced boat drivers who had conducted missions with multiple boats. I did take note of Bob's position as the last in the column—always a dangerous position to be in.

The discussion came up regarding possible air cover, specifically helicopters. The Army major felt that the presence of helicopters nearby while they were delivering the troops would be far too noisy as well as making the helos a sitting target when the Swifts unloaded the troops.

Everyone felt that the Swift Boats could make a quieter stealth approach and provide better gunfire support during the landings. There was the possibility of rapid response if the helicopter gunships were on standby located several klicks away. With multiple boats simultaneously unloading troops, plus the distinct possibility of at least enemy small arms fire, helos overhead sounded like a recipe for disaster. With this much going on, clear fields of fire were difficult to define and could very well generate the risk of being hit by friendly fire. The unanimous conclusion was that the helos would be nearby but called in only at the request of and under the control of the onsite Navy commander.

After the major left, Bob sat down with Bernique, Franke, and Irwin, along with Bob's boss who would be the onsite commander embarked with Mike on the lead boat. Bob's boss was Joe Patton, an outgoing young lieutenant commander, call sign "Captain Marvel." I suspect he either had delusions of grandeur or read too many comic books as a child. More importantly, he was on his second Vietnam tour and had spent the previous one on Swift Boats. This gave them all a sense of comfort because he had firsthand combat experience on the boats and was not some desk jockey who had decided to lead a mission to get a couple of combat citations.

The night before the mission each boat officer briefed his own crew individually and then the onsite commander addressed all of them. After dinner everyone turned in early with the order clearly promulgated: "no booze, no exceptions."

Bob described how they all left the APL the next morning at 0400 to pick up their passengers at a small commercial pier nearby. This timeframe would allow them to arrive just south of the insertion point thirty minutes before first light. Bob got up about 0230 and made sure Singleton had the crew awake and standing vertical. The cooks had laid out food for everyone, nothing fancy—juice, toast and plenty of black coffee. They were on the boats twenty minutes early, checking the engines, radar, radio, and all weapons. All boats had been fueled and rearmed the day before.

All four boats shoved off together with the Mission Commander Joe Patton riding lead on Bernique's PCF-3. Call signs were assigned specifically for this mission: "Mustang Actual" for the Mission Commander, then "Mustang Alpha" (Bernique), "Mustang Bravo" (Irwin), "Mustang Charlie" (Franke) and "Mustang Delta" (Mack). All the boat drivers liked this call sign structure because when the going got tough they could drop, in this case, the prefix Mustang and still understand to whom you were talking. In combat, radio clutter and misinterpreted commands could be deadly.

As planned, the night was no-moon black as the four boats proceeded slowly across the harbor, without running lights and with only their radar on. They were running in a column formation about 200 feet apart, so they could just make out the boat ahead.

Arriving at the pier, they saw that it was a good-sized cement structure that had been built for commercial cargo, so the troops had arrived by truck and were parked above and waiting for the Swift Boats. The pier was more than big enough so that all four boats could tie up at the same time, bow to stern along the floating dock beside and below the pier. The Vietnamese Special Forces troops came down a ramp and were quickly loaded on board. They moved aft near the mortar mount where there was room for them to sit and remove some of their gear. As far as Bob could tell, they had their weapons but nothing additional other than canteens of water and extra ammunition. Each group had two M-60 machine guns, four M-79 grenade launchers and everyone else carried an M-16. Not heavy firepower but certainly adequate for a light and mobile force conducting a search and destroy mission. This group was definitely not equipped to stay on the ground for several days and the back-end pick up by the Swifts was an integral part of the mission plan.

You could never know, especially at a commercial pier in a non-military location, where there might be a Viet Cong sympathizer who would quickly report the events taking place to the enemy. With a minimum of conversation, all boats took in the mooring lines and maneuvered quickly away from the pier and headed out of the small harbor toward the mainland.

"Mustang Actual" Joe Patton came up on the radio and gave the order for all of them to form a line abreast alongside him, 150 feet apart. This

*Running in a column upriver.*

formation was a heads-up move on Joe's part because running side by side each boat would paint more clearly on the other boat's radar. In a high-speed column formation, the wake of the boat ahead would often obscure the radar contact of the boat itself, increasing the possibility of a collision. Also in the dark, you were a lot less likely to hit a boat running alongside of you than you were to run up and over a boat traveling ahead of you if that boat unexpectedly slowed or stopped.

Joe in the lead boat instructed everyone to crank the speed up to about 20 kts, which would get them to the pre-insertion point with enough time to conduct a final briefing, check their gear and go to General Quarters. When this was completed, at first light, they would enter the river mouth at full speed proceeding to the designated drop zone by 0530. The rendezvous was somewhat of a waste of time because Joe was justifiably leery of using the radio to communicate so close to the enemy. Any radio transmission, even in code, would tell the enemy that some action was about to take place, just radio chatter itself can be valuable intel.

Everyone had hoped that the seas would be calm enough so that they could briefly tie up alongside and talk. The wind, however, had come up and the waves were building two to three feet high. Therefore slamming the boats together, especially with extra passengers on board, was not considered a smart move. As a solution, Joe directed Mike Bernique as the skipper of PCF 3 to pass astern of the other three while they were facing the river mouth. That way, each boat skipper had an opportunity to exchange any last-minute comments or concerns. There were none.

A faint orange and red glow on the eastern horizon had just begun to show and Bob proceeded toward the pilothouse fully expecting Joe to commence the operation and start the run upriver. They had agreed the previous day that all four boats would transit upriver in a column formation with 150-foot intervals, thereby bringing all guns to bear on the shoreline at the same time. The boats would alternate port and starboard in terms of their weapons covering the shoreline. Mustang Alpha would provide cover to starboard then Bravo to port, Charlie to starboard and Delta to port.

They would run in at close to 25 kts with the actual speed being set by the lead boat. Basically, it was going to be "follow the leader" and then each boat would adjust the intervals accordingly. Running at this speed with twenty tons of boat and not much light was tricky, so concentration by all hands on all boats was critical. Bob was in the helmsman's chair in the pilothouse, right hand on the top of the big aluminum wheel, left hand on the throttles, the radio microphone and speaker right overhead. Singleton was watching the radar scope but traveling at high speed with four boats this close made for a confused and cluttered radar display.

In accordance with the mission's operations order, once the boats entered the Vinh Te Canal river mouth, it was "guns free" because this was confirmed enemy territory with no good guys around. That said, they did not want any over-active trigger fingers unleashing the hell fire from all four boats, thereby sending a clear signal of their approach to the enemy.

Bob was at the helm in the pilothouse, needing to be near the radio and to look forward to see firsthand the position of the other three boats charging upriver ahead of him.

Meanwhile, the Special Forces troops were on their own, aft by the mortar, but Bob sensed they were experienced enough to remain seated and hold on during some of the winding turns that were rapidly approaching in the river. While the tight turns in the river could very well conceal an enemy ambush, they also provided some cover for the Swifts as they approached. The distance between the turns in the river would also define the potential ferocity and duration of any firefight.

Another serious consideration was the risk of a high-speed grounding in a shallow riverm which could be disastrous, leaving you stranded on a damaged boat and surrounded by the enemy. All eyes were locked on the boats ahead. Hearing was fine-tuned to the radio with each skipper grabbing an occasional glance out the open pilothouse doors as the shoreline raced by.

Bob described surfing along the foaming white wakes that were generated by the three boats ahead. Each wake rolled then crashed along the riverbanks with the waves quickly being dispersed by the dense

*No margin of error in Bernique's Creek. (Courtesy Michele Bernique)*

root structure of the mango trees. The river was no more than 200 feet wide in this section. He realized that there was no way any boats could drop forty or more troops in this environment because they could never penetrate the tangle of tree stumps, roots and branches that came right down to water's edge. Joe Patton as the mission commander had to know where there was a clearing and a convenient drop-off zone, one location big enough for four Swift Boats to land at the same time.

So far so good, no enemy fire, but the shoreline was so dense with trees, jungle and vines, Bob figured the VC couldn't operate in this area either. Suddenly, the radio speaker over Bob's head crackled to life and Joe transmitted, "All units, this is Mustang, stand by for touchdown."

Three "Roger outs" followed in quick succession with the appropriate call signs attached, Bravo, Charlie, and Delta.

Bob immediately relayed this info to gunner Simonson who was sitting above him in the gun tub manning his twin .50s. As previously agreed, in less than two seconds he had relayed the "touchdown" message back to the rest of the crew as well as the Special Forces troops on the aft deck. Bob trusted that he had not lost any of his passengers on the trip upriver.

Joe Patton was riding on Mike Bernique's Alpha, the lead boat, and Bob saw it abruptly slow down and watched his big white wake disappear to a rolling ripple under the stern. Virg Irwin in Bravo, Bill Franke in Charlie and Bob Mack in Delta immediately pulled back their throttles and followed suit.

The lead boat, now at idle speed, made a quick 90° turn to starboard, heading toward a small open marsh area that was approximately fifty yards wide and another fifty yards deep, before the dense green jungle closed in again. Joe was a resourceful guy and perhaps he had found this spot in some local Vietnamese AAA tour guide book marked: "ideal for troop landings."

No sooner had the first boat touched the shoreline then a crewman ran to the bow and tossed over the cargo net. The troops quickly moved toward the bow of his boat, ignored the cargo net, and jumped off onto the soft marsh grass. The other three boats quickly followed and all troops were off in what seemed to be less than five minutes. The troops quickly moved out of the open area, disappearing into the underbrush, and that was the last they saw of them. Mustang came on the net with a simple message: "All units be advised, Mustang departing." Each boat replied, "Roger that."

Next, Virg backed out hard into midstream followed by Bill and then Bob last in the Delta slot. Staggering the departures would keep the order of boats the same as before although Bob was now situated farthest downstream. Using heavy throttle, port and starboard juxtaposed, Bob swung the wheel and twisted his boat to line up last in the column and then pushed both throttles forward. The trick, which came from experience driving, was to push the throttles aggressively forward but not to accelerate so fast that the inertia and weight of the boat caused the diesels to stall out. These were heavy boats, not sports cars—love 'em and they loved you back, push 'em too hard and they crapped out at just the wrong time.

As agreed, each boat departed the area at full speed not worrying about establishing an interval between the boats, until later on. The goal was three fold: Eliminate time in enemy territory, present multiple high-speed moving targets to any onshore enemy and try to minimize the risk of anyone seeing the drop-off point. Each boat maintained the same assigned gunfire coverage alternating port and starboard, which they had used on the trip upriver. Again this brought maximum firepower to bear on both sides of the shoreline just in case there was an enemy ambush waiting around the next turn. Adrenalin was still running high as was their concentration as each boat twisted and turned, running at close to full speed downriver. Only part of the job had been completed and that may have been the easy part.

## CHAPTER 24

# THE RETURN AND PICK UP

After about twenty-five minutes of high-speed running time, all boats exited the river mouth by Ha Tien into open water. The plan was to have two boats head north and two boats head south and conduct routine junk traffic inspections. As a result no Vietnamese boat traffic in the area would see four Swift Boats clustered together, attracting attention.

The weather had not deteriorated further, so on Bob's boat, Singleton decided to make a late breakfast or perhaps an early lunch for the crew. The time of day made little difference because the menu was the same as it was up north: thickly sliced baloney, iceberg lettuce with yellow mustard served on Wonder Bread. Black coffee or the alternative drink was Navy "bug juice" considered a distant cousin of Kool-Aid. Not the Ritz but always well received. Because Swift Boat patrols were usually no more than thirty-six hours long, they used the small onboard refrigerator and were able to avoid eating those delicious Army and Marine field rations.

Bob was assigned to the northern patrol with Bill Franke and both agreed to transit the fifteen-mile area slowly and to give their crews some time to sleep. With two boats working together, this seemed to make good sense. Before starting the patrol, they stopped and tied up alongside each other, turning the sterns of the boats into the sea for stability. This gave them the opportunity to review the morning's events and discuss the afternoon's upcoming extraction plan. Also, it presented some time for their crews to jawbone, lowering the tension level and allowing for the exchange of personal observations that were often quite valuable.

Both agreed that the insertion operation had gone extremely smoothly, most likely because they had caught the enemy by surprise. Either the bad guys were not in the operating area or they did not have time to launch any counter offensive. Both skippers felt that the extraction operation would not be as simple, especially if the Special Forces had disturbed some hornet's nest, which was the goal of their mission. They were looking to identify any enemy positions, do an aggressive hit and run, then keep moving through the area, eventually being extracted by the Swifts. If the enemy was caught by surprise, hit hard with significant casualties, they were unlikely to pursue them, but if the enemy remained strong or had other units in the area, this could present a significant challenge for the extraction operation. Bottom line, no one expected the withdrawal part of the mission to be the same cakewalk that the morning had been.

The mission plan called for all four boats to rendezvous at the river mouth at 1500. Bob and Bill arrived on station and were joined by Joe Patton still riding Mike's Alpha boat, and Virg nearby on Bravo. Joe informed the others that he had received one radio call at 1200 from Green Giant, the U.S. Army liaison officer. He reported that they had made light enemy contact only, but were moving south based on some local intel which said there was an operating base there with over 100 regular NVA troops. This meant enemy troops that were better trained and equipped with more firepower than the Viet Cong. As each boat maneuvered close alongside, Joe explained that the extraction was tentatively scheduled for between 1800 and 1900—there would still be light, and the location would most likely be downriver from the morning drop off. This appealed to everyone for several reasons: It was closer to the river mouth, not in the same area as the drop off and was south of where the Special Forces had been operating, in summary, closer to the exit.

All four Swifts started approaching the river slowly about 1700, waiting for the call from Green Giant. The challenge was that they wanted to be nearby to quickly respond, but the river mouth was not an area where you wanted to be noticed or be traveling at idle speed. Four Swift Boats traveling together was not the Pacific Fleet but they were likely to be noticed by the locals whom could be counted on to relay the information to the VC or NVA.

At 1740, Joe got Green Giant's extraction call. The location was going to be a point about three miles downriver from the morning's drop-off site. Green Giant said they had been successful in engaging the enemy but were most likely being pursued and wanted out, *fast*! The Special Forces were not adequate in size or well-armed enough to remain in a static combat position. "Hit and run" was their mission, plus they had been on the move since the morning drop off.

Joe gave the visual high sign and each boat went back to General Quarters with all guns manned and armed. He took the lead and the other boats fell in behind, building to full throttle. They entered the river itself at 1810, closer this time with about a fifty-yard interval between boats. Each crew sensed the danger and they were locked on to the shoreline, all guns at the ready. In a river, the enemy was most likely hidden around the corner waiting for you just a couple of hundred feet ahead.

Back in the pilothouse, Bob heard Joe using his Mustang call sign to give a heads-up call to the standby helos "Black Diamonds," saying they might well need backup and air support. The choppers were a Navy group that had worked with the SEALs so they were familiar with Swift Boats' special ops as well as close-in air support.

Naturally, their laconic response was classic airdale, "Mustang, We are Black Diamonds at your service."

Joe radioed to the boats, "All units this is Mustang, 5 minutes to touchdown," and got the prerequisite "Roger that" in response.

No margin for error at this speed. Wagoner, in the gun tub above, heard the radio message from below and once again bellowed it to the rest of the crew.

A round was in the chamber of every weapon as soon as they entered the river mouth, a finger on every trigger. Bob gave his watch a quick glance. Four minutes to go, nothing yet. Up ahead in the river was a sharp turn to port. Without slowing, the first two boats quickly disappeared from view as Bill and Bob followed close behind. Bob swung the wheel hard to the left with his eye on the stern of Bill's boat and felt it lean into the turn and waited for the sound, any sound.

*Black Diamonds ready for action.*

The river abruptly turned straight again and he could see almost a mile dead head before the next turn. He calculated that at 25 kts of speed it was approximately two minutes to a mile. At the turn, Bob estimated he was less than two minutes from "Touchdown."

Where was the best ambush location? This depended on whether the original group pursuing Green Giant had somehow gotten ahead of the good guys? Was there another enemy unit in the area that had been instructed to cut off the movement of Green Giant and the Special Forces? Did they know about the extraction and that Swift Boats were involved? If so, had they figured out that the Swifts needed an open section of shoreline to land four boats? Did they already have an accurate location for the extraction and were they now hidden waiting in ambush?

All these questions churned over in Bob's mind. He knew Joe in command would be running "guns tight" and not risk opening fire at a "might be" target, which would absolutely confirm their location to the enemy.

Mike's boat, with Virg's right behind, entered the right turn and Bob watched their wakes roll out to break on the opposite shoreline. Bill followed in the third position with Bob close behind. They were each fast approaching the turn in their respective Charlie and Delta positions. Bob had his left hand locked on the throttles and assumed that Bill just ahead was doing the same, ready to pull back and slow down rapidly on Joe's command. Then the radio roared at high volume.

"All units, this is Mustang. Touchdown, touchdown, come full right."

There was no radio response to Joe's message because the shoreline erupted with machine-gun fire primarily aimed at Bill, as he made the tight turn to starboard following the first two boats. Bob couldn't see whether Bill was slowing or continuing at full speed, perhaps even passing the touchdown.

It was obvious to Bob that the enemy had let the first two boats pass by and make their turn toward shore, waiting to fire on the second two boats in hopes of cutting off any escape route.

Bob's crew opened fire to starboard with the crack of the first enemy round. The twin .50s forward and the single .50 aft let loose with a steady round of fire. The hot spent brass shells from the .50 calibers firing in the gun tub above jumped from the breech of the gun and rained down into the pilothouse, clanking as they rolled around on the deck, making a racket of falling metal. The big .50 caliber rounds were tearing up the jungle cover—leaves and dust were flying everywhere. You could tell from the sound that the enemy had lighter, more mobile weapons. They were hidden, while the Swifts were very much in the open. Bob could see the wake ahead from Bill's boat, which now had gone around the corner, but he had no trouble hearing his gunfire. He soon saw Bill's ( 50 cal.) rounds tearing up the shoreline and splintering the trees, around what he assumed to be the enemy position – the same positon which was now coming up fast on Bob's starboard beam.

Bob was not concerned about the fire from Bill's guns hitting his boat because of the large angle between them. He did hope that he had a similar safe firing angle on the two Swift Boats located just upriver. Neither skipper wanted their rounds going through the dense jungle to the extraction position. Bob still had not completed the full turn because he had made the decision to slow down and engage the enemy full on, rather than simply charge by. Bill, just ahead on the Charlie boat, was firing at the same location as Bob, confirming this was the right decision. The result was two Swift Boats with six guns blasting away resulting in a decent crossfire. They were engaging the enemy while providing cover for the other two boats, which they hoped were at the extraction point and loading troops.

All the while, the enemy continued to fire with their rounds still coming at the Swifts hard and fast, with an alternating *ping* or a *thunk* when they hit the boat's hull. So far, there were no casualties on board and Bob's crew kept firing nonstop.

As Bill and then Bob finally entered the turn, the full picture came into focus. Alpha and Bravo were bow first on to the shoreline of the clearing and loading fast. In the loading instance, the cargo nets over the bow worked well because the sides of the Swift Boat were too high to climb up unassisted, especially when stepping off the soft river bank. Neither boat was firing because the Special Forces were still coming out from their concealed jungle positions into the clearing and the risk of hitting friendlies was too great. Meanwhile, the .50 caliber gun on the stern of each boat was trained across the river but not firing.

Bob kept up his fusillade while making the turn slowly to starboard. Bill, still moving at half speed, stopped firing while he passed the extraction point, and did a 180° turn in the narrow river without even slowing. Again, he passed the extraction point and was now heading back downriver toward Bob with all his guns firing broadside at the ambush point. The enemy had been smart in their setting of the ambush with a plan to cut off the Swifts' departure. They had not calculated that the last two boats (Charlie and Delta) could bring fire to bear on them from two opposing angles and still not threaten the extraction effort.

Now Bob (heading upriver) and Bill (heading downriver) were closing each other bow to bow with six .50 calibers firing nonstop. Bob told me he grabbed the radio mike and yelled.

"Charlie, this is Delta. Cease fire and pass me port to port, I will maintain fire."

Bill's response was immediate, "Delta, this is Charlie. Wilco, coming past you at half speed."

Meanwhile, as Bob approached the extraction point, he could see that the other two boats upriver were still loading but there were a lot of troops already on their fantails.

At that moment, Joe Patton came on the net, "This is Mustang. All units be advised, extraction complete. *I say again extraction complete.* Charlie and Delta, provide maximum cover."

Bill and Bob both came back with "Charlie Wilco" and "Delta Wilco." This was a gutsy ball play on Joe's part. Rather than take the firing pressure off the enemy, he had loaded all the troops on just the first two boats so that the second pair could maintain maximum firing cover.

As he passed along the side of Bill's boat, Bob noticed that his crew had elevated their hot guns to avoid any weapons cook-off (firing by themselves), which could have been deadly. Once clear, Bill let loose again, this time firing to port as he headed slowly downriver. Bob didn't know the status of his own ammo, but he heard behind him the more junior members of his crew, Simmson and Poons, climbing up on to the cabin top dragging two belts of .50 caliber. Each belt was 454 rounds linked together and weighed 30–40 pounds.

Wagoner had the guns open and was already slamming the first round of each belt into the breach. In seconds, he would be ready to commence fire again. Bob was now almost abreast of Joe Patton and Virg and he saw they were backing off the beach so he yelled to his crew, "Cease fire, hold on, hard left turn."

This way he turned first and therefore did not crowd Joe Patton (in the Alpha boat) and Virg Irwin (in the Bravo boat) as they finished their rotation in the river. Just as important, this was not the time or place to lose someone over the side.

After completing his turn, Bob was now headed back downriver with Bill about fifty yards ahead of him. Both boats were now going in the same direction with Bill's crew walking their .50 caliber fire left then right along the shoreline. Bob assumed their boat was also taking fire but simply couldn't hear it above the racket of his own guns firing and the *zing* and *snap* of the close-by enemy rounds.

In the next instant, three streaks of white grey smoke appeared, breaking through the jungle cover. They were handheld rockets, highly mobile, somewhat slow, but very effective. The first rocket, aimed at Bill's boat, passed harmlessly fifty feet off his bow. Wes Symmes RD-2, his lead petty officer, was in the gun tub and immediately turned the twin .50 calibers following the exhaust plume back to shore and commenced fire. Unless this guy was very fast, that was his last shot.

The two rounds fired at Bob's boat were better aimed. The first landed right in front of his bow and might have hit it. He couldn't tell with the explosive flash and the plume of water. The boat rose up by the bow as if it had hit something under water. A second later the other round hit his boat amidships with a deep-throated explosion. Then a cloud of black smoke came spiraling out from the port side of the boat. The hull rolled to starboard from the impact and then settled back on a level keel. In seconds, the fifty-foot boat, weighing twenty tons, had been lifted out of the water by the bow and then rolled sideways about 45°. All this time, his crew had never stopped firing.

Bill Franke shifted into overdrive. *What was Bob's status? Had they suppressed enemy fire on shore...? For how long...? What was the status of the other two boats?* His last question was answered quickly.

"Delta, this is Mustang. We are astern of you and are commencing fire port side with all guns both units." Having seen the rockets fired from shore Joe continued, "Interrogative, the status of Delta, over?"

Bill, listening to his radio on board the Charlie boat, simply didn't know. Bob had not responded but his radio could be out. The boat now appeared to be stopped, dead in the water, which was not good.

Bill transmitted, "All units, this is Charlie proceeding to assist Delta. Request you provide maximum cover."

"Maximum cover" it was. The other two boats had their six .50s clanking away in unison but in addition, both groups of Special Forces were flat on the aft decks providing fire cover with their automatic weapons. Overloaded with troops, they were moving slowly downriver to the ambush site. Within five minutes the firing from shore had ceased. Joe ordered a cease fire and all crews moved to rearm their weapons.

No one knew how long the NVA had been at that location and Bill wondered if they could possibly be well dug in. For a moment, he considered asking Joe for permission to use the mortar on board his boat, which would fire a heavier round and could penetrate the jungle from above. Bill dropped the mortar idea and shifted his focus back to Bob. He yelled for his crew to cease fire and elevate their guns as they went alongside Bob's boat, which was now stationary about two boat lengths behind them. The smoke was dark and heavy but there appeared to be no flames which made Bill feel better about the risk of any ammo cooking-off. The engine hatches were open and he could see Singleton and someone else leaning in with the fire extinguishers. Just then, Wagoner came up from the main cabin dragging a mattress. This had to mean they were taking on water.

This accounted for three men but there was still no sign of Bob and the other two men. Bill's crew, led by his bos'n Tex Stokes, had brought up their fire extinguishers and were standing along the port side as they approached on Bob's starboard side. Bill told his crew to ready some docking lines including breaking out the big nylon tow line that was stored on the back side of the stern ammo locker.

By now, Bill had moved from the pilothouse to the aft steering station so he had a better view and could easily communicate with Bob's crew as well as his own. Symmes was in their pilothouse to handle any radio traffic.

Bill still saw no sign of Bob. He decided that the fastest way to assess the situation was firsthand and he jumped onto their boat. They told him they had taken a hit from the second rocket forward in the engine room knocking out the diesels. Smoke, no fire but a good-size hole, port side which looked to be below the waterline, therefore the mattress.

Bill went below using the aft cabin door and saw Bob lying on the deck in the main cabin. He was conscious but bloody. His other two crew members were with him, applying a pressure bandage to control the bleeding. The head wound looked serious; Bob appeared groggy and was in a lot of pain from his arm.

The first rocket round had hit near the bow of the boat, broken the windshield into a million fragments, and a piece of shrapnel had caught

Bob (at the helm) on the side of the head. On closer inspection, it would require stitches but would have little long-term impact on his youthful hairline. The second blast had knocked him down the two stairs leading to the main cabin, with enough force to badly break his arm.

Fortunately, despite the amount of red-hot lead that the enemy had been firing from all directions, there were no other significant personnel casualties on Charlie or Delta. There was no question, it was time to "di di mau" out of that location before the enemy regrouped for another attack.

Bill radioed a sitrep (situation report) to Joe Patton as mission commander: "Mustang, this is Charlie. Recommend we leave the wounded short-term on the Delta boat and attempt to tow it from the immediate ambush site."

Joe ordered Mike Bernique as skipper on Alpha and Virg Irwin on Bravo, to remain astern of the other two boats that were not moving and to provide fire cover, but Joe wanted to see Delta under tow in ten minutes. All of them knew the risk of staying in one place, thereby

*Returning to pick up the troops. (Courtesy Michele Bernique)*

giving the enemy valuable time to regroup. As senior officer on the mission, Joe made the decision that if they missed the departure deadline, Bill was to move Bob onto his Charlie boat, then disable the weapons and engines on Delta with their high-temperature thermite grenades, essentially leaving the enemy an unusable hulk.

Symmes and Stokes had begun rigging a towline from Bill's stern to the bow of the Bob's boat. This was a complicated task even without the enemy watching you on shore less than a football field away. It required rigging a bridle and a towline that was slowly paid out to avoid any shock that might break it.

Feeling the clock ticking and most likely a very unfriendly audience nearby, Bill suggested to Stokes that instead they do an alongside tow. The Charlie boat would tie up alongside with a slight overlap to Bob's Delta boat. With several lines going backward they would essentially be pulling his boat forward. This towing method was slower underway but quicker to rig. Under the circumstances quicker to rig won out.

Meanwhile, Bill went to see the status of the hole in Bob's hull from the outside. Leaning overboard while holding onto the railing, he estimated it to be about a foot across. Either they had to make it watertight inside or any type of tow was not going to happen. Joe Patton's ten-minute countdown was still under way.

Symmes knew Singleton, his counterpart on Bob's crew, and they were both sharp and dependable. Bill looked into the engine room and saw the duty mattress had been stuffed in the rocket hole and held in place by what looked like a couple of mop handles and a short piece of pipe (origin unknown). All this was braced against some empty .50 caliber ammo boxes jammed against the diesel engine block. In the Navy, damage control was not an exact science. This rig wasn't going to win an MIT engineering prize, but they assured Bill that it would hold and he could start to move downriver with this rig. They were working to get the pumps going to drain the water from the bilge.

Because the boat had essentially stopped moving when the rocket hit just at the waterline, the water in the bilge from the hole had risen to less than a foot. This was a significant bit of luck because the boat was only sinking slowly and the flow of water was not constant, but once under tow the all-purpose mattress patch had to hold against the increased pressure from their forward movement.

Their time was up and Joe was back on the net. Bill confirmed with him that Bob, his crew, and the Delta boat were stabilized and Bill was ready to commence towing alongside. Joe said he would pass by and take the lead leaving Virg in the last position providing cover astern. Only those two boats (Alpha in front and Bravo at the rear) could provide fire cover because Bob's boat was alongside Bill's, essentially blocking his field of fire. Swift Boat firepower was now at fifty percent.

Bill radioed to Joe that he would like to start the tow at no more than 5 kts, almost idle speed, increasing it slowly. He also informed him that his boat was clear to provide .50 caliber fire cover to starboard if there was trouble from that side of the river. Everyone hoped that if trouble did occur, it would not be from both shorelines.

Bill decided to transfer Bob to his boat, along with most of his crew, in case they needed a quick breakaway. He left Wagoner at Delta's aft helm station to steer and stabilize the tow. Bill figured he could do any release of lines in an emergency solely from his boat with an axe nearby. Meanwhile, Bob had been given a shot of morphine. He was pleased that his crew was OK, but pissed off that his boat was being towed.

No more than fifteen minutes had passed since the rocket attack, and the enemy ceasefire had continued at least for the time being. Most likely this was a direct result of the hellfire fusillade from the Alpha and Bravo boats accompanied by the sharpshooter fire from the Special Forces riding on both boats.

Never assuming victory was at hand, Joe instructed Virg as the last boat in line to commence mortar fire with his 81mm mortar along the shoreline, basically abreast of their position, working behind them and back upriver. Meanwhile, Joe directed Mike Bernique and his crew on the Alpha boat to do the same, in this case start abreast of the group but walk his mortar rounds downriver several hundred yards ahead of them. They used VT fuses, which meant that the rounds went off above ground. This firing maneuver created a moving but deadly rectangle of

*Extraction complete. (Courtesy Bob Shirely PCF 45)*

high-explosive mortar rounds exploding onshore in front of and behind the departing Swifts. The enemy would have a tough time assembling an ambush ahead of them or catching them from behind, despite their slow departure speed.

As soon as they cleared the actual ambush site, Joe radioed the Black Diamond helos and informed them of the mission's status and what action they were taking. They immediately volunteered to provide air cover during transit or even medevac Bob. Joe advised them that a medevac from a Swift Boat was not worth the risk and that Bob was stabilized. He said air cover would be appreciated and asked them to patrol only off the starboard side of the Swifts because they were firing their mortars over the port side of the river.

The Swift Boats, the onboard Special Forces and two choppers nearby presented a formidable but not invincible force. Surely the enemy was very unhappy about a penetration so deep into their territory, and the heavy casualties they were taking.

The group was not able to do much more than 10 kts with the mattress patch in the hull of the Delta boat, so the five-mile trip was a long, very long thirty-minute commute to open water. En route, Joe radioed a destroyer offshore and requested his assistance.

The destroyer captain asked their ETA then moved his ship closer to shore and offered to take Bob on board his ship where they had a corpsman and helo deck that could be used to medevac Bob ashore. As they cleared the river mouth, Virg, his boat still carrying her double load of Special Forces, came alongside Bill, picked up Bob and headed for the destroyer at full speed.

Fortunately, the seas were calm as two boats remained overloaded with the other two in a towing formation. Joe continued to ride on Mike's boat and came alongside Bill to brainstorm the next course of action. The destroyer probably had a welder on board, but it was unlikely they could do aluminum welding below water. The alternative was for Virg to bring back better patching equipment than the two mop handles and mystery pipe that were currently being used. Mike radioed the destroyer and confirmed the welding problem, but they told him not to worry. Proper damage-control gear was already being loaded on Virg's boat, as was a self-contained high-capacity pump. Also, one of the Navy Black Diamonds had just landed on the destroyer's helo deck to pick up Bob. This was teamwork in action.

When Virg arrived back, the crews unloaded the gear while the Vietnamese Special Forces lent a helping hand. Virg had gone to damage control school on his first ship so he provided some guidance as they patched and braced, then shimmed and hammered in the wedges for additional pressure. Just to be safe, they started the pump on the main deck, set its throttle at idle speed then ran the water pick-up hose overboard so the pump would not overheat.

All units continued their slow trek back to base, which took about two hours at 15 kts. Despite the long day, no one asked to sprint ahead.

*Heading home. (Courtesy Bob Shirely PCF 45)*

*Good day at An Thoi. (Courtesy Larry Irwin)*

Between the four boats, there was enough ice cream and cold Cokes for all hands on board. A couple of Vietnamese Army types even finished off the Swift Boat culinary trademark sandwich.

After transferring the Special Forces troops ashore and sharing congrats all around, all boats arrived back at the An Thoi APL. Finally tying up at the repair dock marked the end of a long and strenuous trip for all hands.

Demonstrating their seafaring skills, Bill and Virg decided it would be a very good idea to put out multiple inch-and-a-half nylon mooring lines, making sure the boat didn't sink alongside the dock. With these additional lines, they were confident the pier itself would provide adequate flotation and lift. Bill instructed the roving pier security watch to conduct an onboard check every thirty minutes. Symmes and Singleton, both senior petty officers, took responsibility for thoroughly checking the hull patch in the engine room one last time. Lastly, they positioned the large pump from the destroyer nearby on the pier, gassed up and ready to go, if need be.

The firefight that day had been one of the worst; men were wounded and a Swift Boat had almost been lost. However, shipmates working together, not heroes, had carried the day.

# Section VI
# All in a Day's Work

CHAPTER 25

# A TALE TO TELL BACK
# IN DA NANG

When Bob finished his story, I had to admit that I was forced to take a couple of deep breaths just to catch up. He said that certain parts of the story, such as patching the hole in his boat and its being towed back to An Thoi, were unknown to him until he returned to the APL from the hospital in Saigon, several days later. Without question, he was extremely proud of his own crew but, understandably, also had the highest praise for all the other crews that provided damage control, towing services, and gunfire support. Each man was a professional in his individual efforts, but also critical as part of a combat team.

It was close to restaurant closing time and I had a plane to catch the next day as did Bob. He mentioned that in the next month or two he would need additional orthopedic surgery, most likely in Japan, and was intending to meet his wife Connie there. Unfortunately, the new Miss Emily was too young to make that long a trip. Not seeing his new, first-born baby must have been unbelievably hard for him.

I was certainly glad that I had made this brief trip, even though I was taken aback by Bob's injuries and the intensity of the fire-fight. Often, understatement or even denial of combat takes place by those involved. Sometimes that is healthy and others times it is not. Understatement can be effective mental health management, while denial is usually dangerous, so I felt good about my candid discussions with Bob.

The next day, I hitched a ride to Tan Son Nhat, which was Saigon's major airbase. Flights, especially to Da Nang, were frequent and—provided you were not choosy about seating and the type of aircraft—you could catch a ride fairly easily. In my case, it was a two-engine cargo plane, an Air Force C-123 Provider, which in terms of basic utility was right up there with Henry Ford's Model T.

Swift crews did not wear the usual in-country jungle greens, so I was traveling in a traditional Navy khakis work uniform. At least for this flight, I had on shoes instead of my usual Top-Sider boating shoes. Though no one cared, I was looking sharp wearing my personalized Swift Boat blue baseball cap and aviator sunglasses.

Prior to the flight, I had been informed that the first-class section was completely sold out, so as a result I was ensconced basically in cargo class. This meant sitting on well-worn, dusty and sagging Air Force-grey canvas bench seats that were hung from the plane's exterior bulkhead. A minimum load of cargo was at the rear of the aircraft, held in place by heavy nylon webbing. Along the way, I had ample time and was in a pivotal position to gaze up and down the plane, studying my fellow passengers.

Sitting across the way were a couple of desk jockeys, resplendent with their .45 caliber pistols, which caught my attention. I wondered if these guys had ever fired those guns or whether they even knew how to clean them. From my seat, I could see that most of their leather holsters looked so stiff that I doubted they could even draw the weapon without five minutes' prior notice. When that did take place, they probably stood a decent chance of shooting themselves in the foot. I also noticed that many of my fellow travelers seemed to be carrying leather briefcases. Most likely these were packed with top secret military documents, accessible only to those individuals well above my lowly pay grade. Conclusion: maybe I should have been wearing my boat shoes after all.

As we approached Da Nang, we were still running straight along the coast, passing over China Beach directly below. This was an in-country R&R site for the Marines, later to become the basis of a TV series called *China Beach*. Slowly our plane rolled left and began a banking turn to port, passing to seaward of Monkey Mountain, which was topped with its massive aircraft-control sites bristling with radar and radio antennas.

*Fully loaded F-4 Phantoms heading north.*

*Sure, I can fly this thing!*

They were responsible for controlling and coordinating all the aircraft for hundreds of square miles, including flights into North Vietnam.

Looking down through the plane's scratched and dusty window, I could see that Da Nang harbor, as usual, filled with cargo ships of all sizes, each waiting its turn to proceed to the deepwater piers and unload. As we continued our descent, I was able to catch a good view of the Swift base, a mile or so off to our left. Then we made our final landing approach in a westerly direction, coming in low over the water.

With no more than one light bump, followed by a roaring racket as the pilot switched the propeller pitch, we touched down at this massive Air Force facility. A quick look around once again gave me another perspective of the magnitude of this war effort. Both day and night, Air Force and Marine fighter-bombers loaded with ordinance were constantly rolling down the tarmac. Some of these planes provided close air support for our troops in-country but other planes had assigned targets deep inside North Vietnam. This group often shared enemy targets with the Navy jets launched from the aircraft carriers steaming several hundred miles to the north, off the coast of North Vietnam, assigned to Yankee Station. It was a sad truth that the majority of the brave men captured as POWs when they were shot down over North Vietnam were pilots from these locations.

Other planes at the Da Nang base were cargo planes carrying troops, ammunition and all types of supplies to the more remote bases throughout South Vietnam that were not reachable by water or safe enough for road transport. The Air Force had two major workhorses: the larger four-engine turbo prop C-130 Hercules and its smaller sister the cargo-carrying two-engine C-123 Provider, which I was currently flying on. Both were high-wing aircraft designed for short takeoff and landing in rugged conditions. In real hot spots near the DMZ, the Provider would simply roll out supplies, including ammunition, on pallets from a lowered ramp in the plane's tail. They taxied along the runway, slowing but never stopping. This technique of rolling and unloading was used to minimize the chance of becoming a sitting target for enemy sniper fire or a pre-targeted rocket. This was the type of mission where the aircrew and the loadmaster, without question, earned every dollar of their flight

*No Smoking, Explosives Nearby.*

and combat pay. I assumed or hoped that on this flight we would come to a complete stop prior to unloading.

Scattered among the bombers and cargo planes were an assortment of unmarked aircraft that did other things, primarily for the CIA. This often entailed clandestine troop or supply missions along or beyond the borders of Vietnam.

Ironically, parked in the midst of this assortment of combat-related aircraft, you would frequently see a large clearly marked commercial Boeing 707 jet belonging to Pan Am or World Airways. These planes were chartered to transport troops to or from the war zone, or often utilized for R&R trips. Only senior airline crews were assigned to this demanding duty, no trainees. Managing the apprehension of new combat arrivals and the elation of departing veterans were all part of their job description. Their ability to continually switch roles between being a concerned nursemaid and traffic cop was indeed remarkable.

As our plane rolled to its assigned parking spot, a truck from the Swift Boat base was waiting nearby to pick me up because I radioed ahead my arrival time. With only one small bag, I climbed in front to ride shotgun. The departure route out of the airbase was secure, so "shotgun" was a figure of speech only, besides, heavily armed Marines were scattered at checkpoints all along the way. The trip home took us along a memorable five miles from the airbase through war-torn downtown Da Nang, across the well-guarded bridge over the Da Nang River and on past Camp Tien Sha. This last tourist attraction was the massive home base of our good friends and admirers, the Naval Support Activity.

I looked across the tidal marshes and salty meadows, which someone less poetic might have described simply as swamps. I saw the APLs tied up and beyond them the commercial cargo loading ramps. These water-front ramps were used by smaller landing craft, such as LSTs for their roll-on and roll-off cargoes, which they transported along the coast and up the rivers to the various Marine installations. Fifty yards beyond them were the massive concrete and steel deepwater shipping piers. These facilities were equipped to handle large ships and their never-ending volume of container traffic which was loaded onto tractor-trailers and flatbed trucks. These piers are still in use today.

Living so close to where they unloaded hundreds of tons of ammunition and bombs on a daily basis we felt gave our neighborhood some real panache. It was not really what one might call the high-rent district, but certainly was a distinctive location and, understandably, one surrounded by plenty of open landscape.

As we approached the Apple the verse, "Home is the sailor, home from the sea," briefly crossed my mind. "Home" being a relative term. I had been living on these barges on and off for five months and on board were shipmates who would be my friends for a lifetime. We pulled up nearby in our corporate limo because parking was never a problem. I climbed the outside ladder/stairway to the second deck.

We were utilizing this deck of the Apple because Swift Boats had no chief petty officers as part of their crew and each of the thirty or so Da Nang boats had at least one commissioned officer using them, so we needed significant living space. The Apple would never qualify as glamorous, but was definitely functional, with a good kitchen and the all-important central air-conditioning.

As I came through the door, many of the troops were there and rose to greet me. Eldon Thompson and Jay Fleming suspended the card game and were quick to inform me that from a social-calendar standpoint they had no more *Repose*/nurse stories to report.

Off to the side, I saw good friend Ed Bergin, who was visiting from Chu Lai "only to get a new engine in PCF 79," he quickly explained. Larry Myer was his usual effervescent self and as our self-appointed historian informed me that he expected a full report on all I had learned in Saigon and a run down on operations out of An Thoi. Bottom line, it was good to be back even from a short trip.

Ed had gotten my brief radio message before I left Saigon about Bob's boat taking several rocket hits and his being badly wounded. I shared the details of that story but I told Ed that I did not know his longer-term prognosis after surgery in Japan. Would he resume duty or be sent stateside was the question. Knowing Bob, the latter would not be an attractive option even considering his married and new father status.

Later, I was glad that I was able to talk privately with Ed and express, for the first time, my sincere sympathies about the death of his bos'n, Bobby Don Carver. Obviously, this was weighing heavily on him and it showed. Carver had been close to my Bos'n Bill Fielder, who likewise felt the loss of a shipmate and friend. You do not spend hours, days, and months with someone and not build a unique and lasting friendship, based on good times as well as bad.

Along the way, someone passed me a tall Canadian Club and water which was much appreciated. Dinner had already been cleared but sandwiches were always left for the arrivals from any late patrols. Starvation was not a high risk in the U.S. Navy.

Before the movie, I shared with the other boat skippers a relatively complete rundown on the enemy activities and operations down south especially out of An Thoi. This included the layout of their patrol areas, all of which Bob had covered during our dinner. Most everyone knew someone at every other base, either from Boat School days or from time they spent rotating between various base locations, so there was ongoing interest in the story.

Catch up continued for about an hour even though my trip had only been a two-day turn-around; then the nightly movie began. Movie time was sacrosanct, regardless of how bad or old the flick was. I think the flickering light and poor audio quality had some mentally soothing impact, as did Eldon's poignant and often humorous commentaries in his other role as "Movie Master." Any book reading or letter writing took place off to the side in a lighted corner of the room, albeit in the same uncomfortable grey metal chairs. If you tilted these chairs it provided some angle of ergonomic relief, but any prior liquor consumption, combined with the waxed floor, presented a significant risk of slip and crash.

During our pre-movie discussions, I learned that the small Cua Viet base had not been reopened after the sinking of my boat PCF 76 and, about a week later, of PCF 14. This meant that the area was still being patrolled out of Da Nang, which required a ninety-mile transit north to those operating sectors. Currently, the weather was still being impacted by the tail end of the winter storm season, so I knew that this trip could be a long one in stormy seas. The last several weeks had been so bad that the Da Nang boats stayed in port about five days, simply because of the danger of high seas. The Apple was a good place to eat and sleep, but hardly somewhere you wanted to spend several days of downtime. Even the Coast Guard WPB (82-foot cutters), which were larger and better designed boats, had remained in port and those guys thrived on rough weather.

The problem with the patrol areas from Da Nang heading north was that there was little if any shelter from bad weather to be found anywhere along the almost straight coastline. Nor were there any islands offshore to hide behind when the weather turned really nasty. The Hue and Cua Viet rivers, with their raging surf and shifting sandbars at the river mouths, were definitely not a sanctuary. We had proven that conclusively with the loss of three boats and four men in a twelve-month period.

If you were patrolling at the DMZ and the weather turned foul, which could happen fast in just a matter of hours, the ninety-mile trip south back to Da Nang could be a long and arduous one. It could often be well over six hours of hard work and holding on, plus it was very tough on the nerves. Seas often were well over ten feet of rolling and cresting white water, as you climbed up one side and slid down the other, with horizontal rain and zero visibility. Regretfully, this was something we would confront again in the weeks ahead.

MoTac, my new boss, arrived just before the movie started. He had walked over from his office on the Ops barge farther up the pier. He welcomed me back and said he expected me to start my new job as Maintenance Liaison Officer (MLO) the next day. We had discussed this several weeks previously, so it came as no surprise and also presented no problem. I mentioned that the first thing I wanted to discuss with him was how my crew was going to be utilized to make sure I kept them in the loop. Later, I checked in briefly with Boats to ensure our troops were OK and he assured me they were. We agreed to meet mid-morning and then I would give him a full update on our new assignments.

CHAPTER 26

# NEW JOB, MAINTENANCE MANAGEMENT

The next day Mike Tackney and I had breakfast together and walked over to the boat maintenance piers. These were located just fifty yards away tied to the shore perpendicular to the APL. Not really a pier but rather a series of large barges that were tied together, each one maybe 200' × 75' wide. Some had sheet metal structures built on top of the barge hull that contained several small offices, but mainly the space encompassed shops for repairing electronics, doing welding or rebuilding our big 12-71 Jimmie diesels. Tied farther out, extending the pier, were two more barges with more open deck space where Swift Boats could be lifted out of the water onto heavy steel cradles. Here hull work on rudders and props took place along with painting and full engine replacement. Lifting the boats and engines required a massive floating crane, which was brought alongside the pier by a tug when needed.

All this was all managed by the Naval Support Activity which did an outstanding job supporting the Swifts and some of the harbor patrol craft. These young sailors were simply the best, most knowledgeable and an unbelievably hard-working group. Most of the repair sailors at the pier were well trained as enginemen, electronic techs, welders, etc. They all reported to a mustang lieutenant (former enlisted) named Sam MacCune. Sam was a grisly 200-pound, six-footer of Scottish heritage who hailed from the landlocked state of Wyoming. He started wandering as a twenty-year-old and never stopped until he hit the coast of

California and joined the Navy. He was one of those people you could count on no matter what. Standard jobs got a "No problem." Real challenges received a "We'll find a way" response from Sam.

As Mike explained it to me, part of my job was to schedule the work on our Swift Boats and ensure that everything went smoothly. That meant diplomacy, bribes or whatever it took to get the job done. Therefore, any boat officer or crew member who screwed up this finely tuned diplomatic relationship was in deep shit, no exceptions. Sam and I hit it off over the first cup of coffee, black, no cream, no sugar. I had been well trained by Boats.

These Naval Support Activity repair guys had a critical job and did it well. Despite being part of the same organization, they displayed none of the self-important attitude that existed among the officer-level paper pushers back at Camp Tien Sha, their main Da Nang base. Fortunately, we had little contact with them except for our fashion nemesis Ball Cap Smithson.

With the demanding patrol schedules we maintained, the wear and tear on the boats was considerable. The Swift crews were responsible for fueling and rearming the boat after each patrol, along with the frequent oil changes to the main engines and the generators, every 100 hours, no exceptions. This work was done at the outermost ends of the pier where more boats could be tied up alongside each other, often three abreast and another three bow-to-stern. Before a patrol, boats were driven over and moored alongside the Apple to pick up food but everything else was done at the repair dock. For security and quick response, at least three boats were tied up each night alongside the Apple, with their crews designated and ready to roll for any red alert.

The other part of my new job was to fill in with my crew when we were needed, especially on the night patrol in the Delta area just north of the harbor. This was the location where several months ago we had discovered the top secret "Beauty Sleep," our submarine and frogman friends. The Delta patrol was, in most cases, not a demanding one. With a full day's work followed up by the patrol that night it could be a load, but Mike usually allowed some flexibility during the day.

After I digested the breadth of my new job responsibilities, it occurred to me that my new boss had not been completely forthcoming in our

*Dan Daly, the new MLO and the duty truck.*

initial discussion of my job description. Regardless, MoTac was an extremely competent officer with a good sense of humor, which made the day and the tasks flow smoothly. He came from a Navy family, was an Annapolis grad, had been a Swift Boat skipper and brought with him a positive sense of reality.

My crew would continue to patrol with me and would serve as fill-in on other boats. Boats, because of his seniority, would work for me in the maintenance area and be the lead enlisted man on any boat as needed. His competence was well known and therefore I hoped he would still be available to me. There could be no better roving ambassador, political lobbyist or "cumshaw devotee" than Boats. Working to our advantage, each member of our crew had less than two months left in-country and most boat skippers wanted and were assigned permanent crew members.

*"Good as new, Mr. Bergin."*

"Musical crew members" was in my opinion a risky strategy in combat, especially on a Swift Boat that required specific skills and team cohesiveness. That team effort, based on training, competence and trust, had saved our butts more than once.

Back at the Apple later that night, over a drink, I ran my list of job responsibilities by Ed Bergin. In his most fatherly fashion, Ed put his arm around my shoulder and asked me with a big grin, "Mr. Maintenance, I know you are extremely busy but perhaps you could tell me, what is the current status of PCF 79 and my new engine?"

He continued jerking my chain, "Please understand, my presence is desired ASAP down south at Cos Div 16. You remember Chu Lai? The land of no paperwork and Navy bullshit." Ed was once again displaying his sensitive and understanding side.

## CHAPTER 27

# PUFF THE MAGIC DRAGON

Several days later we were scheduled for the next night-time Delta patrol. Our crew had not been together on patrol for over a week and we were anxious to get back together and function as a team. We were using Jay Fleming's PCF 13, so we knew it would be in top-notch condition.

After dinner, we got under way and the sun began to gradually set across the harbor, just touching the east end of the runways at the airbase. Great sunset, not so great a backdrop, was my thought as we headed slowly across the harbor. Once outside, we turned off our running lights and headed north for the short run to the Delta area. All was quiet and we expected no activity that night based on the conversations and briefing we had had with Article before we got under way. Tonight, my only concern was that it was once again dark of the moon and the level of enemy activity had been increasing steadily for several weeks as the calendar approached the celebration of the Vietnamese Lunar New Year (Tet) at the end of January.

Boats had the first watch, with Snipe sitting lookout above in the gun tub keeping the twin .50s company, while Buck was in the pilothouse on the helm. I turned in around 2100 prepared to relieve him at midnight. We set the patrol parameters, 10 kts, a thousand yards off the beach. Because the shoreline formed a large deep semicircular bay, there was little commercial junk traffic through the patrol area, only an occasional fishing junk or perhaps a submarine. Around 2300 Boats approached the northern half of the patrol area where a small village was located at the opening to an inland waterway meandering five miles north to join the Hue River. The water was colored dead black and the sea glassy calm, with no moon above and little light except for the stars.

Shattering the silence, about 30° off our port bow, were two large flashes onshore, quickly followed by the explosions that rolled out across the water. They were of sufficient magnitude that they woke me up and most definitely caught Boats' attention, who was immediately back at the wheel in the pilothouse ready for action. I immediately rolled out and jumped down from the top rack yelling: "General Quarters," waking up Muller and Newcomer and getting everyone to their battle stations. As I stuck my head in the pilothouse, I told Boats to remain at the wheel and drive slowly toward the shore and the fires that had now broken out in the village. I told Guns (Muller) to man the twin .50s forward and yelled to Snipe, who had taken up his position on the aft .50, to carefully scan the shoreline off our port side for any movement or muzzle flashes. Buck said he was going aft to help Snipe, and Newcomer was below at the radio listening for any messages. I gave the order "Guns Free." The enemy onshore most likely could not clearly see us but there was no doubt they could hear us. Without any wind to distort sound, the rumble that came from our two diesels, even at low speed, would provide a good target to track, especially as we approached the beach.

I grabbed the radio microphone and reported what we had just seen to Article. It appeared that several good-size rockets had been fired from close range into the village. While sending the message to Article, I remembered that there were Marines either in the village or nearby working with the South Vietnamese to provide security.

Within minutes, Article radioed back that he had contacted the Da Nang Marine Operations Center. They informed him that there was a small Marine detachment residing in the village with whom they had recently spoken. Those men said they were under attack from the south by rockets. Article suggested I radio the Marine detachment directly on their frequency, utilizing their call sign "Red Rover 1-2."

"Red Rover 1-2, this is Enfield Cobra Delta, U.S. Navy patrol boat near your location. Can we assist, over?"

Their response was immediate: "Affirmative, Navy, we are taking heavy enemy rocket fire from the peninsula just south of us across from the river mouth."

They further described this as the same position from which they had received enemy sniper fire earlier in the day. Assuming that the Marines knew the Swift Boat's armament, I informed him that firing our .50 calibers at the enemy would be too dangerous, possibly sending rounds into the village and hitting friendlies.

I radioed that we could safely and accurately fire our 81mm mortar avoiding the village and at least keep the enemy's heads down, thus possibly suppressing another round of rocket fire.

Time was of the essence, before the enemy reloaded. I did not feel we could accurately determine our own position, that of the Marines, as well as the enemy's location quickly enough to calculate a good firing solution. Therefore, I suggested to Red Rover that we fire several illumination rounds which the Marines could observe and then from their location adjust our fire for accuracy. After that, we could rapidly follow up with high-explosive rounds. The illumination rounds would be unlikely to injure anyone below unless they were hit by a falling piece of metal from the exploding flare component.

I took over the wheel from Boats and sent him back aft to fire three illumination rounds from the mortar at thirty-second intervals. I gave him an approximate range and a relative bearing for the weapon. The first round was away and burst in about five seconds, 500 feet in the air and then hung from its parachute for about ten seconds. The Marines gave their corrections in general terms, which were hundred yards closer to the beach and 100 yards farther south of our airburst. I yelled to Boats the rough changes in target position and he quickly adjusted the mortar range and bearing to hit the target. Definitely not by the book, but I knew we were clear of friendlies and we would be firing some rounds at least close to the enemy. I decided this was the fastest and best course of action. We also had to assume that the enemy was on the move.

The next two rounds of illumination were called satisfactory and Red Rover gave us permission to commence fire.

"This is Red Rover 1-2. Commence fire, five rounds, high explosive, fire for effect."

To confirm, I repeated Red Rover's message verbatim. Then I yelled to Boats, who had already laid out the rounds and set the fuses, to drop-fire five rounds in rapid succession. Meanwhile, I told him I was going to slowly twist our boat to port, which would result in a spread as the rounds hit the ground. No sooner had we stopped firing when two more rockets were launched from a position farther down the peninsula, south of our current location. Once again, both rounds slammed into the village igniting more fires.

My conclusion was that these were larger weapons, not shoulder-fired RPGs (Rocket Propelled Grenades), though the ones they were using were still mobile and of significant size. Most likely they were multiple enemy units on the peninsula or they were sprinters able to outrun our mortar fire. If the enemy was investing this amount of ammunition, it was probably their intent to follow up with more troops and overrun the village, perhaps gaining control of the opening to the inland waterway.

There were no other Swift Boats nearby for support nor were there any destroyers offshore on the gun-line to give us additional firepower. Therefore, I made the decision to get on the radio and request air support. My initial call to Article was immediately acted upon, most likely by some Air Force air controller located on top of Monkey Mountain, about ten miles to the south on the eastern edge of Da Nang harbor.

He immediately came on our frequency and asked the size of the enemy force, the weapons they were utilizing, and the general location of the target. When Swift Boats called for air support like this, it was usually provided by the Air Force simply because the Navy was hundreds of miles to the north, operating from aircraft carriers. The Marines, with limited aircraft, usually could only support larger Marine operations. However, in our experience, the Air Force usually had plenty of hardware airborne and was always willing to help out. In this case, their response took less than five minutes when "Puff the Magic Dragon" came on the net saying he was nearby and asked for target coordinates.

Puff was a very serious and deadly piece of airborne hardware. It was a converted twin-engine DC-3 propeller aircraft used by the military

*"This is Puff 3-5." (Courtesy Douglas Aircraft Company)*

*Three mini-guns inside Puff. (Courtesy Douglas Aircraft Company)*

for decades to transport cargo and personnel. This version carried three mini-guns on one side of the aircraft firing 7.62 caliber slugs from each gun at a rate of 6,000 rounds per minute. The impact description of this weapon was: "In a football field, Puff could put one round in every square foot." The rounds were small with a minimum of penetrating power but, for any enemy out in the open or lightly concealed, the result was deadly.

I suspected that the enemy was operating in multiple independent units scattered around the peninsula, each with a series of rockets. So, Puff was the ideal air support. My concern was the proximity of the village and also the risk to our boat that was now positioned about 200 yards offshore.

Puff 3-5 (his call sign) checked in again and I could hear the drone of his engines as he circled slowly overhead, but I couldn't see him because there was no moon and few stars, plus he had a camouflage paint job. This effect in itself was a bit unsettling. I knew these guys were really good and would not go "guns free" until I gave them the go-ahead. Next, I contacted Red Rover onshore to outline what was about to take place so that he would not think the world had ended.

My attention focused on keeping our Swift Boat out of the line of Puff's deadly fire. I got on the radio and transmitted, "Puff 3-5, this is Enfield Cobra Delta. Interrogative, do you know what type of unit we are, over?"

His response was, "Delta, Roger that. You're one of those Navy gun boats."

This was delivered with that laid-back southern twang that seemed to be used by most pilots regardless of their geographic origin. My better judgment suggested I be somewhat more specific.

"3-5, this is Enfield Cobra Delta. Roger your last. Reference my position, we are located approximately 200 yards off the beach. I will illuminate the white and blue star located on my cabin top with our searchlight."

Immediately, I turned on our searchlight. His response was once again in that slow drawl, combined with that casualness that all pilots seem to have regardless of the circumstances.

"Roger Delta, I see you there good buddy. You are just a trifle too close, suggest you stand off about another klick (1,000 yards) just to be on the safe side."

He asked if I could mark the northern end of the target zone to avoid any onshore friendlies. I said that I had the capability to fire a white phosphorus mortar round but was concerned about hitting him. The laconic response:

"Well Delta, I certainly appreciate that. I will make a slow turn out to sea beyond your position and then you fire away."

As he flew over us, I could clearly hear him slowly turning and at that altitude could just make out above us the threatening dark shadow of this deadly machine. The whole thing was surreal in the pitch-black night.

We fired one round of "Willy Pete" that marked the northern end of the target zone, which I also confirmed with Red Rover from his position in the village. Puff 3-5 came back, "Target marked and identified, request you cease fire. Pull back and I will commence my attack." I immediately responded "Puff 3-5, this is Enfield Cobra Delta. I am pulling back 1,000 yards, have ceased firing and I am guns tight."

The response was a simple, "Roger that, Navy."

Within a minute, quite literally, all hell broke loose. The sound was not one of machine guns firing but rather like multiple chainsaws all roaring together. As the rounds rained down, a certain number were tracking red tracers that looked like a stream of red water coming from the sky.

The entire beach and peninsula immediately erupted and became covered in sand. As the rounds continued to tear up the landscape, a cloud of dust drifted slowly overhead across the water toward us. Puff made a slow second circle banking the aircraft in toward the target area and fired again. The only way anyone could survive that fusillade was to have dug a deep hole with some protection overhead like a steel plate. Out in the open, there was no way you could avoid being hit, most likely multiple times.

The next message was, "This is Puff 3-5. Mission complete, Navy. My guns are tight. Interrogative, additional targets?"

My response was, "Negative Puff 3-5. No additional targets this time, many thanks." Red Rover onshore came up on the same frequency with a similar message. The response from Puff was a simple, "The United States Air Force at your service, out."

I checked in again with Red Rover and told him we would stay in the area and patrol along the surf line using our night vision scope to make sure that no enemy troops were lurking in the shallow water, working their way north to Red Rover's position. We carried the Starlight Scope, the high-tech spyglass (1968) with light-enhancing capability so we could see the outlines of any figures moving along the shore. Having witnessed Puff in action, I seriously doubted there was going to be any activity in the area for the foreseeable future.

At dawn, we informed Red Rover of our intention to return to port. He thanked us for our assistance and gave us the always appreciated Marine Corps, "Semper Fi." As we turned to the south, off our port side we could see the sun just starting to glow below the morning horizon. So much for another quiet patrol and good night's sleep in the Delta sector.

## CHAPTER 28

# HAWAIIAN RENDEZVOUS

After about two weeks in my important new job as Maintenance Liaison Officer (MLO), I received a letter from Kate saying that she would be able to take leave in about ten days and meet me in Honolulu. The *Repose* was in Japan for maintenance and therefore her workload was significantly less than when the ship was operational. She knew this was short notice but it was the best she could do, but she understood if I could not join her.

I had previously discussed this possibility with my boss MoTac, so he was not completely surprised. As expected, his response was simply, "Let's make this happen," and he picked up the phone to pull some rank with the R&R scheduler. Within two hours, my letter with confirmation and arrival time in Hawaii was in the mail to LCDR Kate Hancock.

Ten days later, I was on an R&R flight making its final approach to the island of Oahu, Hawaii. The main airfield was in Honolulu and military and commercial airlines both used the same runways. The official name on the military side was Hickham Air Force Base and Honolulu International on the commercial side. I arrived on the Air Force side of the terminal, despite the fact that my flight had been a chartered Pan Am commercial flight.

Arriving at midday, I checked in at an assigned room at the terminal that was part of the required R&R arrival. There all the troops from our flight received the standard military behavior "This is civilization" speech, after which I confirmed my return flight seven days hence. Officers were pretty much given a free rein with some basic guidelines: "Do not get arrested and do not miss your flight back to Vietnam."

I took a taxi downtown to the Surfrider Hotel, which was located directly on Waikiki beach. In our various letters Kate had suggested, in her own subtle way, that we get two rooms overlooking the beach. By any standards, this was not unreasonable considering that the most physically intimate we had been to date was shaking hands. Arriving at my fifth floor room, fronting directly onto Waikiki beach, I quickly unpacked, then did a recon of the hotel lobby and surrounding area. This mission included an ice-cold Budweiser beer and a civilian-quality cheeseburger cooked medium rare with french fries, all consumed on the beachfront patio.

The next day, I awoke early after a truly outstanding night's sleep with my patio door open wide, while listening to the rolling surf below. Sunrise beckoned so I went downstairs for an early morning swim. I have always enjoyed swimming since our family summers on Cape Cod and this looked like spectacular water. In Vietnam, whenever we had the opportunity we would stop the boat for a swim. There is no question in my mind that this quasi-mandatory training regimen was at least partly why everyone had survived when we lost PCF 76 several months earlier at the Cua Viet River mouth.

After breakfast, I selected from my somewhat limited civilian wardrobe, a short-sleeve shirt, grey slacks and leather boat shoes. We traveled in uniform, but civilian clothes were mandatory on R&R. I suspect this was especially true in Hawaii where the military spending was well received but the military presence was downplayed, even more so in Honolulu itself.

Here I was, waiting at a Pan American Airway's gate for the commercial flight which Kate had taken from Japan. Before leaving the hotel, I had purchased an orchid lei not realizing that many commercial flights were greeted by Hawaiian girls who presented leis to the arriving passengers. Regardless, I concluded it was the thought that counted. Despite my tan from constantly being on the water, my short haircut and aviator sunglasses shouted military, not native.

They announced the flight's arrival and I double-checked to ensure that I was at the correct gate. Soon the big 707 jet taxied to a halt at the gate and they wheeled out the stairs. To my dismay, I saw that five Japanese businessmen were the first off. I briefly thought she might have missed the flight with no way to communicate that information to me.

Then, she appeared at the plane's doorway stopping at the top of the stairs in her tropical white uniform looking, in a word, outstanding. Despite this being a commercial non-military flight, I assumed she was in uniform to receive the military discount.

She stood briefly on the stairs all alone and to me she could have been a picture in a recruiting poster. Without question, I would have signed up. I learned later she was actually searching for me with the same concern that I might have been unable to make my flight. We were at war and our time and schedules were often not our own.

I raised my hand and waved enthusiastically. Any goal of appearing cool at the time was not a consideration. Spotting my wave, she gave me that special smile. It was much later that I learned that her father was a dentist. Now as I looked up, the sun was shining even brighter in that crystal-blue Hawaiian sky as she began her walk down the stairs. I moved my way politely up the line of greeters on to the tarmac toward her. As I held up the lei to put around her neck I made sure that I didn't knock her cover off.

"Welcome to Hawaii," I said and kissed her lightly on the cheek. I had thought about this beforehand and felt it was a relatively low risk but heads-up move. She said nothing but with a gentle brush returned my kiss.

It occurred to me that while we both may have been caught up in the moment, we were not filming a movie scene and we were in fact blocking traffic. I reached out and took her carry-on bag, which felt like she had packed her barbell set. In response, she linked her arm in mine, not a bad trade-off. Though we were not on the movie set, we damn well looked the part.

Up to now she had not said a word to me and then she turned and whispered, "Hey sailor, going my way?" I responded with a smile and a definite, "Yes ma'am, I am."

We quickly retrieved her one checked bag at luggage arrival. Outside the terminal, we hailed a taxi to the hotel and covered the short trip with flight updates and pre-departure horror stories. She had been training a new trauma team, having unexpectedly seen both Emily and Betsey transferred stateside in a two-week time frame. The result was she had a new team to train and the best time was in port just before she left. As I looked more closely in the taxi she had a touch of what my mother would describe as that "grey look," which came from too much stress and not enough sleep. I hoped with luck, the next several days would provide the cure.

At the Surfrider, she checked in and then I carried her bags upstairs after giving a couple of bucks to the bellhop to keep the peace and let me handle the heavy lifting. I expected our arrival at her door to be an awkward moment but Kate set the tone. She said she wanted to unpack, take a long shower after her flight and would meet me in front on the beach in two hours. This was followed by another kiss on the cheek and I was sent on my way.

I walked down the hall to my room, rapidly turning the sequence of recent events over in my mind. My conclusion: we were not two hot-blooded college undergraduates trying to wow each other, but two adults understandably feeling our way along in this absolutely unique relationship. I was good with where we were.

After getting on my swimsuit and a jersey, non-military green, I took the beach elevator downstairs. The beach front was built up, even in 1967. While it was lined with mostly high-rise hotels, the actual beach was not overly crowded. It was spotlessly clean without a fallen leaf or scrap of paper anywhere in sight, right down to the edge of the magnificent clear and sparkling blue water. There were small waves cresting offshore, with each one gently rolling to the beach and brushing the shoreline. Despite the calm conditions, both surfers and outrigger canoes were riding the waves.

I moved two beach chairs together in the area that appeared to belong to the Surfrider Hotel. Next door, I saw the Royal Hawaiian Hotel with its pink-painted stucco walls and tile roofs. This was another postcard picture right out of a WWII movie. The Royal Hawaiian had been the location or backdrop for numerous films that had been made during and after the war. I made a mental note for us to stop by for a drink or even have dinner in their main dining room. Either would make for a memorable evening.

A beach attendant soon brought me two large towels, I presume based on my relocating the two lounge chairs. Thanking him, I stretched out in one of the very comfortable chairs.

Sitting for a moment, the mental rush came at me. I used to feel it in combat and now it had returned. In this case, it was not the anticipation of battle demanding razor-sharp concentration, but rather a muddled sense of bewilderment. Here I was 6,000-plus miles from Vietnam and maybe a similar distance from home. I was sitting on one of the most beautiful beaches in the world, staying at a luxurious hotel, waiting for a woman with whom I had spent a total of less than ten hours.

Never had I considered myself a shallow person or one who made important decisions casually. If anything, time in combat had reinforced the opposite. Yet, here I was. I had no regrets and I truly had feelings for Kate. Perhaps, I was reacting this way because events were evolving, not really beyond my control, but certainly with less reflection than usual on my part. Over the years, in school and especially in the military, I had trained myself to take a series of slow deep breaths and that would help get the anxiety under control. It also occurred to me that Kate might well be having similar feelings and this should be factored into my thinking.

No sooner had I completed this mental exercise then I heard from behind me, "Dan, I almost missed you hidden in the chair."

I turned around to see an image I can clearly recall even today. Here was a vision of loveliness, casually walking across the warm white sand. There was no confusion, this person was definitely saying my name and she was in fact walking toward me. Suddenly, there was that smile and I saw the special sparkle was again back in the eyes. The black two-piece bathing suit with the beach jacket slung casually over her arm only added to the picture. It was topped off by a floppy straw beach hat with a bright orange-colored band that she must have purchased in the hotel lobby, definitely not Vietnam vintage.

Surprising myself, I had the presence to ask Kate how she felt and she responded, "Not there yet but gradually winding down."

In return, she asked how I was doing. My response was basically the same but I mentioned I had an eighteen-hour lead on her. Before sitting down, she carefully spread out one of the towels on the chair.

For a moment, we both sat in silence simply looking down the white sand beach, then out across the sun-sparkled water that stretched to the horizon. Where sea and sky finally met there were a couple of fair-weather clouds drifting above. We agreed, it was one of the most peaceful and beautiful views either of us had seen in a very long time. This was despite the fact that the property located just behind us was dense with multi-storied hotels. Time in combat situations demands you compartmentalize things and on Waikiki beach, this was a skill that served the two of us well.

This was Kate's first trip to Hawaii but my second. My first trip, three years earlier, was also courtesy of the U.S. Navy, on a summer NROTC cruise while in college. I had spent over two months on the aircraft carrier *Ticonderoga,* off the coast of Vietnam. On the way back, they had allowed us stop over for several weeks in Hawaii, at our own expense, and then they gave us the flight back home. "Join the Navy and See the World," was how the recruiting slogan went and it often worked. I am not quite sure how my Swift Boat duty fit in with that recruiting tagline.

For the next half hour we both read. I had a murder mystery and she had some historical novel set in seventeenth-century Europe. For a moment, I thought she might have been a pseudo-intellectual but she had told me earlier that she had been a history minor and still enjoyed those readings. I mentioned to her that I was an economics major and found that subject not the least bit enjoyable but that I might change my mind in the future.

Kate suddenly dropped her book and said, "That water looks too good to waste."

Having been swimming earlier in the morning, I was able to report in response, "It's outstanding."

She then sprinted to the water's edge and without a pause charged right in. People who have grown up on the ocean do things like that; pool people do not. A step behind, I crashed forward as a small breaker hit the beach. Diving underwater as far as my breath allowed, I surfaced about twenty feet beyond her. My next move, again underwater; was back to her, ending in a tackle around the legs. I came in low caught the ankles, pulled and over she went.

Suddenly, it occurred to me that this was not Cape Cod and she was not "one of the girls." My antics might well be seen as obnoxious or worse. As I broke the surface fully prepared to apologize, there was no sign of Kate. Wham, I was hit from the starboard side, not only knocked over, but pulled down by the knees. I surfaced and was greeted by my attacker who smiled and simply stated, "Younger brothers."

After this ritual of defining our mutual waterborne competence, we spent the next half hour swimming out and then body surfing in. Neither effort was particularly demanding because the waves were small and consistent.

As we arrived back at our beach chairs and toweled off, I think we both felt the wind down had begun to take hold. I made the suggestion that we eat dinner at the Royal Hawaiian next door. She knew about its long history and thought this was a great idea. I volunteered to walk over to the hotel and talk in person to the manager of the beach bar. I said I would try and play the veteran card if there were any reservation problems. Securing the reservations was going to be a solo mission because she was going to her room and would be ready for cocktails in an hour and not before. The trauma nurse in her certainly had no problems with decision-making.

Arriving at the bar, I needn't have worried because the manager was clearly identified in his blue blazer, obviously in charge. When I asked about dinner reservations his singular response was, "Vietnam?" Obviously, my haircut and sunglasses had again been the tip off.

"That's right," was my somewhat defensive response.

"Who and where?" was next. I wasn't quite ready for twenty questions but went along with it: "Navy Swift Boats. Da Nang, Chu Lai and Cua Viet."

His response was a succinct, "The Corps." After a pause, with a quick look at the table board, "Will 1930 on the patio be acceptable, sir?"

Things were definitely looking up, at least on the dinner front. I then introduced myself to Gunnery Sergeant Brownell ("Gunny"), thanked him and heard "Semper Fi" as I walked away.

I knocked on Kate's door at 1815, the appointed hour. I was in my blue blazer, grey slacks, no boat shoes but some well-worn loafers, a white shirt with a blue and gold stripe tie (Navy colors). I knew dinner at the Royal Hawaiian was not casual.

The door opened and for a moment, again I just stared. This woman had no end to her surprises. She had on a floor-length bright colored print dress cut in Hawaiian style. Her auburn hair was pulled back with a flower above her ear, port side. I was sophisticated enough to say, "You look lovely," but not much more.

It was becoming very obvious to me that my time in Swift Boats was raising hell with my finely tuned Boston social skills. Once again, as she had done at the airport, Kate took my arm, a practice that I was thoroughly enjoying. Hand-holding was for high school or walks on the beach, but then again even that wasn't something I really felt strongly about.

We walked through the Surfrider lobby, crossing slowly through the outside tropical gardens complete with orchids of every color, cascading bougainvillea and other flowering plants, well beyond the level of my East Coast horticultural competence. The pathways blended into the Royal Hawaiian property and we went in through the formal brass and glass main entrance.

It wasn't just my imagination, heads turned and they were not looking at me. I was 6' 3" and in heels Kate was close to 5' 10". In her Hawaiian dress, she was stunning. As we entered the main lobby, I quickly recalled some of the famous names, both civilian and military, who had walked through this very same room: FDR, Truman, Nimitz, Halsey and MacArthur, and literally hundreds of famous presidential and military personnel.

We headed down the hallway to the main dining room and introduced ourselves to the maître d'. He mentioned that our table had been set on the patio and would be available now or when we had finished cocktails. The night was mild, with a light wind off the water, so he recommended we spend at least some time at the beach bar watching the sunset.

Gunny Brownell, ever the good Marine, spotted our approach and greeted me with, "Good evening, Lieutenant."

Somehow he must have figured out that I was an officer and that Swift Boat skippers were lieutenants. Not to be outdone, I took Kate by the elbow and said. "LCDR Hancock, let me introduce Gunnery Sergeant Brownell, United States Marine Corps retired."

Without missing a beat she extended her hand and responded, "It's a pleasure Gunnery Sergeant Brownell."

We had the best seat in the house, actually, in the bar. Palm trees, white sand, rolling surf and the sun falling toward the horizon just for us.

"Will it be a cocktail tonight or might I suggest a split of champagne for the occasion?"

This guy must have received his theater training alongside Bos'n mate Fielder, he was that good. I got the nod from Kate who signaled me, never question a Marine gunnery sergeant. Champagne it was. As expected while he poured, Gunny was able to get all the intel on Kate and was suitably impressed. Her business was saving lives, and often they were Marine lives.

The next hour was beyond belief in its beauty. The sun fell slowly at first than rapidly below the horizon, followed by nautical twilight which lit up the one or two clouds that remained above into blends orange and pinks. Somehow our split of champagne never quite bottomed out. I suspected a Marine Corps plot.

It was time for dinner so we thanked Gunny for his hospitality. I saw that the bill did not reflect the consumption incurred and tipped accordingly. Somehow, I knew this was far from a typical business transaction. With his back to me, he thanked Kate and said several of his men had been on board the *Repose* and he knew the quality of treatment they had received. Turning to face me, he shook my hand and said, "Lieutenant, keep your butt down and your powder dry."

Then he gave me a wink with a nod in Kate's direction.

My response was a simple, "Gunny, I read you loud and clear. Semper Fi."

We found out later that the Gunny had done two tours in Vietnam, he was well decorated and had been assigned to the Marine airbase on the other side of the island as his final duty station. Our source said that upon retirement, he decided to never leave Hawaii. So he took the job because it was outside, near the water and he had total control.

We moved across the patio to the more formal dining section, somewhat protected from the wind, but still with beautiful views of the beach, framed by flaming torches. Two steaks, medium rare, baked potatoes, sliced fresh tomatoes with peppercorn dressing. The wine was a domestic red which we were informed had been sent over by Gunny. It was full bodied and excellent, but we would have enjoyed it even if it was paint thinner.

Gunny, Kate and I were brothers-in-arms and that's how it was.

It was a December Saturday night, so somewhat off season, yet they had a good-size band playing inside. I asked Kate, the history buff, if she remembered Guy Lombardo. She rolled her eyes and said, "Absolutely," but she doubted he was still with the band.

Despite this intellectual put down, ever the gentleman, I stood up and asked if she would care to dance. A long pause seemed to hang in the air. Had I, so to speak, just put my dance foot in my mouth, perhaps betrayed by the Marine Corps claret? She was charming, had good looks, with a pleasing personality; I assumed, of course, she could dance, or so I hoped.

She turned in her chair, lifted her right hand to mine, while ever so subtly pushing her chair backward away from the table with the other foot, rather than waiting for me to move it. Perhaps, she was concerned that I might just flip the table over while trying to get her out smoothly.

As we walked to the dance floor, she was doing that arm-in-arm move, which I was really starting to enjoy. I was committed to the dance floor and would make the best of whatever the situation brought forth.

There was absolutely no need to worry; she immediately picked up the beat of the band and settled into my arms as we moved across the floor together. Big band music, which this definitely was, in most cases was easy to dance to because of its strong and consistent beat. While I was bred on rock and roll and thoroughly enjoyed it, finding the consistent drum beat could be a challenge in that genre.

Kate was incredibly smooth and able to anticipate my moves, which on occasion could be described as somewhat creative. Holding her and feeling her light touch was wonderful. She glided with grace; there was no sense of "the tug boat push," as we used to refer to it in college.

As the band announced a waltz, we realized we were the youngest couple in the room by far. Without question, we were also at the low end of the income scale, especially judging by the outfits and accompanying jewelry on the women. Kate gave me a knowing look with a nod. As we moved to the center of the floor, all I could think of was my summer cruise on the aircraft carrier and that all-important command, "Stand by to launch aircraft." It was obvious, I needed help.

The waltz began and we were off, our feet moving smoothly even with an occasional cross-over step, arms extended, upper body rigid, with her head turned slightly to the side. There were others on the floor more competent but I just didn't happen to notice them. We held our own as evidenced by the fact that we received several compliments from the older generation as we returned to our table. Knowing Kate was from Virginia, as I held her chair, I asked, "Cotillions?"

"A couple, how about you?" was her response.

"In my corrupt youth," I said with a smile, confirming that I felt we had most definitely made our mark on the dance floor.

Most stories have two versions, so it is only fair to hear Kate's side of this one:

*I was sitting in the lobby of the Surfrider with Dan at 0830 and we were talking to a travel agent. There was a poster in the window with a picture of the island of Kauai describing it as the "Garden Isle," perhaps the most beautiful in the world. We were scheduled to get on a plane in two hours to spend a couple of days at the Hanalei Bay Plantation where they had filmed segments of the movie* South Pacific.

*Had I lost my mind? Last night had been perfect—champagne, a steak dinner and wonderful dancing. This was followed up by a shoeless walk on Waikiki beach toward Diamond Head with a sparkling backdrop of stars stretching uninterrupted down to the horizon. Dan had kissed me fully for the first time and this was something I hoped that I had responded to. Later as we returned to the hotel, I mentioned to him that I really had to turn in. Even though it was 2230 Hawaiian time, I was still on a Japan schedule and tired from my ten-hour flight.*

*He appeared to take all this in stride which separated him from many of the men previously in my life. Was he really this smooth, he appeared strong but gentle or perhaps he was just mellow being away from combat? Regardless, he had my attention and a lot more.*

*Dan had agreed after dinner last night to take the side trip to Kauai. I had made it clear in my letters to him that all expenses were to be split 50/50, no exceptions. This made me feel somewhat less guilty about the extra expense— "somewhat" being the operative word. A flight was available that would get us there by noon and we locked in a return flight two days later because Dan's military charter flight left before my commercial one. I knew his departure was an absolute "must make" in the Navy's eyes.*

*The travel agent knew we were both military and gave us a discount but then asked, "Rooms or a cottage?*

*I responded "Cottage" perhaps a little too quickly, to which the agent replied, "Good choice."*

*Out of the corner of my eye, I saw that Dan had a smile on his face, perhaps amused by the speed of my response.*

*Our flight was a short one, less than an hour, and as we approached the runway on Kauai all you could see was green everywhere. We touched down, got our bags and Dan rented a Jeep. He explained to me that this was not some military flashback, but the fulfillment of a longtime college desire. Having been the instigator in this project, I was happy to take the shotgun seat as he consulted our map to the hotel. Having met Bos'n Fielder in Da Nang, I had little concern in that department. Driving the jeep on back roads (there appeared to be no main roads) was a treat and within thirty minutes we saw the sign for the town of Hanalei and shortly thereafter the plantation itself.*

*As with everything on this odyssey I was not disappointed. The main house was "livin' on a hillside, lookin' on an ocean, beautiful and still," which I think were the words from one of the* South Pacific *Broadway songs. The view was spectacular. It looked down to the palm-studded beach below and across to a beautiful small bay and peninsula lush with green growth, sharply contrasting with the bluest water of the bay. We checked in and left the jeep at the main house. The cottages were located below and we would be driven down in a small cart. Dan, looking at the steep hill, made some comment about survival school and another forced march, but I chose to ignore him.*

*A cottage was the appropriate description. They were all separate units and the hill sloped sharply enough so that each one looked out over and above the unit below. Inside, our cottage was one big room with a generous screened-in seating/ eating area facing the water across from a kingside bed with opaque hanging drapes. Behind was the bath and off to the side a small kitchen area.*

*Dan had tipped the driver and carried in our two bags. Dropping them on the floor, he picked me up in his arms, kissed me with a definite measure of passion, and then he literally tossed me onto the bed.*

*"Swim Call" was what followed as he sat down on the bed and kissed me again, saying "Great choice on the Plantation."*

*We walked down the hill to the beach forsaking the tram-like machine that ran down the hillside. At the bottom of the hill, there it was the beach from* South Pacific *and across the way the mystical Bali Hai.*

*The water was as clear and beautiful as Waikiki but not surrounded by high-rise hotels or any buildings for that matter. This beach fronted onto an enclosed bay, so the calm water allowed us to swim farther from shore. Dan was in good shape, a fact not lost on me, and he had a strong stroke which made me comfortable in strange waters. Other than two couples, there was no one else on the beach that stretched nearly a mile to our left and a half mile to our right.*

*We stayed in the water for almost two hours after which we strolled down the beach to look at some boats tied up near shore. They could be rented, so we reserved a catamaran sailboat for the next day. Foolishly, I asked Dan if he knew how to sail, to which he responded with a smile, "Kate, I am a U.S. Navy Swift Boat skipper, you know."*

*Shaking my head, I knew I should have anticipated that response and simply taken a pass on my question. After cleaning up for dinner, we took a slow walk up the hill to the main house. Dan felt the exercise would be good for us. "Exercise, what you think we were doing all afternoon?" was my comment.*

*We finally made it to the top and sat at a small outside cocktail table on the circular stone patio that I had first noticed when we arrived. From this location, the expansive view took our breath away; we paused to take it all in. It encompassed a panorama of almost 270° of natural beauty at multiple levels ... lush greenery, sandy beaches, and water that mixed greens and blues as the depth changed offshore. All this was blended with a warm and gentle breeze that caressed us as it climbed up the hill from the bay below.*

*We each had a glass of crisp white wine which seemed the perfect accompaniment for this vista before us. When ordering, Dan mentioned he would take a pass on his traditional Jack Daniels Tennessee Sippin' Whiskey because he felt it would struggle rather than meld with our surroundings. I got a kick out of his comments; they began to tell me a lot about this man I was here with in paradise.*

*Dinner inside was enjoyable but not as tasteful as the previous night at the Royal Hawaiian. This was understandable as this was a small island without a large population. Despite the beautiful weather, it still was off season, though it made no difference to us. There were enough people in the dining room to make it feel alive and we all enjoyed the four-piece band. We finished eating and danced at little closer than we had last night, but this time there was no dance contest.*

*Much to Dan's horror, I asked the band to play several songs from* South Pacific *which they gladly did. As I suspected, this was not an unusual request. My partner joined right in and held me quite tight on one particularly romantic number, which was wonderful. After an hour, we decided to walk around the grounds. I agreed but only if I could go barefoot. I informed him that I had not brought my hiking heels.*

*The paths were soft grass, wet with dew and felt great without shoes. The gardens had low lighting which was perfect at night and added to the effect of all the flowering plants and vines. This was indeed the "Garden Isle."*

*We slowly headed back to our cottage making our way carefully down the hill. We stepped inside and my friend went over to the side board and produced a bottle of VSOP cognac, along with two snifters.*

*Reflecting back on our first champagne Swift Boat ride in Da Nang, I concluded there appeared to be no end to the resourcefulness of these boat drivers. He opened the bottle then covered slightly more than just the bottom of the snifter with the amber liquid, giving it room to breathe. Passing me a snifter we swirled our glasses, inhaled, looked at each. Then we each took a breath from the snifter, a short swallow and started to laugh. He gave me a big hug which said it all. I then asked if he would excuse me for a moment. As if on script, he said, "Hurry back."*

*Ten minutes in the bathroom and I returned to the scene of the crime. My "Uniform of the Day" was black lace which I had picked up in a fancy shop in The Royal Hawaiian lobby.*

*There was a twinge of fear that tingled through me as I turned the corner looking at Dan, but I had my line rehearsed, "Hey sailor, going my way?"*

*In response, the warmth of his smile said it all to me. Despite all my planning and bravado, I simply fell into his outstretched arms, and the two of us let that multitude of emotions from the past few days simply flow away.*

*The next day we swam and sailed across the bay to the mythical Bali Hai. We pulled the boat up on the beach and spread out our hotel-prepared lunch, complete with chilled wine, a beach blanket and jungle backdrop. Later that night we danced at dinner and laughed, hoping the magic could go on forever.*

*Back at our cottage, sitting on the deck, as the stars came out, my afternoon sailing partner, who did in fact know how to sail, plied me with cognac. Next, he convinced me to go for a moonlight swim. Fortunately, there was no moon and by the time we got to the bottom of the hill, I was having some trouble just seeing the stars.*

*My Naval officer, showing his true colors, convinced me of the merits of swimming naked. I recall his saying it was a mental health exercise. Making love at the water's edge was a once-in-a-lifetime experience. Sand yes, but also the owner's horses roamed free at night and our antics soon caught their attention. Heavy breathing, not our own, caused us to turn and see our new rather large equine friend who had come by to investigate. Dan, my hero, decided we should immediately retreat and swim for deeper water. I was no expert but had some riding experience and I slowly stood up. Hopefully, the horse was not as shocked as my partner. I spoke softly and gently patted the animal. As I suspected, it was very tame and simply curious as to what was going on. The horse waited around while we got dressed and then quietly left as we walked up the hill, hand in hand. As the song goes, "Love is a many splendored thing."*

Kate was still sound asleep when I awoke at around 0630 showered, shaved, made coffee in the room and ordered some breakfast from the Main House, which arrived soon after. Under the circumstances, I felt I had no choice but to announce to my shipmate, "Reveille, reveille, rise and shine, the ship intends to get under way at 0830 hours."

Despite the cleverness of my Navy call to duty, I was greeted with only a grunt from across the room. The beautiful creature had arisen. As she passed by, I believe I heard a mutter that sounded very much like, "Physical abuse of a senior officer," as she closed the bathroom door. Ten minutes later the shower stopped and there was a bellow, "LT Daly, coffee black and on the double!"

In response, mug in hand, I knocked formally on the door requesting, "Permission to enter?" I was confronted by a towel-wrapped, wet-headed sea nymph, who grabbed my head in her hands, kissed me on the lips while dripping all over my shirt. Within seconds the coffee was snatched from my hand and the door was closed smartly in my face. All of this was followed by a muffled, "Permission denied, but thanks."

After twenty minutes Kate emerged. "Plan of the day?" was her first question. At least she said it with that special smile, but I detected no sparkle in those eyes. I responded in my best military fashion that our flight to Honolulu was to depart at 1000 hours arriving at 1045.

"Before leaving, we have to check out and turn in the jeep. My charter flight leaves Hickham at 1500 and your commercial Pan Am flight is scheduled to depart Honolulu International at 1830. We have a room reservation at Fort Derussey in the BOQ where we can change into our uniforms and take taxis to the airport. This schedule will give us more than adequate time."

Without missing a beat, coffee mug in hand and with a totally straight face she looked me in the eye and said, "Good briefing LT, but what about artillery cover and who is handling secure communications and air support?" There is no question, I could grow to love this woman.

We checked out of the Plantation and had a quiet ride to the airport in the jeep. Both of us were alone with our thoughts, but some of mine were of the last several days and what lay ahead. We dropped off the jeep, thanked it for its faithful service and went to the gate to board our plane.

The Honolulu flight, mid-week and mid-morning, was half full so we had plenty of privacy. I took the lead and said, "Kate, can we talk seriously for a moment while we have some time?"

"Please" was her response as she turned toward me, putting down her third cup of morning coffee.

"The last several days have been special in my life, very special and now we are returning to reality, most likely with no let up for the next several months." I continued, "I would like to try and make this relationship go forward in time, not surrounded by palm trees and white sand beaches but just you and me together."

Not a great speech but it was what I felt deeply. Next came a pause that I clearly remember being hours in length, when in fact it was mere seconds.

She placed her hand on mine, turned and looked into my eyes and simply whispered, "Yes."

We sat just like that for at least five minutes not moving or speaking. I for one was at a loss for words and just wanted to savor her answer. My life, hopefully our lives, had started down a new path.

Kate then resumed the conversation with a more practical thread— we had a busy afternoon and then two long flights, hers to Japan and the *Repose* and mine back to Da Nang and Swift Boats. We were in agreement that we would look three to four months ahead and think about what was in our individual futures and how that would impact our relationship. We could discuss this by frequent letter writing and meet again, if we could possibly schedule it somewhere during that time. We both knew this was unlikely to happen.

I digested this and it appeared to be a realistic plan. The reality of the situation was that we were talking about possibly the rest of our lives and casually saying let's get together in a couple of months. This hit me hard and I suspect it was the same for her. I could do nothing else but lean over, kiss her, and say, "Deal."

We checked into the BOQ at Fort DeRussey and had a quick lunch in the bar. Then we went to the room and pulled out our respective uniforms for the trip. They looked like they had been crammed into a suitcase for the last several days, most likely because that was the case. The room had an iron and ironing board; undoubtedly, we were not the first ones to go down this road. I started ironing my shirt after seeing that my pants were at least acceptable to travel in. Within a minute, I was relieved of duty and brushed aside with the comment, "Just remember, I'm not your mother."

I put my full LT bars on the shirt, having been promoted right before I left Vietnam. Kate seeing them for the first time commented that my new rank made her feel much more comfortable about leading a junior officer astray.

She stayed in civilian clothes because her flight was later that day. Then together, we walked outside and grabbed a cab for the airport. The terminal was packed with several charter flights scheduled to leave at about the same time. Because it was Hawaii and U.S. soil, there were many more families present here than at other foreign R&R destinations. Husbands, wives, children and girlfriends were everywhere, so the two of us didn't stand out during the check-in process. I remember clearly thinking that this was not a happy place, despite the fact we were in paradise. Lives and families were being disrupted, troops were returning to a combat zone and many would be going in "Harm's Way."

We stood at the gate beside a salty Marine sergeant with a chest full of ribbons, a beautiful wife and two blonde children, about four and six, holding their father's big hands. He was ramrod straight but

I could see some moisture in his eye. I was not far behind as his wife took the older child's hand and locked her arm in her husband's. To this day, I can clearly recall that family picture and the ultimate sacrifice it represented.

Kate saw it too and it actually helped us move through the moment. The line started to creep toward the door, so we passed the Marine with a simple nod.

We had said our goodbyes previously in the terminal, which under the circumstances were quite restrained. At the gate itself, I turned to Kate, pulling her gently toward me and hugged her while she whispered in my ear, "God Bless."

## CHAPTER 29

# TET IN THE DA NANG RIVER

After my return from Hawaii, reality set in as the grey winter months progressed. I remained relatively senior among the boat drivers and had only a month or two left in-country. MoTac (Mike Tackney) wanted me to continue as maintenance liaison officer working with the boat repair and maintenance men from the Naval Support Activity. During the day, my responsibilities entailed getting our boats repaired as fast as possible and back out on patrol. This could involve anything from fixing electronics to hull repairs and even engine replacements.

During this time, the enemy threat level around the harbor was building as the Tet New Year holiday approached at the end of January. In addition to my day job, my crew and I were often assigned to nighttime patrols. One of these was down the Da Nang River preventing enemy infiltration from the south side of the city. Because of the weapons on a Swift Boat, we were well suited to provide security in the waterway located below the main bridge that crossed over the river leading to downtown Da Nang and the massive airbase beyond. Each night, a duty boat would be designated and by dusk the pilothouse, forward gun tub and after .50 caliber mount would be surrounded by sand bags for protection. The significant increase in weight decreased the boat's speed and stability, both of which could be a significant factor in combat. As a result, this boat was limited to patrolling the river and the inner harbor lest it roll over in any rough water.

One evening there was a heavy rocket attack on the main airbase and we received a call from the Commander, Third Marine Amphibious

Force (III MAF), using his personal call sign "Big Daddy." We were instructed to proceed immediately to a position in the Da Nang River near his headquarters. This was a call from the man himself, a three-star Marine general, and an order that would be promptly complied with. I had the duty and my crew and I took the sandbagged boat, cast off and headed full speed down the river. I was at the wheel in the pilothouse while Newcomer tuned the radar. Muller and Buck were in the gun tub above and Snipe was aft with Boats by the .50.

Several weeks prior to this trip, the radar was a little slow warming up and in the pitch black we missed the tricky left turn to the entrance of the river. We put the boat smartly up on the nearby sandbar at 25 kts. Two props, two rudders and two shafts were the casualties, all repaired by 1000. This was all smoothly undertaken thanks to a finely tuned team lead by the MLO and that would be me. On my own authority, I concluded that maintaining any work orders or related paperwork to this incident was not a good use of my time in this demanding combat environment, and so the job was completed with all due haste.

Tonight, our intent was to be much more careful. Da Nang was lit up by fires and the ongoing explosions from the rocket attack, as well as by illumination flares being dropped by friendly aircraft overhead. These activities, combined with the radio request that used Big Daddy's personal call sign, emphasized the level of urgency. While enemy fire from the shore was always our concern, tonight we had to worry about friendly aircraft operating overhead who were not accustomed to seeing high-speed water contacts operating at night, especially in a combat zone. On the pilothouse roof of all Swift Boats was a white star with a blue background which we illuminated with our spotlight because a helo overhead with rockets or a mini-gun with a confused or inexperienced crew could ruin the evening. Fortunately, our short trip downriver at full speed was uneventful. We arrived on station and monitored the Marine radio frequencies for any specific assignment and slowly patrolled the lower end of the river.

There were several risks associated with this mission: the first was from the large parachute flares which resembled square coffee cans each weighing four to five pounds and made of white phosphorus, which

*A sandbagged Swift ready for river patrol.*

were dropped by Air Force planes circling overhead. Falling slowly, these burned for several minutes and made a half-mile area look like high noon. By the time the flare container hit the ground it was usually extinguished, but the parachute itself was big enough to cover our entire boat. As a result you could get smashed on the head by the empty flare canister, and at the same time suffocate under the parachute, providing, of course, you didn't fall overboard draped in the chute and drown. All this came from friendly forces flying above. The chutes were for dropping cargo not personnel, so they were dark colored and tricky to see at night especially when the flare had burned out, but not before it had ruined your night vision.

The other threat was passing under the Da Nang bridge where Marine security guards were stationed, tasked with the job of preventing enemy frogmen or sappers from blowing up the bridge. Therefore on a dark night, when the city was under attack, any Swift Boat proceeding under the bridge had to make it extremely clear that we were friendly and not some vessel being utilized by the Viet Cong for river insertion. A new Marine, in the confusion of battle, could very well toss some sort of anti-swimmer explosive device (like a grenade or stick of dynamite) off the bridge onto a Swift Boat fully loaded with fuel and ammunition. Establishing verbal and visual communications with those on the bridge above was critical.

Any Swift Boat operating in the river beyond the bridge made an excellent target for the enemy in the marshes if they were equipped with a standoff shoulder-launched missile. The boat, because of its significant firepower, would be an effective deterrent against any swimmer in the river or enemy troops moving through the open marshes. However, the attack this night seemed to focus more on the airfield not the city or any headquarters operation. So receiving no additional instructions from "Big Daddy" as dawn approached, we proceeded back upriver to our base.

Listening to our own radio frequency, I learned that several of our boats had run into problems that night patrolling close in by the airfield. One had gone aground but floated free with propeller damage and

*A direct rocket hit on an airbase hangar.*

another one was still entangled in the floating hose used to unload fuel from anchored offshore tankers. This required the assistance of our frogmen friends and their underwater acetylene torch.

Breakfast and sleep would have to wait because my morning would be relatively busy in my role as the MLO, getting these boats towed back to base, repaired and back on line as soon as possible. Also, in the finest tradition of Swift Boats, once again, any investigation would be kept to a minimum by employing the policy of 3Fs: Find them, Fix them, and Forget the paperwork.

I was sitting on the repair barge reporting the night's events to MoTac when he received a call from the Naval Support Activity. Up until that moment, after a long night, the morning's black coffee had been outstanding. The repair crews, although they didn't report directly to us, were performing their commonplace but remarkable Swift Boat repair magic. The frogmen had succeeded in cutting loose the boat that had become entangled in the fuel hose at the airport and this problem would soon disappear in short order.

However, I did notice that Mike appeared rather serious as he took the phone call.

"Yes sir, we did have a boat down the river last night during the attack."

He mouthed the words "Ball Cap Smithson" to me, covered the bottom of our phone and then shared the earpiece with me. Ball Cap was obviously in a state of significant agitation.

"You Swift Boat morons have really stepped on your dicks this time. One of your boats went down the river so fast last night that its wake lifted the Admiral's launch so high it smashed into a pier piling and now there's a 2' × 2' hole in the port side. And, "he continued, "The Admiral is really pissed."

Suddenly, it occurred to me that with full fuel, ammo plus the sandbags, my wake must have easily been five feet plus when we passed the Admiral's headquarters. This happened to be directly across from the Marine Corps headquarters (Third MAF), which was our assigned destination.

Ball Cap continued, "I want to know what Swift Boat idiot was driving that boat and why he felt he could charge down the river at full speed."

Ball Cap ranted on, convinced he was playing a winning hand. MoTac, as usual, assumed that ever-respectful Naval Academy tone but concluded that it was useless to continue the discussion.

So he responded, "Commander, with all due respect, sir, you should be aware that this particular Swift Boat was responding to a direct call and request from Big Daddy Actual."

A significant pause, then within seconds I heard the slamming of the other phone. Even though they were built to battlefield specifications, the sound was explosive.

Once again, Swifts had survived head-to-head combat with the evil Commander Ball Cap Smithson, based on our (MoTac's) keen and razor-sharp wits. However, in less than two hours, the Admiral's barge was sitting in the small dry dock nearby and being repaired. True to Ball Cap's description, it did indeed have a 2' × 2' hole in the port side, which in fact might have been a somewhat conservative estimate of the damage.

Understandably, oversight of this repair project did not come under my purview as the Swift Boat Maintenance Liaison Officer. Discussing the events, MoTac and I concluded that this would probably mean that we were off the invitation list for the Admiral's upcoming Navy Day cocktail party.

## CHAPTER 30

# TOUGH TRIP TO NORTH VIETNAM

The next two months went by quickly as I divided my time between my maintenance responsibilities, night patrols downriver and one or two standard patrols along the coast. Our crew had never been a group of short timers, but now they were understandably talking in terms of the weeks left in our tour.

Fortunately, since we had returned from An Thoi, everyone in the crew had a shot at taking an R&R. For each of them, it was a good chance to see a part of the world that most likely they might never see again, such as Hong Kong, Japan or Kuala Lumpur in Malaysia. In Boats' case it was a week-long trip to Australia. I was pleasantly surprised when he returned without being in shackles and chains, so my questions covered no more than, "Did you have a good time?"

Toward the end of January, there had been several days of stormy weather keeping the boats in port. That gave all of us a short break before resuming patrols. We were assigned by MoTac to the Alpha patrol, ninety miles north of Da Nang, with the DMZ marking its most northern boundary. Because of the transit distance involved and the fact that there were no other Swift Boats to the north, this patrol usually went to a senior crew and thus we received the nod. Having patrolled out of Cua Viet in better times, we knew the area well. The Cua Viet River marked the southern border of the DMZ, while the enemy-controlled Ben Hai River marked the northern border. Beyond that was absolute bad-guy territory, it was North Vietnam, complete with its radar-controlled artillery pieces located along the coast. Other weapons covered the rivers from the caves securely located high in the bluffs above.

We had patrolled this sector as recently as Christmas Day and knew it could be a relatively quiet area but could also turn hostile—due to weather or enemy activity—in a very short time. On Christmas Day, we had come alongside the USS *McCormack*, a destroyer on the gun line. The captain came down to the main deck to wish us Merry Christmas and asked if we wanted to come aboard for Christmas dinner. He would tow the Swift Boat and his crew would maintain our radio watch. It sounded like a great offer which I was tempted to accept, but then he stated that he had to head offshore ten to fifteen miles for an underway replenishment of fuel. When I heard this, my decision was relatively easy—we simply could not, under any circumstances, travel that far outside our assigned patrol area. Regretfully, it was too early in the day for hot turkey but he provided us with an outstanding selection of desserts.

In most cases, the captain or at least the executive officer of any destroyer would come down to the main deck to personally ask if we needed any supplies. Occasionally, we did and our shopping list was immediately filled. The captain would always introduce himself using his first name. Although, I would always refer to him as captain, it was nonetheless flattering to any boat skipper to be recognized as a peer by someone significantly senior.

This Alpha patrol would most likely be our last one to the north. We had asked Jay Fleming (Malibu Foxtrot) again for his boat PCF 13, knowing it would be in top-notch shape. We loaded up with fuel, filling the tanks right to the top because the duration of the trip had resulted in almost dry tanks by the time we returned to base.

Today, we simply kept track mentally or on a piece of paper how fast we were traveling and took stick measurements of what we saw remaining in the fuel tanks. Hardly scientific, but there were no gauges for the tanks. All in all, one more item to put on the worry list.

We shoved off from Da Nang at about 0700 with a light wind out of the northeast generating a short chop of one to two feet. We exited the harbor and headed north at about 1900 RPMs, approximately 25 kts. There were no speedometers. The speed depended on how clean the bottom of the boat was and the last time the engines had been rebuilt. Again, not exactly rocket science, but after ten or eleven months you got the hang of how the system worked.

The day had that wonderful flat-grey monsoon look. It was somewhat like being under a blanket that extended down to the horizon, broken up only by a constant parade of menacing cumulus clouds that rolled overhead. The larger they were, the darker they appeared, the slower they moved—all were indicators of trouble ahead.

After about three hours of travel time, we arrived on station and relieved Larry Myers (Surf Rider) in PCF 16 a few miles north of the Hue River mouth. He informed us that due to the weather there were few fishermen along the coast and they had inspected only one cargo junk heading south after it had exited the Hue River. We knew that there was no commercial water traffic that proceeded north of the Hue River and anyone heading south from the DMZ was by definition a bad guy coming down from North Vietnam.

Larry mentioned something we had already heard in our briefing when we met with Article before leaving Da Nang harbor. The U.S. Navy had pulled all our large warships (destroyers and cruisers) off the gun line along the North Vietnam coast as a peace gesture. (This was early 1968, during the Tet offensive. Apparently the peace gesture was not well received.)

From our standpoint, this event had two very significant impacts: first, if we got into trouble there were no friendlies nearby to help out. Second, in the past, we were always able to get weather conditions from those destroyers when they were operating a hundred or more miles to the north off North Vietnam. Normally, the weather would travel south and we would get some lead time before we got clobbered. Now, the only weather forecast was from the carriers that operated so far to the north that their weather information was of little use to us.

With these happy thoughts in mind, we commenced patrolling the ten miles of Alpha sector, about a thousand yards off the beach, and observed little activity. At the same time, we monitored the Marine frequencies in case they wanted us to do any firing along the coast or within the DMZ itself. Around 2200, I took the first watch so Boats and his team could get some rack time. The wind was picking up slightly to around 12–15 kts and the seas were building accordingly. I decided to move off the coast almost a mile simply because at night when the surf was up it was difficult to get an accurate radar range from the beach. The last thing I wanted to do was to approach close in to the surf line along the DMZ.

It was about 2300 when Article came on the net with a coded message. Newcomer copied it and after decoding it read: "Enfield Cobra Alpha, this is Article. Possible steel-hulled contact reported vicinity of [chart coordinates]. Request you investigate and report."

A steel-hulled contact in this neck of the woods was definitely nothing to ignore. So I woke up Boats, told him to decrypt the message again and plot the reported contact. When you had been in-country as long as we had, you were able to keep a rough running fix of your current location in your head. Referencing that skill set, I knew this reported contact was nowhere that I was particularly interested in visiting. Boats, with the chart in his hand, came up from the main cabin and his first words were, "Holy shit, Skipper, this bogie is ten miles north of the DMZ, well into North Vietnam waters."

After referencing the chart again, the position of the reported target required that we transit into enemy territory, a distance well beyond any previous patrol. Considering this location, along with headquarters' decision to pull the larger ships off the gun line, we were very much alone on this one.

With these factors in mind, I set General Quarters and we headed north, but far enough offshore to avoid any artillery emplacements. While they might spot us on their shore-based radar, it would be difficult for their guns to reach us. At least that was my rough calculation.

I sat on top of the pilothouse in front of Muller who was manning the twin .50 calibers while I looked through a pair of the 7 × 50 binoculars, the best-size glasses for night work.

Boats was in the pilothouse driving, with Newcomer's eyes glued to the radar scope. This was definitely the time to have the senior team on look out. Regretfully, there was no moon to provide even the least bit of background light. The seas were black and building, but not so high that they eliminated the advantage electronic detection (radar) had over visual. With the binoculars resting on my knees for stability, my butt in the middle of the pilothouse roof, I scanned slowly from our starboard beam across the bow to our port beam. Any reflection, any spark of light or even a shadow might provide us with some critical early warning. We even checked our radar to see if the electronic pulse of the enemy artillery radar might be transmitting at a frequency that might show up on our scope. It did not. Despite our distance off the beach, I looked for any changes in the darkened shoreline that might indicate a vessel was hugging the coast to avoid detection. This was big-time enemy territory and surprises were not acceptable.

I immediately recalled that Don Schwartz (call sign "Gramps 29," reflecting his age) in PCF 95 had wandered north of the DMZ several weeks ago and had almost bought the farm. He was traveling between half a mile and a mile off the coast and a mile north of the Ben Hai River when North Vietnamese artillery opened up and began firing on his Swift Boat. These were not small arms but real artillery pieces with five-inch shells—all radar controlled.

The guns had locked onto Don's boat, commenced fire and were bracketing him with artillery rounds, as their radar tracked and recalculated his movement. There was a splash to the left, then a splash to the right, each one getting closer and more on target. One round of that size would have been all that it would take. Don was an experienced driver and perhaps had seen enough World War II movies that he did several things correctly. First, he slammed the throttles full forward and headed perpendicular to the shore, away from the enemy. Next, he steered his boat for the last shell explosion and splash. A Swift Boat, being only fifty feet in length and relatively fast, could beat the calculations of the radar-controlled artillery piece, or so Don hoped at the time. He made it, but when he returned to Da Nang seven hours later, he was still white as a ghost and started breakfast with a double bourbon, straight up.

With this scenario in mind, I took over the helm and gave Boats and Snipe each a pair of binoculars with Buck as backup. I radioed Article our current position and informed them that we were proceeding to investigate the contact. I wanted somebody back at Da Nang to know exactly where we were and where we were going in case anything happened, such as taking a hit and sinking. Swimming ashore to North Vietnam, in my opinion, was not really an option and friendly territory was now ten to fifteen miles to our south.

I told the crew I wanted all eyes and ears on the shore for two things: any muzzle flash or the whistle of an artillery shell heading our way. We had survived an artillery attack onshore from these same guns when we were operating out of the Cua Viet base and one does not quickly forget the whistle of an artillery shell heading toward you. The shorter the whistle, the lower the pitch, the closer you are to being the target. We were too far offshore to worry about small arms fire and correspondingly our machine guns would have little impact against a major weapon which was most likely hidden in a cave onshore.

I told Boats to give the binoculars to Newcomer and instead lock onto our radar scope and scan carefully for any target ahead in a 180° sector. The radar was very sensitive and certainly would pick up a steel-hull target at least out to five miles. The seas still had not yet built high enough to present a problem by concealing this type of target. Boats turned the scope so it faced him directly, which ended my view, but it was more important for him to have a clear view and I did trust his capability on the scope.

I brought the engines up to 20 kts, yelled "Hold on," and headed for the location of the possible contact we had received from Article. Unfortunately, that position was about two miles off the beach rather than the five miles offshore position that I would have preferred. I guessed that any vessel coming down from the north would hug the coastline, hoping to blend in with the shoreline both visually and on radar. Dark of night, a growing sea state, and our target potentially a mile or two off the beach, combined with the knowledge that no U.S. ships were on the gun line as a possible backup, wore steadily on our nerves.

Boats reported nothing on the scope out to ten miles, which was a realistic detection range that I trusted. The rest of the crew continued to report no visual contacts. Now we were approximately two miles from the reported position of the enemy bogie standing just off the high bluffs that made up the North Vietnamese coastline in this area.

I pulled the engines back to about 5 kts, not wanting to stumble upon an enemy contact with the possibility that they might detect us first. I wasn't concerned about the sound of our engines because we were heading into the wind and at General Quarters. We displayed no lights except for the occasional red flashlight in the pilothouse for chart work. For a brief moment, I considered firing illumination rounds ahead of us in the general direction of the contact as we approached it. I discussed this with Boats and we both concluded it was a bad idea because we still had not detected any contact which should have shown on the radar if, in fact, it was a steel hull. More important, our firing of illumination rounds would send an engraved invitation to the enemy onshore that we were nearby. This would just be inviting enemy artillery fire.

We continued our approach from the south, driving right through the reported position of the contact and finding nothing. I proceeded another two miles north and then turned south traveling back through the original position of the reported contact. All the while, we continued to look carefully along the coast to see if possibly there was any movement in the surf line. Much to my relief, there was none. Cruising at idle speed, we criss-crossed the area one more time with a 360° visual scan, all the while maintaining radar surveillance.

I picked up the radio to report to Article that I was at the position of the reported contact.

"Article, this is Enfield Cobra Alpha. We have criss-crossed the target area multiple times, found nothing suspicious either visually or on radar. Nothing detected along the coast and nothing farther out to sea to a distance of ten miles. We are returning to normal patrol."

"Roger out," was Article's somewhat terse response. Our conclusion was faulty intelligence.

Article probably correctly assumed that my next move was to get the hell out of Dodge and do it fast. I yelled for the crew to once again "Hold on, full right turn." Then smartly I swung the wheel to starboard, turning our stern 90° to the coastline. Jamming the throttles forward, I was relieved when those big Jimmie diesels spooled up. Cruising all alone one or two miles off the coast of North Vietnam, where I knew there was heavy artillery, was the last place I wanted to be.

There was some conflict in my decision because I knew our full-speed departure might well show up as a solid contact on the enemy radar as the boat left behind her large white wake. The boat at 30 kts traveled a mile every two minutes and I was looking to put maximum distance between us and the enemy. Their artillery most likely had a range of five to ten miles and probably became less accurate with each mile. At about five miles, I gradually turned right 90° and started heading south, still maintaining 30 kts. Fuel consumption was going to be a problem at this speed but I would address that more fully in about thirty minutes. We passed the mouth of the Ben Hai River, ran parallel along the four miles of the DMZ and finally slowed off the mouth of the Cua Viet.

During the entire trip, from the position of the elusive contact to when I finally slowed down, was probably a total of twenty miles, which took around forty minutes. I believe the only words spoken were mine when I said "Hold on, full right turn," as we headed south.

Boats let out a big sigh along with Newcomer and Snipe as they came in the pilothouse, while Muller and Buck leaned down through the opening in the gun tub mutually muttering.

"Skipper, glad that was a false alarm." Images of survival school and POW camp were all too vivid in my mind.

Rather than be upset about what appeared to be a wild goose chase, we instead relished the fact that we were not slugging it out with some enemy cargo ship while sitting under the gun barrels of North Vietnamese artillery. We knew from Ed Bergin's earlier trawler capture that these enemy ships were well prepared for any Swift Boat, as well as being heavily armed.

Intel can be somewhat of a military oxymoron and certainly is not an exact science. Where this contact report may have originated, I have no idea. It could have come from a U.S. patrol aircraft operating many miles to our north and the position we received could have been the result of an extrapolated but not verified course/track for that vessel. Also, the vessel could have come from one of the rivers or harbors along the North Vietnamese coast intending to make a quick run south. For some reason, it might have turned back, possibly even knowing that we were in the area.

It was now around 0200 and the wind and waves had picked up substantially. We were still ninety miles north of Da Nang and our high-speed run from North Vietnam had consumed a fair amount of fuel. There were no Chevron Oil stations nearby, so I decided that we would proceed slowly from the northern end of the patrol sector and start heading south, hopefully arriving near Da Nang at 0500 or 0600.

From 0200 to 0300 the weather deteriorated significantly. The hard part was that we did not know what was in store for us coming from behind because there were no friendlies anywhere to the north of us relaying weather forecasts. The seas were now rollers around eight to ten feet, dead astern with the occasional crest on top.

The hull of a Swift boat had almost a flat bottom with very little V for stabilization. As a result, in a following sea with the waves behind, the boat tended to be very unsteady. The flat stern of the boat often surfed down the front side of a wave after the boat had climbed up and over the back side. The result was a disconcerting lack of control. The worst case could result in a broach, as we had already experienced, whereby the boat was pushed down the front of a wave and then twisted sideways in the trough, sitting sideways between two waves just as the next wave hit.

Boats was at the helm in the pilothouse as this surfing motion began to increase. At the same time the diesel engines added RPMs as the waves literally pushed the boat along and increased the speed of the propellers. We had the sensation of sliding down a hill, with the increased noise from the engines to reinforce the message, all taking place in the pitch black.

The short bow of the Swift Boat, with the pilothouse being located so far forward, served to increase the feeling that we were diving head first into a deep dark hole. I soon saw that Boats wasn't comfortable and offered to take the helm, but soon the falling sensation and lack of control was also getting to me. I knew that PCF 76 being turned over in the surf back in November had to be on everyone's mind as well as mine own.

Out of the corner of my eye, I saw the radar flicker then the screen displayed a series of bright flashing rings followed up by total darkness on the scope. Our radar had just crapped out.

The radar was one of our basic tools of navigation, which we used to maintain a certain distance off the coastline. In this case, we used it to follow the coastline south. Without the radar we would not be sure how close we were to the shoreline. As a last resort, we could use the depth finder to make sure that we remained at a constant depth, as we paralleled the coast. No radar left me dependent on our compass to follow a steady course south. This is OK if the coast is straight. You just calculate your course at the beginning of the run and follow it. However, over a ninety-mile trip, the coastline had several zigs and zags along its contour, which had to be factored in.

After about an hour it was obvious the weather was continuing to deteriorate. The crew was gathered in the vicinity of the pilothouse and Buck asked, "Skipper, mind if I put on a life jacket?"

Understandably, my response was based on our life-changing experience when we sank PCF 76. Our crew had every right to be somewhat gun shy in heavy weather. "Absolutely, break one out for everyone and toss me one here in the pilothouse."

No sooner had the big orange life jacket landed at my feet then a big wave lifted the stern, driving the boat downward into the trough causing it to broach slightly to port. Just as this happened, the mount for the compass in front of me cracked, probably from the slamming and twisting of the boat and the compass broke loose from its mount. Fortunately, the compass was intact and I was able to grab it before it hit the deck. A compass does not have to be in a mount to be effective, but you have to know basically where the top of the compass is and ideally that should be heading toward the bow of the boat.

Assessing the situation, we had no radar, the compass was operational but with its mount broken it would have to be held by one of the crew. It was obvious that a decent-sized storm was bearing down on us from the north, with foul-weather capability never being a strong suit for a Swift Boat.

I said the hell with it and decided to drive back aft. I passed Boats the compass and told him to sit on the deck near the back door and try to keep me on a straight course. I asked Buck for a short piece of line and sprinted out the back door onto the aft deck while putting on my life jacket. I pulled the shaft engaging the steering wheel, grabbed it and quickly tied myself to the two handrails on the cabin top after wrapping the line twice around my waist. The rest of the crew came out on the aft deck, sat down on top the engine covers and leaned against the cabin side facing aft all in life jackets. Boats held the compass sitting on the steps to the cabin below. For safety, I had Newcomer sit one step below Boats where he could dash to the radio if we needed it.

The swells now were ten to fifteen feet high, still primarily rollers but some with the occasional crest breaking on top as the wind increased. From my aft position, now I could look to either side and astern and at least see the waves around us which made me feel a lot better. I could then adjust my course and speed to ride over them in a more stable fashion. In a small boat in heavy seas it was not enough to just hold on, you had to continually work the waves with both rudder and throttles or you could quickly get in trouble. The goal was to climb up the back of the wave, then slowly go over the top, and then maintain control as you slid down the front side. Looking around, I could see the crew agreed that being all together outside was better than being crammed into the small pilothouse, riding the front end of what was quickly becoming a dangerous roller-coaster ride.

Now our problems were twofold: where were we relative to Da Nang harbor which was our eventual destination, and how far were we off the coast? The compass would hopefully help us maintain a reasonably straight line, but would provide us no indication of where we were relative to our destination or the coast.

Around 0400 some faint light appeared in the east and I was becoming more comfortable that it was unlikely we would unsuspectingly drive up onto the beach. At the same time, I knew we should be approaching the Da Nang harbor mouth using a basic calculation of time versus our speed, but that was at best a very rough estimate because I was inputting our speed simply as *slow.*

The clouds remained dark, still low on the water and now heavy rain had commenced. My immediate concern was simply missing the harbor mouth—despite it being almost three miles wide—and continuing to the south. This would add more time to our trip and require battling the seas head-on if we had to turn around.

Since Boats was engaged in the management of our very sophisticated compass navigation, I yelled for the rest of the crew to turn all eyes to starboard and see if they could see anything along the coast that might look familiar and give us some indication of where we were. This exercise went on for about an hour with no results.

We were wet, cold, beaten up and I was beginning to have some serious concerns regarding our fuel status, although our current slow speed should have provided us with an adequate margin of safety. Running out of fuel meant a loss of engine control that I did not want to risk happening in heavy seas. Without an accurate position, it would be very tough for another boat to locate us in this weather. We didn't have GPS in 1968.

I heard Snipe yell something about seeing lights, which I didn't really understand. He pointed toward shore, but his finger was also pointed up in the air. Seconds later, we were all very happy to learn that, through a break in the clouds, a very short break, Snipe had seen the security lights that surrounded the top of the Monkey Mountain aircraft control site. I knew that if these lights were off our starboard beam we were about half a mile below the southern rim of the harbor mouth. At 5 kts it would take sixty minutes to go five nautical miles. So a quick calculation said one mile would take around twelve minutes and around twenty minutes would put me close enough to the middle of the harbor mouth that I could take a 90° turn safely to port.

Once again, I yelled, "Hold on, I'm going to turn to starboard 180°."

I knew things were tense when I heard a full round of, "Aye, Aye, Skipper."

I picked a smaller wave and started my turn to head back north. Before the turn, I asked Boats to call out our current compass heading, then add 180° and that's the course we would steer for a position off the harbor mouth.

The next twenty minutes were long and wet as we smashed bow first into each oncoming wave despite our slow speed. White water was coming over the pilothouse. I worked the throttles so that we climbed up through the crest with enough power, but not so aggressively we barreled over the top down the backside. This is a challenging task at any time but was made more difficult by the darkness that still remained. Fortunately, dawn was starting to break and I was beginning to get some visibility from the aft steering station. The weather and visibility were not fully cooperating so our concentration and calculations had to be on target.

After about twenty minutes, I carefully turned 90° to port, running along the troughs avoiding any breaking waves into what I assumed was the Da Nang harbor mouth. After about fifteen minutes, I hoped that we had turned correctly. The seas were diminishing so I figured we were inside. In the harbor, the clouds had lifted slightly so we could get some idea where we were and as we approached shore our sightlines became even clearer. We were not going to make any high-speed arrival, but at least we were heading home and our destination was a mile or two ahead.

To give us a "get home kick" I asked Boats to put on a fresh pot of coffee and all hands volunteered to help. I untied my survival lines and all of us removed our life jackets and tossed them below, not so much to make a fashion statement but rather because they were damn cold and wet. Vietnam at this time of year was not guaranteed tropical.

We approached the pier and as we tied up we found out that most of the other boats, because of the weather, had come in during the night and we were the last boat to arrive. After we tied up, cleaned the boat and refueled, Jay Fleming, despite the bad weather, came by in his foul-weather gear to check on his property.

I told him that we'd had a delightful cruise well into the North Vietnam chasing some mysterious enemy bogie. His compass had broken loose and, as casually as I could, I mentioned that the radar had crapped out at around 0300, just as the storm was building—all making for a delightful cruise home.

Jay, not to be outdone, looked up and down at PCF 13, took another slug from his coffee mug, smiled and said, "Glad the boat worked out well for you guys."

# Section VII
# Homeward Bound

## CHAPTER 31

# FINAL ORDERS, PACKING UP

It was in mid-March when MoTac told to me that our orders home were going to be cut in the very near future so he was pulling all of us off the patrol schedule, which was standard operating procedure. This week off gave the crews time to wind down, say goodbye to shipmates and pack up their personal belongings for shipment back home. The Navy policy was that when you were in-country a year you could ship just about anything home designated as household goods, except perhaps a Swift Boat. In most cases, this was clothing, stereo and camera equipment, and a few war trophies purchased or legitimately acquired.

As I mentioned earlier, our crew had never been a group of short-timers focused on counting down the days remaining in-country. That said, even though we knew it was coming, when it was confirmed that we were leaving, it did come as a shock. In our case, we had been operating at close to full speed, with a constant load of adrenaline for a long time and all of a sudden everything stops or downshifts into slow motion. Adding to this, the winter weather had finally broken and the days were becoming warm and beautiful. The enemy Tet offensive, at least in the Da Nang area, had failed despite the media stories to the contrary. Being onshore was basically secure again.

When I informed the crew that we were indeed "heading home," we all kind of looked at each other, took a deep breath and sat down on the edge of the pier to discuss what this, in fact, meant. The first thing was that we were "heading home." We had four out of six wounded; fortunately, no one seriously. We had survived the sinking of PCF 76 and had our share of combat experience. Just as important, we had survived as a team and were close to completing a job we could all be proud of. Not necessarily in chronological years, but certainly in experience, we were a lot older than we had been just a short fifteen months ago when we first met in Coronado.

I told them that they were basically on their own for the next several days, but we would meet outside the maintenance office after breakfast every morning just to exchange schedules and news. With some seriousness in my voice, I mentioned that some individuals in Swift Boats had undertaken action that had delayed their departure from Vietnam. I told them to enjoy themselves, but to make sure that when the plane left they were going to be on it.

We were fortunate in Da Nang because China Beach was only a few miles away, an in-country R&R location with a beautiful beach, good food and drink, in a secure location. This would be available to them on a limited basis.

I fully understood that returning to the U.S. would be a challenging adjustment for all of us. My men had not seen family and friends for over fifteen months. In Swift Boats, especially with our crew, we had become a tightly knit team, practically family. Focused on the mission, protecting our crewmates and striving to be the best were the guidelines we followed. The Swift program had definitely developed its own sense of flash and flair, some of which was legitimate, other parts of which were "legends in our own minds." Regardless, back home this would not be the case. Hopefully, family and close friends would provide the support and the welcome home, but after that who knew where the road would lead.

In 1968, most of our country was not pleased with our involvement in Vietnam and a good deal of this angst was placed on the shoulders of the returning troops.

This was the first time that deadly combat was seen nationwide on TV, often the next day after the battle. Body counts and KIAs became nightly statistics alongside the ball scores. There were no pictures of returning troops stepping off the plane, smiling and being greeted by cheering crowds waving American flags.

There was little any of us could do to prepare for this. At best, I discussed it in general terms with the crew, emphasizing the pride each of them should carry forward in terms of what we had accomplished together.

For myself, I wanted to determine the status of Ed Bergin and Bob Mack, their respective crews and departure times, which I suspected would be relatively close to ours. Ed was easy to confirm with a short radio message to Chu Lai. He informed me that he and his crew had orders as we did and they would be departing from Da Nang, possibly on the same flight as we were.

I knew that Bob Mack, after spending some time in Japan recuperating from reconstructive surgery, had asked to return to An Thoi to finish out his active-duty Swift Boat tour. Bob could have asked for duty back in the states, especially considering that his arm was going to be either in a cast or sling for several months, which would eliminate any at-sea duty. However, taking the easy route was not Bob's style and they assigned him to be the Operations Officer at the An Thoi base for the remaining two months of his tour.

After several futile attempts, I was finally able to raise him by radio late one night on our longer-range frequency. I was truly ecstatic to learn that he was heading home at about the same time we were scheduled to leave. Bob mentioned that his crew might have an opportunity to leave a week or two earlier, but he was training his replacement and therefore could not join them. Bob told me that he would try to fly north and join us in Da Nang, ideally taking the same flight back to the States. In his typical make-it-happen fashion, he said that based on his executive position and a handy typewriter, he could probably generate his own transfer orders. He would let me know in two days.

The possibility of Ed, Bob and I joining up again after all these months we had spent patrolling along 1,000 miles along the coast of Vietnam was something to really look forward to. It would be even better if we had a day or two together in Da Nang.

As ridiculous as it sounds, I had trouble winding down and it only took me a day to transfer my Maintenance Liaison Officer responsibilities to Larry Meyer (Surf Rider). I read quickly through a couple books, took my personal gear to downtown Da Nang for shipment home and then spent some time working on my tan on the roof of the APL, even though it was March. The bottom line was—I could not turn off as quickly as I would have liked, not an uncommon experience.

Over dinner one night, Dick Jankowski (call sign "Red Ryder") suggested that I hop a flight with the Army "Cat Killers," a light reconnaissance and spotter aircraft that flew out of Monkey Mountain. It sounded like a good idea at the time, so the next morning I grabbed a helmet, flak vest and M-16 and hooked a ride out to the Monkey Mountain Airbase.

I met Army Warrant Officer Nick Henderson who was going to be my tour guide and we did a quick walk around of his aircraft. Describing it as a "Volkswagen with wings" would be a significant exaggeration. During his lengthy (two-minute) pre-flight instructions, he informed me that it would be a better idea if I sat on the flak vest rather than wear it because the aircraft had absolutely no armor and the most likely shot from the enemy would come directly from the ground below.

*Cat Killer: the ultimate flying machine.*

With my extensive briefing complete, I climbed into a seat behind him entering through the cockpit cover/window. They seemed to be one and the same. Despite my size and being a trifle awkward, I somehow made it into the economy-class row and strapped myself in.

He fired up the engine, not quite the powerful roar I expected. Again, the Volkswagen analogy returned to mind as we taxied out onto the runway. It was easy to see why these planes operated out of the helicopter base at Monkey Mountain rather than the larger Da Nang Air Force Base. A plane this small could easily become lost or simply be run over by some fighter-bomber or cargo behemoth. It only needed about 150 feet of runway and a little headwind to get airborne.

We catapulted down the tarmac with the prevailing wind providing us almost as much lift as the thrust of the engine. Over the internal radio, Nick informed me that the first stop in our mission was to deliver the mail to one of the small islands three miles offshore.

As we approached the island's grass runway, I noticed there were four or five cows grazing across our touchdown point. Sensing my concern, Nick said this was never a problem because one quick low-level pass usually cleared the animals off to the side.

Indeed, they appeared terrified by the roar of our approach as I observed the cows swinging their tails, casually strolling away after our first fly over. We landed smartly, despite a sequence of three-foot-high bounces. Even to my untrained eye, it quickly became obvious that we were about to run out of runway. The beachhead below was a three-foot drop and it was rapidly approaching. Once again, I learned that in the nuances of flying small aircraft, challenges such as these were never a problem. With approximately 100 feet left in our roll, Nick simply jammed his rudder to the right which spun the aircraft around leaving us headed in the opposite direction.

We taxied back to the point near our touchdown and were greeted by a waiting pickup truck. Pulling alongside the truck with the wing overlapping, Nick flipped up the canopy and passed out the mail. The individual at the wheel was wearing the usual Vietnam fashion statement—jungle greens, but he had no name or markings on the uniform. As we took off, Nick informed me that he was some sort of a "private contractor," whatever the hell that meant. With three days left in-country, I concluded that my "need to know" requirement was at a very low level.

As we gained altitude, perhaps 200 feet, we banked sharply to the north over a small village where the structures were built of cement block topped off with government-issue metal roofs. My pilot handed me a bag containing candy and instructed me to toss it to the children playing nearby in an open field. Evidently, this was standard operating procedure. This task complete, we headed back along the coast. I asked if we could fly south so that I could observe the dune lines south of Da Nang.

When Swift Boats patrolled close in along the shoreline, we were always concerned about any enemy activity going on behind the dunes. This might include building a bunker or some fortified emplacement where an ambush team or sniper could be concealed just waiting for you drive on by. After all, this type of intel gathering was the underlying justification for me taking this foolhardy trip.

In my defense, because the enemy had begun stretching their operations closer to Da Nang (now nicknamed Rocket City), this airborne reconnaissance on a regular basis might be a worthwhile trip. I made a mental note, that when I returned to the base I would suggest this idea, along with the need to carry a chart/map. This could be used to record the location of any suspicious activity rather than try to remember what you saw and where, when every sand dune below looked the same.

Up ahead offshore, I saw a Swift Boat on patrol in what I guessed was either the southernmost Da Nang patrol area or the northernmost Chu Lai designated Same Drink Alpha. I couldn't be sure who it was because I couldn't see the boat's number, which was painted on the top of the stern ammunition locker. Regardless, this was a great opportunity to say hello, which I relayed to Nick on the internal radio.

Ever the small aircraft pilot, he needed no further instructions. He banked the plane sharply to the left, circled a mile or two out to sea and came in hard and low, approaching the Swift Boat from its stern. We were flying at about 100 feet at best. At this time of day, most likely no one was asleep but our flyover would eliminate any possibility of that. Out of the corner of my eye, I saw what appeared to be a hostile gesture from someone in a khaki uniform, who I assumed was the officer-in-charge. I recognized the gesture as belonging to one Eldon Thompson (Mary Poppins) in PCF 22.

Switching frequencies I radioed, "Mary Poppins, this is Megaphone Bravo circling your position at this time. Request a ready deck and permission to land?"

My attempt at humor was based on the fact that I remembered that sometime in his naval career Eldon had served on an aircraft carrier. In response, I received Eldon's now famous "Whisky, Tango, Foxtrot, Oscar," response which loosely translated meant, "What the fuck, over?"

I knew by his response I had made his day and that this would be the cornerstone of the dinner conversation later that night. I dutifully informed him, "We have reconnoitered the nearby shore and dune line from the air and observed no immediate enemy threats." I felt this was especially relevant considering Eldon was traveling a mile and a half off the beach. Obviously it was lunchtime.

With this critical component of our mission complete, Nick said he wanted to show me something close to the Laotian border. This side trip had not been mentioned in our flight manifest but I reluctantly agreed and we headed west. As we closed the shoreline he dropped down to the deck and flew inland, rolling up a small estuary at palm tree level. I knew this to be a somewhat unfriendly area but he informed me that this high-speed, low-level approach over the water was the safest. Even if the enemy heard you coming they couldn't see you soon enough to shoot. With this questionable logic in mind, after approximately one minute, I was relieved when we climbed back up to about 500 feet and continued our journey west.

After a short flight, he pointed out the cockpit window to the edge of the grassy field over which we were flying. I saw, now dead ahead, a rather large tree with multiple thick branches. He casually informed me that the tree was the location where he had left his last plane when he ran into engine problems a month ago.

For the past hour, having been part of Nick's barn-storming approach to flying, I had few doubts that this part of the story was anything but true. He described how in the crash the wings were damaged but the plane was so light it dangled in the tree. After it stabilized in the branches, he was able to climb out of the aircraft, slide down the tree limbs and was picked up shortly thereafter by a rescue helicopter.

At the time, I was not aware how close our current position was to the unfriendly Laotian border nor was I overly anxious to find out. My recurring thought was, "*Why the hell did I ever take this flight with forty-eight hours left in-country?* Much to my relief, Nick now banked the plane sharply to the right and while climbing announced, "Let's head back, it's cocktail time and I'm a little low on fuel."

This decision received my hearty support and off we went, arriving back at Monkey Mountain in less than thirty minutes. As we touched down and started to taxi, we rolled by a large open hangar and he pointed inside. "See, Dan, look in there, that's my plane."

Inside the hangar was an exact replica of the aircraft in which we were currently flying, minus the wings.

Climbing out of the aircraft, I reached back inside to remove my flak vest from the seat, and thanked Nick for a most enjoyable flight. Shaking his hand, I said any time he wanted to ride in a Swift Boat, he should just drop by our base.

"Way too dangerous, but thanks anyway," was his response. Once again proving, in combat, everything is relative.

Arriving back at the Apple, I saw that Ed Bergin had arrived from Chu Lai.

"Let the games begin!" he proclaimed.

We quickly commenced the cocktail hour and put together a small group to head downriver to the Stone Elephant for a pre-departure dinner party.

Adhering to an old Swift Boat tradition, which upon reflection may have just been established that night by our freeloading friends, Ed and I bought several rounds of drinks. We toasted our fellow boat skippers, who regretfully we had to leave behind. Two members of our group had patrols the next day so they left shortly after dinner. As a result, our party had shrunk to six in number, but this was more than enough to carry on in appropriate fashion.

Club closing time was 2300. This was a smart policy to ensure that the Officers' Club did not become part of the surrounding combat zone. We had arrived by Swift Boat, but the early departees had taken it back to the Apple. Thus, we had little choice other than to take to the road. It was well over a three-mile hike so we decided to hitch a ride, but considering the time and location, there was little casual traffic.

Ten minutes into our forced march, our very good friends, the United States Marine Corps, pulled up alongside in a large 6X truck. They asked if we could use a ride and would we mind riding in back which was filled with supplies but there would be enough room if we sat on top. Considering our condition and the challenges of the road ahead, we gladly agreed. After a short trip, accompanied by several back-breaking bounces, they let us off at the end of the dirt road leading to the boat piers.

We thanked them for the ride and Ed asked in a casual manner, "By the way Sergeant, what was that uncomfortable cargo we were sitting on?"

With a big grin on his face, the grisly Marine at the wheel responded, "High explosives, Sir. We're transporting the load to the nearby cargo ramps for transport to the grunts up north."

## CHAPTER 32

# WELCOME HOME?

Bob Mack was scheduled to arrive mid-afternoon the next day on a flight from Saigon, so Ed and I borrowed the duty jeep to pick him up at the Da Nang Airbase. Neither of us had seen him in more than three months.

Stepping off the plane it was obvious he had lost some weight but other than that, he looked good. We immediately saw that his arm was still in a sling with a small cast on his wrist. However, his spirits seemed high and with a casual flip of his good hand he ordered us, "Boys, my bags if you'd be so kind." We knew then little, if anything, had changed.

We all piled into the jeep. Ed, as expected, took the wheel, once again claiming seniority. Bob, because of his sling, got to ride shotgun, so I climbed in back with Bob's gear. The short ride back to the APL was mostly filled with an update on Bob's condition, his wrist operation in Japan and his meeting with Connie. Upon arrival, Ed and I struggled topside, climbing the outside ladder/stairs with Bob's bags which we unceremoniously dumped in the bunk room.

Moments later, Ed reappeared with a bottle of twelve-year-old scotch along with a bottle of seven-year-old bourbon. He called all present in the room to rise and stated:

"Gentlemen, join me in drinking a toast to a returning war hero."

"Hear, hear," the booming response from the gathering, always game for a celebration.

In short order, glasses and ice appeared all around. Ed had engineered this toast earlier in the day and the impact on Bob was heartwarming to see. Bob, we found out later in the evening, had been working right up until the moment he climbed aboard his flight with absolutely no down time. To be with two old shipmates and another twenty comrades-in-arms, albeit in the unglamorous but relaxing environment of the Apple, was just what the doctor ordered.

As the second round was poured, the outside door opened with its traditional resounding crash as it swung back hard against the bulkhead. In stepped Eldon displaying that wall-to-wall grin followed up by his now notorious arrival greeting,

"Well let's hear it. What the fuck, over? Let's have a drink. You know some of us have been out all night on patrol!"

We were scheduled to depart with our crews late afternoon the next day, so we decided that discretion was the better part of valor and ate dinner on board. We had adjusted the dinner calendar to make it steak night in recognition of Bob's arrival. With twenty boat drivers in attendance, the first two bottles were soon dry and others, with a more humble heritage, had arrived by the time the movie commenced.

The big day had arrived and after breakfast, Ed and I both rounded up our crews and confirmed that we were all ready to depart at 1100. "Heading home on the big bird." For all of us, the reality was setting in slowly that our Vietnam tour was drawing to a close. We would say goodbye to our respective crews at Travis Air Force Base in California because Bob, Ed and I had agreed previously that we would return for several days to San Diego where it had started, rather than proceed directly home.

Connie Mack was scheduled to meet Bob in San Diego along with Emily, the new baby. Ed wanted to check in with a few old friends, presumably female, and show them that he had indeed returned home safe and sound. Although I was anxious to see my family in Boston after fifteen months, I also wanted to share my U.S. arrival with my shipmates. Connie and the baby would be there and the presence of Ed's female fan club would be an added bonus.

Each of us was well aware that while loved ones and close friends would be there to greet us, there would be few others. There would be no flags, no banners, and no welcome home handshakes from a grateful nation.

For the past two weeks, I had been trying unsuccessfully to reach Kate to determine her status and location. Since Hawaii, we had been writing back and forth and had exchanged letters about every two weeks. I had informed her of my intention to retire from the Navy and return to Boston to attend graduate school or start a job, most likely during the summer. That timeframe would provide me a month or two to adjust and hopefully get started in an appropriate direction.

Kate was ambivalent about remaining in the Navy, but she certainly wanted to continue her medical career. Both of us were proud to have served and agreed that our respective experiences were extraordinary and valuable. However, the relocations and bureaucracy associated with a long-term military career were not really attractive to either of us.

Within the last month, she had written to me that she was scheduled to leave the *Repose* shortly and transfer stateside where she could retire or extend her naval commission on a short-term basis. Her nursing skills were in such demand that she had considerable employment flexibility, which did not exist for former Swift Boat drivers.

I informed her of my departure schedule and when we would most likely arrive in San Diego. As soon as it was available, I would try to telegraph her with some contact information. It was not an ideal arrangement but the best we could do under the circumstances.

Bob, Ed and I were assembled outside the Apple with our respective crews.

"All men present and accounted for, Skipper," was the traditional report from Boats, accompanied by a crisp salute with just the right smile.

At times like this, I knew the loss of Bobby Don Carter was never far from Ed's thoughts. I was blessed with my crew: Fielder, Wells, Newcomer, Muller and Buck, all together standing tall, all survivors, and all seasoned combat veterans.

The first leg in our trip home turned out to be on a school bus parked outside the Apple. It was painted in the prerequisite battleship grey with "U.S. Navy" painted boldly in twenty-inch letters on the side. Perhaps this designation was to ensure that our vehicle would not be confused with some Greyhound bus that might also be departing the Da Nang area. More realistically, it was meant to discourage our Marine

*Heading home with ball cap and aviator sunglasses.*

Corps friends from doing a bit of midnight vehicle requisitioning. Prior to boarding, I did give it a quick look to see if "U.S. Navy" had been previously painted over "USMC."

Loading onto the bus, all spirits were understandably high and building. This continued right onto the Da Nang Airport tarmac as we approached the Pan Am charter flight that was scheduled to take us home. As the bus stopped near the bottom of the loading steps, everyone on board the bus became strangely silent when one of the Pan Am stewardesses climbed on board.

She told us about our departure time, flight schedule, where we were stopping to refuel and our ETA CONUS (Continental United States). She further told us that we were the last group of troops to board this particular aircraft and because we were all part of a defined unit, seats had been set aside so that we could all sit together. That brought forth more than a few cheers from the troops. The crews from Pan Am and the other airlines that were assigned these "going home" flights, as well as the R&R trips, were simply the best. They understood where your head was at, nothing shocked them and in most cases they treated you as royalty. This was a message unfortunately not to be repeated, but one that was certainly well received at the time.

Mostly in silence, each of us stepped down from the bus and slowly climbed the plane's boarding steps. Along the way, just about everyone took a moment or two to slowly glance around to take in that final snapshot of the country where we had spent the last year together. I suspect there were some that believed this day would never come. A few were even disappointed to be leaving and did return later. For some sadly, only their memory would make the final journey home.

It was not until we were all in our seats that the conversations really started to flow again. Not being a shrink, I am only speculating that this occurs because you are always fearful that something is going to happen, for some reason, the plane will not be leaving or you will be called back.

In short order, the cabin hatch was closed, and then the pilot announced that we were taxiing out onto the runway. For a moment, we had to hold as a group of F-4 Phantom fighter-bombers rolled down the runway, afterburners belching flames, wings loaded with deadly ordnance. This made for a fitting and final image that we were leaving an active war zone. As the Phantoms clawed their way skyward, we were next in line. We then turned off the taxiway onto the runway and immediately started to roll with the four engines of the Boeing 707 pushed to full throttle. There was the usual *thunk* as the wheels left the ground and shortly thereafter the pilot announced to a cheering crowd, "Wheels up, heading home."

At that instant, I was deeply moved and I remember how I felt to this day. Most everyone took a moment to gather their thoughts, which I suspect were similar to mine. I was incredibly thankful to see my entire crew sitting several rows in front of me and then beside me, Ed and Bob, two friends who would remain so for many years.

The flight home took more than twenty-four hours with one refueling stop, several above-average meals, a book and a half and no liquor. Twelve hours into the flight, boredom set in, as did an insatiable desire to finish this trip and get my butt off the plane. Since there were many more hours to go, the majority of us soon shifted into that "we will survive" mode of mental discipline that we had developed over the last twelve months.

We touched down at California's Travis Air Force Base, outside of San Francisco, late morning. One by one, we each walked slowly down the stairs from the aircraft. At the bottom of the steps, most of us took a moment just to look around, take in a deep breath and slowly take it all in. More than few knelt down. We were home, we were home.

There was definitely no reception committee but some local military families were there to greet the arrivals who would not be traveling on. For most of us, this was just the first U.S. arrival point and we would require another one or two commercial flights to get home. My troops all had their tickets home and we were going to be bused to the San Francisco Airport about two hours away.

We had some extra time to regroup and I decided that Travis was a better place to say our goodbyes then during the rush to various gates at the San Francisco Airport. For each member of the crew I had framed a 5 × 7 picture of PCF 76, along with a picture of our crew taken on board our Swift early in our tour of duty. They, in turn, had made up a wooden plaque painted ebony black with a centered gold crest listing all of their names below PCF 76 and presented it to me as their skipper. No trophy or award has ever meant as much to me.

This was before the days of "man hugs," but there were strong handshakes, sincere thanks and best wishes for the future, all around. Many years later, I can clearly recall each of those handshakes and picture the smiling faces, along with the pride I felt being part of the team of Fielder (Boats), Wells, Newcomer, Muller, Buck and Daly. No question, squared away sailors and combat veterans. We had survived.

Shortly thereafter, we boarded separate buses that were grouped by airlines and destinations so the decision to say our farewells at Travis had been a timely one.

Ed, Bob and I travelled on the same bus to San Francisco and had reservations for a 1500 American Airlines flight to San Diego. We checked in, dumped our bags and had just enough time to make the gate. Seeing us sprinting in uniform, the gate attendant motioned for us

*PCF 76: a seasoned crew. L to R: Dan Daly, Oscar Wells, John Muller, Bob Buck, Bill Fielder, Michael Newcomer.*

to slow down and informed us, "The pilot has no intention of pushing back from the gate until the three of you are on board."

As we walked down the stairs from the terminal and headed toward the plane we saw the pilot slide open his small side cockpit window. Out stretched his arm, his left hand giving us the big thumbs-up signal; we returned the salute. Like many airline pilots, he was undoubtedly a veteran and his was a well-received "Welcome Home."

On board, they gave us three seats together in coach. This was 1968 and there was no corporate policy of upgrades for returning military personnel. We did, however, have an enjoyable lunch and a couple of *very cold* Budweiser beers. Understandably, Bob was close to ecstatic about seeing his daughter Emily for the first time. He walked us once again through his entire picture collection. Emily was just over one year old and Connie had told him she was starting to walk. Ed, on the other hand, was highly secretive regarding who was greeting him at the airport. I was basically along for the ride, but I had no doubt it would be an enjoyable one.

We touched down right on schedule. As the plane rolled toward the gate, as previously agreed we would change our regulation covers, so we reached in our carry-on bags and pulled out our blue Swift Boat ball caps. The day was still sunny, so for a touch of theater, we all added our aviator sunglasses.

As we walked forward toward the exit hatch, the pilot stepped out of the cockpit, shook hands with each of us and said, "Air Force, welcome home." He looked at the blue ball caps and said, "Navy?" Ed replied "Swift Boats" which brought a smile and a subtle but knowing shake of the head from the pilot.

The stewardess at the top of the stairs was next and repeated the greeting with a similar smile and enthusiasm. Out of the corner of my eye, I did notice that some passengers behind us were frowning at the delay caused by the plane crew's special greeting to us. Regardless, at that moment, life was good and we were home.

It was a short distance across the tarmac to the stairs leading up to the terminal and only a handful people were in front of us, so we picked up the pace. In fact, we damn near sprinted up the stairs and down the short hallway into the terminal itself.

Suddenly, I heard a high pitched multi-voice scream, "Eddie!"

It appeared to be emanating simultaneously from a blonde, brunette and redhead, all with their arms extended. My first thought was rock star but then, as they ran over to Ed, I understood that some things just never change.

Off to the side, while the crowd rushed to depart, I saw Connie Mack who was holding the tiny hand of beautiful little girl dressed all in white with a big red, white and blue bow placed in her blonde hair. In her other hand was a small bouquet of three short but ruby red roses, one for each of us.

Bob approached them, stopped about ten feet away and went down on one knee and held out his good arm to hug his daughter for the first time. I noticed he had removed his sunglasses so as not to frighten Emily. No question, Bob was going to be a great dad.

In Hollywood contrast, "Lord Mort" was indeed enjoying his role as the returning warrior. I had met two of the girls before but the redhead was new, regardless there were hugs all around.

Even little Emily gave me a smile.

Connie took control and suggested we move our little welcome home group away from the departing crowd, which seemed like an excellent idea. Ed certainly had his hands full and Bob was holding Emily, so Connie and I had the carry-on bags. It mattered little because we were home!

Despite my being alone, I did not feel that way even for a moment because I was with my shipmates, their friends and loved ones, Brothers Swift. Also, Connie was one of those unique individuals who instantaneously made you feel like you belonged, because in her mind, you did.

Altogether, our colorful little band of eight started down the crowded walkway, largely ignored or possibly even resented by those other travelers who silently rushed by. We rounded a corner and were following the signs toward the baggage claim when I heard a voice off to my right side call out to someone, "Hey sailor, going my way?"

I stopped, grabbed a breath, instantly recognizing the voice while turning rapidly towards its source, all at the same time. Standing there against the wall, just around the corner was Kate. She was dressed in civilian clothes, dark slacks, starched white blouse and the coordinated light blue sweater casually hung over her shoulders. Civilian clothes were the reason I had completely missed her. I had trained myself to anticipate the unexpected, but this was different. Kate meeting our plane had not even been a remote consideration.

This woman was someone who, in a matter of a few months, had become so special in my life that the shock of seeing her literally left me (Megaphone Bravo) speechless, and almost unable to move. Seeing my befuddled reaction, without hesitation she moved smoothly across the walkway toward me. Slipping her arm gently through mine she whispered, "Welcome home, I thank God you are safe."

She kissed me lightly on the cheek. Despite my absolute joy at seeing her, I was still struggling to move in any direction.

Then from the roar and applause of my nearby friends, I knew I had been set up, most likely orchestrated by Mrs. Mack. I was most appreciative of this noisy distraction because at the moment my carefully maintained "Mr. Cool" patina was definitely showing some cracks. Kate, never one to make a scene, kept one arm in mine and suggested we continue on. At the same time reacting to the noise, Emily had started to cry but Bob appeared to deal with her fright in a very competent fashion, especially for a first timer.

Undoubtedly anticipating my list of questions, Kate leaned over and whispered in my ear that she would explain everything in due time. Meanwhile, she quickly informed me that she was temporarily assigned to San Diego but was soon to leave active Navy duty and was already applying to hospitals in the Boston area. Did I need to know more?

Gradually adjusting to what had just taken place, I looked around me and knew who the primary instigator in this drama was. However, by their smiles and knowing looks I suspected that all of them were co-conspirators on some level. Connie was smiling, displaying that ultimate "gotcha" look and indeed she had.

I looked first at Bob then over to Ed and they just nodded. Both had heard me speak fondly of Kate but neither had met her. Despite the stress of the moment, introductions were one social interaction I was able to carry out. Each of us knew that we were feeling similar emotions—we were home and we had done our job. We had survived and here we were, all together again, surrounded by people who meant the world to us. Sadly, as we were beginning to realize, the rest of the world didn't seem to care, but at that moment to us, it didn't really matter.

The redhead with Ed, named Linda (no call sign), brought along a lot more than her camera. Holding it in her right hand with her left, she pushed the three of us together for the arrival photo.

With a touch of drama, Bob and I replaced our sunglasses. Ed, ever the Hollywood star, with his surrounding entourage, had left his on. As other passengers rushed by, most of them ignoring us, Ed, Bob and I stopped for a moment, standing side by side in the walkway. Then each us, with more than a little pride, adjusted his blue baseball cap embroidered in gold, respectively Officer-in-Charge PCF 79, 56 and 76.

We were Swift Boat sailors and we were home!

# EPILOGUE

Upon their arrival home in the late 1960s, there were no banners and bands to greet those men and women who had served their country. They were mostly ignored but on occasion scorned by their fellow Americans, many of whom had no concept of the sufferings, demands and scarring of combat.

In Vietnam, over 2.7 million served and over 58,000 gave their lives.

Today's returning veterans are portrayed differently. The media shows groups of strangers in the middle of the night enthusiastically greeting the planes of returning veterans as they first touch down in the United States. Along highway overpasses, there are banners welcoming home family members who have served. Ships arrive in port, greeted by throngs of people joyously awaiting their return. Small towns hold parades for the returning heroes and mourn those who will not return.

In this book, I tried to tell the stories not of heroes but of one small group of men who served in Swift Boats. Over six years, fewer than 3,500 officers and enlisted were in the program. Their strength of brotherhood remains today. Small evidence of this is their biannual reunion which draws over 500 crew members and spouses from across the country.

Now, *America has it right*. The men and women who serve deserve our appreciation and support. The rights and wrongs of war are based not on their decisions but on those of our elected officials.

Today, Americans speak two simple phrases that apply to all those veterans who have served. "Welcome home" and, more importantly, "Thank you for your service."

No matter how awkward it may sound to those who say these phrases, they will always be well received by all those who have served.

Dan Daly, 2015

# THE CREW OF PCF 76:
## CURRENT LOCATIONS

---

Bob Buck, married, retired postal service, hospital volunteer—Washington

Dan Daly, married, business consultant, author—Massachusetts

Bill Fielder, deceased—Texas

John Muller, single, farmer, heavy equipment operator—Idaho

Michael Newcomer, married, retired, Boeing, Bonneville Power Admin.—Oregon

Oscar Wells, married, retired, Army officer, minister—Georgia

# SWIFT BOAT SKIPPERS, 2007

*(L to R) Ed Bergin, Walt Doblecki, Jay Fleming, Tom Jones, Dan Daly.*

*L to R: Larry Meyer, Dan Daly, Eldon Thompson.*

# APPENDIX: SWIFT BOAT SPECIFICATIONS

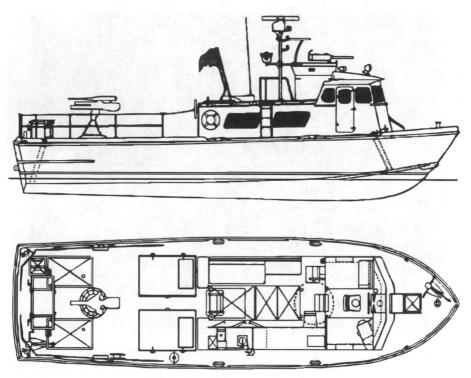

*Mark I Model (PCFs 1 through 104).*

*Manufacturer:* Sewart Seacraft, Berwick, Louisiana
*Crew:* One officer and five enlisted
*Length:* 50'
*Beam:* 13' 6"

*Draft:* 3' 10"

*Weight/Displacement:* Approximately 20 tons

*Speed:* 30 kts, on a good day.

*Engines:* Two General Motors Detroit Diesel 12V71 "N" rated at 480 hp each.

One Onan 3 or 6 KW diesel-powered electrical generator.

*Fuel:* 800 gallons diesel in three tanks.

*Range:* Range at 8 kts: 800 nautical miles. Range at 23 kts, 250 nautical miles.

*Electronics:* One Decca D202 X band surface search radar, DC powered with a maximum range of 24 miles.

One AN/URC single-sideband AM/CW radio 100 watts, primary radio, range up to several hundred miles depending on atmospheric conditions.

One AN/VRC-46 FM radio short range, boat to boat, or nearby shore units.

*Armament:* One twin .50 caliber Browning machine guns manually operated, each capable of firing 450 to 550 rounds per minute. Ammo cans at the mount held up to 600 belted rounds. On board, 20,000 to 25,000 rounds were carried in the main cabin magazines. Maximum range was 7000 yards, effective range 2000 yards.

One 81mm Mark 2 trigger-fired mortar located below one single .50 caliber Browning machine gun. The range of the 81mm mortar was 4000 yards elevated and 1000 yards direct trigger-fired. These weapons were located together on a fixed tripod on the after deck. Mortar ammunition carried on board in a transom-mounted locker was approximately 100 rounds composed of High Explosive, White Phosphorus, and Illumination.

Other onboard weapons would include: M-60 machine guns, M-79 grenade launchers, M-16 rifles, 12-gauge shotguns, .38 caliber pistols and a variety of hand grenades, both fragmentation and thermal.

*Boat armor:* None